# Global Finance Series

Edited by
John Kirton, Munk Centre for International Studies, Trinity College, Canada,
Michele Fratianni, Indiana University, USA and
Paolo Savona, LUISS University, Italy

The intensifying globalisation of the twenty-first century has brought a myriad of new managerial and political challenges for governing international finance. The return of synchronous global slowdown, mounting developed country debt, and new economy volatility have overturned established economic certainties. Proliferating financial crises, transnational terrorism, currency consolidation, and increasing demands that international finance should better serve public goods such as social and environmental security have all arisen to compound the problem.

The new public and private international institutions that are emerging to govern global finance have only just begun to comprehend and respond to this new world. Embracing international financial flows and foreign direct investment, in both the private and public sector dimensions, this series focuses on the challenges and opportunities faced by firms, national governments, and international institutions, and their roles in creating a new system of global finance.

*Also in the series*

**Making Global Economic Governance Effective: Hard and Soft Law Institutions in a Crowded World**
Edited by John Kirton,
Marina Larionova and Paolo Savona
ISBN 978-0-7546-7671-3

**G8 against Transnational Organized Crime**
Amandine Scherrer
ISBN 978-0-7546-7544-0

**Governing Global Derivatives: Challenges and Risks**
Chiara Oldani
ISBN 978-0-7546-7464-1

*Full series listing at the back of the book*

# Debt Relief Initiatives

## Policy Design and Outcomes

MARCO ARNONE
*Centre for Macroeconomics and Finance Research, Italy*

ANDREA F. PRESBITERO
*Università Politecnica delle Marche, Italy*

ASHGATE

Published by
Ashgate Publishing Limited
Wey Court East
Union Road
Farnham
Surrey, GU9 7PT
England

Ashgate Publishing Company
Suite 420
101 Cherry Street
Burlington
VT 05401-4405
USA

www.ashgate.com

**British Library Cataloguing in Publication Data**
Arnone, Marco.
Debt relief initiatives : policy design and outcomes. --
(Global finance series)
1. Debts, External--Developing countries. 2. Debt relief--
Developing countries. 3. Debts, Public--Developing
countries. 4. Developing countries--Economic conditions.
I. Title II. Series III. Presbitero, Andrea F.
336.3'435'091724-dc22

**Library of Congress Cataloging-in-Publication Data**
Arnone, Marco.
Debt relief initiatives : policy design and outcomes / by Marco Arnone and Andrea F. Presbitero.
p. cm. -- (Global finance)
Includes bibliographical references and index.
ISBN 978-0-7546-7742-0 (hardback) -- ISBN 978-0-7546-9473-1 (ebook) 1. Debts, External--Developing countries. 2. Debt relief--Developing countries. 3. Debts, Public--Developing countries. 4. Developing countries--Economic conditions. I. Presbitero, Andrea F. II. Title.
HJ8899.A763 2010
336.3'435091724--dc22

2010021621

ISBN 9780754677420 (hbk)
ISBN 9780754694731 (ebk)

Mixed Sources
Product group from well-managed forests and other controlled sources
www.fsc.org Cert no. SA-COC-1565
© 1996 Forest Stewardship Council
FSC

Printed and bound in Great Britain by
MPG Books Group, UK

# Contents

# List of Figures

# List of Boxes

# List of Tables

# About the Authors

**Marco Arnone** (PhD University of Pavia, MSc University of Warwick) is Director of the Centre for Macroeconomics and Finance Research (CeMaFiR), and has been Adjoint Professor of Economics and Finance of Emerging Markets at the University of Eastern Piedmont (Novara, Italy). He has worked as an economist in the Monetary and Financial Systems department and the African department at the International Monetary Fund, in countries such as Peru, Croatia, Sri Lanka, Lebanon, Kenya, Zambia, Angola, Mozambique, Lesotho. His recent books and articles (with co-authors) include: *Primary Dealers in Government Securities* (IMF 2005), *Venture Capital for Development* (Vita e Pensiero 2006), *Banking Supervision Quality and Governance* and *Financial Supervisors Architecture and Banking Supervision* (Edward Elgar 2007), *Central Bank Autonomy: Lessons from Global Trends* (IMF 2008), *Anti-Money Laundering by International Institutions: A Preliminary Assessment* (EJLE 2008), *Central Bank Independence, Accountability, and Transparency: A Global Perspective* (Palgrave Macmillan 2009), *Anti-Money Laundering: The Transnational Criminal Framework and Regulation* (ICFAI 2009). Dr Arnone is also Founder and Executive Director of the Arnone – Bellavite Pellegrini Foundation, which provides financial support for developing countries students, and Vice President of Prometeo onlus, a not-for-profit organization of liver transplant patients, their families and friends.

**Andrea F. Presbitero** (PhD Università Politecnica delle Marche, MA University of Sussex) is Assistant Professor at the Università Politecnica delle Marche, where he teaches International Monetary Economics. He is affiliated to the Money and Finance Research Group (Mo.Fi.R, Ancona) and to the Centre for Macroeconomics and Finance Research (CeMaFiR, Milan). He was an intern at the Economic Policy and Debt Department (PRMED) of the World Bank and he is consultant at the World Bank on debt relief and growth strategy issues. He has been a visiting scholar at IRISS-C/I at CEPS/INSTEAD (Luxemburg). His research interests cover development economics, banking and finance, and international economics. He has published in international refereed journals, such as the *Journal of Economic Geography*, the *Journal of Financial Intermediation*, the *Review of Finance*, the *Development Policy Review*, the *Economics: The-Open-Access, Open-Assessment E-Journal*, the *Journal of International Development*, the *Cambridge Journal of Regions, Economy and Society* and the *International Economic Journal*.

*To Vincenzo Mazzaferro, Laura Gangeri and the Staff at the Liver Transplant and Nuclear Medicine Units at the Istituto Nazionale dei Tumori in Milan, Italy.*

*And to Alessandro Prati, he would have known why – M.A.*

*To Chiara, Bianca and Alice – A.P.*

# Foreword

It has now been 14 years since the official launch of the Heavily Indebted Poor Country (HIPC) initiative – at that time a radical program agreed upon by the governing boards of the World Bank and the International Monetary Fund. HIPC was designed to coordinate large reductions in the external debt burdens of the world's poorest countries – with the explicit purpose of helping them get onto the path of sustainable growth and meaningful poverty reduction. The 1996 HIPC I was followed by HIPC II in 1999, under which debt relief was made faster and more generous and accessible, and then by the Multilateral Debt Relief Initiative in 2006, under which a large group of the poorest countries had all their debt to the IMF, World Bank (International Development Association), and the other multilateral banks completely wiped away.

These programs were in large part the outcome of an impressive debt relief movement of international civil society, faith-based organizations, and celebrities, which gathered steam in the 1990s in the run-up to the Jubilee year of 2000. The movement for debt relief attracted support from the left and the right in the West. In the United States, the Clinton Administration supported HIPC I, championed HIPC II and the Bush Administration championed MDRI. Across the world, the movement galvanized the technocratic, think tank, and academic communities – for debt relief and in the cause of development more broadly. For the first few years of the twenty-first century, the end of poverty, to use the title of Jeffrey Sachs's 2006 book, suddenly seemed possible because of the apparent success of the debt relief movement.

In many ways, the Center for Global Development owes its existence to the debt relief movement. It was the debt burden of the poorest countries of Central America that triggered the determination of our founding benefactor and current Board Chair, Edward W. Scott, Jr., to create an independent center to speak truth to power on debt and other development policy issues.

For that reason alone I am pleased to have the opportunity to introduce readers to this impressive book.

The authors of this book address fundamental questions using careful and clear technical analysis. Their answers will generate considerable discomfort among the debt movement's supporters. Did debt relief programs help countries increase spending on education and health programs – a fundamental objective of supporters keen on reducing poverty? In some HIPC countries pro-poor expenditures did increase, but not in others. Either way, it is outcomes that should be assessed – not expenditures. Did debt relief trigger higher private investment and faster economic growth? No, not in and of itself, though the economic reforms (mostly improvements in macro-economic management) that in many HIPC countries did make a difference were probably encouraged by the conditions set by the international community for HIPC eligibility. Did debt relief improve lives in benefiting countries? Maybe, but we really cannot be sure. There is little, if any, systematic evaluation that relates debt relief as an input to improved lives as a key outcome.

That is not surprising. Reductions in poverty and gains in well-being are tough challenges unlikely to yield obviously or quickly to a one-time reduction in a country's debt obligations – particularly given that most HIPC countries prior to the program had already been receiving more aid in new loans each year than they were paying out in debt service.

The authors are honest and clear in puncturing unrealistic expectations and explaining the mixed results of past debt relief programs. That provides a solid foundation for their ideas about debt financing in the present and the future.

They ask – and sometimes answer – good questions. Are poor countries still at risk of an overload of public debt? Yes probably – but in part because their governments are resorting too much to high domestic borrowing, about which the IMF and others were not (until recently) sufficiently wary. Moreover the increase in internal financing in HIPC countries – which if interest rates rise risks crowding out bank lending to the private sector and public investment in infrastructure and social programs – may be an unintended consequence of the HIPC initiative. Are the multilateral institutions (in my own view never held sufficiently accountable for defensive lending in the 1980s and early 1990s) overdoing it again? Perhaps, they suggest yes, under the pressures created by the global financial crisis. Are the recent tweaks to the standards they use to "permit" more lending (so-called debt sustainability analysis) an improvement? Or is this debt sustainability analysis, as the authors argue, too complicated, opaque, and driven by assumptions about future growth that are too optimistic? Did official multilateral debt relief make it too easy for poor countries to attract more costly loans from China and western export credit agencies anxious to support their own exporters? Should the international community not be organizing now to reach agreement on global rules to discourage and even eliminate vulture fund awards? Why is that coordination problem not now being addressed?

The authors have sensible proposals for how the IMF and the other international financial institutions could do better. One is to target debt relief exclusively to countries with good policies and institutions (an initial HIPC principled honored largely in the breach); they show that it is only in those countries that high public debt has been a binding constraint to investment and growth. Another proposal of theirs deserves far more attention from debt activists, i.e. emphasis on reducing debt service (flows) rather than only or almost always on reducing poor countries' debt stock. This focuses attention on increasing domestic resources for poverty reduction (versus repaying external debts), particularly as a kind of insurance against negative shocks. This is an approach I proposed with John Williamson in CGD's first publication (*Delivering Debt Relief: From IMF Gold to a New Aid*

*Architecture*, 2002), in the simple and transparent form of ensuring debt service never exceeds 2 percent of GDP.

But the strength of this book is less in its proposals for how to do better in the future, and more in its honest and technically thorough assessment of what hasn't been fully absorbed in the policy community about the past. The book is a worrying reminder of how little evidence scholars have amassed about the causes and consequences of debt overload in low-income countries and the impact of the recent massive international effort to relieve unsustainable debt. Debt and debt financing are a fundamental source of development investments – and poor countries should not be denied access to such financing solely because they are poor. But this book constitutes a subtle indictment of the failure of the international community to make lending institutions more accountable for their lending decisions, low-income countries more accountable for managing their development programs, and scholars, policy analysts and activists far more focused on systematic assessment of the outcomes for people on the ground of the borrowing-lending-debt relief cycle. HIPC-style debt relief, after all, should be a last resort not a recurring habit. I hope this book reinforces that view.

Nancy Birdsall<br>President, Centre for Global Development<br>Washington, DC

# Preface

This book is a must read for researchers, policy-makers, and debt relief activists. The authors achieve the almost impossible objective of combining the concerns and views of soft-hearted members of the debt relief movement with those of the hard-headed economists who populate the international financial institutions. The book includes a rigorous treatment of the economics of debt relief but never loses sight of the plights of those who should ultimately benefit from debt cancelation.

The book starts with a review of debt relief initiatives. The starkest message of this section is that activists should never give up. Many policies and initiatives which are now taken for granted were deemed impossible to implement when initially proposed. Consider the case of the HIPC Initiative. It now seems natural and even insufficient, but when it was initially proposed the first reaction of the official sector was "this cannot be done, it would create moral hazard and, anyway, we do not have the resources". With these considerations in mind, it is now time to push the agenda towards a substantial revision of the IMF/World Bank debt sustainability framework (DSF).

I feel that the DSF suffers from a number of major shortcomings. Many of these shortcomings are discussed in the book, but this is a subject on which I am much more critical than the authors. My main issue with the DSF exercise is that it gives the impression that we know something when we know almost nothing (how reliable are growth forecasts over a 20 year period?). This may give policy-makers a false sense of security and end up doing more harm than good. Thus, the DSF reminds me of Mark Twain's famous quote "It ain't what you don't know that gets you into trouble. It's what you know for sure that just ain't so."

Related to this point is the debate on the choice of the ideal blend between grants and loans. Currently, the World Bank sets its grant-loan mix by using the DSF to establish a country's ability to repay. However, past experience shows that repayment capacity is very difficult to asses. Therefore, the DSF might be a very imperfect crystal ball. A possible solution to this problem would be to allocate concessional credit on the basis of country's needs (assuming that the country will be able to repay) and then set the repayments as a fixed percentage of borrower's GDP. This would be equivalent to moving from *ex-ante* to *ex-post* grants and would result in a system in which grants are allocated only to the countries which really need them. Besides eliminating the need of conducting unreliable long-run forecasts, this scheme would also provide the right incentive to lenders, without necessarily generating moral hazard on the borrower side .

The second part of the book focuses on the role of domestic debt in low income countries. This is an important topic that until recently was completely disregarded by the research and policy community. I remember that when Eduardo Borensztein, Eduardo Levy Yeyati and I started working on Living with Debt (Borensztein, Levy Yeyati, Panizza 2006), we had to convince the management of the Inter-American Development Bank that the book should include both domestic and external debt. We also had to work hard to collect data on the level and structure of domestic public debt in Latin America. It is now accepted that there are important interactions between external and domestic debt, and that the latter should be included in all debt sustainability analyses. However, there are still important obstacles in terms of data availability and quality. The official sector should intensify its efforts in collecting and disseminating these data. This is also a field in which debt activists have been absent. Statistics may seem dry and boring, but good data help in formulating good policies. Building good statistical offices may end up saving more lives than other, more fashionable, policy interventions.

The third part of the book is somewhat technical but is extremely helpful for readers interested in a concise and up-to-date review of the theoretical and empirical literature on the macroeconomic consequences of debt and debt relief. This part, especially Chapter 8, also contributes to the literature on the effect of debt relief with a set of new and provocative results on the effects of debt relief under the HIPC initiative and on the interaction between debt relief and the rise of domestic debt.

The book closes with a discussion of the impact of the current crisis on debt sustainability and touches on several hot topics such as the allocation of grants and loans, the role of vulture funds, and the treatment of odious debt. It seems that the authors have a well- planned and ambitious research agenda and I am looking forward to reading their next book.

In concluding this brief preface, I would like to join Marco Arnone in remembering Alessandro Prati. We all learned much from Alessandro and could have learned much more.

Ugo Panizza<br>
Chief of the Debt and Finance Analysis Unit<br>
in the Division on Globalization and<br>
Development Strategies, UNCTAD<br>
Geneva

# Authors' Note

The idea of this book originated in Washington, DC when Marco Arnone was at the IMF and had the opportunity to work directly (and often jointly with the World Bank) on external debt sustainability and debt relief under the Heavily Indebted Poor Countries Initiative in countries such as Mozambique and Zambia, and on domestic debt/government securities and monetary management in Angola, Lebanon, Peru and Sri Lanka. Direct work on the minute (and often not sufficiently known outside the policy circles) details of these areas provided highly valuable "food for thought" both at the time and later. Our gratitude goes to the team colleagues and friends whose great work and experience made these missions highly rewarding, and to local colleagues, national authorities, NGOs, trade unions, the business community, local research centres and civil society members in these countries for frank and stimulating "out of the box" discussions: we hope that the richness of these exchanges has been – at least partially – reflected in these pages.

We wish to thank colleagues and friends at the IMF, the World Bank and the Inter-American Development Bank: Andy Berg, Tito Cordella, Domenico Fanizza, Aart Kraay, Shonar Lala, Bernard Laurens, Gian Maria Milesi-Ferretti, Vikhram Nehru, Jean-Francois Perrault, Mark Plant, Abha Prasad, Alessandro Rebucci, Luca Ricci, Martin Sommer, Volodymyr Tulin, Gallina Vincelette and participants to the seminars "Debt Relief, Institutions and Growth in Poor Countries", given on March 26 and 27, 2009 at the IMF and the World Bank, for their invaluable feedbacks and suggestions – often based on unique direct experience – on earlier drafts of parts of this book. We are also grateful to participants to several other seminars, where draft chapters have been presented, given at the World Bank, the Bankers' Association in Lima (Peru), the Catholic Universities of Milan and Piacenza, the Università Politecnica delle Marche, the University of Eastern Piedmont, the University of Perugia, the University of Bergamo, the School for International Relations at the University of Trento, the Italian Economic Society in Naples, the Associazione degli Economisti di Lingua Neolatina (Italy), the annual conference on Development Economics of the German Economic Association in Berlin (Germany), the Universities of Warwick and Manchester (UK), the University of Lusaka (Zambia) and the Central Bank of Zambia, for useful comments and discussions.

We are especially indebted to Luca Bandiera, Michele Fratianni and two anonymous referees for discussions and suggestions on the issues addressed here and their encouragement in pursuing this project.

Andrea Presbitero wishes to thank his colleagues at the Università Politecnica delle Marche and Mo.Fi.R, and especially Piero Alessandrini, Luca Papi and Alberto Zazzaro, for their support and suggestions. A special thanks is for my great co-author Marco Arnone, who introduced me to the topics addressed in this book and continuously guided and encouraged me. I have learned a lot from him, and not only on economics. My gratitude also to the students at the Università Politecnica delle Marche and the University of Bergamo (Master in Microfinance), whose challenging questions helped shaping the book.

Marco Arnone wishes to dedicate a special thought to a close friend and exemplary economist, Alessandro Prati, who left us in June 2009. His bright mind, the stimulating discussions, his great dedication to applied research in an institution with global responsibilities like the Fund and, above all, his friendship and human touch – especially in tough times – will always be in our hearts and minds.

*Author royalties from the sale of this book will be donated to SAVE THE CHILDREN.*

# List of Abbreviations

| | |
|---|---|
| AfDB | African Development Bank |
| BIS | Bank for International Settlements |
| BLEND | IDA-eligible country but credit-worthy enough to borrow from IBRD |
| BOP | Balance of Payments |
| CIA | Central Intelligence Agency |
| CIRR | Currency-specific Interest Reference Rate |
| CPIA | Country Policy and Institutional Assessments |
| DAC | Development Assistance Committee |
| DEC | Debt and Exchange Rates |
| DeMPA | Debt Management Performance Assessment |
| DMF | Debt Management Facility |
| DR | Democratic Republic |
| DRF | Debt Reduction Facility |
| DSA | Debt Sustainability Analysis |
| DSF | Debt Sustainability Framework |
| ECF | Extended Credit Facility |
| E-HIPC | Enhanced HIPC |
| ESF | Exogenous Shock Facility |
| FDI | Foreign Direct Investments |
| GDF | Global Development Finance |
| GDP | Gross Domestic Product |
| GFS | Government Financial Statistics |
| GMM | Generalized Method of Moments |
| GNP | Gross National Product |
| HIPC | Heavily Indebted Poor Country |
| HIPC II | Enhanced HICP (*see* E-HIPC) |
| IBRD | International Bank for Reconstruction and Development |
| IDA | International Development Association |
| IDB | Inter-American Development Bank |
| IFI | International Financial Institution |
| IFS | International Financial Statistics |
| IMF | International Monetary Fund |
| IV | Instrumental Variables |
| LIC | Least Income Country |
| MIC | Middle Income Country |
| MDG | Millennium Development Goals |

| | |
|---|---|
| MDRI | Multilateral Debt Relief Initiative |
| NGO | Non Governmental Organization |
| NPV | Net Present Value |
| ODA | Official Development Assistance |
| OECD | Organization for Economic Cooperation and Development |
| OIR | Over-Identifying Restrictions |
| OLS | Ordinary Least Squares |
| PNG | Private Non-Guaranteed |
| PPG | Public and Publicly-Guaranteed |
| PPP | Purchasing Power Parity |
| PRGF | Poverty Reduction and Growth Facility |
| PRGT | Poverty Reduction and Growth Trust |
| PRSP | Poverty Reduction Strategy Paper |
| PVC | Present Value Constraint |
| RCF | Rapid Credit Facility |
| SBA | Stand-By Arrangement |
| SCF | Standby Credit Facility |
| SDRM | Sovereign Debt Restructuring Mechanism |
| SME | Small and Medium Enterprises |
| SOE | State-Owned Enterprise |
| SSA | Sub-Saharan Africa(n) |
| TFP | Total Factor Productivity |
| TOT | Terms Of Trade |
| UN | United Nations |
| UNDP | United Nations Development Program |
| WB | World Bank |
| WDI | World Development Indicators |
| WEO | World Economic Outlook |
| WGI | World Governance Indicators |

# Introduction

*When a country is well-governed,*
*poverty and a mean condition are things to be ashamed of.*
*When a country is ill-governed,*
*riches and honour are things to be ashamed of.*
(Confucius, 551-479 BCE)

*A policy is a temporary creed liable to be changed,*
*but while it holds good it has got to be pursued with apostolic zeal.*
(M. K. Gandhi, 1869-1948 AD)

After the major debt build-up and defaults in Latin America in the eighties, the nineties witnessed the accumulation of new debt in the world's poorest countries: most of them in SSA and a few in Central America and Asia. This latest debt accumulation was (and is) particularly harmful because it occurred in countries with per capita income often below the subsistence level. Debt accumulation had the unwelcome aspect of being connected to a life-saving supply of aid and often to natural disasters, wars and volatile commodity prices. Therefore, there is a strong humanitarian dimension to high external debt in poor countries, which is not necessarily associated with other occurrences of high indebtedness.

At the end of the nineties, despite several rounds of debt relief, many poor countries still had large external debts and debt-service obligations – that are generally perceived as constraints to economic growth and poverty alleviation – even though they kept on receiving net positive resource transfers from the IFIs, unlike countries during the Latin American debt crisis of the eighties. The debt burden was clearly unsustainable from both an economic and a humanitarian point of view. Large chunks of existing debt were not going to be repaid and the flows of repayments (if they were taking place) were a strong burden on countries with limited liquid resources. Also, we should not underestimate the critical voice of public opinion requiring from national governments and IFIs not just to address the financial dimension of external debt in poor countries, but especially to relieve the human suffering associated with poverty, malnutrition, failing health and poor education. Additionally, it is worth remembering the spread of HIV-AIDS to many African countries: not certainly alone in having this plague, but probably the ones paying the heaviest toll. After rounds of restructuring and rescheduling it became evident that coordinated action was required to reduce the debt burden substantially.

As a consequence, the international community promoted concerted action for coordinated debt relief under the so-called HIPC Initiative, where not only sovereign countries (Paris Club members) would agree to grant debt relief, but also the multilateral institutions were participating in granting relief on concessional debt to promote long-term debt sustainability and poverty reduction. In 2005, during the G8 meeting in Gleneagles, the MDRI was created: the IMF, the WB, the AfDB and the IDB committed themselves to provide complete debt cancellation to countries that had graduated from the HIPC process.

In the last ten years the HIPC Initiative and the MDRI have been the most relevant multilateral programs in the area of debt sustainability and debt relief, also augmented with bilateral initiatives. The international community has spent for the HIPC Initiative 74 billions of US dollars and the MDRI will add other 45.

Debt relief for poor countries is one of the most important and critical issues of political economy, as it affects the life of about 600 million poor people across the world. The great efforts undertaken by many NGOs, campaigners and civil society, especially in the years before and after the year 2000, have raised a lot of attention and enthusiasm on debt relief and have brought great pressure on rich countries' governments. This large mobilization resulted in a deeper commitment to debt reduction and has pushed forward the debt issue in the political agenda.

However, an efficient use of these resources requires a careful cost-benefit analysis, so that the HIPC Initiative has not been immune from criticisms. The renewed interest in debt relief gave more emphasis to the aid effectiveness debate among academics, campaigners and practitioners. Here, we choose not to enter what is now called the *Easterly-Sachs debate*, which has been very provocative and passionate. However, at the risk of oversimplifying, it is worth recalling that the most important distinction is between those arguing for a much broader and deeper debt reduction, as the only solution to reduce poverty and those who claim that more conditionality and selectivity is needed in order to avoid providing additional resources to corrupt governments. Both lines of reasoning have their merits and have in common the underlying idea that debt relief – at least until now, as we show in Part 3 – has not been able to foster a strong path of economic growth, which is the core element for poverty alleviation and debt sustainability. On the one hand, many activists and NGOs call for a complete debt write-off, on the ground that the current level of aid is not enough to fuel a growth process: complete debt cancellation without increased foreign aid is calculated to be not nearly enough to meet even the basic health expenditures (Sachs 2002), while additional resources are required for other basic needs and social infrastructures. Given these premises, Sachs has called for a radical change in the creditors-donors point of view, in the sense that debt reduction should be directly linked to an assessment of debtor-specific requirements for meeting their essential needs. On the other hand, this approach have been harshly criticized on the ground of decades-long experience of unsuccessful foreign assistance (Easterly 2006; Rajan and Subramanian 2008; Moyo 2009). Instead, building on the role of sound institutions and macroeconomic policies for the process of structural change and economic development (Acemoglu and Robinson 2008), another part of the literature and several commentators call for increased conditionality and selectivity in debt relief, that "will only help reduce debt burdens if government policies make a true shift away from redistributive politics and toward a focus on economic development" (Easterly 2001a: 22). When given to corrupt governments, lacking resources and know-how for budgeting, monitoring and accounting for public resources, debt relief does not provide the right incentives to implement better economic policies and structural reforms. Debt relief granted to irresponsible governments is at best ineffective and possibly a danger: giving resources to corrupt and undemocratic governments means weakening the rule of law by supporting those very responsible for breaking it; worst still, in the presence of civil tensions and/or ethnic differences (quite common features in several African countries, although not only there), indiscriminate debt relief or financial support often means that more resources could be used by the recipient group in power in order to discriminate, suppress or weaken another group in the same country. Additionally, debt relief to corrupt or undemocratic governments might also represent a lost opportunity to help better governed countries eradicate poverty.

In our opinion, a stronger financial commitment by donors – associated with heightened attention to macroeconomic and competition policies, and a sensible allocation process between loans and grants – is highly desirable to avoid poor countries being forced to fill their financial gap by issuing domestic debt or relying excessively on non-concessional borrowing. As we discuss in Part 3, it seems unambiguous that, on the whole, the current amount of resources freed up by debt relief is not enough to reach the MDG. Additionally, the destination of a large share of scarce resources to a limited number of countries, lacking some of the most basic infrastructures and institutions to trigger economic growth and permanently exit from debt dependence, means that less resources are made available to assist other poor countries better equipped to profit from external assistance: as a matter of fact, there is evidence of some positive results at country level, mostly in the presence of sound policies and good institutions. Thus, even abstracting from ethical considerations and looking exclusively at the economics of debt relief, we argue that corruption, poor macroeconomic management and bad governance must be taken into account in the allocation process: debt relief has to be granted only to countries for which the debt burden represents an actual constraint to economic growth, following a *growth diagnostic* approach (Hausmann, Rodrik and Velasco 2005). Finally, through an appropriate selectivity mechanism based on *governance conditionality* (Radelet 2005a; Collier 2007), debt relief can also be used as an incentive mechanism to encourage countries to undertake structural reforms and improve their governance. The *ex-ante* institutional improvements should enhance the effectiveness of debt relief, driving the allocation of resources freed up towards productive investments and pro-poor and social spending.

Our work blends together our different backgrounds, merging an academic approach with operational and institutional expertise, in order to provide an evaluation as complete and balanced as possible on the effectiveness of debt relief in fostering economic growth, reducing poverty and reaching debt sustainability.

This book merges theoretical analysis, empirical evidence and policy experience. It reviews and assesses key elements of the policy design (*ex-ante*) together with policy implementation and outcomes (*ex-post*), providing extensive and original empirical evidence on the successes and failures of debt relief programs, raises words of concern on specific issues that can derail the overall success of debt relief in HIPCs, and suggests a more comprehensive approach to debt sustainability and debt relief programs.

Part 1 of the book provides the background concepts. We start with a brief review of recent debt crises in developing countries, and show descriptive evidence of debt accumulation and debt relief in HIPCs. We then illustrate the mechanics of the HIPC Initiative and the MDRI, their targets and how they work.

In Chapter 2 we deal with debt sustainability. We begin by presenting the original *external* debt sustainability approach, as well as subsequent modifications leading to the DSF. We extensively review the literature on debt sustainability, discussing the different suggestions to improve the standard DSA and the empirical models proposed to assess debt sustainability. Finally, we consider the effects of concessional lending to LICs on debt sustainability, stressing some unintended consequences of a rise in foreign assistance and the importance of the appropriate mix between grants and loans.

Part 2 analyzes the evolution of *domestic* PPG debt, after the inception of the HIPC Initiative. We show that the adjustment programs required by the Initiative have been successful in reducing inflation, but the slow fiscal adjustment, together with the (program-imposed) lack of access to international capital markets and adequate inflows of concessional lending, forced governments to tap domestic markets to finance their primary deficits. This inappropriate policy mix resulted in a steep increase in real interest rates, which could undermine overall growth and public debt sustainability. This Part also presents a new empirical evaluation of public debt sustainability in a simple accounting framework. We use data on (multilateral and bilateral) external public debt and an original dataset on domestic public debt to show how the inclusion of domestic debt into the analysis undermines the sustainability target.[1]

After a general presentation of the role of domestic markets for government securities in poor countries, we present some descriptive evidence of the dynamics of domestic debt, together with its cost in LICs and MICs over the last 20 years. We look at the potential effects of domestic debt on economic growth and investigate the risks of fast-growing internal debt in HIPCs, selectively reviewing the existing literature and presenting new empirical evidence.

1 Regarding the substantial amount of data in tables, graphs and the econometric exercises presented in the book, it is generally updated to what is available as of the first quarter of 2010. However, as the group of HIPCs has changed several times and the various debt relief programs have evolved, the data used and presented may not necessarily include the same group of countries nor the same time periods across the book, but is always internally consistent in each of the instances presented.

We stress the limits of the current DSF and the need to include domestic public debt into the analysis. The standard sustainability analysis does not take into account the fully-fledged government budget constraint and the feedback effects of the fiscal and monetary adjustments required by multilateral programs. The switch from foreign to domestic borrowing and rising domestic real interest rates are likely to jeopardize the overall sustainability and the success of debt relief programs.

The evolution of domestic debt during the last decade confirms the need for its inclusion in a fully-fledged macroeconomic framework. Even if its level is not yet excessive, its costs are already a constraint to macroeconomic and monetary management. The benefits from external debt cancellation could be offset by the adverse effects of domestic debt (credit squeeze, crowding out of investment due to higher interest rates, inflationary pressures, and a reduction in social and pro-poor expenditure due to the increased domestic interest payments).

Part 3 discusses the relationship between debt and macroeconomic performance. It consists of three different chapters. The first one selectively reviews the theoretical and empirical literature on the economic consequences of excessive debt in developing countries, focusing on investment, GDP growth, productivity and capital flight. The bulk of the discussion concerns the debt overhang hypothesis, which, discourages public and private investment, predicts that higher debts are detrimental to economic growth; and its empirical validation, which is illustrated by the Debt-Laffer curve. The crowding out of investments due to external debt service and the high level of uncertainty and macroeconomic instability created by a large indebtedness are also considered.

We stress the specificity of the current debt crisis, so that the standard arguments developed as a response to the Latin-American crisis of the eighties have to be adapted to the specific characteristics of the HIPCs. In particular, positive net resource transfers are likely to weaken the disincentive effects of large external debts, while an unsound institutional framework and an unstable macroeconomic environment are likely to be the binding constraints for overall economic performance, since they discourage long-term investment and structural reforms. The empirical evidence is generally mixed, with the Debt-Laffer curve being poorly identified, even if there is some evidence of debt overhang and crowding out.

In Chapter 7 the estimation of a growth model on a panel of developing countries suggests that policies and institutions are likely to cause simultaneously debt accumulation and low economic growth rates. The debt-growth nexus clearly depends on a country-specific institutional framework: debt overhang is effective exclusively in countries with good policies and institutions. On the contrary, external debt seems to be growth-neutral for countries with weak institutions. These results indicate that debt reduction is likely to be effective only in countries with sound institutions, so that debt relief policies should be tailored in order to consider country-specific characteristics, following the same approach adopted in the DSF.

Chapter 8 explicitly focuses on the *ex-post* assessment of debt relief. A new and promising strand of literature inspects the direct effects of debt relief on a number of macroeconomic indicators in poor countries, generally finding that reductions in external debt are not associated with significant improvements in economic performance (when there are positive effects, they are likely to be conditional on a sound institutional framework). We add extensive new empirical evidence and analysis, especially with respect to investment, GDP growth, pro-poor public expenditure, foreign investments, institution building and domestic borrowing. Our results show that debt relief is only weakly associated with subsequent improvements in economic performance in HIPCs, while it is clearly correlated with increasing domestic debt, which undermines the positive achievements (where and when they are present) from reduced external debt service. There is some – albeit limited – evidence that, since the launch of the HIPC Initiative and the stepping-in of multilateral institutions, donors are moving towards a more sensible allocation of debt forgiveness, rewarding countries with better policies and institutions.

Part 4, firstly discusses the transmission of the current economic and financial crisis (2008-2010 global recession) to LICs and its possible implications for future debt sustainability in HIPCs. Secondly, it draws the main implications from each of the above chapters in order to propose a comprehensive approach to debt sustainability and debt relief. In particular, we propose to extend the current DSF, arguing that a comprehensive DSA requires a fully-fledged government budget constraint, which should include not only the external position, but also public domestic debt and the feedback effects from the exchange rate and the choices of deficit financing.

We also suggest to consider uncertainty and the risk of default, to carefully evaluate the resources required to finance poverty reduction policies and to develop a legal framework to deal with private creditors and vulture funds. As a result, debt relief should be tailored to specific country needs and should be part of a more comprehensive development policy – aimed at promoting donors' coordination, spearheading growth and reducing poverty – built on the fully-fledged government budget constraint and designed to provide an incentive to strengthen institutions and policies.

With reference to debt relief policies, the current approach to debt relief is based on a uniform treatment of indebted poor countries by donors, apart from new lending allocated between grants and loans according to the DSF. However, the evidence discussed in Part 4 suggests that policy-makers should avoid one-size-fits-all solutions and consider different countries other than the HIPC-eligible ones, targeting additional financial resources to countries with relatively good governance. Our empirical analysis of the key role played by institutions and policies suggests that for debt relief to be effective on growth and social expenditures it must be conditional on a certain level of institutional quality. Also, a governance conditionality-based policy design that makes differential amounts of debt cancellation conditional upon actual improvements in institutional quality would act as a strong incentive for recipients to strengthen institutions and policies.

Overall, we focus almost exclusively on the economics of debt relief, looking at the effects of the debt burden on economic growth and at the relevance of domestic debt for the overall debt sustainability and for the effectiveness of debt relief policies; we also choose to provide new original empirical evidence. In our opinion, these are the areas where more research is required to assist a sensible and effective decision-making process. The renewed interest in internal financing among academics and practitioners, and some recent studies on the consequences of debt relief seem to support our view.

Other open issues are worth considering, at least briefly. We refer to some of them in Part 4: the role of odious debt and vulture funds is briefly discussed, jointly with new lending policies and the role of non-concessional borrowing in HIPCs. The development of prudent lending policies, especially coupled with the effects of the global crisis, is critical to maintain debt sustainability over the long term. As additional data are made available, it will be possible to empirically test the behaviour of donors and borrowers after the MDRI relief. Debt management and monetary and fiscal policy coordination are other areas which should draw increased attention.

Lastly, the presentation of the history of past debt reduction initiatives has been kept short as it falls outside the scope of this work. For readers with a specific interest, the WB and the IMF websites and publications, together with some of the references mentioned throughout this book, offer a broad range of descriptive and explanatory materials.

# PART 1
# Multilateral Initiatives and External Debt Sustainability

## Overview

The first part of the book briefly illustrates the history of recent debt crises in poor countries and the responses by donors and IFIs (Chapter 1).[1] Initially, the approach to the debt crisis by western countries was to adopt a series on non-concessional debt flows reschedulings hoping that this would provide LICs with the required fiscal space to start growing and repaying their debts. However, what was originally perceived as a liquidity crisis turned out to be a solvency problem and, therefore, required a structured and comprehensive approach. Through a number of agreements, the Paris Club increased its commitment to debt relief and debt reduction in the late eighties and the nineties, until the launch of the HIPC Initiative in 1996 by the WB and the IMF. The Initiative, which has evolved into the MDRI in 2006, targets 40 poor and severely indebted countries, deals for the first time with multilateral external debt and is aimed at achieving a permanent exit from unsustainable debt positions and a reduction in poverty.

In Chapter 2 we focus on the issue of public debt sustainability, which is the core of the HIPC Initiative. Since the identification of indicators of fiscal and external sustainability is not straightforward – depending on a lender- versus a borrower-based approach, *ex-post* versus *ex-ante* definitions of sustainability, and the consideration or not of basic-needs financing – we review the different approaches, highlighting their major advantages and drawbacks. In particular, we consider the approach adopted in the IMF-WB DSA, analysing the evolution of the definition of debt sustainability implied in the analysis, the IMF-WB responses to several criticisms to their original approach and the establishment of the DSF in 2005 and subsequent proposals for reform, which bring a number of elements of novelty into the DSA. In particular, there is a shift from a focus on *ex-post* identities to a forward-looking approach, adopting prudent lending policies.

1 The book deals exclusively with the debt problems of HIPCs. The theoretical and the empirical literature on sovereign debt, default and growth is extremely vast and at least few contributions are worth mentioning for the interested reader. Panizza, Sturzenegger and Zettelmeyer (2009) provide a very extensive and recent review of the economics and law of sovereign debt and default; Panizza and Levy Yeyati (2010) deepen the analysis of the relationship between defaults and output growth in emerging countries; finally, Reinhart and Rogoff (2009) present a broad historical (but also quantitative) picture of debt crises.

However, we stress that even the current approach is not immune to criticisms, its main weaknesses being a limited attention to the endogeneity issue, to domestic debt and exchange rate dynamics, including the maturity and currency composition of public debt.

Finally, we take into consideration the issue of concessional lending to poor countries, which plays a key role for public debt sustainability. Some commentators call for a scaling up of foreign assistance, which is one of the usual commitments by donors. However, there are reasons to believe that a surge in aid could undermine debt sustainability because of lower revenues and a contraction of the tradable sector due to an exchange rate appreciation and a rise in inflation or in interest rates. Debt sustainability can also be affected by the grants-loans mix in aid allocation. The shift toward grants suggested by the Meltzer report has put forward on the policy agenda the debate on the appropriate grant share in concessional lending. In the final section of Chapter 2 we discuss the different positions in this debate, arguing that any choice on the grants-loans mix should take into account a minimum target of resources for poor countries to finance their basic expenditures. This is needed to avoid the recourse to alternative sources of financing, such as the issue of local-currency denominated government securities, which, under certain conditions, could have a negative effect on debt sustainability.

Chapter 1

# The Heavily Indebted Poor Countries and the Multilateral Debt Relief Initiatives: Description and Issues

## 1.1 The Debt Build-Up and the First Responses

As of April 2010, the HIPC and the MDRI target 40 low-income and highly indebted countries, mainly located in SSA, but also in Latin America and Asia.[1] Debt relief is delivered in two stages (decision and completion points), with countries that graduate from the second stage receiving 100 percent debt cancellation under the MDRI. Therefore, according to the specific characteristics and performances under the HIPC initiative, different countries are at different stages of the program: 28 countries have already reached completion point (Uganda was the first one in 2000, while Congo DR, Afghanistan and Liberia have been the last ones in the first half of 2010), seven are in the interim period and have received partial debt relief, and five (Comoros, Eritrea, Kyrgyzstan, Somalia and Sudan) have still to reach the decision point (Figure 1.1). On the whole, HIPCs are home to more than 600 million people, whose annual GDP per capita in 2008 was equal to 548 dollars (1,210 at PPP) and are affected by widespread poverty and hunger, poor sanitation and low levels of education. Over 117 billion dollars have been committed or delivered under the HIPC and the MDRI initiatives to tackle global poverty and this effort has been associated with a major reduction in the external debt burden and with an increase in poverty reduction expenditures. However, as we discuss in the following chapters, the picture is quite heterogeneous and the identification of a nexus of causality between the input – debt relief – and different outputs – poverty reduction and economic growth – is not at all simple.

The debt crisis in the HIPCs is a long lasting phenomenon that hindered economic growth due to creditors' lending policies – driven by increasing bilateral loans at commercial interest rates and concessional lending – imprudent debt management policies, lack of macroeconomic adjustments and structural reforms in debtor countries, and a number of exogenous domestic and international exogenous shocks, such as the secular decline in the TOT, vagaries of the weather, social unrest and wars. As a result of these adverse conditions, these countries

1 Differently from the HIPC Initiative, the MDRI includes also Tajikistan and Cambodia as additional beneficiaries. Nonetheless, we focus exclusively on the original sample of HIPCs, as done also by the WB in its official statistics.

started accumulating external debt, reaching very high ratios of debt to GDP and exports in the nineties (Figure 1.2).

At the beginning of the seventies HIPCs had, on average, a level of external debt equal to total exports and to around a fourth of GDP. By the end of the eighties, the stock of debt became equal to the annual GDP and to more than five times exports, notwithstanding the extensive use of non-concessional flow rescheduling granted by the informal group of 19 sovereign bilateral official creditors (the Paris Club): between 1976 and 1988 they agreed on 81 non-concessional flow rescheduling with 27 countries that allowed for payments close to 23 billion dollars to be delayed (Table 1.1). The initial creditors' behavior towards the debt problems of LICs resembled the experience of the Latin America debt crisis and was motivated by the desire to increase the likelihood to have their original claims paid back through a rescheduling of debt service, which would have given time and resources to borrowers to grow out of their debt problems.[2] The initial reluctance of donors to agree on actual debt reductions is aimed at limiting moral hazard by indebted governments. The donors' preference to avoid disbursements of untied aid to countries with bad institutions is also part of the story: debt relief, contrary to other forms of assistance, is basically untied budget support, and recipients are generally countries with weak institutions. However, what was perceived to be a liquidity crisis started to reveal itself as a solvency one. The increasing external debt and its associated debt-service payments, raised from 15 percent of export in 1980 to 30 percent in 1986 (Figure 1.3), were seen as unsustainable and determined a number of debt reduction initiatives, introduced during the late 1980s and the 1990s, according to which bilateral donors agreed to rescheduling on concessional terms and introducing the option of stock-of-debt cancellation.[3]

The launch of the Strategic Program of Assistance to Africa (now called the *Strategic Partnership with Africa*) at the 1987 IMF-WB Annual Meetings represents the first coordinated response of multilateral institutions to the debt crisis in LICs and it could be perceived as the forefather of the HIPC Initiative, since it included concessional lending and debt relief as channels to address BOP problems in poor countries. The shift from debt relief to debt reduction by the Paris Club happened in the same year at the Venice G7 meeting, when for the first time they recognized that "the problems of some of the poorest countries, primarily in Sub-Saharan Africa, are uniquely difficult and need special treatment. [...] For those of the poorest countries that are undertaking adjustment effort, consideration should be given to the possibility of applying lower interest rates to their existing

2 As noted by Gamarra, Pollock and Primo Braga (2009), the agreements with Ghana (1974) and Indonesia (1970) were two notable exceptions, since they were settled on concessional terms, considering the importance of debt sustainability.

3 See Daseking and Powell (1999) and Gamarra, Pollock and Primo Braga (2009) for a detailed discussion of the history of debt relief and Table 1.1 for a brief synopsis of the Paris Club agreements.

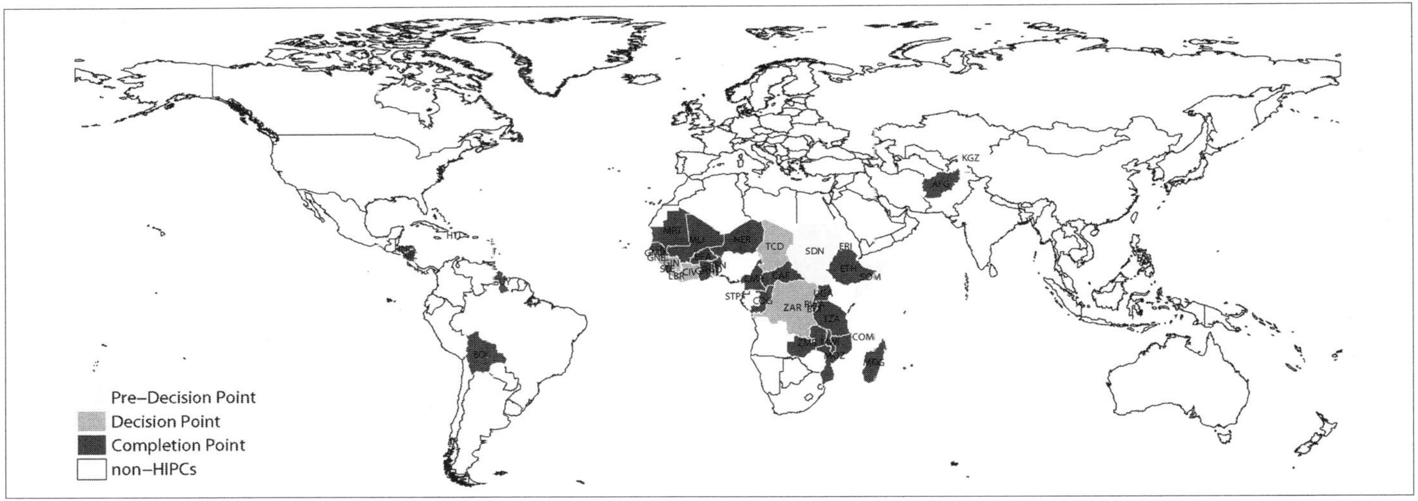


**Figure 1.1 Heavily indebted and poor countries**
*Source*: Authors' elaboration on WB data on HIPCs' status (as of April 2010).

debt, and agreement should be reached, especially in the Paris Club, on longer repayment and grace periods to ease the debt-service burden".

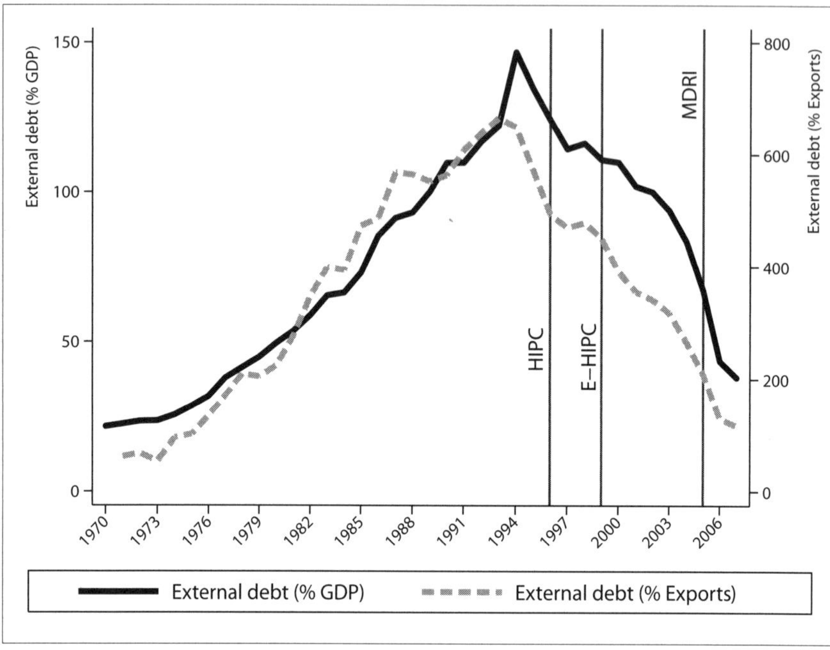


**Figure 1.2 External debt in HIPCs**
*Source*: Authors' elaboration on the 2009 GDF and WDI. Data, when available, refer to the sample of 40 HIPCs.

As a result, under the so-called Toronto (1988) and London (1991) terms, donor countries started providing debt relief with outright cancellation or through concessional rescheduling of debt service (setting the interest rate on residual claims after debt restructuring at below-market rates), in order to address what was still perceived as a liquidity problem.[4] Under the Toronto terms, 20 LICs received debt reschedulings, amounting to almost 6 billion dollars of payments falling due being either partially cancelled or rescheduled on a concessional basis. However, as the stock of external debt kept increasing, the Paris Club realized that for LICs the high levels of external debt and debt service did not represent a liquidity but a solvency issue. Donors devised new rules to address this "ability-to-pay" problem,

4 In 1990 the Paris Club introduced the Houston terms, but only for the debt of lower middle-income countries. Among the HIPCs, only Congo DR, Côte d'Ivoire and Honduras benefited from the Houston terms.

by offering new debt rescheduling agreements – the Naples (1994), Lyon (1996) and Cologne (1999) terms – which for the first time covered the outstanding stock of external debt and not only the debt-service flows falling due. Under the Naples terms seven agreements accounted for about 17 billion dollars of debt being partially forgiven or rescheduled on concessional terms and, as a results, the debt service for HIPCs declined to 17.6 percent of exports in 1997. With the Lyon and Cologne terms, the official bilateral creditors agreed on debt reduction in the HIPC framework: by October 2009, Paris Club creditors had delivered more than 20 billion dollars in debt relief to HIPCs, of which almost 8 billion were provided to completion point countries beyond the HIPC Initiative.

**Table 1.1 Paris Club rescheduling agreements**

| Terms | Years | Stock or Flow | Number of Reschedulings | Number of HIPCs | Brief description |
|---|---|---|---|---|---|
| Classic | 1956 | Flow | 67 | 26 | Credits (non-ODA) are rescheduled at the appropriate market rate with a repayment profile negotiated on a case-by-case basis. |
| Toronto | 1988-1991 | Flow | 26 | 19 | For the first time a reduction of part of the debt of poor countries is implemented: the level of reduction was defined as 33.33%. |
| London | 1991-1994 | Flow | 23 | 21 | The level of debt cancellation is raised from the 33.33% as defined in Toronto terms to 50%. |
| Naples | 1994 | Stock & flow | 40 | 29 | Replaced the Toronto and London terms. The level of cancellation is at least 50% and can be raised to 67% of eligible non-ODA credits. Since September 1999 all Naples terms carry a 67% debt reduction. Stock treatments may be implemented, on a case-by-case basis. |
| Lyon | 1996-1999 | Stock & flow | 7 | 5 | In the framework of the HIPC initiative, the level of cancellation is raised up to 80%. This measure goes with specific contributions of the multilateral institutions so that they also reduce the level of their claims on the concerned countries. |
| Cologne | 1999 | Stock & flow | 34 | 26 | Replaced the Lyon terms. The level of cancellation for the poorest countries is raised up to 90% or more if necessary in the framework of the HIPC initiative. |

*Source*: Authors' elaboration on Daseking and Powell (1999) and Paris Club data (available at: www.clubdeparis.org).

Over the same years, LICs benefited also from other instruments aimed at reducing their debt burden, such as: debt relief by non-Paris Club creditors (i.e. Gulf countries) and commercial creditors (London Club); the forgiveness of ODA debt by DAC member countries; several debt swaps and debt conversion bilateral initiatives; and the establishment of the WB Debt Reduction Facility designed to address repayment problems of commercial debt.[5]

By contrast, multilateral development banks and the IMF resisted recommendations to provide debt relief on their concessional loans and maintained their status of preferred creditors, according to which payments of multilateral debt take priority over private and bilateral debt. In those years, the stock of external debt kept growing and, at its peak, its level in the whole group of HIPCs reached 663 percent of exports in 1993 and 152 percent of GDP in 1994 (Figure 1.2). Given the shift of bilateral donors (especially EU countries) from loans to grants started in the 1980s, the Paris Club debt reductions and the scarce capacity of poor countries to attract private lending, an increasing proportion of their external debt was due to multilateral creditors (Birdsall, Williamson and Deese 2002). According to GDF data, the share of multilateral debt in total external debt increased from 11 percent in 1970 to 47 percent in 1996[6] (Figure 1.3). As a result, NGOs and some sovereign lenders (notably, the UK, the Netherlands and Scandinavian countries) put growing pressures on multilateral institutions and western donors to increase debt relief efforts and extend debt reduction to multilateral loans.

The IMF and the WB were initially reluctant, arguing that debt relief was neither necessary nor affordable and that it could generate moral hazard and undermine IMF conditionality (Evans 1999, Teunissen 2004). Nevertheless, under increasing political pressure from their major shareholders, in 1996 the sister institutions endorsed the debt relief policy and launched the HIPC Initiative, which was enhanced in 1999 in order to provide faster debt relief to a larger number of countries. Finally, in 2005, following the G8 meeting at Gleneagles, donors pledged to cancel the whole debt held by the IDA of the WB, the IMF and the African Development Fund of the countries that reached completion point under the E-HIPC Initiative (in December 2006 also the IDB agreed on the 100 percent debt relief). Thanks to these efforts, amounting to over 117 billion of dollars, external debt ratios started declining. Especially because of the steep reduction occurred in the previous five years, in 2007 the average external debt to GDP ratio was reduced to 38 percent and the ratio over exports declined to 116 percent, below the threshold identified as the sustainable level of debt under the HIPC Initiative. Similarly, debt-service payments declined below 10 percent of exports in 2005 and 2006.

5 In 1989 the WB established the IDA Debt Reduction Facility, with the aim of restructuring and buying back commercial debt with IDA credit. Nevertheless, even if sponsored by a multilateral institution, this program was mainly financed by bilateral donors and, more importantly, it concerned commercial and not multilateral debt. The facility is still working and it has gained importance in recent years by helping poor countries dealing with commercial creditors' litigations (see section 10.2.2). See Gamarra, Pollock and Primo Braga (2009) for an extensive discussion on different debt relief instruments.

6 The share of multilateral in total external debt reached 61 percent in 2005, when it started declining (it was 51 percent in 2007).

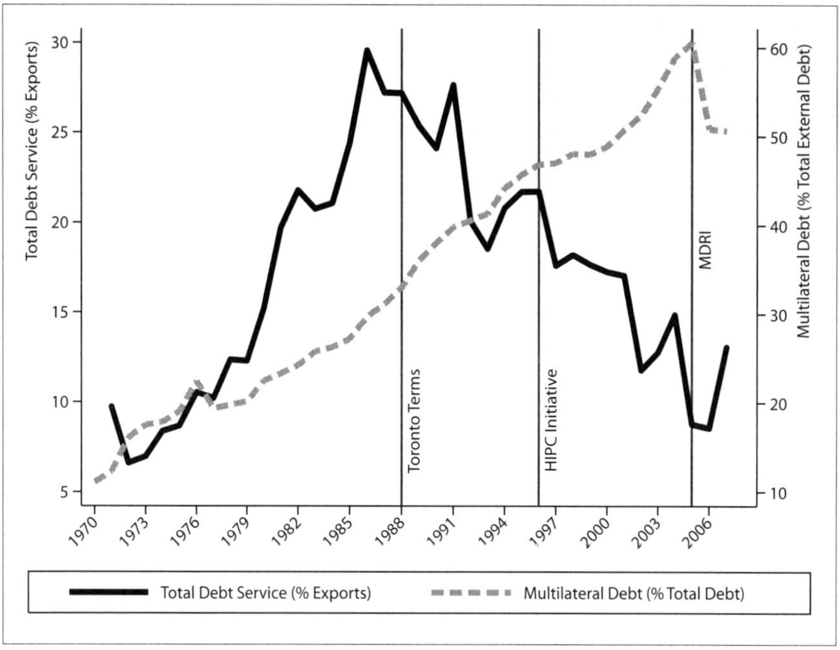


**Figure 1.3 External debt in HIPCs:**
**Total debt service and share of multilateral debt**

*Source*: Authors' elaboration on 2009 GDF data.

## 1.2 The HIPC Initiative

In the 1990s, bilateral official creditors started to negotiate debt reduction programs, at first limited to debt repayment flows and, subsequently, expanded also to debt stock reductions. The threatening evolution of external debt ratios in the early 1990s and the increasing importance of multilateral debt, coupled with increasing political pressures, forced the WB and the IMF to boost debt relief programs through the creation of the HIPC Initiative in 1996, with two main targets: assuring long-term debt sustainability and poverty reduction. With respect to traditional debt reduction programs, this program conveys two key elements of novelty: it deals with debt owed to multilateral institutions, which represents a large share of total debt held by HIPCs, and focuses on debt stocks, which should be reduced up to a low enough amount to reach sustainability.

The Initiative targets poor and heavily indebted countries and each potential candidate should meet three eligibility criteria. The first one concerns the definition of a poor country and requires the per capita GDP to be below a certain threshold: more technically, the country has to be classified as PRGF-eligible by the IMF and as IDA-only by the WB, meaning that its per capita income in 2008 was less than

US$ 1,135 and that it lacks the financial ability to borrow from the IBRD. The second criterion is related with a debt situation perceived as unsustainable, and the third one concerns the presence of an appropriate track record of adjustment and reforms. The most critical element is the second criterion, since, as discussed in section 2.2, debt sustainability is a complex issue and its definition in not unique. Under the original HIPC Initiative "a country can be considered to achieve external debt sustainability if it is expected to meet its current and future external debt-service obligations in full, without recourse to debt relief, rescheduling of debts, or the accumulation of arrears, and without unduly compromising growth" (Boote and Thugge 1997: 17). The eligibility criterion was based on the DSA defined on a case-by-case basis. In particular, debt sustainability was defined as "a position of a country when the NPV of (public and publicly-guaranteed) debt to exports ratio and the debt-service (on public and publicly-guaranteed loans) to export ratio are below certain country-specific target levels within ranges of 200-250 percent and 20-25 percent respectively" (Boote and Thugge 1997: 28). For countries with open economies (export-to-GDP ratio greater than 40) and substantial tax revenue (at least greater than 20 percent of GDP), having a NPV of debt-to-tax revenue greater than 280 is an alternative condition for eligibility.

These thresholds of sustainability were determined on the basis of the past experience of a number of countries, especially those emerging economies that in the 1980s underwent external debt crises: this confusion regarding the different origins and nature of external debt problems in poor countries in the 1990s versus emerging economies in the 1980s did not help the design of the HIPC Initiative (section 2.2). The program was also weakened by the excessive number of years necessary to qualify for debt reduction once the adjustment programs started: by July 1999, the HIPC Initiative had provided actual debt reduction to just four countries – Uganda, Bolivia, Guyana and Mozambique – and only three more – Burkina Faso, Mali and Côte d'Ivoire – were due to benefit by 2001. In 1999, as a response to a number of criticisms raised by NGOs and academics, the Initiative (now E-HIPC, or HIPC II) was modified in order to: 1) enlarge the number of countries potentially eligible for debt cancellation; 2) grant faster debt relief; and 3) create a stronger relationship between resources freed by debt relief and poverty reduction strategies. With the E-HIPC Initiative the eligibility ratios were reduced, but the approach to debt sustainability did not change, since it is still based on debt stocks, ignoring the relevance of debt-service payments on the government budget constraint. The ratio of the NPV of debt-to-exports is 150, while the additional fiscal indicator is lowered to 250 and it applies to countries with a revenues-to-GDP above 15 percent and exports-to-GDP ratio above 30 percent. Lowering the debt ratios aims at providing a deeper and broader debt relief, while the choice of uniform targets removes the country-by-country assessment, providing an unambiguous and simpler tool to define sustainability. However, this choice was widely perceived as unsatisfactory since it comes at the cost of ignoring country-specific factors which could affect the country's ability to manage external debt. Suggestions and criticisms – including those of their own internal evaluation departments[7] – created momentum for the IMF and the WB towards a more comprehensive definition of external debt sustainability. The development of a fiscal and external repayment capacity and the expected flows of grants and lending are included as key aspects for sustainability, together with the existing stock of public debt. In order to "assess long-term debt sustainability, the focus of attention must shift from this single debt indicator [the NPV of external public debt] to a more complex and comprehensive view of the development process in which policies, institutions, exogenous factors and debt management play an integral role over time" (IDA and IMF 2001: 3). This shows that the multilateral financial institutions were sensitive enough to external and internal suggestions, although the speed of their response was not perceived to be fast enough.

In February 2004, the IMF and the WB proposed a new DSF (IDA and IMF 2004a, 2004b). The new DSF, launched in April 2005, has

> a 'forward-looking' approach that aims at guiding borrowing and lending decisions for low-income countries on terms that allow borrowing countries to devote resources toward achieving the MDG, while simultaneously retaining (or accumulating) sufficient means to repay loans. By taking into account each country's specific circumstances, the framework tries to help borrowing countries balance their need for funds with their current and prospective ability to repay their debts. Linking a country's borrowing potential to its current and prospective ability to service debt should help countries avoid accumulating excessive debts.[8]

The DSA carried out under the DSF is based on the determination of country specific debt thresholds, depending on policies and institutional quality. It aims at monitoring the evolution of a country's debt burden indicators and reducing the vulnerability to debt distress through the formulation of an appropriate borrowing and lending strategy (Chapter 2). Given the empirical evidence linking policy variables to the probability of debt distress (Kraay and Nehru 2006), this new operational framework assesses debt sustainability by adopting policy-dependent debt and debt-service thresholds and classifying countries at different risk of debt distress according to their debt ratios. This classification is then used to allocate debt relief and also for future lending policies. Finally, contrary to previous experiences and in light of some criticisms (UNCTAD 2004; Arnone and Presbitero 2007), domestic debt is now considered in the analysis, because of its relevance as a source of vulnerability in many LICs (see Part 2 for details).

The HIPC Initiative now covers 40 countries (see Table 1.2): 35 of them have already benefited from debt relief, while the other 5 countries are potentially

---

7 A report by the WB Operations Evaluation Department (Eaton 2002: 10) states "that there is no current debt level that 'ensures debt sustainability' with any certainty. It all depends on the future behaviour of the country and its creditors".

8 Source: http://go.worldbank.org/4IMVXTQ090 (last accessed April 2010).

eligible for HIPC relief but still fail to meet the conditions required to achieve debt reduction. This difference is due to the specific design of the program, based on a two-step procedure (Figure 1.4):

1. Eligible countries can reach the *decision point* once they have a track record of macroeconomic stability and have prepared a PRSP. The amount of debt relief is calculated at this stage on the basis of the DSA. In the *interim period*, following decision point, countries might start receiving interim relief on a provisional basis on their debt service.
2. Once a country has maintained macroeconomic stability under the IMF's PRGF program, implemented a PRSP and carried out structural and social reforms for at least one year, it can reach *completion point*, which implies that the full amount of debt relief becomes irrevocable.

The policy design is aimed at granting debt relief to countries that reached macroeconomic stability and pledge to carry out structural reforms. The number of conditions attached to the whole program are intended to limit borrowers' moral hazard and stimulate sound macroeconomic and institutional reforms, but, at the same time, they should not be too stringent to avoid delaying the whole process. One of the main early criticism received by the original Initiative, as also acknowledged by the internal review undertaken by the WB (Gautam 2003), was that it was going to be *too little, too late*, so that in 1999 the E-HIPC framework was streamlined, introducing *interim* debt relief after decision point, a floating completion point and the so-called *topping-up*, additional HIPC assistance

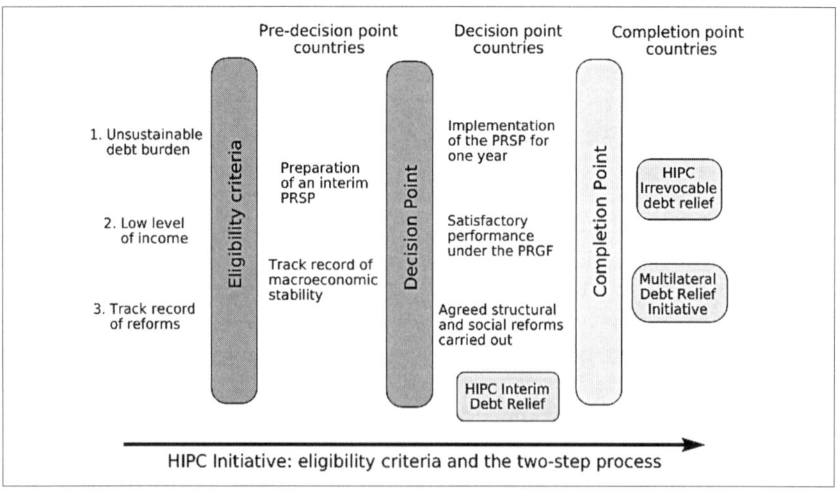


**Figure 1.4 How the HIPC Initiative works**
*Source*: Authors' elaboration.

**Table 1.2 List of HIPCs (as of April 2010), their status and external debt (in percent of GDP)**

| Completion Point | | | | | | Decision Point | | | |
|---|---|---|---|---|---|---|---|---|---|
| | *Year of DP* | *Year of CP* | *Year of MDRI* | *External debt (% GDP)* | | | *Year of DP* | *External debt (% GDP)* | |
| | | | | 1995 | 2007 | | | 1995 | 2007 |
| Afghanistan | 2007 | 2010 | Jan 2010 | 19.67* | . | Chad | 2001 | 58.53 | 29.21 |
| Benin | 2000 | 2003 | Jan 2006 | 82.14 | 15.78 | Congo, Dem. Rep. | 2003 | 271.42 | 142.86 |
| Bolivia | 2000 | 2001 | Jan 2006 | 81.18 | 38.20 | Cote d'Ivoire | 2009 | 188.74 | 73.63 |
| Burkina Faso | 2000 | 2002 | Jan 2006 | 53.62 | 21.73 | Guinea | 2000 | 89.82 | 72.66 |
| Burundi | 2005 | 2009 | Jan 2009 | 117.60 | 154.59 | Guinea-Bissau | 2000 | 380.71 | 213.59 |
| Cameroon | 2000 | 2006 | Apr 2006 | 131.70 | 15.34 | Liberia | 2008 | 765.77** | 442.13 |
| Central African Republic | 2007 | 2009 | Jul 2009 | 85.53 | 57.19 | Togo | 2008 | 116.67 | 80.13 |
| Congo, Rep. | 2006 | 2010 | Jan 2010 | 480.01 | 86.09 | | | | |
| Ethiopia | 2001 | 2004 | Jan 2006 | 136.60 | 13.57 | | | | |
| Gambia, The | 2000 | 2007 | Dec 2007 | 112.97 | 122.85 | | | | |
| Ghana | 2002 | 2004 | Jan 2006 | 86.88 | 29.85 | | | | |
| Guyana | 2000 | 2003 | Jan 2006 | 373.05 | 73.29 | | | | |
| Haiti | 2006 | 2009 | Jul 2009 | 28.13 | 26.08 | | | | |
| Honduras | 2000 | 2005 | Jan 2006 | 131.46 | 28.01 | | | | |
| Madagascar | 2000 | 2004 | Jan 2006 | 143.30 | 22.68 | | | | |
| Malawi | 2000 | 2006 | Sep 2006 | 165.75 | 24.58 | | | | |
| Mali | 2000 | 2003 | Jan 2006 | 122.29 | 30.61 | | | | |

**Table 1.2 continued**

| | Completion Point | | | | | Decision Point | | | |
|---|---|---|---|---|---|---|---|---|---|
| | Year of DP | Year of CP | Year of MDRI | External debt (% GDP) 1995 | External debt (% GDP) 2007 | | Year of DP | External debt (% GDP) 1995 | External debt (% GDP) 2007 |
| Mauritania | 2000 | 2002 | Jun 2006 | 175.34 | 61.98 | | | | |
| Mozambique | 2000 | 2001 | Jan 2006 | 360.55 | 44.01 | | | | |
| Nicaragua | 2000 | 2004 | Jan 2006 | 368.34 | 60.58 | | | | |
| Niger | 2000 | 2004 | Jan 2006 | 86.11 | 23.03 | **Pre-Decision Point** | | | |
| Rwanda | 2000 | 2005 | Jan 2006 | 79.22 | 14.92 | | | *External debt (% GDP)* | |
| Sao Tome and Principe | 2000 | 2007 | Mar 2007 | . | 117.07 | | | *1995* | *2007* |
| Senegal | 2000 | 2004 | Jan 2006 | 82.89 | 23.36 | Comoros | | 92.10 | 64.67 |
| Sierra Leone | 2002 | 2006 | Dec 2006 | 149.00 | 21.37 | Eritrea | | 6.26 | 64.06 |
| Tanzania | 2000 | 2001 | Jan 2006 | 144.64 | 31.39 | Kyrgyz Republic | | 37.49 | 65.03 |
| Uganda | 2000 | 2000 | Jan 2006 | 63.33 | 13.95 | Somalia | | . | . |
| Zambia | 2000 | 2005 | Jan 2006 | 215.07 | 27.94 | Sudan | | 136.25 | 45.88 |

*Note*: * Refers to 2006; ** Refers to 1997; Liberia reached completion point is June 2010. For Somalia there are no data on external debt. Comoros reached decision point in June 2010.
*Source*: Authors' elaboration based on GDF data, the Heavily Indebted Poor Countries (HIPC) Initiative and Multilateral Debt Relief Initiative (MDRI) – Status of Implementation (September 2009) and the WB website: http://go.worldbank.org/48MIDC8BH0 (last accessed April 2010).

at completion point for countries whose debt burden indicators deteriorate substantially due to exogenous factors. The *ex-ante* selection, by contrast, is mainly based on countries being heavily indebted and very poor, while there is limited attention to country selectivity. Apart from the development of the PRSP with the civil society and the presence of a track record of reform under the IMF programs, there is not a specific *ex-ante* conditionality which could reward good performers with specific characteristics, such as good institutional quality and low corruption. The rationale for this choice could be explained by the necessity to include a sufficiently high number of poor countries, which are not generally among the best performers in institutional and policy reforms.

## 1.3 The Multilateral Debt Relief Initiative

Notwithstanding some positive results achieved by the HIPC Initiative, which was able to reduce the stock of external debt in decision point countries from US$ 114 to 57 billions (in 2008 NPV terms), additional debt relief and resources were still required to finance investments in health, education and infrastructures required by poor countries to meet their development goals. Several bilateral donors provided more debt relief than required by the HIPC Initiative, but they also pressed the international institutions to move beyond the HIPC Initiative. Thus, after a period of great enthusiasm and support for aid to Africa and debt relief – as testified by the activity of several campaigners and NGOs and by the work of the *Commission for Africa* chaired by Tony Blair, who called for 100 percent debt cancellation for Africa – in 2005 the G8 Summit held at Gleneagles under the UK presidency proposed the establishment of the MDRI: it grants 100 percent debt cancellation to HIPCs to support progress towards the MDG.

The MDRI does not include bilateral and commercial creditors, but only debt disbursed before end-December 2004 by the IMF, the IDB and the AfDB and before end-December 2003 by the WB. The debt still outstanding at the time of qualification for the completion point under the E-HIPC Initiative is totally cancelled. Moreover, the Initiative applies the criterion of additionality, so that IDA's financial capacity will be preserved, as clearly stated in the G8 proposal for debt cancellation:

> Donors agree to complete the process of debt relief for the Heavily Indebted Poor Countries by providing additional development resources which will provide significant support for countries' efforts to reach the goals of the Millennium Declaration (MDG), while ensuring that the financing capacity of the IFIs is not reduced. This will lead to 100 percent debt cancellation of outstanding obligations of HIPCs to the IMF, World Bank and African Development Bank (and IDB).

The MDRI assistance will amount to US$ 45 billions (in nominal terms) and it will bring the debt burden of the 35 indebted countries that already reached the decision point at US$ 24 billions (in 2008 NPV terms), so that the combined effect of the HIPC Initiative and the MDRI will reduce their debt burden by almost 80 percent.

# Chapter 2
# External Debt Sustainability: Theory, Approaches and Limitations[1]

## 2.1 Introduction

We concur with some authors that debt relief seems to have failed to reach its targets partly because the DSA originally used in the Initiative was weakened by major drawbacks. The accounting approach used in current policy analysis – embodied in the criterion of financial sustainability – presents several shortcomings. Financial sustainability is quite limited a notion for a concept that is, instead, complex and that requires a wider perspective. As we point out, the most important shortcomings of the standard DSA are the endogeneity of the relevant variables, the exclusion of domestic debt and of the essential needs requirements. The macroeconomic impact that many variables have on economic activity requires the implementation of a more comprehensive framework in order to assess long-run debt sustainability. As a response to some of these criticisms, the WB and the IMF went through a revision of their analysis, developing the so-called DSF, a forward-looking tool which incorporates some country-specific factors, deals with rising domestic debt (see Part 2) and begins to address the possible effects of adverse exogenous shocks.

This chapter critically reviews different approaches to external debt sustainability, with a particular attention to the WB-IMF approach, in order to contribute to the development of a comprehensive and appropriate model to assess the sustainability of debt in HIPCs. To do so, we also present few theoretical models, which include some of the main criticisms received by the standard DSA. Notwithstanding some limitations (namely, the exclusion of the current account, domestic debt, and/or lack of feedback between fiscal and current account), these models represent a substantial improvement and they could be considered as a starting point for a more comprehensive approach, based on the fully-fledged government budget constraint.

Nevertheless, long-term debt sustainability in HIPCs is a very difficult target to achieve without structural and macroeconomic adjustment. Since debt sustainability critically depends on the evolution of poor countries' external

---

1 This chapter partially draws on a paper by M. Arnone, L. Bandiera and A. Presbitero, *Debt Sustainability Framework in HIPCs: A Critical Assessment and Suggested Improvements*, 2005 (revised 2008).

(and domestic) financing, we also discuss the consequences of increased foreign assistance, focusing on the widely debated choice between grants and loans in aid allocation.

## 2.2 Different Approaches to External Debt Sustainability

The external debt sustainability issue is widely debated in the theoretical and empirical literature and there are different perspectives to debt sustainability, depending on the economic targets and on the consideration of lender and borrower behavior. The approach used by the IFIs in the HIPC Initiative is just one of the possible ways to address the problem and we will see that it has been criticized under many aspects. The HIPC Initiative is based mainly on the DSA, which concerns the behavior of the borrower country and its willingness and ability to meet its debt obligations. However, the notion of debt sustainability is quite complex and it should generally consider the behavior of both the borrower and the lender. Debt sustainability is achieved by the interaction of the debtor country economy with the investment choices made by creditors in the financial markets. The literature presents different approaches to debt sustainability: a first distinction is made between the lender-based and borrower-based approaches, while a broader classification distinguishes between a simple debt capacity analysis (financial sustainability) and a more complex view that involves the assessment of some basic development targets (economic sustainability).

Another possible distinction between different perspectives used in the literature to address the external debt sustainability problem includes:

- Optimizing models, where the marginal benefit equals the marginal cost of borrowing. This approach was the first one developed by the theory.
- Non-optimizing models: *growth-cum-debt model and "debt dynamics" approach.* In the growth-cum-debt model, the external borrowing is used in order to fill the gap between domestic savings and investments, as in the two-gap model (Chenery and Strout 1966). The condition to be solvent requires that the rate of growth of the economy must be greater than the interest rate (the cost of borrowing). One important shortcoming is the lack of attention to the foreign currency issues. The *"debt dynamics"* approach looks at the external solvency and at the export rate of growth, which is now the parameter that must exceed the interest rate. These models remain unsatisfactory, because the growth paths are assumed to be time invariant and imports are not considered.
- Fiscal space models, which focus on the reduction in public expenditures due to debt service. The lack of infrastructure and public spending has an adverse effect on private investments, which are dismissed, and the result is slower growth. Another way in which the cash flow effect damages

the economy is through import compression, which reduces government investments and, in turn, the GDP growth rate.

- Disincentive effect models: a large stock of debt undermines economic performance through the *debt overhang* effect, which is related to the tax disincentive and macroeconomic stability. In the first case, which reflects the basic idea of the debt overhang theory, a large stock of debt discourages investments because taxes on future income are expected to be used to serve the debt payments. In the second case, the disincentives are related to the possible creation of macroeconomic instability, due to: 1) exchange rate depreciation; 2) increases in fiscal deficit; 3) monetary expansion and inflation; and 4) uncertainty due to exceptional financing.

Large part of the theoretical and empirical analysis has focused on the capacity of a debtor country to service its debt, ignoring the effect that debt and deficit have on the other economic variables and the development requirements. Moreover, the fact that debt sustainability is based on a solvency condition makes the criterion forward-looking, raising a number of implementation difficulties and originating the so-called "impossibility principle" (Wyplosz 2007).

In the following section we present the theoretical background of the two approaches – accounting and present value constraint – of financial sustainability. Some serious limitations of these definitions of debt sustainability and their implementation difficulties, as well as the advantages of a development perspective – based on the adverse effects of a large external debt on the economy – call for a more comprehensive approach to external debt sustainability in the HIPC initiative.

### *2.2.1 Financial Sustainability*

Following the so-called accounting approach (or, borrower-based approach), a fiscal deficit is considered sustainable if it generates a constant debt-to-GDP ratio. This condition just requires the growth rate of the economy to be greater than the real interest rate. In that case, government can run permanent primary deficits, even maintaining stable the ratio of debt over GDP. On the contrary, when economic growth is sluggish (and real interest rates are high), debt sustainability is granted, and explosive debt dynamics avoided, only through substantial primary surpluses. However, since in many LICs the grant element is a large fraction of government financing, a primary deficit may still be consistent with a stable debt-to-GDP ratio.

Differently, the present value constraint approach (or, lender-based approach) is based on the requirement for a government to be solvent. This conditions is satisfied when the flow of the expected value of future government revenues (plus foreign assistance) is at least equal to the face value of the stock of debt. This criterion is different from the accounting one, which imposes an upper bound to the debt-to-GDP ratio (Box 2.1). Under the usual assumption of a real interest rate greater than the rate of growth of GDP, the PVC requires only the real grow rate of debt to be lower than the real interest rate. If the former is between the GDP growth rate and the latter, the PVC is satisfied, but the debt-to-GDP ratio can grow over time. Given that the focus is on the level of deficit which is financeable, this approach does not require the full repayment of the entire debt.

**Box 2.1 Financial sustainability**

According to the accounting approach, the level of primary government surplus (or deficit) which stabilizes the debt-to-GDP ratio – $b$ – can be easily derived from the government budget constraint and, ignoring seigniorage, is given by:

$$BALANCE_t = \frac{(r_t - g_t)}{(1+g)} b \tag{2.1}$$

where $r$ is the real interest rate and $g$ is the rate of growth of GDP (see Ley (2008) for a clear presentation of the arithmetic of debt sustainability). From the equation (2.1) is clear that, as long as the economy grows at a rate higher than the interest rate, it is possible to run a sustainable primary deficit. What really matters is the capacity of the government to raise enough revenues to balance the expansion of the stock of debt. Since in LICs the grant element is a substantial fraction of GDP ($f$), the previous condition should be less stringent, and the primary balance can be defined as:

$$BALANCE_t = \frac{(r_t - g_t)}{(1+g)} b - f_t \tag{2.2}$$

In this way, Cline (2003), assuming a reasonable growth rate of 3 percent, grants equal to 4.5 percent of GDP and the real interest rate equal to 0.5 percent, estimates that HIPC countries do not have to run any primary surplus, but they can incur a primary deficit equal to 7.2 percent of GDP, without boosting the debt-to-GDP ratio above the current level of 106 percent.

The PVC approach (or, lender-based approach) defines a government as solvent if the flow of the expected value of future resources is at least equal to the face value of the stock of debt. It is the classical approach used to evaluate the domestic debt sustainability and it is translated in the following condition:

$$B_0 = \sum_{t=1}^{\infty} \frac{BALANCE_t}{(1+r_t)} \tag{2.3}$$

Where $B$ is the initial stock of debt, $r$ is the real interest rate and *BALANCE* are the future government primary balances, given by the difference between revenues and public expenditures.

Other than these two well-known and widely used approaches, it is worth mentioning the market value approach, which should take into account also the risk of non-payment, including "arrears, rescheduling and 'constrained' refinancing of various sorts" (Cohen 2001: 364). In that way, the market value of the stock of debt is smaller than its face value and its present value and the donors should consider the distinction between nominal and actual debt cancellation. What is generally considered new aid should be, in this perspective, a reported loss. This concept is particularly useful to understand the limited effectiveness of debt relief, since it often concerned debt that was not being serviced, so not freeing resources with respect to a situation without debt relief (Chapter 8).

The most important limits of both the two traditional approaches – the accounting and the PVC – are the assumption of exogeneity of the main policy variables and great reliance on their projections. As well stated by Wyplosz (2007: 6-7):

> Because debt sustainability is a forward-looking concept, it cannot be assessed with certainty. In that sense, debt sustainability analysis (…) is impossible. At best, (…) one can make educated guesses but it is important to recognize at the outset that these are just guesses, no matter how sophisticated they may be.

In this vein, the complete reliance on estimates and projections would make the sustainability of debt changing over time, as it is clear from the sharp revisions of the evolution of the debt ratios over the medium term from one DSA to the following one (this is particularly true when the macroeconomic framework changes substantially, as during the current global crisis, see Chapter 9). The assumption of exogeneity is also critical, since, if it is true that the repayment capacity of debtor countries is a function of their rate of growth of GDP, of exports, of fiscal revenues and of the interest rates, these variables are also, to some extent, influenced by the level of indebtedness (i.e. economic growth is affected, amongst other variables, by the debt burden, see Chapter 7). Gunning and Mash (1998) stress the centrality of forecasts, GDP growth, and real interest rate for sustainability analysis. Moreover, they underline also that what matters are not only economic fundamentals, but also expectations which generates uncertainty and make predictions less reliable.

### *2.2.2 The IMF – World Bank Approach to Debt Sustainability*

The WB-IMF view is strictly connected to the debt capacity perspective: the original DSA was based on the accounting approach and it derived thresholds of solvency. The WB and the IMF were concerned with the external debt and the borrower behaviour and they looked at the country's willingness and ability to meet current and furture external debt service obligations, without incurring into arrears or rescheduling. As already stated in Chapter 1, under the original HIPC Initiative "a country can be considered to achieve external debt sustainability if it is expected to meet its current and future external debt-service obligations in full, without recourse to debt relief, rescheduling of debts, or the accumulation of arrears, and without unduly compromising growth" (Boote and Thugge 1997: 17). This definition is consistent with the standard accounting approach. In a 2002 IMF document, debt was defined "sustainable if it satisfies the solvency condition without a major correction (…) given the costs of financing" (IMF 2002a: 5), explicitly referring to the PVC approach.

However, as stressed by Wyplosz (2007), the WB-IMF definition of sustainability is more demanding than the simple solvency criterion, since it requires: 1) neither major corrections, nor reschedulings, arrears or debt relief, and 2) a stable growth path. The requirement of the absence of major corrections is a fairly vague concept and it cannot be easily translated into an operational framework. Thus, the DSA used in the HIPC Initiative, grounded on the accounting framework, calculated the future evolution of the debt-to-GDP ratio, determining some thresholds of solvency and running several stress tests to evaluate the sustainability of external debt. These indicators of debt sustainability were the ratios of the NPV of external debt to exports and to fiscal revenues (see Box 2.2). These ratios, initially based on historical values, have been subsequently adjusted downwards, to grant higher debt relief to a larger number of countries (Chapter 1). Finally, the original DSA focused exclusively on debt stock indicators to assess debt sustainability, while flow indicators were merely descriptive. In the DSF the emphasis is still on the stock of public external debt, even if debt service indicators are now included among the debt-burden thresholds used to assess the risk of debt distress (see section 2.2.2.2 and Table 2.1).

*2.2.2.1 Early criticisms*

The original HIPC framework for DSA has been subject to many criticisms, which encompass a wide range of issues (Birdsall, Williamson and Deese 2002). In particular, critics stressed:

1. the implied exogeneity of the main policy variables, which ignore, for instance, the negative feedbacks of high interest rates and a tight fiscal policy on the GDP growth rate;
2. the great reliance on (overly-optimistic) projections;
3. the lack of attention paid to domestic debt dynamics and the substitution effect between external and domestic debt (UNCTAD 2004 and Part 2);
4. the need for an explicit consideration of an adequate level of indebtedness as a function of the specific institutional and economic characteristics of a country (Sun 2004; Kraay and Nehru 2006 and, more recently, Wyplosz 2007 and Cassimon, Moreno-Dodson and Wodon 2008).

The limitations of this sort of analysis are recognized also by the WB Independent Evaluation Group (formerly Operations Evaluation Department), which stresses that the debt projections are likely to be biased by the assumptions and the methodology used in forecasting, that does not consider the effects of high external debt and of the required macroeconomic adjustments on growth (Eaton 2002; IEG 2006).

**Box 2.2 The net present value**

The NPV of debt is the sum of all the future debt service obligations – interest and principal – on existing debt, discounted at the market interest rate. Its use is justified because it takes into account the degree of concessional lending. When the interest rate on a concessional loan is below the market rate, the NPV of debt is lower than its face value.

As a general point, Martin (2004) challenges the idea that NPV is the more accurate measure of debt burden, because it does not capture the debt overhang effect, which could depend on the face value of debt. Other authors argue that the appropriate measure of debt is its market value, which considers the risk of non-repayment (Cohen 2001). Furthermore, the NPV compares future debt-service obligations with current repayment capacity without considering the country's growth capacity and it is highly sensitive to the choice of the discount rate.

The discount rate currently used in the HIPC Initiative is the long-term dollar Commercial Interest Reference Rate (CIRR), which is based on the interest rate on the seven-year US Treasury Note. Using a single rate to discount future debt obligations, the DSF tried to find a balance between the desire to keep the discount rate as stable as possible, without de-linking it completely from market conditions (IDA and IMF 2004a). Besides, the choice of a single discount rate addressed previous criticisms about the volatility if the calculation of the NPV of debt, which was originally based on currency-specific, short term, CIRR. This policy augmented the sensitivity of the NPV of debt to the choice of the discount rate, increasing the variability of the assistance and the costs of the initiative and causing an unfair level of assistance, since different countries received the assessment of the debt burden in different periods with different interest rates (Cline 2003; UNCTAD 2004).

In the DSF, the discount rate was originally set at 5 percent at it was subsequently fixed according to a rule which introduce a strong element of inertia: the discount rate can be changed only when the six-month average of the CIRR diverges from the discount rate by at least 100 basis points for a continued period of at least six month. As a result, in many cases debt is actually discounted much more heavily than it should, with the consequence that countries lose part of debt relief. At the end of 2009, the discount rate used in the DSAs was still fixed at 5 percent, but a recent proposal by the IMF and the WB recommends to adjust the discount rate at 4 percent, given the downward trend in global interest rates during the financial crisis (IMF and the World Bank 2009). This change is going to deteriorate the debt burden of many LICs, sometimes increasing their vulnerability to debt distress episodes and adding on other adverse consequences of the global crisis in poor countries.

The use of the ratio of NPV of debt to exports is widely considered inadequate as a sustainability criterion. Hanmer and Shelton (2001: 5) argue that "an increase in exports does not necessarily translate into an increase in government revenue" because exports are highly volatile. Even considering the ratio of affordable debt service to revenue as the unique solvency criterion – as suggested, among other, by Gunter (2003), Martin (2002) and many NGOs – is subject to criticisms, since such a scheme is an incentive for recipient governments to loosen their tax collection effort (Birdsall, Williamson and Deese 2002). As a results, "sustainability needs to be determined by a borrowing level that is consistent with a sustainable external balance and a sustainable government budget" (Hanmer and Shelton 2001: 5).

The original HIPC framework, it is also argued, ignores the current account balance and the foreign exchange constraint, whose relevance is due to foreign currency denomination of public debt. A sharp depreciation or a slowdown in the world trade could reduce the capability of a country to generate enough foreign exchange revenues to service its debt obligations.

Another important aspect that is generally overlooked by the solvency criteria is the feasibility of the adjustments required in order to reach sustainability. Roubini (2001) underlines that the resource gap and the primary gap models provide only a normative rule using the practical criterion of the thresholds. However, in order to stabilize the debt ratio at a certain threshold, a country could have to run a trade (or primary) surplus which, given the expectations on interest rates and economic growth, is practically impossible to deliver, given the volatility of and the reliance on market sentiment of interest rates, exchange rates and inflation.

Finally, the choice of the thresholds and the accounting framework have been subject to many criticisms (among others, Gunter 2003; Hjertholm 2004; Cohen 2001; Martin 2004). The HIPC Initiative is meant to be a permanent exit from future debt rescheduling thanks to the achievement of long run debt sustainability. However, the simple accounting framework does not necessarily ensure that, once a certain NPV of debt to export is achieved, it will be maintained in the long run. There is no theoretical foundation supporting the choices of the specific debt thresholds as level below which the debt is sustainable (Pasinetti 1998): their definition was based on compromises between economic and political interest of creditors and the necessity to cap the overall cost of the initiative (Martin 2004).[2] Moreover, as we discuss in Chapter 6, the empirical literature which tries to provide evidence supporting the presence of debt overhang in HIPCs and the definition of the debt to export ratio at 150 as sustainable is particularly weak. In addition, the original framework assumed that HIPCs would have continued borrowing at very high concessional terms in the medium term and no attention was paid to domestic debt dynamics. More generally, the accounting approach could in principle overcome those problems, but it is weakened by two important shortcomings: 1) the real interest rate and the rate of growth of GDP are generally considered exogenous, while in reality they are affected by government spending and public

2 According to some commentators (Katsouris 1999; Martin 2004), debt thresholds were set at specific levels just to include or exclude some countries. Specifically, the "fiscal window", according to which a country is eligible if its ratio of external debt over government revenues is greater than 250 percent, was devised in order to include Côte d'Ivoire in the pool of eligible countries.

debt dynamics; and 2) the assumptions about the growth rate of liabilities, which ignore the role of lenders.

*2.2.2.2 The DSF and proposals for reform*

As discussed in Chapter 1, as a response to some of the criticism discussed above, in 2004 the WB and the IMF (IDA and IMF 2004a) proposed a new DSF, which addresses some of the shortcomings brought forward by NGOs, academics and by the internal evaluation departments. The new framework, approved in April 2005 and reviewed in April and November 2006, is based on a *forward-looking* approach which stresses the relationship between debt relief and MDG and aims at guiding new financing to avoid the accumulation of excessive debts. Hence, with respect to the DSA carried out under the HIPC initiative, the DSF include a number of improvements and is based on three main pillars: 1) the determination of country-specific debt and debt-service thresholds, depending on policies and institutional quality, measured by the overall CPIA index (Box 2.3); 2) the evaluation of the impact on debt of external shock under a forward-looking analysis of debt and debt service dynamics; and 3) the formulation of an appropriate borrowing and lending strategy that takes into account the risk of debt distress. Thus, there are three debt-burden thresholds, plus two debt service cutoffs, depending on country's institutional quality[3] and the country's risk of debt distress depends on its debt ratios (Table 2.1). As a result, HIPCs are classified as low/medium/high risk or in debt distress and they will receive a specific grants-loans mix in future IDA allocations, according to their performance under the DSA, as suggested by the recent literature (Cassimon, Moreno-Dodson and Wodon 2008). Specifically, on the basis of the CPIA score, "one of four possible risk of debt distress ratings are assigned:

- Low risk: When all the debt burden indicators are well below the thresholds.
- Moderate risk: When debt burden indicators are below the thresholds in the baseline scenario but stress tests indicate that the thresholds could be breached if there are external shocks or abrupt changes in macroeconomic policies.
- High risk: When one or more debt burden indicators breach the thresholds on a protracted basis under the baseline scenario.
- Debt distress: When the country is already experiencing difficulties in servicing its debt, as indicated perhaps by the existence of arrears (irrespective of capacity to repay based on a forward-looking DSA)" (IMF and the World Bank 2009: 9).

3 Furthermore, exports and revenues used as denominators of debt ratios are calculated no longer as three-year backward-looking averages but as single-year forward-looking denominators.

Thus, countries judged to be at high risk of debt distress or in debt distress receive 100 percent grant financing from IDA, while countries at moderate risk receive a 50/50 blend of grants and traditional credits, and countries at low risk continue to receive 100 percent credit financing on standard IDA terms.

A further improvement of the DSF with respect to the original framework is the explicit recognition of the relevance of private external creditors, of domestic debt dynamics, and of the importance of exogenous shocks for total public debt sustainability.

**Table 2.1 DSF and debt thresholds**

| | PV of debt in percent of | | | Debt service in percent of | |
|---|---|---|---|---|---|
| | Exports | GDP | Revenues | Exports | Revenue |
| Weak Policy (CPIA < 3.25) | 100 | 30 | 200 | 15 | 25 |
| Medium Policy (3.25 < CPIA < 3.75) | 150 | 40 | 250 | 20 | 30 |
| Strong Policy (CPIA > 3.75) | 200 | 50 | 300 | 25 | 35 |

*Source*: IMF and the World Bank (2009: 9).

**Box 2.3 The CPIA index**

The CPIA index is a composite index of the quality of policies and institutions, in the sense that it measures the extent to which country policies and institutions create a good environment for growth and poverty reduction. The CPIA indicators are developed by the WB, reflecting its staff professional judgement, based on country knowledge, policy dialogue, and relevant publicly available indicators. The adopted criteria focus on policy actions rather than outcomes, such as growth rates, which are highly influenced by factors outside the country's control, and the scores depend on the level of performance against the criteria, not on changes in performance from one year to the other (IDA 2007).

The CPIA index has evolved since it was first introduced in 1977; early improvements included: 1) broadening their content from strong emphasis on macroeconomic policies to include institutional framework for sustained growth and poverty reduction; and 2) improving the assessment process by making criteria more specific, using external indicators, introducing benchmarking and written rationale for scores. The historical dataset used in the book covers the period 1987-2006 and is confidential. It is often argued that lack of transparency and objectivity could represent potential limitations of this indicator. However, in 2004 the CPIA process and methodology were extensively reviewed by an external independent panel, and the WB accepted most of its recommendations, leading to further strengthening. Starting from 2005, these data are fully disclosed and published in WDI. The main improvements concern: 1) the reduction of the number of criteria from 20 to 16; 2) the review of all criteria and the extension of the rating scale to include 1.5 and 5.5; and 3) the determination of the overall score as the mean of the scores of the four clusters. As a result, now the CPIA index is made of 16 criteria – reflecting a balance between all key factors that foster pro-poor growth and poverty alleviation – grouped in 4 clusters, equally weighted and rated from 1 (low) to 6 (high):

A. *Economic Management*
 1. Macroeconomic Management
 2. Fiscal Policy
 3. Debt Policy

B. *Structural Policies*
 4. Trade
 5. Financial Sector
 6. Business Regulatory Environment

C. *Policies for Social Inclusion/Equity*
 7. Gender Equality
 8. Equity of Public Resource Use
 9. Building Human Resources
 10. Social Protection and Labor
 11. Policies and Institutions for Environmental Sustainability

D. *Public Sector Management and Institutions*
 12. Property Rights and Rule-Based Governance
 13. Quality of Budgetary and Financial Management
 14. Efficiency of Revenue Mobilization
 15. Quality of Public Administration
 16. Transparency, Accountability and Corruption in the Public Sector

Therefore, the broad coverage – the CPIA overall score is available for 136 countries – and the long time horizon (data go back to 1977) makes this indicator very useful for empirical analysis based on panel data (as done in Part 3), since it overcomes the usual problem of lack of historical data for institutional indicators. Another advantage from using the overall CPIA score is that it is currently adopted by the DSF to determine the country-specific debt burden thresholds used to assess debt sustainability and the grants-loans mix. Hence, empirical results can easily be transmitted into actual policy recommendations. Finally, the adoption of the CPIA index allows for identifying whether donors' are actually shifting toward lending strategies aimed at rewarding countries with good policies and sound institutions.

Nevertheless, some shortcomings are still present. Namely, the DSF still does not sufficiently consider the current account balance and foreign exchange constraint in a fully-fledged budget constraint. Even if the new framework for

LICs recognizes the importance of exogenous shocks on the capacity of repaying external debt, these shocks are evaluated only in a partial equilibrium, thus not considering any feedback effect. Besides, the remarks about the feasibility of the fiscal adjustments required to stabilize the debt ratio to a certain threshold are still valid. More recently, Gray et al. (2008) acknowledge that debt ratios do not take into consideration the impact of changes in the currency composition or in the maturity structure of public debt, which instead clearly affect the sovereign risk of the outstanding debt. The same authors also stress the absence of uncertainty in the traditional DSA: in poor countries political risks and economic volatility (also due to the unstable environment due to a large debt burden) are factors that should be carefully considered when running stress tests on debt sustainability. Their valuable proposal for a risk-based framework that builds on the contingent-claim approach overcomes this drawback and it is able to evaluate the impact of a number of shocks. Finally, Cassimon, Moreno-Dodson and Wodon (2008) stress the importance of distinguishing between fiscal and external sustainability and the problems related to the choice of the appropriate debt indicators to be used in any DSA. The DSA should be country-specific and cover the choice between different: 1) definitions of debt (including domestic/private debt; nominal versus present value) and debt indicators (stocks versus flows according to debt overhang or crowding out being the actual binding constraint in the country); and 2) approaches to debt sustainability (the country suffers more from foreign exchange or fiscal gaps?).

In August 2009, the WB and the IMF reviewed the DSF (IMF and the World Bank 2009) identifying some possible critical elements which have to be addressed in the near future. In particular, it is recognized the increasing role of remittances as an alternative source of financing in many poor countries (Ratha and Mohapatra 2009; see also Chapter 9 for some data on their relevance in LICs and SSA countries) and their role in enhancing debtors' ability to manage external debt. Even if data limitations make the inclusion of remittances in the standard DSF for the calculation of debt thresholds very difficult, the WB and the IMF are currently recommending greater flexibility in the consideration of remittances in the DSA. We agree on that and we suggest to look at their effect on a case-by-case basis, focusing on countries where remittances account for a significant share of GDP.[4] The IMF-WB review is also concerned with the long-run relationship between public investment and growth, whose scarce consideration might lead to conservative (and short-sighted) borrowing policies, and to the *threshold effects*: for countries close to the boundaries of the CPIA score, small fluctuations in the CPIA index would imply a change in the assessment of the risk of debt distress and, thus, in the future grants-loans mix.

4 On the contrary, Eurodad (2009) criticizes this recommendation on the ground that it could lead to an expansion of non-concessional borrowing by poor countries and it might undermine debt sustainability, since the inclusion of remittances would lower the risk ratings and allow poor countries to expand borrowing at market rates.

### 2.2.3 Economic Sustainability

The development perspective criticizes the simple framework in which debt sustainability is generally assessed and it proposes two different channels in order to improve the analysis: the consideration of the endogeneity of the main variables and the enlargement of the targets for debt forgiveness. Firstly, following the underlined shortcomings of the traditional approaches, the development perspective investigates the links and the relationships between fiscal deficits, interest rates, economic growth, inflation and balance of payments in order to solve the endogeneity of these variables. Secondly, this approach takes into account the amount of resources needed by debtor countries to reach specific targets of growth and poverty reduction, as done in the MDG and suggested, among others, by UNCTAD (2004) and Gunter, Rahman and Shi (2009).

One of the most important supporters of this view is Jeffrey Sachs, who advocates increased consideration of the financial requirements needed for the basic social and health expenditures (Sachs 2005). His point of view, widely reflected in a number of NGOs documents, is built on the idea that some development targets can be easily achieved just by being able to provide the necessary monetary resources, but ignores the vast economic literature and several experiences suggesting that aid alone is ineffective in economic development. The analysis conducted by the WB and the IMF, on the contrary, does not explicitly calculate the amount of resources that will be redirected to spur economic growth and to reduce poverty after debt relief, even if their debt relief polices are increasingly strengthening the relationship between debt and poverty reduction.[5] Resources freed up by debt relief are assumed to be spent on health, education, sanitation, nutrition and infrastructures, according to the government plans. In that way, there is not a real expenditures target and it is not assured that there will be economic growth and, as a consequence, sustainability. Some authors move the focus from the debt ratios to the debt service payments, which are a more direct indicator of the resources soaked up by external obligations (Martin 2002). Eurodad (2001) calls for a poverty approach to debt sustainability, which gives a lot of emphasis to the resources needed to satisfy the essential human needs, to domestic debt (prioritized with respect to the external debt to favour internal macroeconomic stability) and to other non-essential expenditures. In the same vein, a very recent policy paper by the Jubilee Debt Campaign (2009: 18) states that "Eligibility for debt cancellation should be based on a measure of debt sustainability connected to

5 In the HIPC framework, the use of HIPC savings is monitored only during the interim period, i.e. before debt relief becomes irrevocable. It must be stressed, however, that HIPCs have to prepare a PRSP in consultation with civil society, and this paper is considered key to stimulate ownership. Trying to impose specific constraints on so many items of the government balance sheet could be seen as an undue interference with (and lessening of) a country's sovereignty. Chapter 8 discusses the achievements of debt relief initiatives in terms of poverty reduction and social spending.

human development (… :) at least $400 billion should be cancelled for around 100 countries if they are to be able to pay for essential services for their people without having to tax those below the poverty lines".

We believe that this reversal in the policy design is certainly welcome and worth discussing. On the one hand, it is important to recognize the importance of this approach, which could be used to complement the standard analysis in order to avoid unsustainable and unfeasible interest bills and to give more emphasis on the essential needs of the world's poorest, which must be met regardless of countries' indebtedness. On the other hand, it must taken into account that aid, and debt relief as well, can not be allocated only looking at poverty levels. Other variables, such as country's governance and institutional quality, have to be considered in order to improve aid effectiveness and provide the debtors with the right incentive to undergo the necessary reforms. Moreover, it must be stressed that the possible amount of resources freed by debt relief, even in case of a complete debt cancellation, are not comparable with the estimated financing needs to meet the MDG (Chapter 8). Bearing this in mind helps to avoid unrealistic expectations, which sometimes bring part of the civil society to look at 100 percent debt cancellation as a panacea for all the problems of the poorest countries.

## 2.3 Models of Debt Sustainability

The economic literature presents some models that analyse debt relief and sustainability under a broader framework than the accounting approach. The HIPC initiative aims at reaching long-run debt sustainability mainly through fixing specific thresholds, which are believed to bring the debt burden at manageable levels. However, debt relief seems to have failed to reach a level of sustainability sufficient to enhance and foster economic growth and poverty reduction. One of the reasons is related to the choice of the sustainability indicators, which do not derive from an analytical model and are not connected with any explicit target of economic growth. The theoretical literature presents some contributions in this field: some models take debt sustainability as a target and derive all the macroeconomic adjustments required, while others are more concerned about a growth target. The elaboration of alternative models of debt sustainability has the advantage of developing more nuanced macroeconomic models that take into account the interrelationships between the most important variables, but they present some drawbacks due to the necessity of keeping the models simple and manageable (which implies that some aspects are ignored).

Edwards (2002, 2003) investigates the relationships between debt relief and fiscal sustainability, and debt relief and current account in Nicaragua. He defines macroeconomic sustainability in terms of two key features – fiscal sustainability and current account sustainability – and develops two different dynamic models of sustainability: the first one has a primary balance consistent with a stable debt-to-GDP ratio as a target, while the second a current account consistent with solvency. In both cases, Edwards finds out that sustainability requires strong macroeconomic adjustments (reduced expenditures, higher taxes, devaluation), which are politically difficult to implement and can divert resources from poverty-reducing and growth-enhancing programs. On the one hand, these models consider domestic debt, the distinction between concessional and commercial debt, the inclusion of remittances, aid and grants, as well as seigniorage; on the other hand, the main drawback is a lack of integration between the two papers: in particular, the adjustments demanded for current account sustainability are likely to undermine fiscal stability. The sensitivity of the results with respect to GDP growth underlines the feedback of macroeconomic adjustment on growth.

Fedelino and Kudina (2003) find that the HIPC Initiative does not assure fiscal sustainability, unless fiscal policies change. They start from the Edwards' (2003) approach to fiscal sustainability and modify the budget constraint in order to include: 1) the exchange rate; and 2) the distinction between domestic and foreign debt. Their model implies that donors should provide more grants and aid flows to finance the required (and expected) increased poverty-reduction expenditures, considering that tighter fiscal policy in HIPCs is not viable. The authors conclude that "Unless HIPCs improve their primary fiscal positions or grant financing is sustained at current, or possibly higher, levels, debt sustainability in HIPCs may prove elusive in the long term" (p. 26). Moreover, they show that external debt could be sustainable, but total public debt could not, because of the role played by internal debt. This model has the advantage of including domestic debt into the analysis, but has the same limitations that affect Edwards' models. In particular, it takes the crucial economic variables as exogenous and, then, it derives the effect of a change in those variables.

Burnside and Fanizza (2005) look at the effects that debt relief has on the government budget constraint and on output growth. They analyze the HIPC Initiative from a different perspective: the sustainability of debt and external sector are not addressed, but this model has the advantage of looking at the effect of debt reduction on the economy, without assuming a growth rate target. Government spending, investments, tax revenues and output change in response to debt forgiveness, to the level required by conditionality and *ex-ante* spending decisions. The inclusion of a money demand function allows for the simulation of two different scenarios, depending on monetary policy. If the central bank pursues stable inflation, the outcome is a small reduction in the long-run level of debt and inflation; while a loose monetary policy results in substantial debt reduction, at the cost of higher inflation in the short run. These results confirm the unpleasant monetarist arithmetic highlighted by Sargent and Wallace (1981): lower current inflation implies higher inflation in the long run, or, in this case, lower inflation in the future requires a higher rate of current inflation. However, that conclusion could be mitigated by fiscal reforms: if government increases spending in poverty-reduction programs and cuts other expenditures, there are sizeable gains in terms of permanent reduction of debt and inflation, both with passive and active monetary policy. The relevance of the growth effect denotes the importance of the effectiveness of poverty reduction programmes in raising growth for fiscal sustainability. Even if sustainability is not explicitly considered, this model allows for a broad macroeconomic evaluation of debt reduction. The evolution of the debt stock and the government budget constraint allows to assess the likelihood of future debt distress. The main limitations of this model concern: 1) the disconnection between the monetary and the real part of the model, given that inflation, completely determined in the money market, is not allowed to impact on output; and 2) the exclusion of domestic debt, of the current account and the real exchange rate. A comprehensive framework that addresses these issues requires a fully-fledged government budget constraint that includes both the external and domestic position, and the exchange rate, in order to have a more realistic assessment of debt relief and its impact on the economy.

The empirical assessment of long-run debt sustainability in HIPCs after debt relief provide a mixed picture, highlighting a number of vulnerabilities related to slow economic growth, narrow export base, reduced and uneven fiscal revenue mobilization, weak institutions and poor macroeconomic management (Sun 2004; Yang and Nyberg 2009; Beddies et al. 2009). Since data availability does not allow for the ideal direct comparison between pre- and post-HIPC period, Sun (2004) and Yang and Nyberg (2009) run a cross-country study, in which HIPCs are compared with other LICs.[6] Policy and institutional quality indicators show the highest scores for the completion point countries, while other HIPCs have values lower than the other PRGF countries. However, the quality of the institutional framework varies considerably between countries and shows a declining trend, suggesting that improvement in institutions remains a long-term challenge for HIPCs. With respect to the debt management capacity, the conclusions are similar, with completion point countries performing better, even if all the sample share weaknesses in basic debt management skills. Also export diversification is a structural weakness in HIPCs, where development policies should create broad-based export growth. The HIPCs' exposure to shocks is increased also by the decline in the TOT and by a weak mobilization of fiscal resources. The fiscal issue seems to be severe, since also completion point countries still lag behind other PRGF countries. Long-term debt sustainability is therefore subject to structural adjustments in these sectors and requires a careful mix between loans and grants. Nwachukwu (2008) assesses foreign debt sustainability for a sample of 16 post-completion point HIPCs using a simple growth-with-debt model. The author considers the full debt write-off following the MDRI and shows that, notwithstanding the initial debt reduction, indebted countries are very unlikely to reach a sustainable position, being unable to finance their investments, imports and debt-service obligations out of their domestic savings and foreign-exchange receipts. According to the optimistic

6 In this case, however, results could be biased by the selection bias, since the HIPCs with the best score in institutional indicators and the best capacity in debt management are the first to reach completion point.

scenario where external lending is used to finance the target growth rate (5.5 percent) and does not depend on poor macroeconomic management, the NPV of external debt in post-completion point HIPC will reach 176 percent of exports by 2015 and will decline only after reaching the peak of 242 percent in 2026. In addition, a sensitivity analysis shows that exogenous shocks could generate the accumulation of unsustainable debts. In particular, foreign debt critically depends on the evolution of domestic savings, exports and aid inflows.

## 2.4 Concessional Lending to Poor Countries: Scaling-Up Aid and the Grants versus Loans Debate

LICs and several HIPCs need increased financing to meet their development goals and, at the same time, have to avoid future debt crises and achieve long-term debt sustainability. Among the possible sources of deficit financing, aid inflows receive a considerable attention by the international community, especially after the repeated pronouncements by G8 and OECD countries to increase their aid assistance in order for poor countries to meet the MDG. Foreign aid already accounts for a large share of capital flows to LICs and it amounts to a significant share of SSA countries GDP: between 1980 and 2003 ODA accounted for more than 15 percent of GDP in 8 African countries.[7] The Gleneagles commitments call for a doubling in aid to Africa up to 85 dollar per person in 2010 (Mongardini and Samake 2009).[8] Future prospects of debt sustainability and long-run economic development should take into consideration the possible effects of a surge of aid inflows and a shift from loans to grants in aid allocation.

### *2.4.1 The Macroeconomic Effects of Scaling-Up Aid*

A surge in aid inflows, motivated by the big push hypothesis (Sachs 2005), could affect total public debt sustainability in different ways, depending on how additional aid is used and on its effects on the exchange rate (Gupta, Powell and Yang 2006). The fungibility of aid has often raised scepticisms on the growth effect of aid (Bauer 1971), which is not found to finance investments and, thus, promote economic growth, as predicted by financing gap models (Easterly 1999, 2001b). Recent reviews of the vast literature on aid and growth find very limited support of a positive contribution of aid flows on economic growth, even considering different channels and sources of heterogeneity, such as institutional quality (Rajan and Subramanian 2008; Doucouliagos and Paldam 2009). Similarly, the lack of robust empirical evidence on the presence of increasing returns of aid and of strong non-linearities in the savings-growth and in the productivity-growth

7 See Gupta, Powell and Yang (2006) for more detailed data.

8 The recent evolution, following the unfolding of the global financial crisis, makes the prospects of reaching that target very unlikely (Chapter 9).

relationships does not validate the big push narrative (Easterly 2006; Kraay and Raddatz 2007). Instead of helping poor African countries escaping a poverty trap and reaping the benefit of globalization, the proliferation of aid projects and its associated administrative burden impinge on aid effectiveness (Roodman 2006).

This disappointing conclusions are the result of donor fragmentation and weak selectivity, which channels aid to corrupt governments, large overhead costs of many aid agencies and the use of ineffective channels to deliver international assistance (Easterly and Pfutze 2008). Apart from not necessarily improving the GDP growth rate, aid inflows can cause a real appreciation of the exchange rate, potentially triggering perverse debt dynamics. On the one hand, the exchange rate appreciation reduces the domestic currency value of the stock of external debt and of debt-service payments. On the other hand, it hampers international competitiveness and country's exports, through the so-called Dutch Disease effect, reducing the sources of foreign currency required to service external debt (Rajan and Subramanian 2010). A further negative consequence of scaling-up aid is the raise in interest rates following a possible domestic sterilization of aid inflows, undertaken to reduce the inflationary pressure of increased spending.[9] More foreign aid, particularly when coupled with a shift from loans to grants, could reduce government efforts to collect revenues (Clements et al. 2004). Thus, the fiscal balance may not improve, especially if the surge in aid is not growth-enhancing.

Thus, more aid could result in a worsening of the debt sustainability conditions. However, a recent review of the experience of five Sub-Saharan countries, which went through a surge in aid inflows, does not show any evidence of Dutch Disease and exchange rate appreciation (Hussain, Berg and Aiyar 2009). This kind of evidence is consistent with the model proposed by Adam and Bevan (2006), who limit the Dutch Disease effect to the short term, while in the medium run the raise in productivity in the private sector, due to public expenditures in infrastructures, delivers welfare gains. Hussain, Berg and Aiyar (2009) argue that monetary authorities use a large share of aid to build international reserves, fearing the Dutch Disease effect, while the fiscal policy aims at spending aid inflows. This policy mix could result in a sort of domestically financed fiscal expansion, the only difference being the increase in reserves. However, the surge in money supply forces policy-makers to choose between inflation or higher interest rates (in case of sterilization), with possible adverse consequences on debt sustainability, even in absence of the Dutch Disease effect.

In sum, traditional theory, as well as alternative explanations of the macroeconomic consequences of aid inflows suggest that there are channels through which they can undermine debt sustainability.

---

9 Domestic sterilization generally implies an increase of reserve requirements or the issuance of government securities. The latter policy translates into higher interest rates and a larger domestic debt, which is going to undermine overall debt sustainability (Chapter 5).

### *2.4.2 Grants versus Loans*

Apart from the amount of aid assistance, also its composition matters for debt sustainability and the economic development of poor countries. Moreover, the grants-loans mix is already part of the WB lending to LICs, according to the country-specific risk of debt distress calculated under the DSF. The publication of the Meltzer report in 2000 (IFIC 2000) gave birth to a debate between the US administration, which endorsed the proposal of a shift from loans to grants in development assistance, and European donors, which were concerned about a possible downsizing of the WB and other IFIs lending capacity (Sanford 2002). Some observers and NGOs suggested also that the shift toward grants makes it more likely that some politically-driven donor governments might be tempted to force a "strategic" usage of funds to "shape" recipients' policies in unrelated areas. This would alienate further civil society and public opinion in developing countries, and lead to an inappropriate resource allocation. Abstracting from political and strategic considerations, the grants versus loans debate has important implications not only for economic development and poverty reduction, but also for debt sustainability in poor countries.

The advocates of an increase of the grant share in aid assistance argue that concessional loans alone are bound to undermine external debt sustainability because of the costs of future debt repayments. Poor countries are extremely vulnerable to exogenous shocks which can undermine their repayment capacity and they can often service their debt obligations only by sacrificing social spending. Thus, the use of loans instead of grants could re-start a vicious lend and forgive cycle, providing a bad incentives for borrowers (Daseking and Joshi 2006; Radelet 2005b). Any debt relief initiative could be perceived as a proof of the failure of the soft loan strategy of development assistance (Cohen, Jacquet and Reisen 2007), which is often driven by a defensive-lending approach, according to which lenders keep on refinancing existing loans to avoid a default. However, the empirical validation of defensive lending provides contrasting results: Cohen, Jacquet and Reisen (2007) find that there is no strong evidence of an intrinsic capture of any group of creditors by their debtors, while Marchesi and Missale (2004) show that HIPCs have kept receiving large amount of loans and grants because of their high indebtedness. A similar finding is discussed also by Geginat and Kraay (2007), who focus exclusively on IDA loans. However, they argue that the positive association between disbursements and the existing stock of external debt or its repayments should not be interpreted in support to the defensive lending hypothesis, since the observed correlation is strongly affected by few countries entering in non-accrual status with IDA. Additionally, the authors do not find any evidence of greater IDA disbursements to countries heavily indebted or with a weak policy performance, for which, in case of defensive lending, there should be a stronger interest to lend in order to avoid costly payment difficulties.

Nevertheless, apart from the presence of defensive lending, multilateral concessional loans expand the borrowing capacity of countries which are the least able to absorb international loans. Because of their weak governance, many borrowers have an incentive to maximize their short-term loans ignoring the long-term risks of a debt crisis (Bulow and Rogoff 1990, 2005). Supporters of grants argue that they do not destabilize debt dynamics and, contrary to concessional loans, they are suitable for projects without an immediate tradable output, such as social spending, or with a long time horizon and high uncertainty. However, a shift toward grants does not come without costs. The first and most important issue is that it inevitably decreases the amount of resources available to poor countries, forcing them to find alternative sources of finance. The issuance of government securities or, when possible, international bonds, is costly and generates additional trade-offs that could undermine public debt sustainability (Chapter 5).

The second argument in favor of loans is that, while grants might provide the wrong incentive to recipient governments since they do not have to be paid back, loans should enforce fiscal discipline and make governments more accountable. To validate this claim, Clements et al. (2004) analyse a large panel of countries and find that loans and grants have differentiated effects on governments' efforts to raise revenues. While more loans cause an increase in government revenues, the opposite happens in response to an increase in grants, especially in corrupt countries. Similar findings are also discussed by Odedokun (2004). Even though the theoretical argument appears reasonable, aid assistance policies can be designed to provide the right incentives, for example by tying the renewal of a grant to an *ex-ante* target of fiscal discipline in the recipient country (Cohen, Jaquet and Raisen 2007).

From a review of the advantages and drawbacks of loans it appears clear that a corner solution is doomed not to be the best one, but a mix of the two tools is better suited to provide recipient countries with the appropriate sources of finance. The policy environment, the existing debt burden and the level of economic development affect the way in which the grants-loans mix can foster economic growth: more concessionality improves aid effectiveness in poor countries and in countries with poor policies and higher debt, even if the latter effect is weaker (Cordella and Ulku 2007). Daseking and Joshi (2006) confirm that the optimal solution is a mix of the two ways of financing and suggest that, while the level of assistance should be based on needs and absorptive capacity, the grants-loans mix should be driven by growth expectations and policies and institutional quality. The WB and the IMF have recognized that the grants-loans mix should be tailored on country-specific characteristics. In an influential paper, which constitutes one of the building blocks of the new DSF, Kraay and Nehru (2006) relate the grants-loans mix to the vulnerability to debt distress episodes. The authors state that more grants are required and, for a given institutional quality, their share should increase the higher is the probability of debt distress. However, Kraay and Nehru warn that grants must not replace completely loans because they are difficult to finance and, more relevant, they generate a moral hazard problem. As a result, as discussed in section 2.2.2, the DSF requires the composition of new financing to LICs to be based on the risks of debt crisis, so that the grants-loans mix depends on the level of external debt and on institutional quality, but not on growth prospects and income levels.

Discussing the WB policy towards more grants, Radelet and Chiang (2003) call for a shift towards a higher share of grants in LICs, especially for those with high debt and low growth. They propose to allocate new financing, in absolute terms and with respect to the grants-loans composition, according to four structural characteristics of a country: basic needs, growth prospects, risks, and borrowing capacity. The bulk of grant financing should go to the lowest income countries and, when these countries start sustained economic growth, creditors could pass from grants to concessional loans and then to commercial loans. Radelet (2005b) simplifies the previous proposal and advices the WB to provide grants rather than loans in poor countries (per capita income less than US$ 500). Thus, grants allocation should be based on income levels, instead on debt levels: this shift to grants for the poorest countries is much fairer, ensures that these countries never accumulate debt burdens and allows them to invest resources in their economy, instead of repay the loans. Finally, a different proposal is put forth by Cohen, Jacquet and Reisen (2007), who suggest that debt relief and loans are complementary instruments which are likely to perform better than either loans or grants. In their opinion, it is not only because of poor institutions that LICs do not have access to international capital markets, but also because of their economic volatility. In this respect, state-contingent loans are superior to grants: what is required in the debt relief mechanism is more procedural transparency to avoid the debtor moral hazard.

Following this debate, the IFIs are moving towards a more sensible aid allocation policy, following the main empirical results on aid effectiveness. However, the choice of the grants-loans mix, as it is, does not take into account other sources of country heterogeneity apart from the risk of debt distress. More important, in our opinion, is that the decision of the amount of new lending (and of its composition) should be taken starting from a resource requirement. As in what we have labelled the economic approach to sustainability, it is critical to start from poor countries' basic needs, such as targets in poverty reduction and social expenditures, which can not be reduced, and the required pro-growth investments. Otherwise, given the limited tax revenues (which should be increased providing governments with the right incentive to boost their tax collection effort), it is likely that poor countries will have to rely on alternative sources of finance, such as domestic debt on non-concessional borrowing, undermining total debt sustainability (Part 2). New lending policies by the WB and the IMF should be designed keeping this lesson in mind (Chapter 10).

# PART 2
# HIPCs/LICs and Macroeconomic Management: The Role of Domestic Debt

## Overview

Many poor countries have started developing internal debt markets. The development of a clear picture of the cost and evolution of domestic borrowing is necessary for improving the debt sustainability analysis and understanding the dynamics of key macroeconomic variables, in order to achieve a more efficient resource allocation and suggest policy changes.

On the one hand, the evolution of domestic debt could stimulate the development of deep and liquid domestic financial markets and protect countries from adverse external shocks. On the other hand, the establishment of domestic markets for government securities has to come after the achievement of a certain degree of macroeconomic stability, in terms of credible fiscal and monetary policies, and financial markets liberalization, together with other pre-conditions. If this is not the case, the benefits of domestic debt are likely to be offset by adverse effects in terms of crowding out of the private sector, macroeconomic instability, higher debt service and undermined debt sustainability.

We have collected data for 53 LICs and MICs from different sources for the period 1994-2004, drawing some basic information (debt stocks and interest payments) for as many countries as possible and more detailed data about its composition and structure (maturities, debt by instruments and holders) for different sub-samples of countries. Thanks to this dataset, it is possible to describe the evolution and structure of domestic debt in developing countries.

A descriptive analysis confirms earlier anecdotal observations that domestic debt has been rising, especially since 2000, and is becoming a binding constraint to investments and economic growth. The high cost of financing, associated with short maturities and the absence of a large base of bond holders could pose problems to economic development and overall debt sustainability.

The evolution of domestic debt in a selected sample of 14 HIPCs highlights the high level of dependency on external financing: the lack of access to international capital markets – forbidden under the HIPC Program – is a key reason why a decrease in external lending is associated with an increase in domestic debt. Given the high cost of internal borrowing, foreign assistance should be stable and predictable, at least until the poorest countries are able to adjust their fiscal stance and improve their institutional environment. As a consequence, policy-makers should limit the use of domestic debt until the achievement of macroeconomic stability, especially on the fiscal side, and the development of the pre-conditions for a sound internal market for government securities, with a broad investor base, a sound legal framework and adequate market infrastructure (Arnone and Ugolini 2005).

Part 2 is structured as follows:[1] in Chapter 3 we provide a brief picture of the various sources of deficit financing, stressing on the increasing role of domestic debt in developing countries. We discuss the advantages and drawbacks of the recent shift from external to internal borrowing, with a focus on LICs, reviewing the empirical literature at the aggregate level and also looking at the experiences of single countries. Then, we show how in HIPCs the asymmetric monetary and fiscal adjustments that followed the reform programs ended up in an unavoidable but clearly *ex-ante* predictable rise in domestic debt. Chapter 4 presents the dataset on domestic debt: after a brief discussion on the recent trends in developing countries, we focus on the situation in HIPCs. We present some evidence on the relationship between domestic debt and economic growth in LICs and MICs, showing that – consistent with the discussion of Chapter 3 – the creation of an internal market for government securities is likely to have an adverse impact on the economy, especially in poor countries that, generally, do still not have the required institutional and debt management skills. Most importantly, in Chapter 5 we evaluate public debt sustainability in a simple accounting framework and we show that the switch from foreign to domestic borrowing, and rising domestic real interest rates, are likely to undermine overall debt sustainability and the success of debt relief programs. As a consequence, we stress the necessity to include domestic public debt into the DSF.

1 Part 2 of the book partially draws from and builds on Arnone and Presbitero: "External Debt Sustainability and Domestic Debt in Heavily Indebted Poor Countries", *Rivista Internazionale di Scienze Sociali*, 2, 187-213, 2007.

# Chapter 3
# Domestic Debt in Developing Countries

## 3.1 Deficit Financing in Poor Countries

The ways in which a fiscal deficit affects the economy depend on how it is financed and the composition of government spending. While the effects of deficit financing and fiscal consolidation are well studied in industrialized countries and emerging markets, only limited attention has been given to LICs and their specificities (Easterly and Schmidt-Hebbel 1993; Agenor 2005). Limited administrative capacity and political constraints hinder developing countries' ability to raise tax revenues, especially in African LICs.[1] Other than tax collection, other main sources are seigniorage and domestic and foreign borrowing. Money creation is more frequent in politically unstable countries and has serious costs in terms of higher inflation (Cukierman, Edwards and Tabellini 1992), as testified by several experiences in developing countries, where seigniorage accounted for as far as 5 percent of GDP during the 1990s (Agenor 2005).

Financing public deficits with debt, rather than with tax revenues, could avoid negative effects on consumption and can boost both public and private investment. Assuming that the Ricardian equivalence does *not* hold, fiscal policies could lower consumption as a response to a tax increase, even if the rise in consumption is expected in the future: the evidence from ten developing countries highlights the negative effect that taxes have on private consumption, due to the reduction in disposable income (Easterly and Schmidt-Hebbel 1991). The effect of an increase in tax on private investment is less clear, because of the high dependence on the structure of the economy: in general, privatization, investment in infrastructures and financial sector reform are three key elements that could increase the complementarity between public and private sector, fostering private investment.

However, deficit financing through debt is not without costs. As we discuss in the following sections, domestic borrowing, especially in countries with fiscal dominance, could originate a credit squeeze, since financial intermediaries would prefer lower-risk government securities to lending to the private sector or buying its securities. As a result, reduced credit and public-debt service payments can crowd

---

1 In African LICs, tax revenue is on average about 14 percent of GDP and in many countries the tax-to-GDP ratio is below the 15 percent threshold, which is considered a reasonable target for poor countries (Gupta and Tareq 2008). Strengthening and expanding the tax base could promote social spending and economic stability creating fiscal space, but it takes a number of administrative reforms which can not be implemented in a short time span.

out consumption and investment.[2] The recourse to foreign borrowing, in addition to the cost associated with debt service, generates pressure on the current account balance and interest rates, inducing a real exchange rate appreciation, hampering competitiveness and possibly lowering investment and economic growth (Rodrik 2008). Considering LICs, and HIPCs in particular, foreign borrowing is mostly bilateral and multilateral debt, with a high degree of concessionality (Chapter 1), whose adverse effects on the economy are discussed in Part 3. However, some LICs have recently gained access to the international bond market and to the private debt market, even if the global economic-financial crisis has temporarily frozen these markets (Chapter 9). Ghana accessed syndicated bank loans and issued an over-subscribed US$ 750 million Eurobond in 2007 and similar choices were common in other HIPCs – such as Uganda and Tanzania – where non-concessional financing shows an upward trend over the last decade, contrary to what happens in other non-HIPCs LICs (Hostland 2009, Das, Papaioannou and Polan 2009). Private capital flows could fill part of the LICs' financing gap, helping funding large infrastructure projects, diversifying risks, repaying existing debts and bringing additional benefits in terms of financial market development and macroeconomic discipline (Kose et al. 2009). Nevertheless, international bond issuance could increase the currency mismatch of government liabilities, raise pressures on exchange rate appreciation and expose recipient countries to an increased vulnerability to financial crises, given the pro-cyclical behavior of international investors and the high volatility of private capital flows. More broadly, it should be taken into consideration that, in some poor countries, low savings are not necessarily the binding constraint to economic growth, as weak policies and institutions might be depressing the business environment. In those cases, capital inflows may not be growth-enhancing, but just hamper competitiveness via exchange rate appreciation (Rodrik and Subramanian 2010), as showed by the lack of a systematic evidence of a causal effect of financial globalization on economic growth (Prasad, Rajan and Subramanian 2006). With specific regard to HIPCs, the recent increase in non-concessional borrowing, fostered by the new borrowing space granted by debt relief, raises concerns on future debt sustainability (Chapter 5).

Fiscal deficits are affected by inflation, real interest rates, real exchange rates and output as a result of the debt burden weighing on the economy:

- Inflation is likely to increase the government deficit. This is due to the rise in nominal interest rates, which impinge on interest payments, and to the so-called Olivera-Tanzi effect, which reduces the real value of revenues.[3]

2 The crowding out effect is lower the more elastic is the demand for money, since smaller is the required increase in the interest rate to restore the equilibrium after the deficit-financed expansion of the aggregate demand.

3 The Olivera-Tanzi effect concerns the temporal lags in tax collection and is particularly relevant in developing countries (see Agenor 2005).

However, this negative effect on fiscal balance could be mitigated because inflation reduces the real value of debt in the presence of limited indexation.

- An increase in real interest rates raises interest payments and worsens the fiscal deficit. Financial liberalization increases the sensitivity of deficit to market-based interest rates and the possible rise in the interest rates due to financial liberalization expands the cost of debt.
- The consequences of movements in the real exchange rate are in both directions. A real depreciation enlarges the deficit because it boosts public expenditure (higher payments abroad and cost of traded goods), but it could also reduce the fiscal deficit, because it increases competitiveness and raises public revenues through direct and indirect taxation (especially in countries with SOEs producing tradables).
- Economic growth might not be a solution for fiscal deficit. Easterly and Schmidt-Hebbel (1991) argue that the idea that growth redresses fiscal imbalances is (empirically) flawed because usually higher growth is accompanied by not only higher revenues, but also higher expenditures. Moreover, an economy characterized by public deficit, high inflation and interest rates has little chance of achieving strong economic growth.

Empirical evidence on a sample of LICs shows that fiscal adjustment is positively correlated with economic growth, especially when the adjustment works through a sizeable reduction of domestic financing, suggesting the potential risks of domestic debt which are the core of this part of the book (Gupta et al. 2005).

However, empirical evidence shows that inflation seems to be only weakly correlated to fiscal balances,[4] and the reason could be the non-linear relationship (see Box 3.1) linking seigniorage revenue and inflation. This (possible) relationship has raised a lot of interest also for the relevance of seigniorage revenues in developing countries. However, the case studies show an unfavorable trade-off between inflation and seigniorage. Furthermore, even in developing countries, the magnitude of seigniorage is generally quite limited, although with high inflation it could become an important source of funding for the government.

4 Agenor and Montiel (1999) claim that in the short run there is no correlation between inflation and deficit, while in the long run there is only a weak positive correlation. Among the various arguments proposed to explain this finding, there is the tight money paradox, based on the results of Sargent and Wallace (1981).

**Box 3.1 Inflation and seigniorage**

Inflation and seigniorage revenues are theoretically linked by a non-linear relationship that originates a Laffer curve. As a consequence, policy-makers can estimate the optimal inflation tax, fixing the inflation rate equal to a parameter (1/α) that could be easily estimated. The Laffer curve seems supported by empirical evidence (e.g., Easterly and Schmidt-Hebbel 1991: 42).

Seigniorage is defined as the sum of the change in the real stock of money (m) and of the inflation tax:

$$(1) \quad S = \dot{M}_t / P_t = \dot{m}_t + \pi_t m_t = \dot{m}_t + I_{TAX}$$

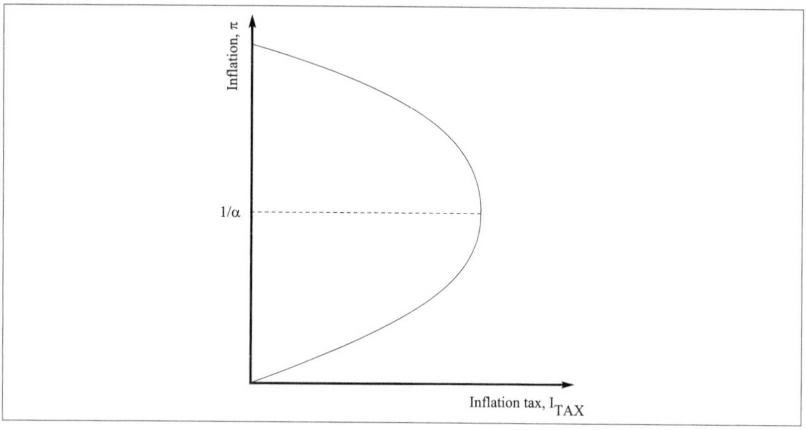


**Figure 3.1 Inflation and seigniorage**
*Source*: Authors' elaboration.

In steady state m does not change and $S = I_{TAX}$. Moreover, inflation is constant at $\pi^*$. Given the usual Cagan money demand function (2) and setting $m_0 = 1$:

$$(2) \quad m_t = m_0 e^{-\alpha\pi^*} \qquad with \alpha > 0$$

$$(3) \quad I_{TAX} = \pi * e^{-\alpha\pi^*}$$

Equation (3) represents the Laffer curve: revenues are maximized at $\pi^* = 1/\alpha$.

Large fiscal deficit could have both an adverse inflationary effect and an output effect. However, these negative consequences can be mitigated if a deficit reflects a raise in public investment and if public and private investments are complementary.

The fiscal approach to the BOP is supported by evidence showing that fiscal and external balances move together (Agenor and Montiel 1999). Fiscal adjustments, reduction in the current account deficit and depreciation are closely associated, confirming that, if the Ricardian equivalence does not hold, a tax reduction, financed by increased internal or external borrowing, boosts private spending and, as a consequence, reduces the trade surplus and generates a real exchange rate appreciation.

### 3.2 Internal Financing

The issue of domestic debt in LICs has been rather neglected by the IFIs, even if it is now clear that its implications for the evolution of domestic inflation, external debt and overall public debt sustainability are critical (Reinhart and Rogoff 2009). Since the seminal contribution by Reinhart, Rogoff and Savastano (2003), the efforts to collect data on domestic debt increased substantially and they originated a very interesting stream of literature which addresses the effects of domestic debt in emerging economies. Panizza (2008) documents a recent shift, over the period 1994-2005, from external to domestic debt common to most developing countries, while Arnone and Presbitero (2007) confirm the same pattern specifically for HIPCs (Chapter 4). Many emerging economies, even having access to international capital markets, increased their share of domestic debt over total public debt. This choice probably started as a response to the financial crisis that hit many developing countries in the second half of the nineties. Policy-makers became aware of the risks of foreign debt, which increases the volatility of GDP growth and capital flows and preferred borrowing domestically in order to avoid the currency mismatch and sudden capital outflows.[5] LICs, instead, were forced to tap the domestic securities market because of lack of access to external resources (being on an IMF Programme limits borrowing at a commercial rate) and to sterilize aid inflows (Hussain, Berg and Aiyar 2009).

Following this renewed interest in domestic financing, in recent years we have seen an increased attention by the IFIs for the development of domestic markets for government securities in developing countries (IMF and World Bank 2001, 2006, Borensztein, Levy Yeyati and Panizza 2007, UNCTAD 2004 and 2008). As a result, policy recommendations and programs in MICs and LICs are also aimed at fostering the development of domestic markets for government securities.

The rationale of these policies lies is the advantages that an internal credit markets could provide to the government and the economy. Financing with domestic-currency denominated government securities – as opposed to external borrowing and banking credit – is likely to reduce the vulnerability of a country

5 Many developing countries can not avoid the so-called "original sin", so they have to borrow in foreign currency, being unable to borrow in the international market in their own currency (Eichengreen and Hausmann 1999, Hausmann and Panizza 2003).

to reversal in capital flows and limit the build up of foreign-currency denominated debt, mitigating the risks of exchange rate devaluations and the monetary financing of government deficits, with its potential inflationary effects. Domestic debt can be managed to reduce the government's exposure to interest rates and currency risks. Furthermore, a market for government securities is likely to support the implementation and the transmission of monetary policy and the development of a domestic corporate bond market, providing a pricing benchmark for corporate bonds. A liquid and deep market with long-term instruments could also help reducing the cost of government financing and mitigate capital flight by providing domestic savers with an alternative to investing abroad. The shift from external to domestic borrowing could mitigate the government's external dependence, promoting political accountability and institutional reforms. All these positive effects and spillovers make the development of a domestic bond market important for strengthening the process of sustained economic growth, since it leads to a more efficient, market-based capital allocation.[6]

Nevertheless, the substitution of foreign with domestic debt does not come without costs, given that the optimal debt structure should take into account the trade-off in terms of risks, costs and externalities that the choice between external and internal borrowing implies (Panizza 2008; Abbas and Christensen 2010). The currency mismatch of foreign debt could substitute a domestic-bond maturity mismatch, given that many developing countries are unable to issue long-term government securities at a reasonable interest rate, since the limited credibility of monetary institutions exacerbates time-inconsistency problems. Considering the strong incentive to monetize the deficit and given that in a number of countries a large share of domestic debt is non-indexed, empirical studies show that large domestic debts have been associated with hyper-inflation episodes and with external debt crisis, such as in Mexico in 1994 and in Russia in 1998 (Reinhart and Rogoff 2009).[7] The positive externalities from the development of a domestic bond market on the private sector are also not assured: lending to the private sector could be crowded out by government borrowing, especially for SMEs and rural borrowers, that have to rely on domestic savings and bank credit; and when banks and institutional investors are "forced" by the government to absorb "too much" domestic debt (Hanson 2007; Panizza 2008). Moreover, different types of holders can have different types of behavior and portfolio allocations, and influence/determine the maturity profile of public debt.[8] In addition to the possibility that

6 For a more detailed discussion of the benefits, costs and risks of domestic bond markets, see IMF and World Bank (2001).

7 Borensztein, Levy Yeyati and Panizza (2006) provide a clear description of how the maturity and the currency composition of domestic debt in Mexico affected policy decisions which were at the root of the 1994-1995 financial crisis.

8 During a banking crisis, for instance, the whole debt held by the banking system, even if composed mainly of long-term government securities, would become instantaneously a *de facto* overnight debt (Panizza 2008).

excessive public debt could crowd out private investment, the cost of domestic debt has become a source of concern because it could absorb a significant share of government revenues, reducing pro-poor and social expenditures and undermining fiscal sustainability (Chapter 5).

Domestic bond markets, as well as other capital flows, are expected to benefit a country only if some pre-requisites are satisfied (Kose et al. 2009). In particular, IMF and WB (2001), Del Valle and Ugolini (2003) and Guscina (2008) underline the importance of some elements:

- A stable macroeconomic environment;
- An efficient money market;
- Broad investor participation;
- The presence of a sound legal, regulatory and supervisory framework;
- A not-distortionary tax system and an updated settlement infrastructure.

The first three conditions refer to the macroeconomic situation and we focus on those, taking into account also the microeconomic aspect of the creation and management of a domestic securities market. In particular, a lot of emphasis is given to macroeconomic and financial stability, which is the priority among the previous conditions. Without a stable and credible government and without sound fiscal and monetary policies, both domestic and foreign investors will be unwilling to buy domestic securities. A weak government will be forced to shorten the maturity structure and raise interest rates to attract investors, thereby reducing the potential benefits of domestic debt. In particular, an empirical analysis carried out on a sample of emerging markets

> … show that unstable macroeconomic environment, poor institutional characteristics, and political uncertainty hinder the development of the domestic debt market and its securitization. In cases where domestic debt market develops despite poor macroeconomic fundamentals, the government might find it very costly to issue long-term local currency non-indexed debt. If investors are unsure about the future, they will demand debt instruments denominated or indexed to U.S. dollar, inflation rate, or debt issued at short maturities. High and volatile inflation, real exchange rate volatility shortens the maturity structure of government debt and/or leads to either foreign currency or inflation indexation. Moreover, foreign currency and inflation indexation linger even after a country has achieved disinflation and fiscal readjustment, reflecting the fact that it takes time to rebuild the anti-inflationary reputation. (Guscina 2008: 31)

Inflationary expectations will be translated into higher nominal interest rates and hinder the development of longer-term instruments, since investors, in a volatile and inflationary environment, prefer short-term securities. Weak fiscal policy, characterized by unstable revenues and uncontrolled expenditures, is also a disincentive to investors and raises the cost of financing because of the perceived country risk due to increased macroeconomic instability. Exchange rate uncertainty is another source of risk which delays the development of a domestic bond markets, because it is part of the risk premium driving the decisions of foreign investors. The investor base is also important and it should be as broad and diversified as possible, including individuals, firms, institutional investors – like pension and mutual funds, usually oriented towards long-term instruments – and foreign participants.[9]

However, our data show that LICs, and especially the HIPCs, do not meet these pre-requisites in their entirety. A look at the historical figures on economic growth, inflation and interest rates shows that the macroeconomic environment is not yet stabilized and, on the contrary, volatility and uncertainty are still major issues. Lack of sound governance and fiscal policies are other elements that increase financing costs and hinder the development of a deep domestic bond market. The concentration of government securities among a few holders, usually in the banking system, is another weakness, which might hamper the formation of a large secondary market. In many LICs a large part of government securities is held by the banking system or other social security funds, when they exist, for several reasons, including the existence of a primary dealers system and the imposition of direct minimum reserve requirements on the banks or indirect requirements on other national funds (Arnone and Ugolini 2005; Del Valle and Ugolini 2003).

For those reasons, in the poorest countries, the increase in domestic debt, even if its overall level is still generally low, is unlikely to bring all the expected theoretical benefits. On the contrary, since domestic securities markets are at the very early stage of development, the cost of financing can be high and the maturity structure skewed to short-term instruments (mainly treasury bills), raising risks of rollover and requiring adequate liquidity management. These concerns are empirically supported (Chapters 4 and 5) and should be taken into considerations in policy recommendations. In other words, the (probably originally unintended) transition from external to internal financing should be gradual and subject to the achievement of adequate standards in fiscal and monetary management and policies, as well as increased government stability and policy credibility.

### 3.3 Domestic Debt in LICs

With the notable exception of some publications by the IMF and WB and a few papers (Christensen 2005, Abbas and Christensen 2010), the literature on domestic

9 However, whether foreign investors can increase competition and market efficiency, they can also bring risks, in terms of market volatility, since they could withdraw their investment if they have expectations of financial crisis, contagion, or deterioration of the macroeconomic framework.

debt in poor countries (especially SSA countries) is still very limited, mainly because of data availability) and not at all conclusive on the effects of domestic financing.[10]

A report by UNCTAD (2004) is one of the first publication to recognize the importance of domestic debt for overall public debt sustainability in HIPCs. This document presents some data on the stock and the cost of domestic debt in HIPCs and discusses some of its possible macroeconomic consequences: it supports the inclusion of public domestic debt into the debt sustainability analysis, since servicing domestic debt is a relevant part of government's fiscal burden and neglecting it could result in underestimating the necessary fiscal effort and the external assistance needed by HIPCs to achieve long-run debt sustainability. By contrast, the focus of the IMF was still limited to emerging markets. The 2004 WEO devotes a chapter to public debt, but it focuses on market access countries, whose experience is very different from the one of LICs. However, some IMF Staff Country Reports present some brief notes and assessments on public domestic debt in LICs and MICs. More recently, the WB and the IMF devoted particular attention to the rise of domestic debt markets in LICs in a paper on the DSF (IMF and World Bank 2006).

A report sponsored by the IDB and coordinated by Borensztein, Levy Yeyati and Panizza (2006) provides an extensive discussion of the role and the effects of total government debt in Latin America and the Caribbean. While the main emphasis is on emerging market economies, the report discusses also some evidence of debt relief initiatives and the evolution of domestic debt markets in Latin American LICs.

The construction of a dataset on domestic debt in 27 SSA countries (Christensen 2005) represents the first cross-country analysis of the structure of domestic debt in LICs. Christensen's findings confirm the general conclusions drawn by the event studies:

- Notwithstanding its relative small dimension, domestic debt is a severe burden to the government budget because of high interest payments;
- The stock of domestic debt is increasing over time;
- Domestic debt could squeeze private investments because of credit constraints;[11]
- The short maturity structure poses high rollover risks and increases macroeconomic instability.

The importance of domestic debt and the less favorable terms of domestic debt with respect to external debt in terms of shorter maturities and higher *ex-post* real

10 By contrast, the evolution of domestic debt in emerging economies is receiving more attention. Hanson (2007) finds that in a sample of 25 MICs over the decade 1994-2004 domestic debt grew faster than GDP and became larger than foreign debt.

11 This happens because the holder's structure in LICs is generally dominated by the banking sector. See the data discussed in Chapter 4 for a sample of HIPCs.

interest rates is confirmed by an analysis conducted by the IMF and the World Bank (2006) on a sample of LICs.

Beaugrand, Loko and Mlachila (2002) look at the choice between domestic and external financing in African countries and develop a theoretical framework which supports concessional external financing. Compared to internal borrowing, it has advantages in terms of financial costs and fewer risks, even considering the possibility of currency devaluation. A limited recourse to the domestic market is still recommended, because it could help mobilize domestic savings and support the development of additional financial instruments.

Abbas (2005) challenges the common presumption about the higher cost of domestic borrowing. He argues that the lack of default on domestic debt may be an insight that "domestic debt servicing might be 'easier' in certain contexts than external debt" (p. 7). Then, looking at Tanzania's experience, Abbas states that, once inflation and the real depreciation rate are considered, the cost of domestic financing could be smaller than the concessional terms granted by donors, and that the government could obtain funds at a lower rate than the private sector. However, Abbas focuses the analysis only on three countries (Ghana, Uganda and Tanzania), which experienced sustained GDP growth rates over the previous decade and he does not take into account the possible adverse effects of higher internal interest rates on the private sector, real exchange rate depreciation and higher inflation on external debt repayments, which could undermine overall debt sustainability.[12]

A significant improvement in this strand of research comes from the build up of a comprehensive dataset on domestic debt in 93 LICs and emerging market countries over the period 1975-2004. Thanks to these data, Abbas and Christensen (2010) are able to deepen the previous descriptive analysis. They estimate the relationship between domestic debt and economic growth in a panel of developing countries, finding that moderate levels of domestic debt have a positive impact on GDP growth. This beneficial effects should be the consequences of the development of financial markets, increased private savings, better institutions and political accountability and improved monetary policy. However, when the stock of domestic debt becomes too large (above 35 percent of banks' deposits), the negative effects of domestic debt (crowding out of the private sector and inflationary pressures) dominate and its contribution to economic growth turns negative. They conclude that this evidence is consistent with policies aimed at substituting foreign financing with securitized domestic debt, given that the latter is cheaper than the former, even after allowing for a 10-15 percent yearly exchange rate depreciation.

12 Furthermore, the three countries considered in that study have more developed domestic bond markets (Tanzania and Ghana have the largest part of domestic debt with medium- and long-term bonds) than most of the other HIPCs for which data is available. Therefore, they could be considered sort of *optimistic exceptions*: as shown in Chapter 5, total public debt, thanks to high growth rates, is sustainable in Uganda and Tanzania (even if the scenario is worsening in Uganda) but not in Ghana, where, however, the situation is improving.

Finally, the IMF and the World Bank (2006) stress the importance of domestic debt for the DSA, especially for HIPCs: there are some countries which, although classified as having a moderate risk of debt distress, have high levels of domestic debt and pay high interest rate to service domestic debt. Moreover, even if limited data availability does not allow for a fully-fledged empirical analysis, some preliminary cross-country evidence indicates that domestic debt matters for the risk of external debt default.

### *3.3.1 Some Country Studies*

Other than the cross-country evidence reviewed in the previous section, the IMF deepens the analysis of the evolution and the macroeconomic consequences of domestic debt for some selected countries: case studies are usually published in the Selected Issues that follow the IMF Article IV Consultation Staff Report at regular intervals. In the following we discuss the evidence for some representative HIPCs.[13]

Ghana is one of the countries in which the management of central government domestic debt is more problematic (IMF 2003), since it increased to 29 percent of GDP in 2002 and this number is even higher when considering contingent liabilities related to debt accumulated by SOEs. The shortening maturity structure is a further problem, because it increases rollover risk. The cost of servicing the debt is very high, so that it crowds out public expenditure and soaks up resources from poverty reduction programs. Recent data confirm the large burden of domestic debt, which, after declining to 19 percent of GDP in 2005, bounced back to 29 percent in 2008, a stock almost equal to the external debt (IMF 2009b).

In Malawi domestic debt sharply increased at the beginning of the millennium, because of a combination of exogenous factors (food shortage in 2002), tight monetary policy and loose fiscal policy (IMF 2004d). The resulting high interest rates make domestic debt service very expensive (interest payments reached 9 percent of GDP) and represent a severe risk for macroeconomic stability and pro-poor spending. More recently, thanks to a strengthened fiscal position under the PRGF arrangement, the spiral of domestic debt was reverted and the stock of internal debt declined to around 15 percent of GDP in 2005-2007 and further down to 11.7 percent at the end of July 2008. Interest payments on domestic debt now account for less than 3-4 percent of gross output, while the interest rate on treasury bills declined from 38 percent in 2002/2003 to about 20 percent in 2007 (IMF 2009l). This debt reduction is a key element of fiscal policy, since it allows for a sustainable increase in spending on high-priority areas, such as health and

13 Even if they are not discussed here because they do not look at LICs, the analysis of public debt in Egypt (IMF 2005a), Costa Rica (IMF 1998, 2004c) and Indonesia (IMF 2005b) confirms the growing interest on domestic debt issues also in emerging markets. Furthermore, they underline how limited data availability is a severe constraint for cross-country studies.

education. Nonetheless, the short maturity structure and foreign participation in the domestic debt market (their stock of treasury bills accounted for 23 percent of banking reserves as of September 2007) expose the government to capital reversal and rollover risks (IMF 2008c).

The same adverse dynamics occurs in Zambia (IMF 2004a), where domestic debt reached 21 percent of GDP and the decline in interest payments on external debt is more than offset by the raise in the cost of domestic debt service, which doubled in the period 2000-2003. In 2004 domestic interest payments accounted for more than 10 percent of government revenues and grants and they were five times larger than interest payments on external debt. As a result, poverty reduction expenditure remained low. In 2006 the ratio of domestic to foreign debt interest payments increased to 10 and domestic debt, which declined to around 16 percent of GDP, was held by non-resident for 13 percent and consisted of short-term securities for more than two thirds (IMF 2008a and 2008b).

The experience of Tanzania (IMF 2004b) suggests the possibility that domestic borrowing may fulfil a buffer role in response to changes in external financing. The evolution of domestic debt does not show any worrying increase in stocks and interest payments, because of adherence to the government's National Debt Strategy. However, some simulations indicate that domestic debt could become an additional source of vulnerability. Even if the fiscal position is manageable in response to changes in the main macroeconomic variables, it is really responsive to changes in external financing: if donors reduce their lending, this will cause adverse adjustments on domestic debt and/or will impose severe fiscal tightening or a reduction in expenditure. Therefore, in the absence of an enhanced revenues system, aid dependence may result in reduced social expenditures. Recent data on public debt dynamics in Tanzania show that the latter represents a good example of the way in which domestic debt could harm economic growth in poor countries, even after the HIPC and the MDRI Initiative: after 2006, debt relief has greatly eased the debt burden, but the increase in domestic interest payments has largely offset the reduction in the interest bill on external debt. As of June 2008, domestic debt amounted to around 14 percent of GDP, half of it is short-term treasury bills (IMF 2009m), which is larger than in 2001, and domestic interest payments accounted for 1 percent of GDP, twice as large than in 2003 and almost ten times the interest bill on external debt (in 2003 the total interest bill was equally shared between domestic and external debt).

Additional recent data on a selected sample of HIPCs show that the increasing trend of domestic debt (documented in Chapter 4) is evident in many poor countries, in contrast to what happened to external debt thanks to the HIPC and the MDRI Initiatives (Figure 3.2). As a result, in some countries (Tanzania and Uganda) in 2008 domestic debt represented the dominant share in total public debt. The prevalence of short-term instruments, a limited and concentrated investor base and high interest rates are a source of vulnerability for macroeconomic stability, economic growth and debt sustainability.

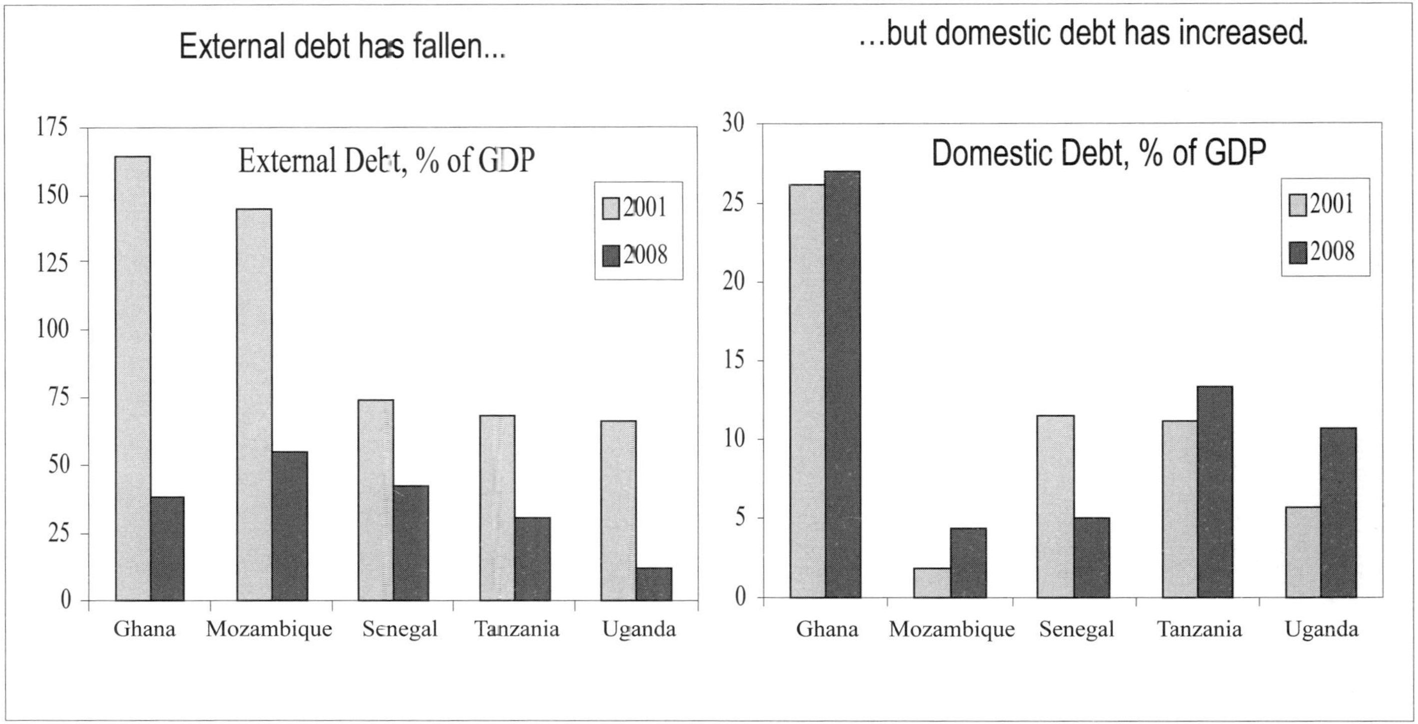


**Figure 3.2 The recent trend in external and domestic debt in five HIPCs**
*Source*: IMF Country Report No. 09/179 (IMF 2009m).

The experience of Latin America countries is similar to the situation described above, because of the large stock of debt, its high cost, which crowds out private investment, and the short-term maturity structure. In addition, the experience of Nicaragua and Bolivia indicates another possible risk posed by domestic borrowing: when a large fraction of domestic debt is indexed to foreign currencies, the dynamics of the exchange rate and inflation add other sources of vulnerability. Nevertheless, those countries have started fiscal consolidation strategies which are improving the profile of public debt, and which should be followed also by other African indebted poor countries.

In 2003 Nicaragua's domestic debt exceeded 30 percent of GDP and was indexed to the US dollar (IMF 2002b). The experience of countries like Nicaragua, where the stock of domestic debt is large and it is very responsive to external shocks, pushed the IMF to stress the importance of considering the aggregate total public debt when assessing fiscal sustainability. Given the threats posed by internal debt, since 2003 a fiscal consolidation is leading to a substitution of costly domestic debt with concessional external financing, even if financing requirements on domestic debt still remain large: the 2006 DSA classifies Nicaragua at moderate risk of debt distress and it still identifies domestic debt as a critical source of distress, given that the overall evaluation of the public debt dynamics is contingent on the continued reduction of domestic debt (IMF 2006b).

In Bolivia the stock of domestic debt increased from 20 percent of GDP in 2002 to 27 percent in November 2008, while the MDRI drastically reduced external debt from a peak of 57.9 percent of GDP in 2005 to 8.1 percent in 2008 (IMF 2009n). In 2003-2004 Bolivia started a gradual trend towards de-dollarization of treasury paper and an extension of the maturity structure, first issuing inflation-indexed instruments and, in 2006, gradually replacing them with non-indexed bonds in local currency. As a result of this policy, the stock of outstanding treasury paper denominated in US dollars declined from more than 90 percent in 2002 to around 25 percent in 2006 and the average maturity increased from 60 weeks in 2004 to 130 in 2006. This positive evolution of domestic debt market is reflected also in the holders' structure, with pension and investment funds holding 45 percent of the outstanding domestic debt and the banking system 18.5 percent, mainly made by non-indexed Bolivianos bonds. Macroeconomic fundamentals and a sound debt management strategy have played a critical role in improving the profile of Bolivia's public debt in recent years (IMF 2007e).

These country studies highlight that the stock of domestic debt is usually small compared to external debt, and that some countries are undergoing a fiscal consolidation or using foreign assistance in order to reduce domestic debt. However, adverse domestic debt dynamics could hinder the positive effect of the HIPC Initiative in term of freeing up resources for poverty reduction expenditures.

### 3.4 The Asymmetric Adjustment of Monetary and Fiscal Variables

The need for internal financing which is boosting domestic debt in LICs is mainly due the asymmetric adjustment process implied by the HIPC Initiative, which failed to reach its target in full because of the different time frames of monetary adjustment as compared to fiscal adjustment. The program is based on the achievement of a track record of macroeconomic stability and structural reforms, but it ignores the fact that fiscal variables are generally much slower to react than monetary ones. The reasons lie in the internal and external lags of fiscal policy and from the fact that, at least in the medium term, large primary deficits in HIPCs cannot be promptly reduced because of low revenues and the inherent political difficulties in reducing public spending in countries where most of the population is already below the (many definitions of) poverty line.

On the one hand, the slow fiscal adjustment, together with the lack of access to international capital markets – required by the HIPC Initiative – and the lack of adequate inflows of concessional lending forced governments to tap domestic markets to finance their primary deficits. On the other hand, monetary aggregates were much easier and faster to control in the context of an IMF program, so inflation in HIPCs has been successfully brought under control, reducing seigniorage and expanding the financing gap of the public sector. The success of the HIPC program in monetary policy coupled with lagging fiscal adjustment was a bad policy mix and had strongly unexpected negative consequences: the need for the government to keep financing its expenditures in the context of rapidly declining inflation led to a steep increase in real interest rates. The unintended consequences of this wrongly-timed policy mix are: 1) a clear increase of the real cost of financing, which has to account also for the limited government's credibility; 2) a drag on government expenditures, investment and growth; and possibly 3) a strengthening of the exchange rate (as foreign banks and investors are eager to invest in high-yield government paper); in turn, this latter could hamper exports whose foreign exchange proceeds are necessary in the medium and long term to service the external debt.[14]

The results of the multilateral programs are illustrated in Figure 3.3, which highlights that the adjustment process was quite successful in terms of reduced inflation, while primary balance kept on deteriorating, apart from the last two years. In other words, monetary policy worked well, while the real sector did not achieved the expected results, also in terms of per capita GDP growth, which is still quite weak and volatile.

---

14 In particular, the exchange rate dynamics are critical for debt sustainability and are affected in different directions by domestic interest rates, inflation and fiscal management. In other words, an exchange rate appreciation could be due to higher interest rates (posing problems on the export side), while unexpected inflation and poor fiscal management could originate a real depreciation (with adverse consequences on external debt repayments).

In conclusion, rising domestic debt in HIPC countries – where financial markets liberalization and macroeconomic stability in terms of credible fiscal and monetary policies might be achieved but not necessarily rooted – puts forward potential problems and risks related to:

- slower economic growth, because of reduced investment, crowded out by higher domestic interest rates and possibly credit constrained by domestic banks, especially when they are put under pressure to absorb government securities (Chapter 4);
- macroeconomic and financial instability, since domestic debt might be concentrated in the financial system and governments are tempted to raise inflation, with subsequent adverse effects on external balance and exchange rates;
- undermined debt sustainability, because of much higher interest rates and lower GDP growth (Chapter 5).

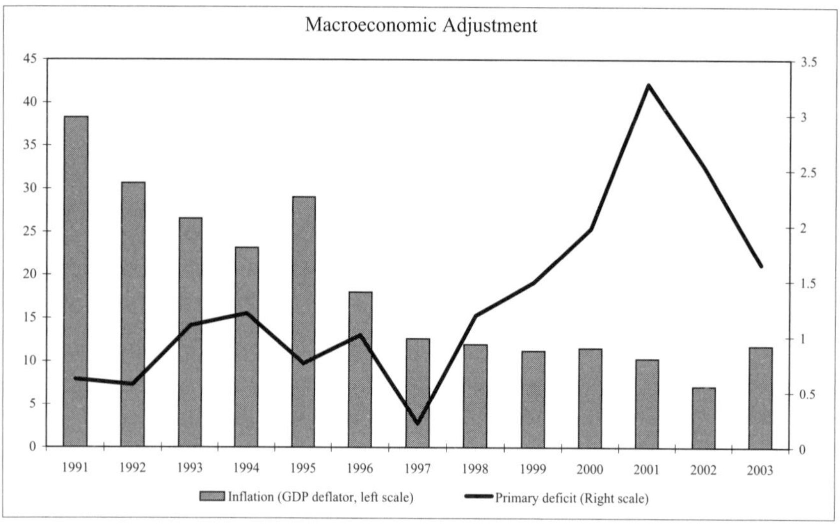


**Figure 3.3 Fiscal and monetary adjustments in HIPC countries**
*Source*: Authors' calculations on a sample of 14 HIPCs. See Chapter 4 for details on the dataset.

Furthermore, the unfavorable evolution of domestic debt could be worsened and exacerbated by a reduction in foreign lending and aid assistance, which is a possibility that should be carefully taken into account, since the ongoing shift towards grants, instead of loans, and the global financial crisis are likely to reduce the total amount of resources that donors will provide in the near future.[15]

15 The standard argument sees foreign aid as an instrument to stabilize or reduce large domestic debt. However, a surge in aid inflows can translate into rising domestic debt: when aid is spent instead of absorbed, the fear of an exchange rate appreciation and of inflationary pressures can push policy-makers to sterilize capital inflows issuing government securities (Aiyar, Berg and Hussain 2009).

# Chapter 4
# The Relevance of Domestic Debt in HIPCs

## 4.1 Definition of Domestic Debt and Data

There is not a clear-cut definition of domestic debt: according to Panizza (2008: 4),

> there are three possible definitions of external (and thus, domestic) debt. The first focuses on the currency in which the debt is issued (with external debt defined as foreign currency debt). The second focuses on the residence of the creditor (external debt is debt owed to non-residents). The third focuses on the place of issuance and the legislation that regulates the debt contract (external debt is debt issued in foreign countries and under the jurisdiction of a foreign court).

While Panizza builds his dataset following the third definition, we rely on the second one, which is the theoretically correct one and consists of data by many IFIs. Thus, according to our approach, domestic debt is defined as debt owed to creditors resident in the same country (the debtor). However, from a practical point of view, the existing datasets highlight the difficulty in defining domestic debt unambiguously (Box 4.1). In particular, the two main issues are related to the choice of: 1) the government level (national, state/regional, municipal); and 2) the liabilities that should be included.

The former issue is relevant because most of the countries considered have local government, decentralized authorities and SOEs, so that there could be a large difference between Central Government and Public Sector domestic debt. For what concerns the financial instruments included in the debt definition, there is a great variety among countries. The definition of domestic debt embedded in the publications and in the data disseminated by local authorities and the IMF includes securities, advances from central bank and commercial banks, loans, debentures, government-guaranteed debt[1] and other liabilities.

Therefore, in order to get a debt stock comparable across countries we refer, when possible, to a definition of Central Government domestic debt which, as in Christensen (2005) and in the BIS statistics, comprises only securitized debt. This

1 Debt guaranteed by the government but obtained directly from governmental or private sector institutions by local governments, autonomous public entities, and public or private enterprises. The government is not directly liable for this type of debt, but it does represent a contingent liability because the government, as guarantor, must assume the obligation in the event of default.

is represented mainly by treasury bills, bonds, notes and government stocks, even if in some countries there are other special securities and consolidated debt.[2]

**Box 4.1 Definitions and data on domestic debt**

The GFS Manual (IMF 2001b) defines debt as "all liabilities that require payments of interest and/or principal by the debtor to the creditor at a date or dates in future. Thus, all liabilities in the GFS system are debt except for shares and other equity and financial derivatives" (p. 129). From the Government Balance Sheet, domestic liabilities are classified into:

1. Currency and deposits
2. Securities other than shares
3. Loans
4. Shares and other equity (public corporations only)
5. Insurance technical reserves*
6. Financial derivatives
7. Other account payable**

Therefore, it is clear that the definition of domestic debt embedded in the GFS figures is broad and embraces different other liabilities other than securities. Furthermore, securities include: bills, bonds and debentures (including convertible bonds), commercial paper, negotiable certificates of deposit, tradable depository receipts, notes, securitized mortgage loans and credit card receivables, loans that have become marketable de facto, bankers' acceptances, and preferred stocks or shares that pay a fixed income but do not provide for participation in the distribution of the residual value of a corporation in dissolution.

With respect to the government level, the GFS is concerned about the balance sheet of the General Government (made by Central, State and Local Government sub-sectors) and the broader Public Sector, which consists of the general government sector plus government-controlled entities.

The IFS relates to the direct and assumed debt of the Central Government and excludes loans guaranteed by the government. The distinction between foreign and domestic is based on residence of the lender (which is a function of the location and not the nationality of the debt holder), where possible, but otherwise on the currency in which the debt instruments are denominated.

2 Christensen's (2005) definition of domestic debt "focuses on gross securitized domestic debt, comprising treasury bills, development stocks, and bonds" (p. 4).

The WEO of September 2003 has a chapter investigating the dynamics of public debt in emerging markets (IMF 2003b). It defines public sector debt according to the most comprehensive measure available in the data. Therefore, it makes use of different definitions for different countries (i.e. Public sector, General or Central Government debt, gross or net debt).

The BIS has a dataset on domestic debt covering 47 countries, mainly industrialized economies, starting in 1989, with annual data until 1993 and quarterly data on domestic government securities thereafter.*** "The domestic debt securities statistics (…) cover data on long-term bonds and notes, treasury bills, commercial paper and other short-term notes issued in the domestic markets of currently about 40 countries (OECD members plus selected emerging market countries). The data are derived from various national sources, such as central banks, national statistical offices, securities registers etc. (…) Domestic debt securities are defined as those that have been issued by residents in domestic currency (with a few exceptions) and targeted at resident investors. (The …) national currencies (values of the amount outstanding) are converted by the BIS into US dollar amounts at the exchange rate prevailing at the relevant reporting date" (BIS Papers No. 14 – Guide to the IFS, February 2003: 16).

*Note*: * They "consist of the net equity of households in pension funds and life insurance reserves, prepaid premiums, and reserves against outstanding claims" (p. 126); ** "Other accounts receivable/payable consist of trade credits and advances and miscellaneous other items due to be received or paid" (p. 128); *** Available online at: http://www.bis.org/statistics/secstats.htm (accessed April 2010).

We have collected data for a sample of 53 developing countries over the decade 1994-2003: all countries have at least 8 observations and there are only 4.15 percent of missing values for the debt stock and 5.47 percent for interest payments.[3] Among the 53 countries, according to the WB IBRD/IDA classification, 27 countries are IDA-only, 20 IBRD-only, 6 BLEND, while 16 are classified as HIPCs (Table 4.1).[4]

3 Data on domestic debt are drawn from a database developed at the WB by J.F. Parrault, A. Presbitero and V. Tulin which cover 79 developing countries for the period 1970-2003. Contingent liabilities, implicit debt and arrears are not included in the definition of public domestic debt.

4 The distinction between IDA, IBRD and BLEND countries are based on per capita income (the 2010 threshold for being IDA-eligible is fixed at US$1,135), country's creditworthiness, and policy performance. This classification affects the capacity of a country to receive credits from IDA, IBRD or from a blend of the two, with the poorest countries accessing exclusively concessional IDA loans and grants, and richer countries having access to IBRD commercial loans.

**Table 4.1 List of countries with domestic debt data**

| Country | Classification | Country | Classification | Country | Classification |
|---|---|---|---|---|---|
| Algeria | IBRD | Guyana | IDA | Philippines | IBRD |
| Belize | IBRD | Honduras | IDA | Romania | IBRD |
| Bolivia | BLEND | India | BLEND | Russia | IBRD |
| Bulgaria | IBRD | Jamaica | IBRD | Rwanda | IDA |
| Burundi | IDA | Jordan | IBRD | Sierra Leone | IDA |
| Cape Verde | IDA | Kenya | IDA | Solomon Islands | IDA |
| Chad | IDA | Kyrgyz Republic | IDA | Sri Lanka | IDA |
| Costa Rica | IBRD | Latvia | IBRD | Swaziland | IBRD |
| Dominica | BLEND | Lesotho | IDA | Tanzania | IDA |
| Ecuador | IBRD | Madagascar | IDA | Thailand | IBRD |
| Egypt | IBRD | Malawi | IDA | Tonga | IDA |
| El Salvador | IBRD | Moldova | IDA | Tunisia | IBRD |
| Ethiopia | IDA | Morocco | IBRD | Uganda | IDA |
| Fiji | IBRD | Myanmar | IDA | Ukraine | IBRD |
| Gambia, The | IDA | Nepal | IDA | Vietnam | IDA |
| Georgia | IDA | Nigeria | IDA | Zambia | IDA |
| Ghana | IDA | Pakistan | BLEND | Zimbabwe | BLEND |
| Guatemala | IBRD | Papua New Guinea | BLEND | | |

*Source*: Data on domestic debt are drawn from a database developed at the WB by J.F. Perrault, A. Presbitero and V. Tulin.

The main sources for data on public debt are the 2005 GDF for external debt, while domestic debt data are gathered from a number of sources: IMF Article IV Consultation and the IMF Staff Country Reports, Statistical Annexes and Recent Economic Development, the IMF GFS and IFS, the WB WDI and Regional datasets, countries' central banks and Ministries of Finance.[5]

5 The IFS definition of domestic debt is similar to ours, so that the IFS data are sometimes used to fill some missing values or extending the time coverage. On the contrary, the GFS domestic debt data refer to a much broader aggregate and, therefore, they cannot be used to fill the gaps found in our main sources. Unfortunately, both these datasets provide only an aggregate definition of domestic debt, without any indication on holders and maturity structure. Moreover, their coverage is largely incomplete, especially in LICs, and they are often inconsistent with data from central bank or other IMF publications. As a result, IFS data are used only when they match (or show a very close similarity) existing data in the overlapping years, in order to extend the time dimension of our database. The WEO is not used as a source of data, since its definition of domestic debt is broader than government securities. The BIS dataset is not taken as an additional source because it covers only few countries of our sample (9), for which we can gather data elsewhere. As a consequence, in order to maintain a certain degree of consistency among the different sources used, we rely mainly on IMF Article IV Consultation and central bank sources.

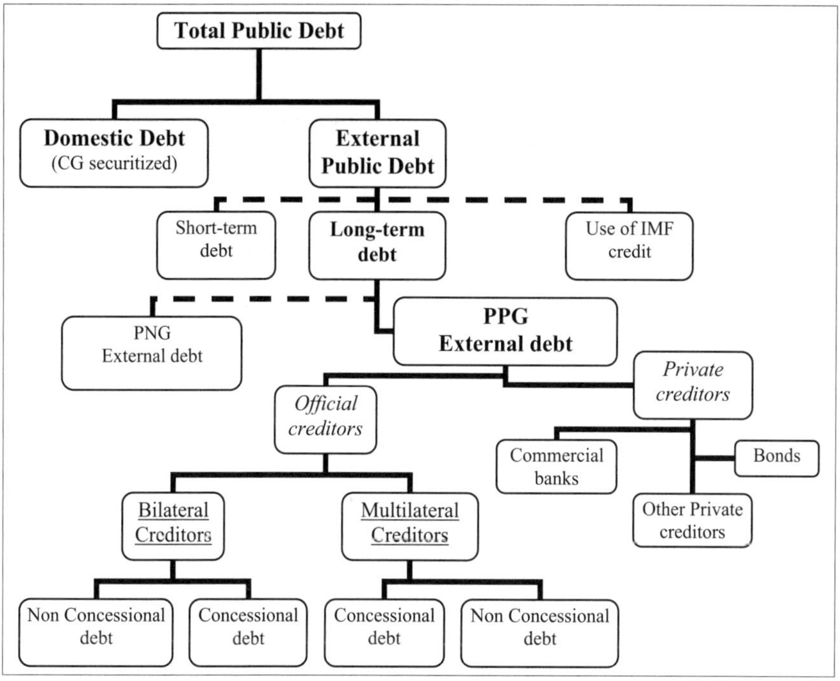


**Figure 4.1 Decomposition of total public debt**
*Source*: Authors' elaboration.

From the original dataset, we are able to build a specific dataset on a sample of 14 HIPCs for which reliable and sufficiently long time series of data on the structure of domestic debt are available.[6] For external debt, data on stocks and flows are available for all HIPCs and they are decomposed in many sub-components. However, with respect to domestic debt, there are panel data only for aggregate debt stocks and interest payments. As far as we know, however, this is the broadest dataset available, since for many countries there are no data at all on government securities, even in the IMF Article IV reports.[7] All other macroeconomic variables

6 The countries are: Bolivia, Burundi, Ethiopia, Gambia, Ghana, Guyana, Honduras, Madagascar, Malawi, Rwanda, Sierra Leone, Tanzania, Uganda and Zambia. The analysis of this chapter is based on 2005 data and HIPC's status.

7 In a few cases, this is because there were no domestic markets for government securities, as in Niger, where the first treasury bills were issued in the summer of 2005. In general it is difficult to distinguish if the lack of data is due to a lack of markets or not. Given the relevance that domestic debt is assuming in poor countries, we underline the necessity for increased efforts in data collection.

(GDP, budget balance, inflation, exchange rates) come from the 2005 WDI and from IMF datasets.

The target of our analysis is total public debt, both external and domestic. Total outstanding external debt is defined by the WB as the sum of three components: 1) long-term debt; 2) short-term debt; and 3) use of IMF credit. However, only the first component is included in the definition of public external debt, since data on short-term debt do not allow for the breakdown between public and private debt. This decomposition is instead available for long-term debt, which is divided into: total PPG and total PNG long-term debt. The former is the object of the IMF-WB debt sustainability analysis; therefore, we will take PPG as a very conservative definition of total external public debt.

A visual representation of total public debt's breakdown is presented in Figure 4.1, where dotted lines connect debt aggregates which are not part of the definition of total public debt (short-term debt, use of IMF credit and PNG debt).

## 4.2 The Evolution of Domestic Debt in Developing Countries

Data on domestic debt for the sample of 53 developing countries confirm the rise of the stock of domestic debt, especially in HIPCs. The latter show a pattern similar to the IDA ones, since they are a sub-sample, but, especially in recent years, their ratios are more volatile and the increase in domestic debt from 1997 is more evident (Figure 4.2). On average (Table 4.2) domestic debt accounts for a larger share of GDP in emerging markets (16.7 percent) than in LICs (12.9 percent).

**Table 4.2 Summary statistics of the domestic debt to GDP ratio (unweighted averages)**

| **Domestic debt to GDP ratio** | *Period* | *Average* | *Median* | *St Dev* | *# countries* | *# obs per year (average)* | *# obs per country (average)* |
|---|---|---|---|---|---|---|---|
| All sample | 1994-03 | 15.69 | 15.18 | 1.88 | 53 | 50.80 | 9.58 |
| IDA-countries | 1994-03 | 12.90 | 12.13 | 2.13 | 27 | 25.50 | 9.44 |
| IBRD-countries | 1994-03 | 16.71 | 16.36 | 1.84 | 20 | 19.60 | 9.80 |
| HIPC countries | 1994-03 | 12.84 | 11.31 | 3.22 | 16 | 15.60 | 9.75 |

*Source*: Authors' calculations.

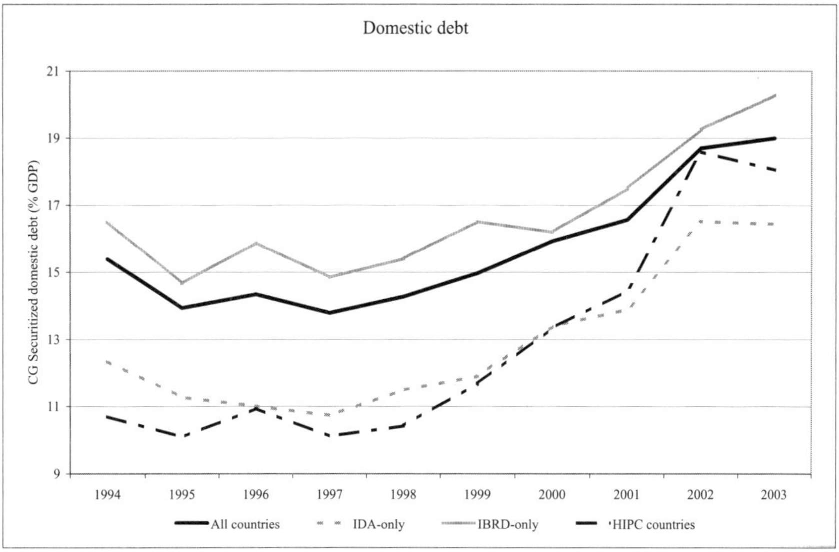


**Figure 4.2 Domestic debt: 1994-2003**
*Source*: Authors' calculations.

With respect to the dynamics of domestic debt service, data show a pretty stable (or declining) evolution of interest payments as a share of GDP, with the notable exception of the HIPCs, whose interest payments increased from a minimum of 1.45 percent of GDP in 1998 to more than 2 percent in 2003 (Figures 4.3). Consistently with the larger stock of debt, also domestic debt service is larger in IBRD than in IDA countries (Table 4.3).

**Table 4.3 Summary statistics of the interest payments on domestic debt to GDP ratio (unweighted averages)**

| **Interest payments on domestic debt to GDP ratio** | *Period* | *Average* | *Median* | *St Dev* | *# countries* | *# obs per year (average)* | *# obs per country (average)* |
|---|---|---|---|---|---|---|---|
| All sample | 1994-03 | 2.24 | 2.25 | 0.15 | 53 | 50.10 | 9.45 |
| IDA-countries | 1994-03 | 1.85 | 1.86 | 0.11 | 27 | 24.80 | 9.19 |
| IBRD-countries | 1994-03 | 2.22 | 2.19 | 0.26 | 20 | 19.30 | 9.65 |
| HIPC countries | 1994-03 | 1.74 | 1.76 | 0.17 | 16 | 15.50 | 9.69 |

*Source*: Authors' calculations.

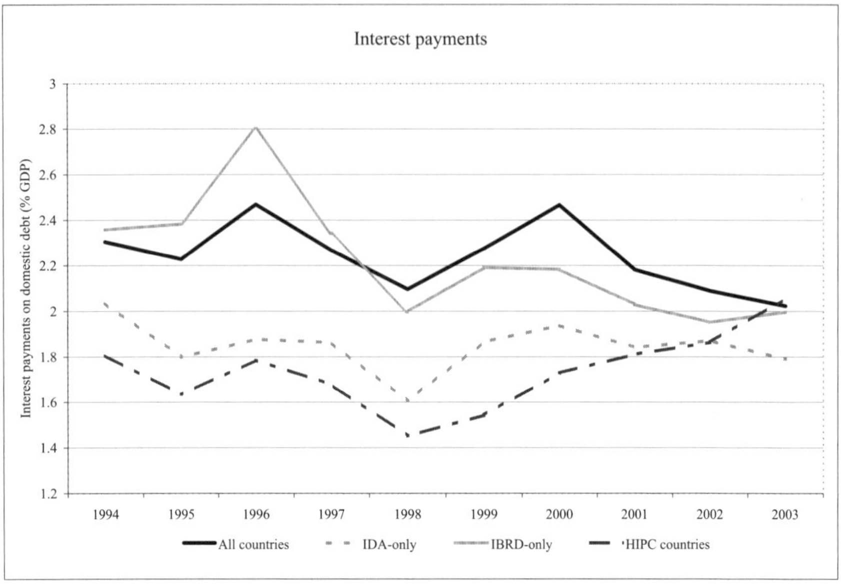


**Figure 4.3 Domestic interest payments: 1994-2003**
*Source*: Authors' calculations.

Data on interest payments allow for the derivation of the implicit interest rate on domestic debt, dividing the payment in the current year by the stock of domestic debt accumulated by the end of previous year. This calculation presents some difficulties mainly due to: 1) the presence of outliers, especially for post-Communist countries, in which the first data available show huge differences from one year to the next; 2) the possible inconsistency between the definition of interest payments and domestic debt.[8] Taking into account these limitations (and, thus, dropping some outliers), we have calculated the implicit rates. They are generally higher in IDA and HIPC countries, than in market-access economies. The most striking feature is that the general decline in the implicit interest rates from the mid 1990s is much more evident for market-access countries, while in HIPCs this declining trend seems to halt in 2000.

To measure the relative importance of domestic debt, it is instructive to look at its share with respect to total public debt, defined as the sum of PPG external debt, converted in local currency, and securitized domestic debt.[9]

8 Unfortunately, we do not generally have a clear definition of what interest payments refer to: payments could also be linked to liabilities other than securities.

9 Data on external debt and exchange rates – DEC alternative conversion factor (local currency unit per US dollar) – are taken from the WB WDI-GDF 2005. The main shortcoming of this indicator of total public debt is that it is composed of PPG external debt,

**Table 4.4 Summary statistics of domestic debt (in percent of total debt, unweighted averages)**

| **Domestic debt as a share of total debt** | *Period* | *Average* | *Median* | *St Dev* | *# countries* | *# obs per year (average)* | *# obs per country (average)* |
|---|---|---|---|---|---|---|---|
| All sample | 1994-03 | 23.46 | 22.91 | 2.65 | 53 | 50.40 | 9.51 |
| IDA-countries | 1994-03 | 15.08 | 14.73 | 2.21 | 27 | 25.50 | 9.44 |
| IBRD-countries | 1994-03 | 30.27 | 30.45 | 3.22 | 20 | 19.20 | 9.60 |
| HIPC countries | 1994-03 | 13.05 | 12.76 | 3.89 | 16 | 15.60 | 9.75 |

*Source*: Authors' calculations.

External debt is the main component of total indebtedness, even if there are significant differences between countries with and without market access (Table 4.4). On average, domestic debt accounts for around 23 percent of total public debt, even if it is more than 30 percent in market-access economies, 15 percent in IDA countries and 13 percent in HIPCs, because of their obvious reliance on foreign borrowing. Interestingly, the latter group shows the highest variability, measured by the standard deviation. The dynamics of the domestic share of public debt over the decade 1994-2003 show a common positive trend. From 1994 to 2003, the ratio of domestic debt to total public debt jumped, on average, from 19.6 to 27.3 percent: specifically, it increased from 11 to 17 percent in IDA countries, from 6 to 16 percent in HIPCs, and from 25 to 35 percent in market-access economies. The stabilization of the ratio in the poorest countries in the most recent period is due exclusively to the sudden increase in external debt, from 78 percent in 2001 to 89 percent of GDP in 2003.

The evolution of the share on domestic to total debt is driven by both the numerator and the denominator. In IBRD countries they moved in opposite directions resulting in a sharp increase in the domestic-debt share, while in IDA and HIPC countries, after the decline in 1994-1997, external debt started increasing again, even if the growth rate of domestic debt was faster. From 1997 to 2003, domestic debt increased by 61.6 percent in IDA countries and 89 percent in HIPCs, compared with an increase of external debt by 21 percent and 20 percent, respectively.

The comparison between external and domestic debt shows an increase in the relative importance of the latter, even if it still remains a small fraction of total public debt. If we compare their costs, measured as the interest payments to GDP ratio,

which measures the public external indebtedness (according to the WDI-GDF definition "Public and publicly-guaranteed debt comprises long-term external obligations of public debtors, including the national government, political subdivisions (or an agency of either), and autonomous public bodies, and external obligations of private debtors that are guaranteed for repayment by a public entity") and by our measure of securitized domestic debt, which refers exclusively to Central Government liabilities.

the picture is different and highlights the real burden of domestic debt. We consider only the countries and the years in which we have observations on both external and domestic payments: Tables 4.5 and 4.6 show data availability and summary statistics for both external and domestic payments in the short and long dataset.[10]

**Table 4.5 Summary statistics of domestic interest payments (in percent of GDP, unweighted averages)**

| **Interest on domestic debt (in percent of GDP)** | *Period* | *Average* | *Median* | *St Dev* | *# countries* | *# obs per year (average)* | *# obs per country (average)* |
|---|---|---|---|---|---|---|---|
| All sample | 1994-03 | 2.27 | 2.28 | 0.16 | 53 | 49.30 | 9.30 |
| IDA-countries | 1994-03 | 1.89 | 1.89 | 0.12 | 27 | 24.10 | 8.96 |
| IBRD-countries | 1994-03 | 2.22 | 2.19 | 0.26 | 20 | 19.30 | 9.65 |
| HIPC countries | 1994-03 | 1.79 | 1.80 | 0.15 | 16 | 14.80 | 9.25 |

*Source*: Authors' calculations.

**Table 4.6 Summary statistics of external interest payments (in percent of GDP, unweighted averages)**

| **Interest on PPG external debt (in percent of GDP)** | *Period* | *Average* | *Median* | *St Dev* | *# countries* | *# obs per year (average)* | *# obs per country (average)* |
|---|---|---|---|---|---|---|---|
| All sample | 1994-03 | 1.53 | 1.54 | 0.13 | 53 | 49.30 | 9.30 |
| IDA-countries | 1994-03 | 1.32 | 1.36 | 0.27 | 27 | 24.10 | 8.96 |
| IBRD-countries | 1994-03 | 1.84 | 1.85 | 0.10 | 20 | 19.30 | 9.65 |
| HIPC countries | 1994-03 | 1.46 | 1.49 | 0.42 | 16 | 14.80 | 9.25 |

*Source*: Authors' calculations.

It is clear from the data that the degree of concessionality on external loans to IDA countries is reflected in interest payments on domestic debt higher than on external debt. Moreover, the breakdown into different sub-samples over time shows that this difference becomes almost zero in market-access economies, where the declining domestic payments at the end of the period are very close to the payments on external debt. On the contrary, in IDA countries, and especially in the HIPCs, the difference between the expenditures for external and domestic interest in recent years is becoming larger, with the HIPCs spending in 2003 twice on domestic than external interest payments (2 percent versus 1 percent of GDP).

10 Table 4.5 is very similar to Table 4.3, the discrepancies are due to the fact that few observations are dropped because of the lack of the correspondent values for external interest payments (in particular, there are no data on Myanmar).

## 4.3 Domestic Debt and Economic Management in HIPCs

In this section we deepen the analysis of the evolution and the macroeconomic consequences of domestic debt in the smaller sample of 14 HIPCs for which there are detailed and reliable data from 1991 to 2003. As already discussed, the HIPC Initiative and the DSA originally implemented in the multilateral programs ignore the role played by domestic debt in poor countries. However, a key requirement for participation in the HIPC Initiative is that it forbids borrowing on commercial terms in the international capital markets; also, monetary financing of the deficit is normally prohibited in IMF programs. Therefore, an important (and probably unintended) consequence of the HIPC design and implementation is that internal financing is becoming more and more important in many countries and this trend is not likely to be reverted any time soon (section 3.4).

Over the period 1991-2003, the stock of debt in the sample of HIPCs almost doubled and the average value is around 18 percent of GDP; given the high variability, there are countries where this ratio is substantially higher (Figure 4.4). The macroeconomic framework of these countries is already encumbered by a huge external debt, so that even a small stock of domestic debt could have an adverse impact on the economy. In particular, governments have to offer high interest rates to raise money on domestic markets. We observe that domestic debt is already more expensive than external debt, in terms of a larger share of GDP that is destined to interest payments, even if the high interest rates could also be the result of illiquid domestic financial markets. From 1991 to 2003 HIPCs moved from a situation in which external debt service is the largest part of interest payments, to an opposite situation, in which the expenditure on domestic interests becomes the greatest share of overall interest bill. In 2003, while interests on PPG external debt were slightly higher than 1 percent of GDP, domestic interests soaked up, on average, more than 2 percent. In some countries this percentages in recent years were much higher, up to 6 percent in Ghana, around 4 percent in Gambia, Guyana, Malawi, and 3 percent in Sierra Leone.[11]

11 It is worth noting that the problem of domestic debt is not limited to the 14 countries in the sample. as reported in a very recent story by Agencia de Informacao de Mocambique, "perhaps the most notable aspect of the Mozambican debt is the growth of domestic indebtedness, through the issuing of high interest bearing long term treasury bonds, and short term treasury bills. Domestic debt was negligible, until the year 2000. In that year, the government had to pay over eight million dollars in domestic debt servicing. The following year the domestic debt service overtook the foreign debt service: the government had to pay 22.5 million dollars to its domestic creditors, and 22.1 million to its foreign ones. Domestic debt servicing rose to 64 million dollars in 2002, falling back to 49 million in 2003 and 22 million in 2004" (http://allafrica.com/stories/200604250643.html, accessed April 2010).

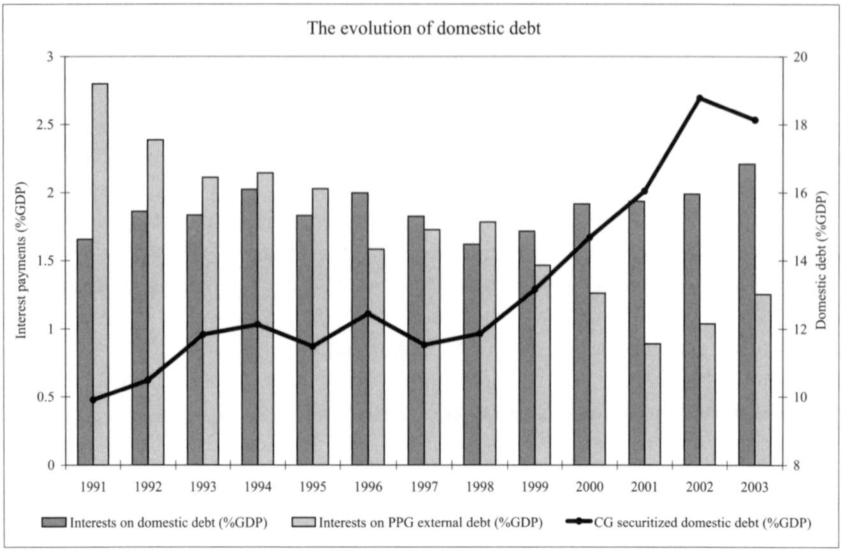


**Figure 4.4 Domestic debt and interest payments on external and domestic debt as a share of GDP (unweighted averages)**
*Source*: Authors' calculations.

Apart from looking at the stocks and flows of domestic debt, it is critical to inspect the debt structure (Table 4.7) in order to point out the potential risks of domestic debt. Our data underline that: 1) maturities are severely biased towards short-term instruments (mainly treasury bills); and that 2) the banking sector is the main holder of government securities, in the absence of a broad investor base.[12] There is the real risk of a credit constraint, since the banking system might (or might be "pressed" to) prefer government securities rather than private sector lending, depending on the allocation of risk and interest rates between public and private sector.

As regards the first point, in six out of 13 countries for which there are data on the maturity structure, short-term securities (with maturity lower than one year) account for more the 90 percent of total debt, and in Guyana, Madagascar and Uganda treasury bills represent the entire stock of domestic debt.[13] With the

12 The lack of a broader investor base could have negative effects on the maturity structure, since potential institutional and foreign investors could prefer long-term securities.

13 There are no data on Honduras. In Guyana and Uganda the share of treasury bills is 99.9 percent, while in Madagascar they are the only kind of government securities. In Burundi, treasury bills were the only instrument from 1996 to 2000, when the government started issuing bonds. In Sierra Leone treasury bills and a one-year bond represent 100 percent of domestic securities from 1996.

exceptions of Zambia, in which the share of treasury bills decreased from 93 percent in 1995 to 32 percent in 2004, Burundi, whose decline is more limited (from 97 percent to 85 percent) and Bolivia, in which the percentage of short-term instruments remained quite stable around 15-27 percent, the other countries experienced a sharp shortening of the maturity structure. On average, the fraction of short-term domestic debt increased by 10 percentage point reaching 69 percent in 2004. The nine completion point countries showed the same pattern, even if their share of treasury bills is, on average, 10 percentage points lower. In particular, the short-term securities increased from 9 percent to 40 percent in Ethiopia, from 18 percent to 50 percent in Ghana (with a maximum at 71 percent in 2000), from 85 percent to 96 percent in Gambia, from 54 percent to 93 percent in Malawi, from 14 percent to 33 percent in Rwanda, from 53 percent to 69 percent in Sierra Leone, and from 12 percent to 30 percent in Tanzania.

**Table 4.7 Domestic debt's structure**

| | *Banking system holding (percent)* | | *Short-term instruments (percent)* | |
|---|---|---|---|---|
| **Country** | **1994** | **2003** | **1994** | **2003** |
| Bolivia* | 88.94 | 32.85 | 27.63 | 21.60 |
| Burundi | 87.88 | 67.81 | 96.97 | 84.90 |
| Ethiopia | 93.29 | 93.78 | 9.92 | 40.29 |
| Gambia** | 29.91 | 40.95 | 85.27 | 94.27 |
| Ghana | 67.1 | 56.3 | 18.77 | 59.24 |
| Guyana | 59.58 | n/a | 99.87 | 99.99 |
| Honduras | 82.8 | 35.07 | n/a | n/a |
| Madagascar | 100 | 65.04 | 100 | 100 |
| Malawi | 50.06 | 52.33 | 54.15 | 90.55 |
| Rwanda | 68.6 | 63.6 | 14.22 | 27.74 |
| Sierra Leone | 75.16 | 61 | 97.05 | 100 |
| Tanzania*** | 81.95 | 59.33 | 12.89 | 23.00 |
| Uganda | 74.29 | 82.3 | 99.98 | 99.99 |
| Zambia**** | 70.89 | 82.71 | 93.04 | 32.28 |

*Note*: * Refers only to the central bank; ** The distribution by holder refers to the overall stock of domestic debt; *** Holders' classification refers only for stock, bonds and notes, no treasury bills; **** Only treasury-bills, no data on bonds by holder. Data available from 1995.
*Source*: Authors' calculations.

With respect to the second point, the central bank and the banking system are generally the main holders of government securities. In seven countries, however, the share of the banking system has decreased, especially in the two Latin

American countries, while only in Gambia, Uganda and Zambia the concentration of securities in the banking sector has become larger.

From the breakdown between central bank and commercial bank holdings[14] we observe a decline of the central bank role as main holder of government securities, whose share fell from 40 percent to 25 percent in 2003. On the other hand, commercial banks slightly increased their share, although they did not completely offset the decline of central bank holdings. As a result, there is an average increase in non-bank holdings, even if the role of non-banking sector remains limited. Besides, in many cases other holders are mainly SOEs of other public sector entities, so that a real diversification of the investor base is far from secured. In Honduras, for instance, the sharp decline in bank holdings is completely offset by the increased role of the public sector, so that the share of the private sector remains marginal. In Sierra Leone, the securities not held by the banking system are generally in the portfolio of non-bank public and public sector enterprises.

Therefore, the analysis of domestic debt in HIPCs shows that the increasing importance of domestic debt is making many of the concerns discussed in Chapter 4 come true. To reap the benefits and limit the risks of the development of domestic markets for government securities countries are required to achieve some basic pre-requisites in terms of sound macroeconomic policies, a legal and regulatory framework for the financial sector, and a fair tax system (section 3.2). Since the CPIA rating includes all these variables (Box 3.2), we expect domestic debt to bring benefits only to countries in which the CPIA rating is high. The 14 HIPCs considered in this analysis have an average CPIA rating of 3.48 in 2004, suggesting that the general quality of policies is far from sound (this value is between the two cutoff points of 3.25 and 3.75 used in the DSF to identify medium and strong policy, Table 2.1).

Figures 4.5 and 4.6 show that the increase in domestic debt goes hand in hand with a worsening of economic and structural policies: this is evident for the 14 HIPCs included in the sample and also for the completion point countries, which have a higher but declining CPIA rating. In particular, from 1998 the quality of institutions and policies decreased, notwithstanding the HIPC Initiative, while domestic debt started to increase sharply (Figure 4.7), moving from 1.65 percent of GDP to more that 2.2 percent.

14 We do not have data on Ethiopia and Madagascar for this kind of decomposition.

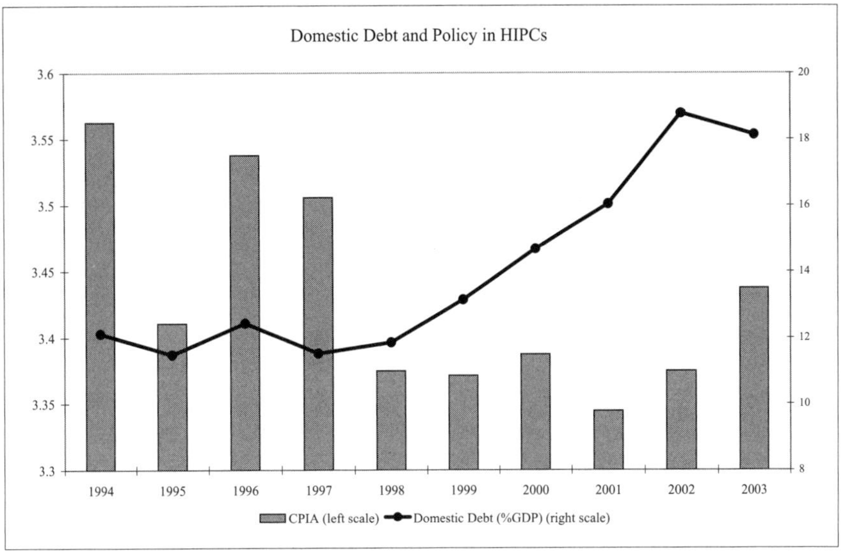


**Figure 4.5 Domestic debt and policy in HIPCs**
*Source*: Authors' calculations.

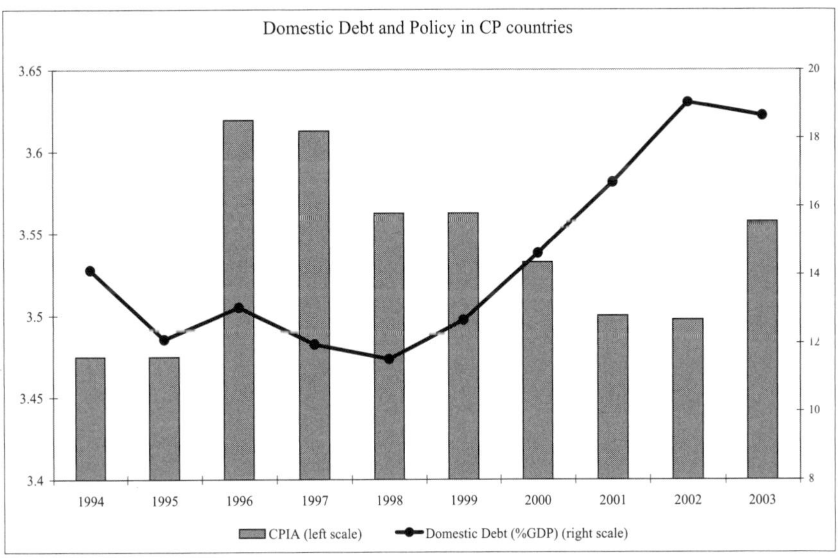


**Figure 4.6 Domestic debt and policy in completion point HIPCs**
*Source*: Authors' calculations.

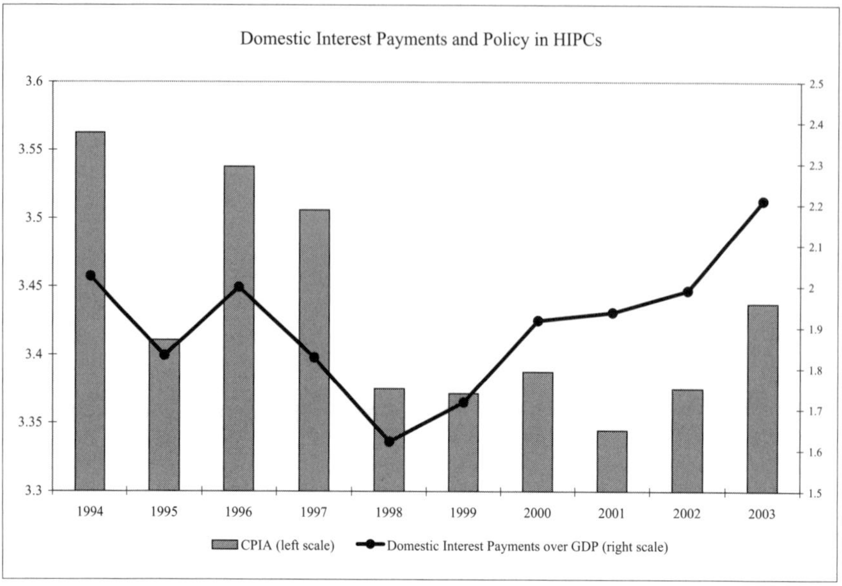


**Figure 4.7 Interest payments on domestic debt and policy in HIPCs**
*Source*: Authors' calculations.

### *4.3.1 The Response to the HIPC Initiative*

In this paragraph we provide a preliminary analysis run in 2005 of what happened to domestic debt in response to the HIPC Initiative and debt relief, while a more detailed, updated and comprehensive analysis is carried out in Chapter 8. Data on domestic debt after graduation from decision point are available only for 15 HIPCs.

From the comparison between the level of domestic debt in the year in which a country reaches decision point and the most recent observations, varying between 2003 and 2004 (Figure 4.8), it seems that in most countries domestic debt slightly increased or remained almost stable (the linear fit is not too different from the 45 degree line). There are some exceptions, notably Zambia, Malawi and Bolivia, whose debt ratios increased, and Ghana and Gambia, where domestic debt actually declined.

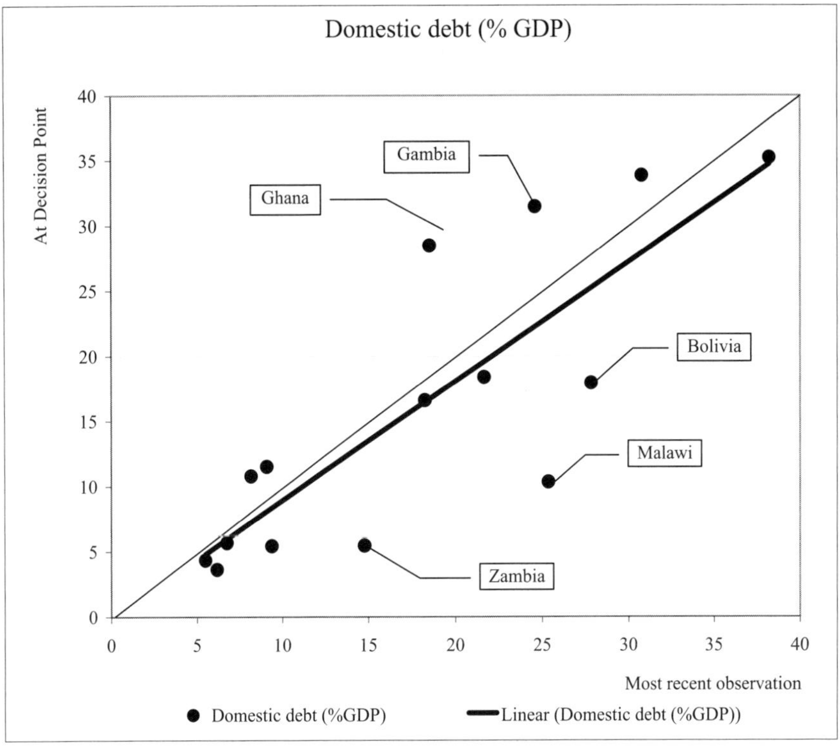


**Figure 4.8 Domestic debt before and after decision point in HIPCs**
*Source*: Authors' calculations.

Figure 4.9, instead, considers the year of graduation from decision point as the year zero, so that we can show the evolution of debt for different countries from that base year. To maintain a consistent sample, we drop Ethiopia, Ghana and Sierra Leone, for which we have only the first three observations of the five-year time horizon.[15] We can observe a sharp increase between the first and the second year, followed by a stable path. Moreover, completion point countries (Bolivia, Guyana, Madagascar, Nicaragua, Tanzania and Uganda) have a debt ratio which is generally 3 percentage points higher than countries at decision point. The last finding could seem counter-intuitive, but it can be explained by the increased borrowing space of completion point countries. In any case, results have to be taken with caution, because of the small sample size.

15 In Ethiopia and Sierra Leone domestic debt increased slightly in the three year after decision point, while in Ghana it decreased from 28 to 18.5 percent of GDP.

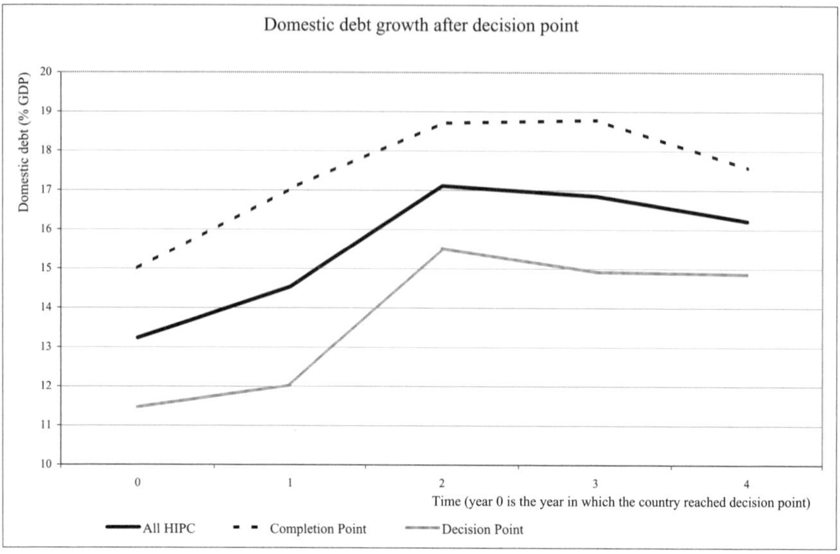


**Figure 4.9 Domestic debt accumulation in HIPCs after decision point**
*Source*: Authors' calculations.

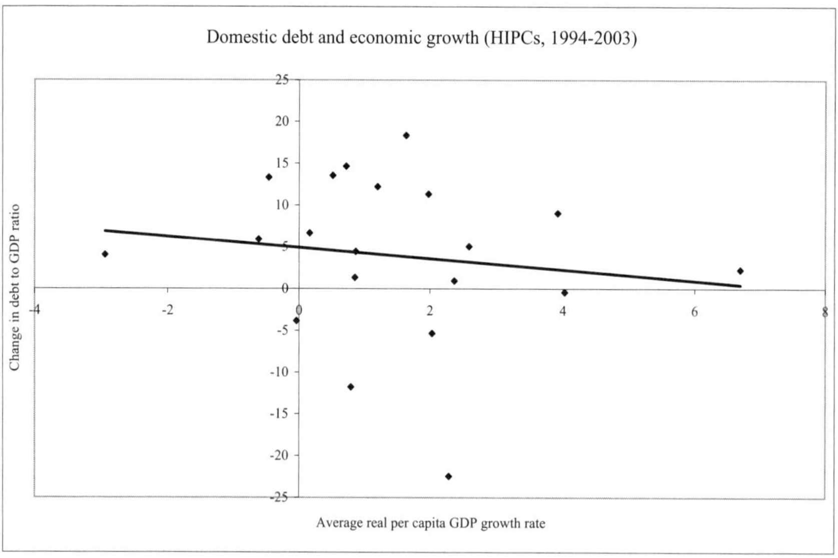


**Figure 4.10 Domestic debt and growth in HIPCs**
*Source*: Authors' calculations.

A descriptive analysis of the data and their dynamics in the last two decades suggests that a rising internal debt could be a constraint to economic growth. The comparison between the change in domestic debt (measured as a ratio to GDP) in the last decade with the average yearly rate of growth of per capita GDP over the same period shows a negative relationship, proxied by the a linear fit (correlation coefficient -0.14; Figure 4.10). These simple finding might support the idea that markets for government securities provide benefits only if some macroeconomic pre-conditions are met and financial markets are somewhat developed. The lack of financial liberalization, weak institutions and macroeconomic instability, which characterizes many poor countries as confirmed by the previous analysis of debt structure, could be the reason why the development of domestic debt is not correlated with higher economic growth. In the next section, we qualify this statement in a multivariate framework, through the estimation of growth regression in which we add domestic debt and its interactions with the quality of policies and institutions. Readers non familiar with the econometrics can skip to Chapter 5 without loss of generality.

## 4.4 Domestic Debt and Growth: A Cross-Country Analysis

It is not possible to run a panel estimation of the effects of domestic debt in developing countries, similar to the one conducted for external indebtedness (Chapter 7), owing to limited data availability; however, we can still exploit the cross-country dimension of the dataset to evaluate whether large and increasing domestic debts are associated with slower growth, even if we are not able to disentangle which are the mechanisms of this possible effect.

The basic approach is the estimation of the model:

$$GROWTH_i = \alpha + \beta_1 \cdot INITGDP_i + \beta_2 \cdot INV_i + \beta_3 \cdot HC_i + \beta_4 \cdot POP_i + \delta \cdot DOMDEBT_i + \varepsilon_i$$

where we include the initial level of GDP (*INITGDP*) to test for the conditional convergence hypothesis ($\beta_1$ expected to be negative), the role of investment in physical (*INV*) and human capital (*HC*, $\beta_2$ and $\beta_3$ expected to be positive), population dynamics (*POP*, $\beta_4$ expected to be negative) and we test for the significance of $\delta$. To capture the heterogeneity of our sample, especially between LICs and MICs, we include a dummy for the former, expecting it to be significant and negative and we also control for differences in the institutional environment and macroeconomic policies, adding the CPIA score (*CPIA*).

For the purpose of washing out part of data variability due to business cycle fluctuations, we use five-year averaging, so that we look at the period 2000-2004 (also lagged variables refer to five-year periods). We estimate the growth equation using the basic OLS estimator, providing a first insight on the partial correlation between domestic debt and economic growth. The dataset is the same used in

Chapter 7 on the relationship between external debt and growth,[16] with the addition of the domestic debt dataset presented in this chapter. The sample of countries and summary statistics are presented in Table 4.8 and 4.9, respectively.

**Table 4.8 Sample of countries for the cross country growth regressions**

| Country | Classification | Country | Classification | Country | Classification |
|---|---|---|---|---|---|
| Albania | MIC | Ghana | LIC | Pakistan | LIC |
| Algeria | MIC | Guatemala | MIC | Papua New Guinea | LIC |
| Armenia | MIC | Guyana | MIC | Peru | MIC |
| Bangladesh | LIC | Honduras | MIC | Philippines | MIC |
| Belize | MIC | India | LIC | Romania | MIC |
| Bolivia | MIC | Indonesia | MIC | Russian Federation | MIC |
| Bulgaria | MIC | Jamaica | MIC | Rwanda | LIC |
| Burundi | LIC | Jordan | MIC | Sierra Leone | LIC |
| Cameroon | LIC | Kazakhstan | MIC | Solomon Islands | LIC |
| Cape Verde | MIC | Kenya | LIC | Sri Lanka | MIC |
| Chad | LIC | Kyrgyz Rep. | LIC | Swaziland | MIC |
| China | MIC | Latvia | MIC | Tanzania | LIC |
| Costa Rica | MIC | Lesotho | LIC | Thailand | MIC |
| Cote d'Ivoire | LIC | Lithuania | MIC | Tonga | MIC |
| Ecuador | MIC | Madagascar | LIC | Tunisia | MIC |
| Egypt, Arab Rep. | MIC | Malawi | LIC | Uganda | LIC |
| El Salvador | MIC | Moldova | LIC | Ukraine | MIC |
| Ethiopia | LIC | Morocco | MIC | Vietnam | LIC |
| Fiji | MIC | Nepal | LIC | Zambia | LIC |
| Gambia, The | LIC | Nicaragua | LIC | Zimbabwe | LIC |
| Georgia | MIC | Nigeria | LIC | | |

*Source*: Authors' calculations.

## Summary Statistics

Summary statistics (Table 4.9) of the main economic variables show significant differences between LICs and MICs: the average MIC is more than three times richer than the average LIC in terms of per capita GDP, measured at PPP, with higher level of primary (HC – prim educ) and secondary education (HC – sec educ), lower rates of population growth (POP), better institutions (CPIA) and slightly higher investment rates (INV). With respect to indebtedness, on average, the poorest countries have the highest external debt over GDP ratios (NPVEXTDEBT), while the level of domestic debt is almost similar, with the average ratio higher MICs

16 All the macroeconomic variables and the overall CPIA scores are taken from WB and IMF datasets.

**Table 4.9 Cross-country growth regressions: Summary statistics**

| Country classification | | GDP GROWTH | DOMDEBT | NPVEXTDEBT | INV | POP | HC – prim educ | HC – sec educ | INITGDP | CPIA |
|---|---|---|---|---|---|---|---|---|---|---|
| MIC | mean | 5.40 | 19.38 | 35.82 | 21.24 | 0.98 | 106.71 | 77.67 | 5113.25 | 3.62 |
| | median | 4.03 | 14.86 | 31.78 | 20.78 | 1.24 | 106.97 | 82.06 | 4640.91 | 3.55 |
| | st. dev. | 3.27 | 16.27 | 24.60 | 4.65 | 1.24 | 8.90 | 16.17 | 1949.52 | 0.40 |
| | obs. | 34 | 34 | 34 | 34 | 34 | 34 | 33 | 34 | 34 |
| LIC | mean | 3.02 | 16.44 | 54.56 | 20.20 | 2.05 | 94.59 | 36.63 | 1530.01 | 3.27 |
| | median | 4.15 | 15.65 | 50.44 | 18.99 | 2.14 | 95.18 | 33.27 | 1477.81 | 3.36 |
| | st. dev. | 3.72 | 9.09 | 26.75 | 8.62 | 0.74 | 21.20 | 20.66 | 731.51 | 0.38 |
| | obs. | 28 | 28 | 28 | 28 | 28 | 28 | 26 | 28 | 28 |
| Whole sample | mean | 4.32 | 18.05 | 44.28 | 20.77 | 1.46 | 101.23 | 59.58 | 3495.02 | 3.46 |
| | median | 4.03 | 15.34 | 38.03 | 20.18 | 1.77 | 102.61 | 61.50 | 3079.52 | 3.45 |
| | st. dev. | 3.66 | 13.49 | 27.06 | 6.69 | 1.17 | 16.70 | 27.40 | 2350.51 | 0.43 |
| | obs. | 62 | 62 | 62 | 62 | 62 | 62 | 59 | 62 | 62 |

*Source*: Authors' calculations.

(almost 20 percent of GDP) and the median higher in LICs. As a consequence, it is reasonable to expect an adverse impact of domestic debt in LICs, not only because of their poorer macroeconomic structure, but also because the same level of debt experienced by MICs in this case has to be added to a very large external indebtedness.

## The Estimates

There are reasons to believe that the domestic debt effects are heterogeneous between LICs and MICs: domestic debt should be a drag on growth in the former set of countries, since they lack the basic pre-requisites in terms of macroeconomic and institutional environment. On the contrary, moderate level of domestic debt could be growth enhancing in market-access economies (Abbas and Christensen 2010). We can test these hypothesis following the earlier approach and including the following in the previous model:

1. An interaction term between the LIC dummy and the debt ratio (*DOMDEBT*LIC*);
2. An interaction term between the CPIA score and the debt ratio (*DOMDEBT*CPIA*);
3. An interaction term between a dummy, that disentangles between bad and good institutions, and the debt variable (*DOMDEBT*GCPIA*), where *GCPIA* is a dummy equal to one (good institutions) for countries whose CPIA score is above the median, and zero (bad institutions) for countries whose CPIA score is below the median value of the index.[17]

We expect the first term to be negative, suggesting a harsher effect on growth in poor countries, while the other two positive, so that the better the institutional quality, the lower the impact of domestic debt.

Table 4.10 shows the OLS estimates of equation (1), augmented with the interaction terms. The standard positive effect of investment and the negative impact of population growth are confirmed, while the human capital indicator is not significant. This last result does not change even considering different measure of education (primary or secondary enrolment rates) and it is consistent with the literature challenging the role of education as a key determinant in the growth regressions (Pritchett 1996; Easterly 2001). With respect to domestic debt, we can see that its impact on per capita GDP growth is always negative and significant, even if we take into account the positive role of institutions, which is strong and significant. In particular, if we test the possibility that domestic debt is a potential source of distress in the poorest countries and in the absence of strong institutions,

17 The median of the CPIA score in our sample is 3.45, which is a threshold consistent with the values proposed by Kraay and Nehru (2006) for the DSF.

the estimates reported in the last three columns provide some preliminary findings supporting this hypothesis: the adverse effect of domestic debt is almost doubled in LICs (column 5), while it is diminishes with improvements in the institutional indicator. Moreover, our findings do not show any positive effect of domestic debt in MICs.

**Table 4.10 OLS estimates**

| GDP GROWTH | (1) | (2) | (3) | (4) | (5) | (6) | (7) |
|---|---|---|---|---|---|---|---|
| INITGDP | -0.41 | -0.49 | -1.21* | -0.58 | -1.19* | -0.59 | -0.60 |
| | (0.45) | (0.36) | (0.09) | (0.27) | (0.07) | (0.26) | (0.26) |
| INV | 4.35** | 4.31** | 3.96** | 3.72** | 3.86** | 3.50** | 3.73** |
| | (0.00) | (0.00) | (0.00) | (0.00) | (0.00) | (0.00) | (0.00) |
| HC | 0.14 | 0.13 | -1.10 | -0.97 | -1.47 | -1.17 | -0.23 |
| | (0.95) | (0.95) | (0.61) | (0.64) | (0.49) | (0.56) | (0.91) |
| POP | -0.28** | -0.27** | -0.26** | -0.25** | -0.26** | -0.25** | -0.26** |
| | (0.00) | (0.00) | (0.00) | (0.00) | (0.00) | (0.00) | (0.00) |
| DOMDEBT | | -0.86* | -0.94** | -0.83* | -0.80* | -3.49** | -1.18** |
| | | (0.06) | (0.04) | (0.06) | (0.07) | (0.01) | (0.02) |
| LIC | | | -1.77 | | | | |
| | | | (0.11) | | | | |
| CPIA | | | | 1.72* | | | |
| | | | | (0.07) | | | |
| DOMDEBT*LIC | | | | | -0.70* | | |
| | | | | | (0.06) | | |
| DOMDEBT*CPIA | | | | | | 0.77** | |
| | | | | | | (0.03) | |
| DOMDEBT*GCPIA | | | | | | | 0.43 |
| | | | | | | | (0.12) |
| Observations | 62 | 62 | 62 | 62 | 62 | 62 | 62 |
| F-test (p-value) | 0.00 | 0.00 | 0.00 | 0.00 | 0.00 | 0.00 | 0.00 |
| Adjusted $R^2$ | 0.43 | 0.45 | 0.47 | 0.47 | 0.48 | 0.49 | 0.47 |

*Note*: P-values are in brackets; * = 10 percent level of significance; ** = 5 percent level of significance. The model includes a constant.
*Source*: Authors' calculations.

Given the point estimates of column 6, if the CPIA score is bigger than 4.53, the actual effect of domestic debt on growth becomes positive. However, since we have a sample of LICs and MICs where the highest value of the CPIA score is 4.39, we can conclude that domestic debt has an overall negative impact on economic growth. Nonetheless, the bottom line is still that better institutions and policies are able to reduce the negative impact of internal debt. The last column is consistent with this interpretation, even though the point estimate of the interaction term is not significant, but it has the expected positive sign.

It is worth recalling that our estimates are a simple description, in a multivariate context, of the partial correlation between domestic debt and GDP growth. Hence, we can say nothing about causality, since our estimates are likely to be affected by serious problems of endogeneity and omitted variables. In order to partially address the endogeneity affecting the model, which makes the OLS estimator biased and inconsistent, we follow two different paths. Firstly, we estimate the growth equation using the stock of domestic debt and the CPIA score at initial period (in 2000). In this way, we test whether more indebted countries experienced subsequent lower rates of growth, after controlling for investment, human capital and their initial level of GDP. Secondly, a further robustness check requires the use of the IV technique in order to control for the potential endogeneity of domestic debt. We instrument the contemporaneous debt variable (and the interaction terms) with its lagged value in the previous five-year period.[18]

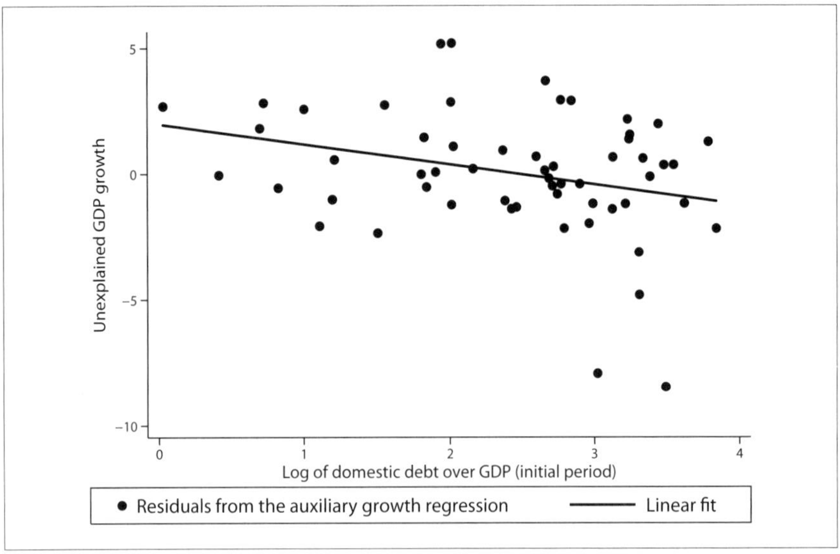


**Figure 4.11 Domestic debt and growth in LICs and MICs**
*Source*: Authors' calculations.

18 Clearly, this strategy is not sufficient to solve the endogeneity issue, since past debt ratios can still be endogenous and also the other right-hand-side variable are not exogenous. Ideally, one would need an exogenous instrument for domestic debt or, at least, the availability of a long panel dataset. However, data limitation is a serious problem and we believe that the simple evidence we have discussed serves our purpose of showing that the negative association between domestic debt and economic growth is heterogeneous depending on policies and institutions.

Results are not reported for the sake of brevity, but they confirm the adverse effect of domestic debt on economic growth, as shown in Figure 4.11: this represents the scatter plot of the unexplained rate of growth and (the logarithm of) domestic debt at initial period. Moreover, the point estimates are, in absolute value, slightly larger than the OLS ones and the coefficient on the interaction between *DOMDEBT* and *GCPIA* become positive and significant, confirming that the negative impact of internal financing is limited by sound institutions, as discussed in Chapter 3. Finally, apart from the growth effect, the rising cost of domestic debt could also affect public debt sustainability in HIPCs. The following chapter investigates this hypothesis.

# Chapter 5
# Domestic Debt and Debt Sustainability

## 5.1 The Accounting Approach to Total Public Debt Sustainability

To evaluate the sustainability of total public debt, we follow a simple empirical strategy, based on the basic accounting approach, according to which a fiscal deficit is considered sustainable if it generates a constant debt-to-GDP ratio (Chapter 2). Using the accounting approach (equation (2.1) in Chapter 2), a policy-maker should consider the real interest rate on the total public debt and not the one on external debt only (Fedelino and Kudina 2003). By doing so, one can observe the critical role played by the inclusion of domestic debt on the solvency condition – the difference between the real GDP growth ($g$) and the real interest rate on total public debt ($r$); the latter is defined as:

$$r = \frac{i - \pi - \alpha\left(\pi_{US} - \pi\right)}{\left(1 + \pi/100\right)\left(1 + \pi_{US}/100\right)} = \frac{i - \alpha\pi_{US} - (1 - \alpha)\pi}{\left(1 + \pi/100\right)\left(1 + \pi_{US}/100\right)} \tag{5.1}$$

where $i$ is the nominal interest rate on the total public debt, $\pi$ is the country's inflation rate, $\pi_{US}$ is the US inflation rate (adopted for simplicity, since a large part of external debt is denominated in US dollar), and $\alpha$ is the fraction of external on total debt.

As highlighted with the data discussed in Chapter 4, the implicit nominal interest rate on domestic debt is much higher than the concessional rate applied on external debt, so that the resulting nominal interest rate on total public debt is larger than the one used in the standard DSA. Central governments, especially in the presence of fiscal dominance, will be tempted to raise inflation to reduce their future payments (inflation tax). However, higher inflation could: 1) trigger further increase in nominal interest rates to keep domestic debt attractive, thus crowding out investment; and 2) have an adverse effect on external debt sustainability, through the exchange rate, because the real depreciation will make debt service on external debt more expensive in domestic currency. Thus, the advantages of a domestic price increase might easily be offset by its costs.

The simple accounting approach, if extended to take into account the overall public debt, points to the necessity for a comprehensive DSA to look at the fully-fledged government budget constraint, without ignoring the feedback effects of deficit financing on expected inflation, domestic nominal interest rates and exchange rates. Higher inflation, rising interest rates and a real depreciation are likely to have adverse impacts on the macroeconomic environment, reducing GDP growth, which is the other key variable of the solvency condition. The strength of the potential adverse impact of domestic financing on total public debt sustainability is also confirmed by the empirical evidence showing that a higher domestic debt is correlated with lower economic growth and a greater likelihood of debt distress (IMF and the World Bank 2006).

The accounting approach to fiscal sustainability is generally presented without an explicit consideration of the presence of both domestic and foreign borrowing. We start from a simple extension to Agenor (2005: 95-99), so that we can explicitly look at the effects of different sources of financing on debt sustainability. Consider the government budget constraint denominated in local currency (1): the primary deficit (PD) and the interest payments on domestic (DD) and external (FD) debt are financed through internal and external financing and money creation (M is the monetary base). E is the nominal exchange rate, while $i^D$ and $i^F$ are, respectively, the domestic and foreign nominal interest rates.

$$PD_t + i_t^D DD_{t-1} + i_t^F E \cdot FD_{t-1} = \Delta DD_t + E \cdot \Delta FD_t + \Delta M_t \qquad (5.2)$$

For simplicity, we ignore seigniorage revenues, on the ground that this simplification does not change the basic sustainability result of the accounting framework. Then, we express the budget constraint in real terms, dividing (5.2) by the GDP deflator (P) and by GDP (Y). Using the identities (5.3) (5.4) and (5.5), we can rearrange equation (5.2) into (5.6), in which lower-case letters refer to real variables as GDP ratios:

$$P_{t-1}/P = 1/(1+\pi) \qquad (5.3)$$

$$Y_{t-1}/Y = 1/(1+g) \qquad (5.4)$$

$$z = \frac{EP^F}{P} \qquad (5.5)$$

$$pd_t + \frac{i_t^D}{(1+g)(1+\pi)} dd_{t-1} + \frac{i_t^F z}{(1+g)(1+\pi^F)} fd_{t-1} = \Delta dd_t - \frac{1-(1+g)(1+\pi)}{(1+g)(1+\pi)} dd_{t-1} + \\ + z\Delta fd_t - \frac{1-(1+g)(1+\pi^F)}{(1+g)(1+\pi^F)} z \cdot fd_{t-1} \qquad (5.6)$$

Taking into account the identity (5.7), which defines the real interest rates (domestic and foreign) in terms of nominal interest rates (domestic and foreign) and inflation (domestic and foreign), equation (5.6) could be easily rearranged into (5.8):

$$1 + r = \frac{1+i}{1+\pi} \qquad (5.7)$$

$$pd_t + \frac{\left(r_t^D - g\right)}{(1+g)} dd_{t-1} + \frac{\left(r_t^F - g\right)}{(1+g)} z \cdot fd_{t-1} = \Delta dd_t + z\Delta fd_t \tag{5.8}$$

In order to have the overall change in total debt on the right-hand-side of the equation, we must consider the effect of changes in the real exchange rate *z*. The overall change in foreign debt, denominated in local currency could be approximated by (5.9), in which $\dot{z}$ represent the rate of depreciation of the real exchange rate:

$$\Delta(z \cdot fd)_t \approx \Delta z_t \cdot fd_{t-1} + z_{t-1} \cdot \Delta fd_t = \dot{z}\frac{z_{t-1}}{z} z \cdot fd_{t-1} + \frac{z_{t-1}}{z} z \cdot \Delta fd_t \tag{5.9}$$

From equation (5.9) we can find an expression for $z\Delta fd_t$ and substitute it into equation (5.8), so that we can have an expression (5.10) for the overall change in total public debt (*td*):

$$\Delta td_t = \Delta dd_t + \left(\frac{z_t}{z_{t-1}}\right)\Delta(z \cdot fd_t) = pd_t + \frac{\left(r_t^D - g\right)}{(1+g)} dd_{t-1} + \frac{\left(r_t^F + \dot{z} - g\right)}{(1+g)} z \cdot fd_{t-1} \tag{5.10}$$

From equation (5.10), we can observe the usual sustainability condition, which requires the growth rate of real GDP to be larger than the real interest rate in order to have a non-increasing debt to GDP ratio. However, we have also underlined the role of the exchange rate on the cost of servicing public debt. We can represent the sustainability condition in a more compact way (5.11), defining $\alpha$ as the share of external debt in total public debt:

$$\Delta td_t = pd_t + \frac{\left[(1-\alpha) r_t^D + \alpha\left(r_t^F + \dot{z}\right)\right] - g}{(1+g)} td_{t-1} \tag{5.11}$$

Thus, assuming a primary balance, a non-increasing public debt to GDP ratio requires that the economy grows at a rate greater than a weighted average of interest rates on domestic and foreign debt, which takes into account also the depreciation of the exchange rate. From (5.11) it is easy to derive the financeable primary deficit (*fpd*, expressed as a share of GDP) consistent with a non-increasing debt-to-GDP ratio:

$$fpd_t = -\frac{\left[(1-\alpha) r_t^D + \alpha\left(r_t^F + \dot{z}\right)\right] - g}{(1+g)} td_{t-1} \tag{5.12}$$

As a consequence, the accounting approach is a useful and simple tool to assess *ex-post* debt sustainability. The general condition deriving from (5.12) states that, as long as the economy grows at a rate higher than the interest rate, it is possible to run a sustainable primary deficit. With respect to the standard DSA, in equations (5.11) and (5.12) it is clearly stated the adverse role played by an increase in domestic interest rates and a real exchange rate depreciation. From the descriptive analysis of the previous section, we expect public debt sustainability to be undermined by higher interest rates and by possible inflationary pressures, which impact the real exchange rate.

For the empirical evaluation of debt sustainability, in the next section the difference between the real interest rate on public debt and the GDP growth rate is considered the sustainability criterion, together with the comparison between the financeable and actual primary balances.

## 5.2 Discussion of Results

To evaluate debt sustainability in HIPC countries, according to the model presented in the previous section, we compare: 1) the growth rate of GDP and the real interest rate on total public debt, as in equation (5.11); and 2) the actual primary balance of the government with the financeable primary balance expressed by equation (5.12); we use the dataset on domestic debt in 14 HIPCs over the period 1991-2003 described in Chapter 4, and data from the WDI and the WEO database.

For the empirical analysis we express the budget constraint in local currency and we calculate a weighted interest rate on the entire stock of public debt ($r^{TOT}$), taking into account the fraction $(1-\alpha)$ of domestic debt, the part $\alpha$ of external debt held by private and official creditors. Then, we estimate the implicit interest rates on each aggregate – $r_t^D$ and $\left(r_t^F+\dot{z}\right)$ – as the ratio of current interest payments on domestic and external debt (*DINT* and *FINT*) on the respective stock of debt of the previous period, as in (5.13):

$$r_t^D = {DINT_t}/{DD_{t-1}} \qquad \left(r_t^F+\dot{z}\right) = {FINT_t}/{FD_{t-1}} \tag{5.13}$$

In this way, the adverse effect of a depreciation (or appreciation) on the cost of external debt servicing is embedded in the analysis through the conversion of debt flows and stocks in local currency.[1]

The following figures confirm the presumption that, if the target of the analysis is the fully-fledged budget constraint, debt sustainability, on average, is not achieved in the 14 HIPC countries included in the sample.

Figure 5.1 depicts the evolution of the implicit interest rates – on domestic, external and total debt – over the last decade, from 1991 to 2003. Notwithstanding a slight decline in the historical path, what is important is the considerable difference between the interest rates on total and external public debt. Even though

1 A real depreciation makes debt service more expensive, since interest payments have to be met in foreign currencies. Comparing interest payments in local currency in the current period, with the stock of external debt in local currency in the previous period we are able to include the exchange rate effect in the determination of the implicit interest rate.

the fraction $(1 - \alpha)$ of domestic in total debt is generally small (but increasing to more than 0.16) the great difference between the implicit interest rates on domestic (ranging between 16 percent and 20 percent in the last five years) and external debt (ranging between 1 percent and 2 percent in the same period) is reflected in a larger interest rate on total public debt than the one used in the standard DSA. As a result, the real interest rate that has to be considered for debt sustainability is more than twice higher than the interest rate on external debt, and the difference is rising over time, because of the increasing degree of concessionality embedded in official loans.[2]

This difference between the two interest rates significantly influences the evaluation of debt sustainability: once domestic debt is included in the government budget constraint, overall debt sustainability cannot always be guaranteed for the HIPC countries in the sample. From the diagram in Figure 5.2, it is clear that the answer could change substantially depending on the choice of the specific interest rate.[3] Thus, if we consider the interest rate on PPG external debt, as done in the standard DSA, we observe that, from 1995, the GDP growth rate is generally higher than the interest rate. This favorable result, however, does not hold when looking at total public debt. In this latter case, the average interest rate – which is around 2 percentage points higher than the one on external debt (Figure 5.1) – is closer to or even larger, in some years, than the real growth rate of the economy.

The representation of the sustainability condition ($g - \left[(1-\alpha) r_t^D + \alpha\left(r_t^F + \dot{z}\right)\right]$) at country level (see Figures 5.4 in the Appendix) points out the substantial effect of internal debt in several countries, such as Bolivia or Ghana. In the last five years, only in three (Rwanda, Tanzania and Uganda) out of 14 countries the difference $g - r^{TOT}$ was positive every year, while in six countries the sustainability condition was not satisfied for at least three years.[4] Besides, the time trend is not encouraging: the comparison of the change between the last two four-year periods (1996-1999 and 2000-2003, see Table 5.1) highlights that the average situation worsened in 8 HIPC countries and in other two countries (Burundi and Ghana) the difference $g - r^{TOT}$ decreased (in absolute value), but it is still negative.

2 The share of concessional debt in PPG external debt increased from less than 70 percent at the beginning of the 1990s to almost 90 percent at the end of the period.

3 In Figure 5.2, as well as in Figures 5.3, 1994 and 1995 appears to be outliers with respect to the entire period. Because of the small sample, this is due to the effect of the results of a single country – Rwanda – which was affected by a dramatic civil war and genocide. In particular, the national accounts show that the economy collapsed in 1994 (GDP went down by a half and more than two million people left the country or were killed), while in 1995 GDP grew by 35 percent. Nonetheless, our main results are not affected by this outlier, as confirmed by the same calculation done excluding Rwanda (diagrams, excluded for the sake of brevity, are available on request from the authors).

4 In Bolivia and Ghana the difference was negative in each of the five years, in Guyana in four years and in Malawi it was positive only in 1999.

Two caveats are worth stressing to complete the discussion of our results: 1) the definition of domestic debt, limited to government securities, is likely to underestimate the overall burden of internal financing, so that the real situation could be worse in a number of countries; and 2) the presence of constant and large budget deficits aggravates the macroeconomic framework.

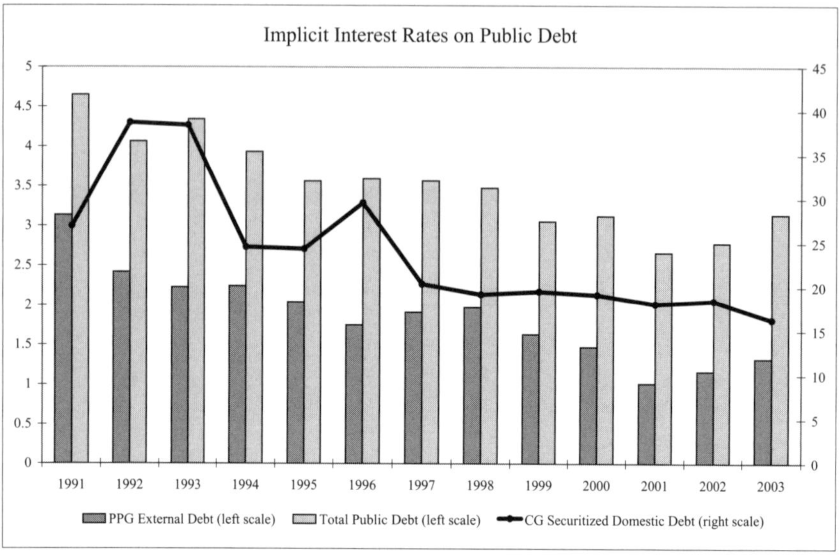


**Figure 5.1 Implicit interest rates on public debt (unweighted averages)**
*Source*: Authors' calculations.

To address this second concern, we estimate the financeable primary balance, as defined by equation (5.12), and compare it with the actual primary deficit (Figure 5.3). The *ex-post* assessment underlines that, in the last decade, the average country should have generally reached a primary surplus (or a small deficit), while the actual outcome was a long sequence of budget deficits. Furthermore, only in 1995 and 1996 the outcome was a sustainable primary balance, while, with the exception of 2003, the difference between the actual and the financeable primary balance increased thereafter, up to a maximum spread of 3.7 percent of GDP.[5]

5 The exclusion of Rwanda does not affect the results and the dynamic of primary balances, even if the 1994 outlier is reduced.

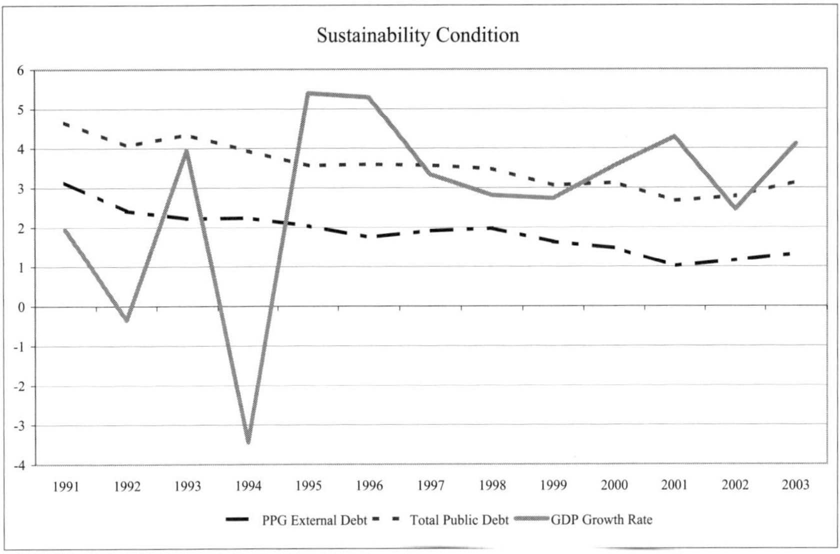


**Figure 5.2 Real interest rates on total public debt and GDP growth rates (unweighted averages)**

*Source*: Authors' calculations.

**Table 5.1 Total public debt sustainability (difference between GDP growth rate and real interest rate, four-year averages)**

| Country | 1996-1999 | 2000-2003 |
|---|---|---|
| Bolivia | -0.19 | -1.48 |
| Burundi | -2.73 | -0.26 |
| Ethiopia | 3.52 | 1.65 |
| Gambia, The | -0.15 | -0.74 |
| Ghana | -4.16 | -2.95 |
| Guyana | -0.71 | -3.42 |
| Honduras | -2.86 | 1.21 |
| Madagascar | 1.24 | 0.27 |
| Malawi | 0.41 | -2.74 |
| Rwanda | 9.47 | 5.43 |
| Sierra Leone | -7.96 | 2.28 |
| Tanzania | 1.23 | 4.53 |
| Uganda | 5.05 | 3.97 |
| Zambia | -0.52 | 0.52 |

*Source*: Authors' calculations.

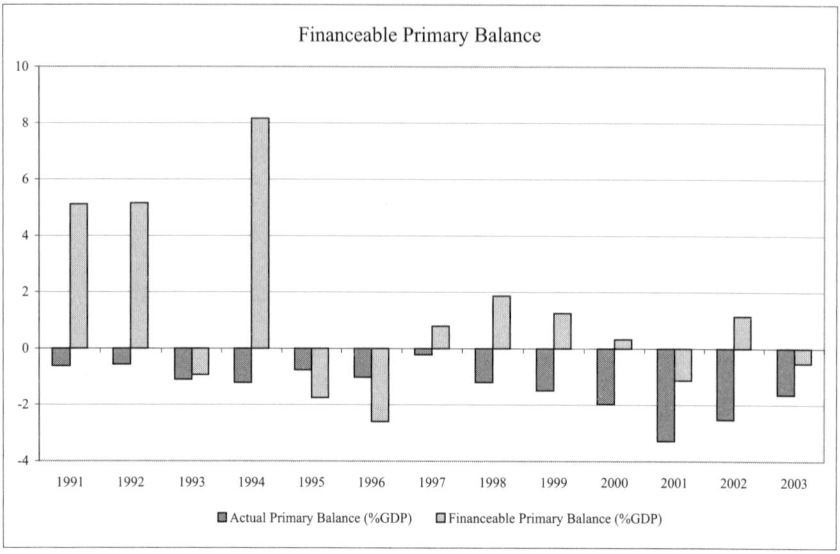


**Figure 5.3 Actual and financeable primary balance (unweighted averages)**
*Source*: Authors' calculations.

In conclusion, apart from the ex-post evaluation of the sustainability criterion, it is worth noting that the presence of a large and increasing domestic debt in these countries is an additional source of concern because central governments, especially in the presence of fiscal dominance, have a strong incentive to use the inflation tax to reduce the future interest payments on domestic debt. This behavior would have detrimental consequences on the economy as a whole and on debt sustainability in particular. A spike in inflation would generate an increase in nominal interest rates and a real exchange rate depreciation, which increases the nominal value of the stock of foreign currency-denominated external debt and the cost of servicing it. Even if data on inflation seems to suggest a limited use of inflation tax, for some countries the level of inflation was very high (i.e. Gambia, Ghana and Zambia experienced inflation rates ranging between 20 percent and 28 percent in 2003), and, more in general, this remains a risk which could seriously undermine investors' confidence.[6]

6 In our sample of 14 HIPCs, inflation in 2003 started to increase after a decade long declining trend (Figure 4.1) and, in 2004, inflation was higher than in the previous year in half of the countries in the sample.

## 5.3 Policy Implications for Debt Sustainability

In this chapter we have highlighted one of the possible risks introduced by the recent trend in domestic debt in developing countries. The evolution and the development of government securities markets could bring benefit to LICs, because they diversify the sources of financing and it helps insulating poor countries from external shocks. Nonetheless, it is worth stressing that these benefits occur only when countries have reached a sufficient level of macroeconomic stability and financial liberalization. If this is not the case, potential risks of default and rollover, a narrow investor base and specific country risk increase the cost of domestic debt. Governments which are not committed to sound fiscal and monetary policies can only borrow internally at short term and at high cost. As a consequence, the rise in interest rates jeopardizes the overall debt sustainability and economic performance, because of the possible credit crunch, crowding out of investments and the constraints on fiscal budget. Government could also be tempted to use inflation to reduce the real value of the stock of debt, worsening the macroeconomic environment.

The analysis of the recent trend of domestic debt and interest rates in the first years of the new millennium in 14 HIPC countries confirms this scenario. Domestic debt, even remaining a small fraction of total debt, is increasing and, more important, interest payments on domestic debt show an upward trend. The maturity structure is severely skewed towards short-term instruments and the banking sector is still the main holder of government securities, in the absence of a broad investor base. Additionally, the increase in domestic debt is not coupled with an improvement in policies and institutions, as shown by the evolution of the overall CPIA score, but is associated to higher costs. As a consequence, internal debt service is actually soaking up more resources than external debt, undermining pro-poor investments and social expenditures. The IFIs are concerned about the achievement of debt sustainability keeping into account country-specific conditions, as testified by the DSF (IMF and World Bank 2006) and by the IMF's Medium-Term Strategy (IMF 2006a). In a document[7] presented at the 2006 Spring Meetings, the Fund acknowledges that:

> The Fund's strategy for low-income countries requires more work in the following areas: i) focus and flexibility – the Fund should focus on macro-critical issues tailored to individual country circumstances, broaden its division of labor with the World Bank, and offer more flexible lending facilities; ii) aid and the MDGs – the Fund needs to assess whether projected aid flows are consistent with macroeconomic stability and the estimated costs of achieving countries' development goals, and also be more forthcoming with donors; and iii) debt relief – the Fund needs to ensure that the beneficiaries of debt relief do not again

7 IMF, *A Medium-Term Strategy for the IMF: Meeting the Challenge of Globalization*, April 2006; www.imf.org/external/np/exr/ib/2006/041806.htm.

> accumulate excessive debt. Countries' public expenditure management systems need to be strengthened.

In the Fund's Medium-Term Strategy the IMF sets the priorities and gives great emphasis on its engagement in LICs: successful debt relief is one of the three targets, which should be pursued focusing on public spending management and sustainability, integrating "in the PRGF a framework for the design and adoption of a medium-term debt strategy, consistent with sustainability" (IMF 2006a: 18).

The increasing stock of domestic debt in countries that do not have access to international capital markets is a symptom of a pitfall in the design of the HIPC Initiative: given the asymmetry in the adjustment process of fiscal and monetary variables, the Initiative has achieved good results on the monetary side (lower inflation), but the slow fiscal adjustment, together with the HIPC-imposed prohibition to use non-concessional financing, is pressing local governments to finance their budget deficit issuing domestic debt (Chapter 3). The resulting stock of domestic debt and interest payments are becoming an additional constraint to the budget balance. Moreover, the comparison between the financeable primary deficits and the actual ones confirms that HIPC countries were not able to close their financial gap, while debt sustainability requires the average country to run a primary surplus.

Against this background, we propose: 1) to look more carefully at the evolution and the structure of domestic debt, for which the lack of data is still a constraint for economic analysis; 2) to include domestic debt in any DSA, taking into account the feedback effects of internal financing on the main macroeconomic variables; and 3) to evaluate the HIPCs financial needs in order to avoid a massive recourse to internal financing, considering the risk of a larger use of inflation tax, which could undermine exchange rate stability and total public debt sustainability.

## Appendix

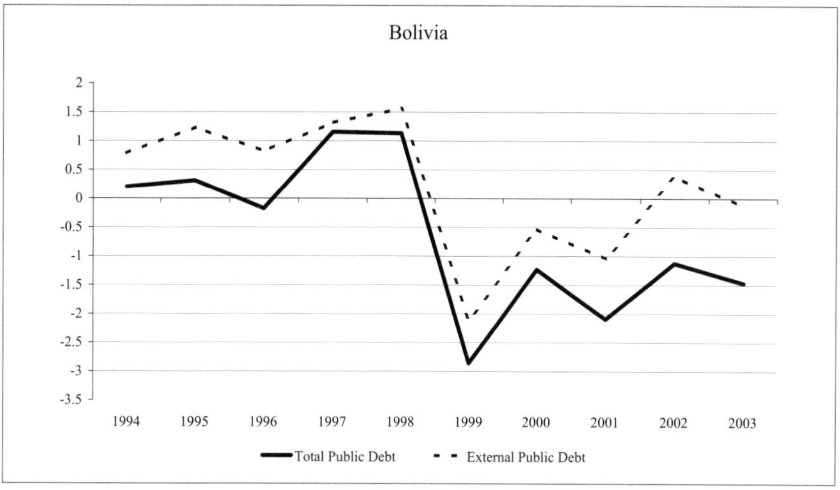


**Figure 5.4a Sustainability condition in HIPCs – Bolivia**
*Source*: Authors' calculations.

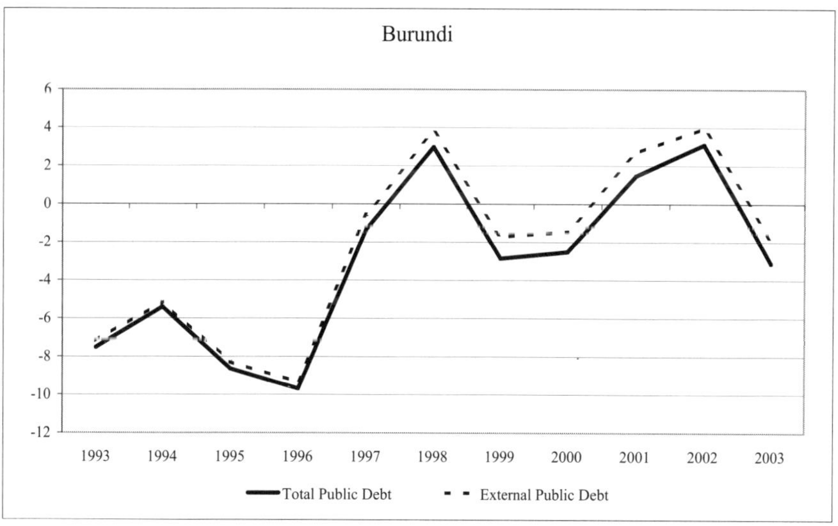


**Figure 5.4b Sustainability condition in HIPCs – Burundi**
*Source*: Authors' calculations.

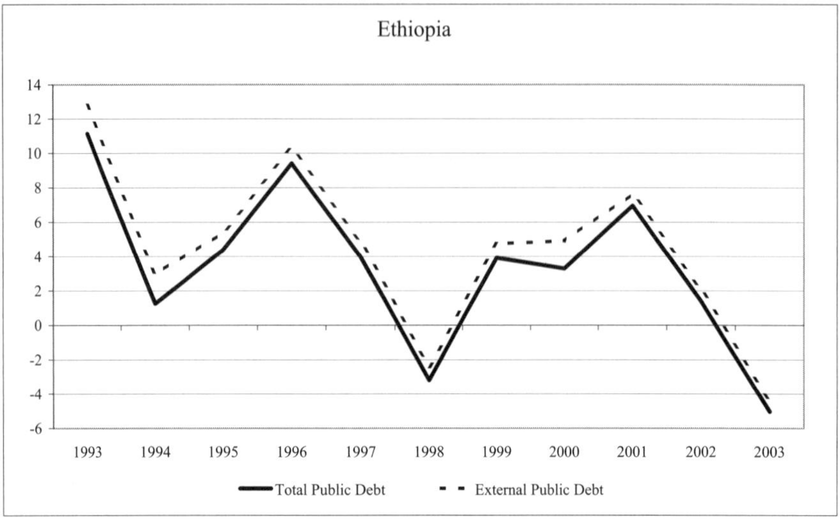


**Figure 5.4c Sustainability condition in HIPCs – Ethiopia**
*Source*: Authors' calculations.

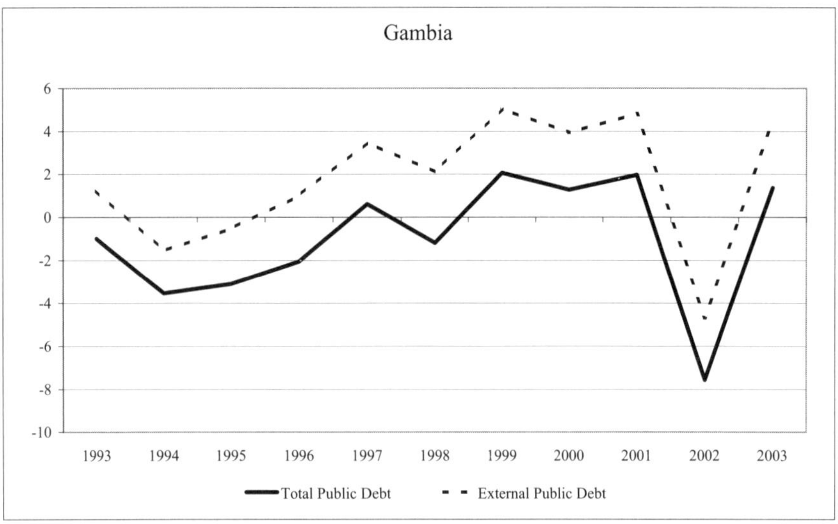


**Figure 5.4d Sustainability condition in HIPCs – Gambia**
*Source*: Authors' calculations.

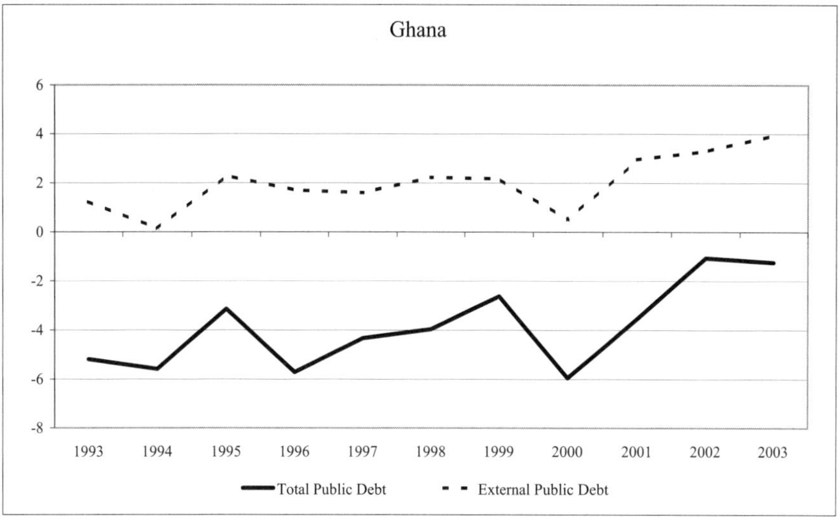


**Figure 5.4e Sustainability condition in HIPCs – Ghana**
*Source*: Authors' calculations.

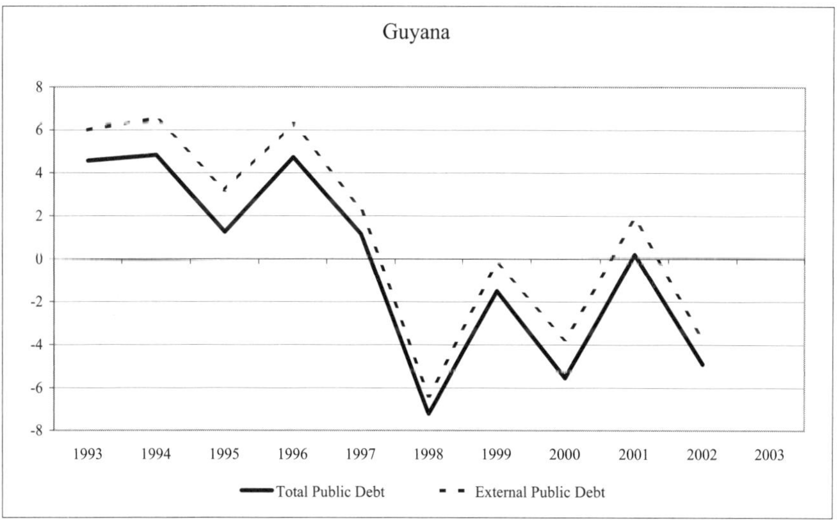


**Figure 5.4f Sustainability condition in HIPCs – Guyana**
*Source*: Authors' calculations.

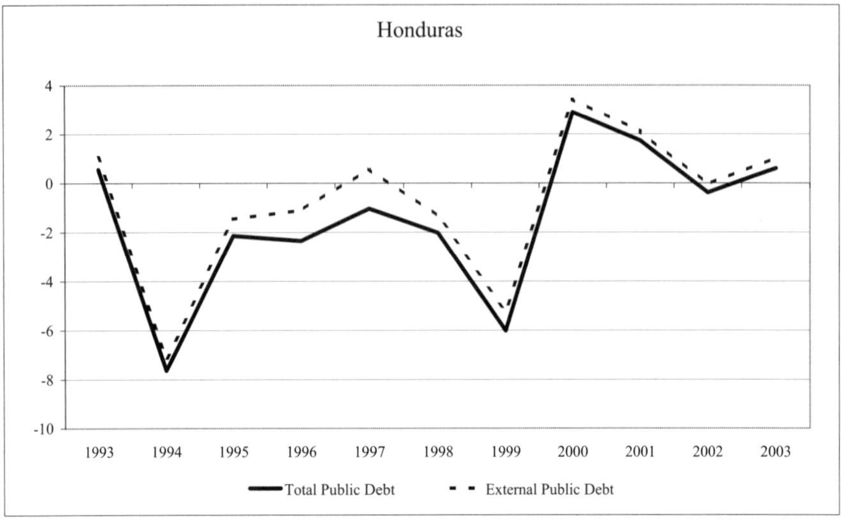


**Figure 5.4g Sustainability condition in HIPCs – Honduras**
*Source*: Authors' calculations.

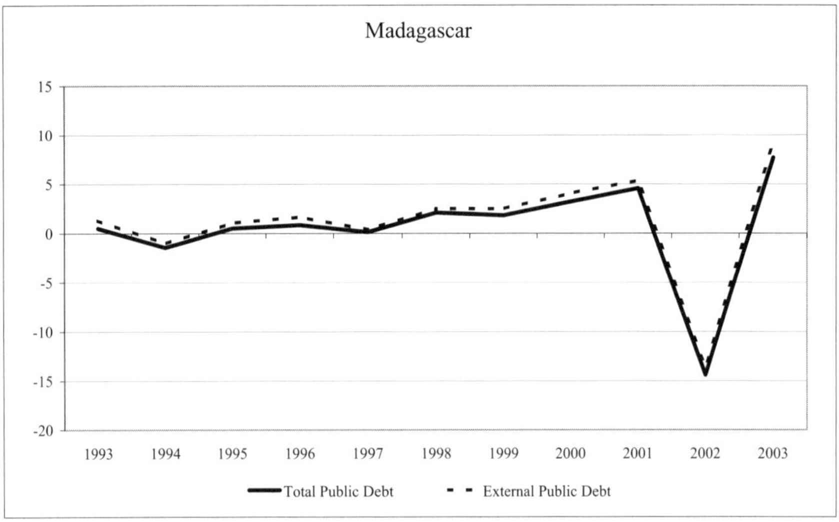


**Figure 5.4h Sustainability condition in HIPCs – Madagascar**
*Source*: Authors' calculations.

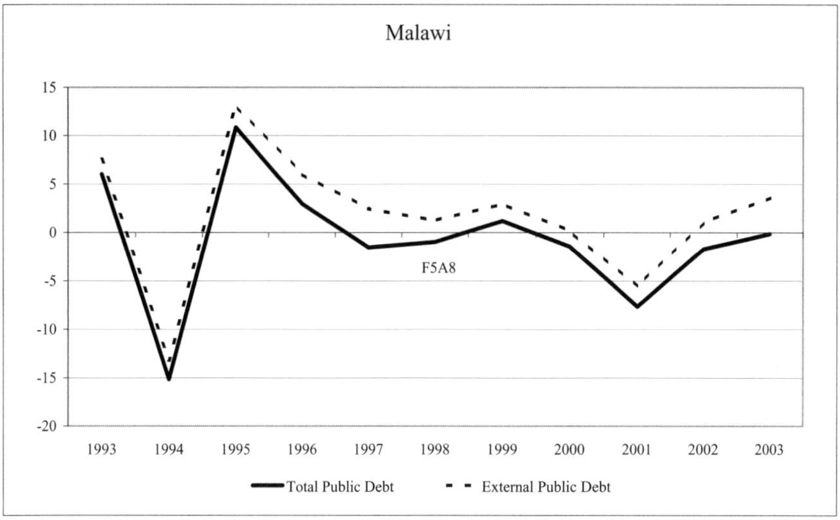


**Figure 5.4i Sustainability condition in HIPCs – Malawi**
*Source*: Authors' calculations.

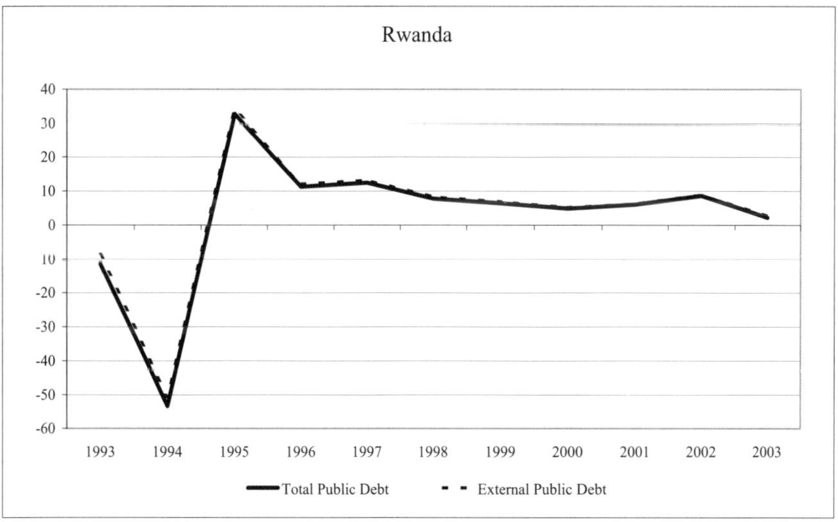


**Figure 5.4j Sustainability condition in HIPCs – Rwanda**
*Source*: Authors' calculations.

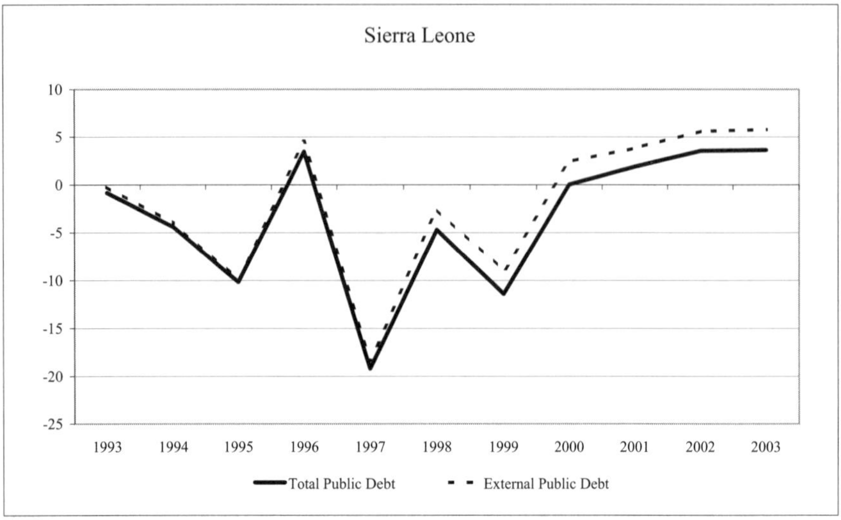


**Figure 5.4k Sustainability condition in HIPCs – Sierra Leone**
*Source*: Authors' calculations.

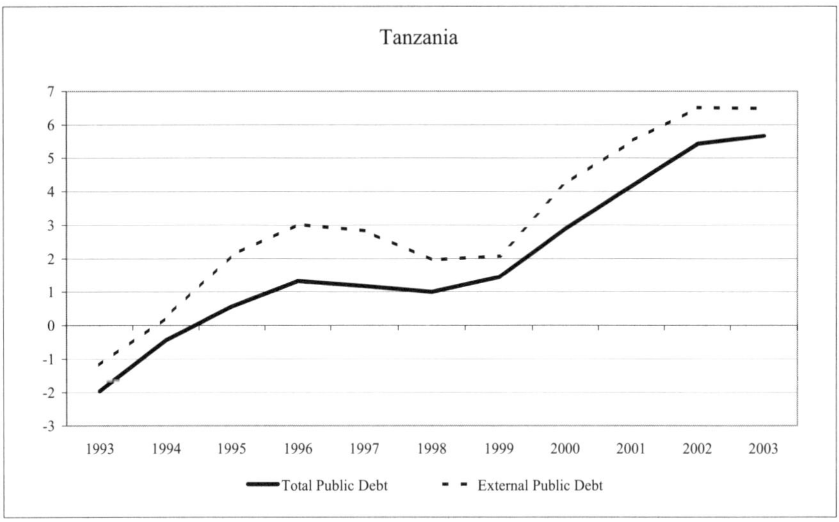


**Figure 5.4l Sustainability condition in HIPCs – Tanzania**
*Source*: Authors' calculations.

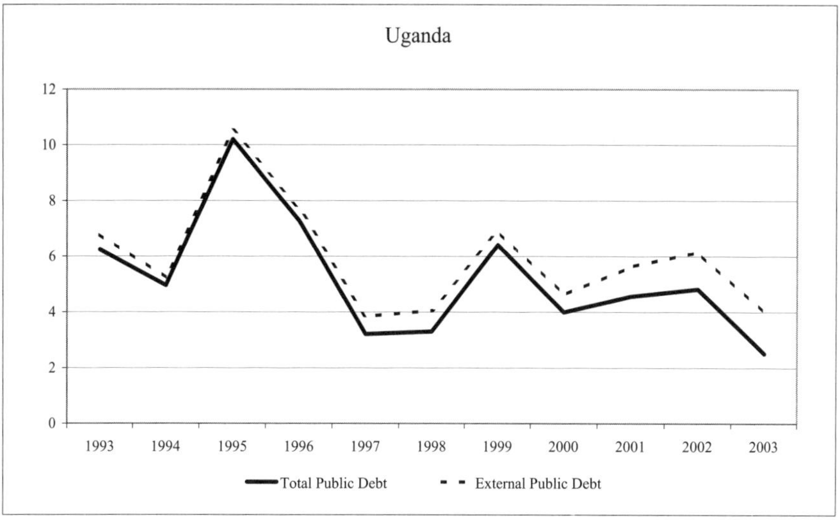


**Figure 5.4m Sustainability condition in HIPCs – Uganda**
*Source*: Authors' calculations.

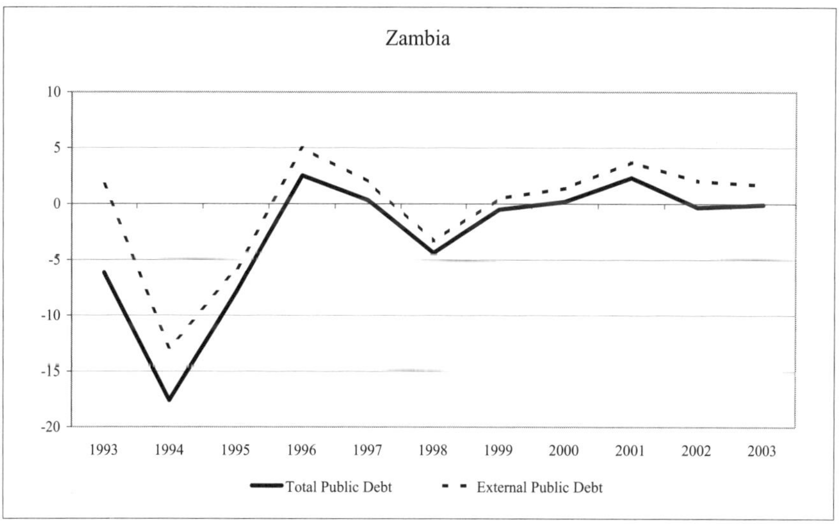


**Figure 5.4n Sustainability condition in HIPCs – Zambia**
*Source*: Authors' calculations.

# PART 3
# External Debt and Macroeconomic Performance

## Overview

Part 3 deals explicitly with the macroeconomic consequences of excessive debt in developing countries and proposes a first tentative evaluation of debt relief initiatives. We discuss the economic rationale for debt cancellation policies, which in our opinion should be grounded on a *growth diagnostic* approach. Specifically, we aim at providing an answer to the following questions: while it is true that reducing external debt and promoting growth is necessary to achieve sustainability, is it also true that lower debt causes faster GDP growth? Is external debt the binding constraint to investment and growth? Which are the channels through which external debt could possibly be a drag on economic growth? Which are the macroeconomic dynamics and consequences of debt relief? Does it actually foster investment and growth? Does the institutional framework matter and is debt relief a good instrument to shape institutions and policies?

In Chapter 6 we discuss the theoretical reasons why a large external debt might impinge on economic performance, focusing on: 1) the debt overhang effect, which is related to the stock of debt; 2) the possible crowding out of investment due to debt service; and 3) the consequences of the unstable macroeconomic environment induced by excessive borrowing. Although some theoretical arguments are not always easily adaptable to the current debt crisis, the common wisdom implies a negative effect of large external debts on economic growth. However, the empirical validation of these theoretical assumptions provides a mixed picture. A large and growing body of literature focuses on debt overhang but, while earlier findings were generally consistent with the presence of a Debt-Laffer curve, more recent evidence is less conclusive. We argue that it is reasonable to assume that the debt-growth nexus is less straightforward than implied by some early studies. Those analysis looked exclusively at the direct relationship between external debt and GDP growth, without taking into account country-specific characteristics. However, institutions and policies shape the government's debt management capacity, affecting debt accumulation and economic growth. Thus, the identification of the direction of causality is not clear *a priori*.

In Chapters 7 and 8, we argue that there is a complex relationship linking economic growth, external debt and the institutional framework. Firstly, we try to identify the causal impact of external debt on economic growth, taking into account institutional heterogeneity across countries and over time. Secondly, in Chapter 8 we focus on the way in which the institutional setting shapes and is affected by debt relief policies, analysing the determinants of debt relief and its macroeconomic effects.

In Chapter 7 we provide an empirical investigation of the relationship between external debt and economic growth. The first contribution is directly targeted at assessing the robustness of the Debt-Laffer curve and our results show that the inclusion of institutions as additional control wash out the non-linearity, confirming that the institutional framework matters for build-up of debt and for economic performance as well. On average, external debt has a linear and negative effect on economic growth. In an earlier contribution, Presbitero (2006) shows that this effect works mainly through a decrease in TFP instead of lower capital accumulation. These findings support an extensive interpretation of debt overhang, meaning that the debt burden can harm the economy in several ways: 1) acting as a disincentive on long-term productive investments, such as those in human capital and innovation; 2) obstructing a government's effort to adopt structural reforms and make fiscal adjustments; 3) reducing a country's creditworthiness and attractiveness in international capital markets; 4) promoting the growth of the informal economy. The second contribution concerns the hypothesis that debt overhang could depend on the policy and institutional framework; we find that the economic consequences of external debt depend on a country's institutions. Specifically, the empirical evidence is consistent with the presence of debt overhang exclusively in countries with sound institutions and a track record of good policies. By contrast, high external debt is not a binding constraint on economic growth in countries with poor institutions, being probably the latter the real constraint to investment and growth. This evidence has important consequences for the design and the effectiveness of debt relief policies, which should not follow a one-size-fits-all approach, as discussed in Chapter 10.

The indications which could be drawn from both strands of this theoretical and empirical literature suffer from a drawback related to the fact that they are not based on a direct estimation of the effects of debt relief on economic performance. The recent availability of data on actual debt relief in HIPCs and other LICs allows for the identification of the direct effect of debt reduction on economic performance. In Chapter 8 we review the existing (limited) literature on this subject and discuss new empirical evidence on the direct effects of debt reduction on a number of indicators related to overall economic performance. In addition to testing the direct effect between debt relief and economic growth, we are specifically interested in finding out whether the resources freed up by debt relief have been channelled to poverty reduction expenditures, social spending and public investment. From a policy perspective, it is also relevant to assess whether debt relief is perceived as a positive signal by international investors, in order to attract private capital flows and FDI. The empirical results are consistent with the existing literature and anecdotal evidence in finding a very limited positive effect of debt relief on investment and growth. This is true even considering possible sources of heterogeneity, such as the quality of institutions. The latter result is in apparent contradiction with the main finding of Chapter 7 about the presence of debt overhang in countries with sound institutions. However, the two pieces of evidence could be explained by the differences in the sample. In particular, the average CPIA rating for the LICs analysed in Chapter 8 and which received debt relief was substantially lower than the threshold identified in Chapter 7 as the one below which debt overhang is effective. Moreover, it should be kept in mind that debt relief might require a longer time period to show its benefits. Instead, we find evidence of a rising domestic debt in response to external debt relief, with the likely adverse effects in terms of rising debt service and crowding out of investments, as discussed in Part 2.

In Chapter 8 we also inspect the correlation between institutional quality and the amount of debt relief granted in order to assess the lending behaviour of donors. Results suggest that, at least since the launch of the HIPC Initiative, debt reduction has been granted to countries which have proved to undergo structural adjustment and institutional improvement. Moreover, we find some evidence supporting the hypothesis that debt relief is an effective policy tool in fostering institution building. On the whole, it seems that, with the active participation of IFIs in debt reduction initiatives, the selection process has improved and has been able, on average, to provide countries with the right incentives to reform and improve their governance.

Chapters 7 and 8 are based on original applied research. We choose to deal with these topics with the usual methodological standards. The reader not interested in the economic details can skip sections 7.2 and 7.4 in Chapter 7 and sections 8.4.1.2 and 8.4.2.2 in Chapter 8 without loss of generality. Similarly, in Chapter 6 we describe three models of debt relief in the boxes 6.1, 6.2 and 6.3, which can be skipped by the not-analytically-minded reader.

# Chapter 6

# External Debt and Growth: Mixed Evidence

## 6.1 External Debt and Economic Growth: Theoretical Considerations

Debt relief initiatives are grounded on the assumption that a large external debt is a constraint for the development process of poor countries. The economic theory identifies a number of channels through which excessive debts could shrink economic development and GDP growth rates, at least going back to Keynes' (1919) discussion on the war reparation imposed to Germany. The standard debt overhang hypothesis focuses on reduced investment, but it could also be extended to include the disincentive effects on government leading to poor macroeconomic policies: inflation tax and a high level of uncertainty are likely to occur with a large outstanding external debt. Additionally, excessive debt could lead to (a combination of) capital flights, high tax rates and continuous over-borrowing, with a negative effect on growth. Finally, the interest payments on external debt could crowd out public investment, putting on hold the building of important infrastructures, and reduce social spending in health and education.

A possible classification of the different linkages between external debt, its forgiveness, and economic performance is the following, based on Claessens et al. (1997):[1]

**Disincentive effects**

- *Debt overhang theory*: when the stock of debt is too high (debt exceeds future repayment ability), the expected debt service is a positive function of the aggregate output. This squeezes investment, because returns are "taxed away" by foreign creditors.
- The stock of debt has another negative effect on economic performance, due to the level of *uncertainty* on the fraction of debt service that will actually be repaid with a country's own resources as an outcome of debt rescheduling negotiations.

1 It is worth noting that high debt has different effects, not only related to macroeconomic performance, but also to political and institutional aspects. It could undermine the effectiveness of structural reforms aimed at enhancing growth and poverty reduction. Permanent fiscal weakness and heavy administrative burden – due to the number of rescheduling and different creditors (at least 31, in HIPCs) and to the large number of currencies (at least 26) in which debt is denominated – can undermine the development of sound institutions and render them incapable of making optimal choices (Moss and Chiang 2003, see also Chapter 8).

**Cash flow effects**

- Debt reduction could facilitate the access to the *international financial markets* and the repatriation of flight capital (increasing private investment and the efficiency of the investment selection).
- *The "crowding out"*: debt service payments soak up resources and reduce the current level of investments, for any given level of future indebtedness.[2]

**Moral hazard effects**

- With debt relief, debtors might believe that creditors have eased their position and will be more willing to forgive any future debt, when the likelihood to obtain a repayment becomes very low. Thus, debtor countries will have incentives to pursue over expansionary policies, undermining macroeconomic stability. Moral hazard can be reduced by implementing a once-and-for-all cancellation or adopting conditionality, which, however, is effective only when the threat is credible (i.e. off-track policies translate into no more funding).

The economic literature has generally investigated and tested empirically three main channels through which external public debt affects economic growth: 1) the debt overhang effect; 2) the liquidity constraint effect; and 3) the uncertainty effect (see, among others, Addison, Hansen and Tarp (2004), Clements, Bhattacharya and Nguyen (2004), and Elbadawi, Ndulu and Ndung'u (1997) who include also the lack of access to international financial markets). More generally, and considering the flow and stock channels, a large public debt should compress public expenditures and affect the mix of public spending, with growth and welfare effects. Looking at the composition of government spending, the decline in fixed capital formation is sometime associated with more resilient social expenditures (Hicks 1989; Baqir 2002; Mahdavi 2004). However, a large external debt might impinge on social expenditures because of fiscal adjustments and public expenditures reductions aimed at honoring debt obligations and because of limited room for future external financing (Lora and Olivera 2007).

Finally, it is worth stressing that the adverse consequences of public debt are not likely to be the same across countries. Specifically, external debt might act as a constraint to investments and economic growth only in countries with a sound institutional framework, while where institutions are weak, bad policies and not debt should hinder investment and growth.

### *6.1.1 The Debt Overhang Effect*

The debt overhang is defined as a situation in which creditors do not expect to be fully repaid because of the presence of a large stock of debt. The literature about

2 The adverse effect of external debt service on economic performance and investment is also called "liquidity constraint" effect.

the debt overhang theory starts generally from two papers by Krugman (1988) and Sachs (1989); they analyze what happens to a country which is unable to service its debt payments in full without new borrowing. "A country has a debt overhang problem when the expected present value of potential future resource transfers is less than its debt" (Krugman 1988: 255). In a situation like that, the borrower has little incentive to follow policies that may be costly in the short run and growth-enhancing only in the long run, since the payoff will be taxed away to repay foreign lenders. Hence, the debt overhang hypothesis predicts that a large stock of external debt reduces the incentive to invest, given that the associated costs are sustained by the indebted country, while the returns in terms of increased output will be used to pay back foreign creditors. This argument, based on the Ricardian equivalence, can be applied both to public and private investments, the former being directly discouraged by future debt service obligations and the latter by the future increases in taxation to raise revenues to serve the external debt. Furthermore, possible complementarities between public and private investment, which are likely to be at work in developing and emerging countries for public investment in infrastructures (Blejer and Khan 1984; Greene and Villanueva 1991; Khan and Kumar 1997; Lora 2007), could strengthen the debt overhang effect.

The presence of this stock of debt changes the incentives of both creditor and debtor, and debt relief could benefit both (Box 6.1). In the absence of debt relief, the latter has a disincentive to invest because he perceives that all the gains will be used to pay the lender, the former could have an incentive to keep on lending in order to avoid a loss, with the hope that the recipient will work to improve its economic conditions and repay all its claims in the near future. Therefore, with debt relief the lenders could increase the likelihood that the remaining obligations will be serviced and the debtors could reduce the distortions given by the presence of the debt burden on investment choices.

The possibility of this double benefit coming from debt relief is illustrated also by the so-called Debt Laffer curve, which represents the expected repayments as a function of the face value of the debt (Figure 6.1).[3] When the debtor country is on the right side (the "wrong" side) of the curve, a debt reduction increases the likelihood of repayment: this situation is analogous to the one discussed in Box 6.1 – the movement from point A to point O' in Figure 6.1. Thus, as long as the stock of debt is higher that the critical value D* (Figure 6.2), both creditors and debtor will be better off after debt relief.

3 The literature makes use of the term Debt-Laffer curve also with different sets of variables. Cline (1995) traces the curve in the space expected value – face value of debt. The rationale is the same, but in the latter case it is possible to show that the secondary market value of the debt could be seen as an indicator of inefficiency (Cohen 1990). The line from the origin tells the market price of debt and its slope is generally less than unity. Debt overhang starts when the curve diverges from the 45° line: when the curve has a negative slope, any additional debt imposes a disincentive so large that the expected repayments decrease.

**Box 6.1 The Dooley's model of debt relief**

Dooley (1989) clarifies in a simple framework how debt relief can benefit both creditors and debtors, thanks to an increase in investments and, as a consequence, in debt repayments.* Using a very simple two-periods two-countries model with intertemporal consumption, Dooley defines consumption in the second period ($C_2$) as a function of investment in the first period ($I_1$), which is given by the difference between the initial endowment ($E_1$) and consumption ($C_1$):

$C_2 = f(I_1)$, where $I_1 = E_1 - C_1$

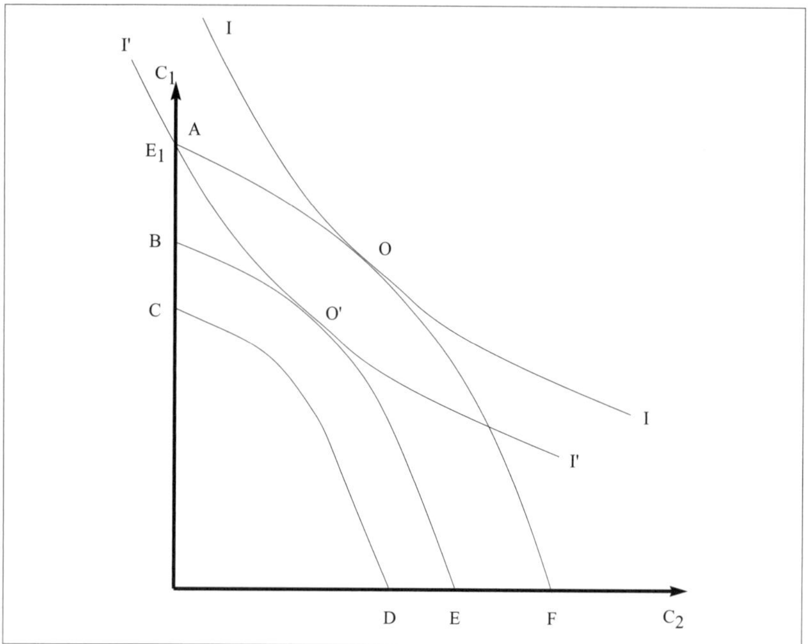


**Figure 6.1 Dooley's model of debt relief**
*Source*: Authors' elaboration on Dooley (1989).

Figure 6.1 shows the transformation curve AF in the simple case with no debt. With the usual indifference curves (II), the optimum will be given by the tangency condition, the point O, where the countries will choose its combination of current and future consumption. In the presence of an inherited stock of debt (the line DF), the new transformation curve (ACDF) will be shifted to the left and it is made by the line ACDF. As long as the outcome of the investment undertaken in the first period is less than the stock of outstanding debt DF, consumption in the second period remains zero, because all the new resources are used to repay the creditors. From the diagram is now easy to see that, given the indifference curves (I'I'), the optimum is a corner solution, with the country choosing the equilibrium A. This situation is unsatisfactory because the debtor does not invest ($C_1 = E_1 \rightarrow I_1 = 0$) and the creditor will not receive any repayment on the existing debt. Therefore, it is straightforward to show that debt relief could make both sides better off. A debt reduction equal to DE moves the transformation curve on the right (it becomes ABEF) and the new optimum shifts to O'. This change is a Pareto-improvement and increases the overall welfare, since the debtor is on the same indifference curve as before but he has an incentive to invest and the creditor country is better off, since it is repaid. Clearly, a debt relief greater that DE will move the debtor on a higher indifference curve, at a higher cost for the creditor, who will receive a smaller repayment but is still better off than without debt relief. The final equilibrium would depend on the bargaining power of the agents.

*Note*: * Dooley analyzes also the problems of the leveraged buy-out of existing debt and of the issue of coordination between creditors. Here, we keep the problem as simple as possible because the aim is to show that debt relief could benefit both sides. Nevertheless, the problem of free riding is critical, as we discuss in Chapter 10. Readers non familiar with economic models can easily skip this box.

The implication of the debt overhang hypothesis is that the implicit tax that weighs on the debtor has a distortionary effect on investment choices and reduces economic growth. This distortion could be avoided or limited by debt reduction up to a point (D* in Figure 6.2) where the expected repayments will increase with the debt outstanding. As discussed by Krugman (1988, see Box 6.2) the extent of foreign aid flows and the criteria for their determination could increase or decrease these adverse effects.

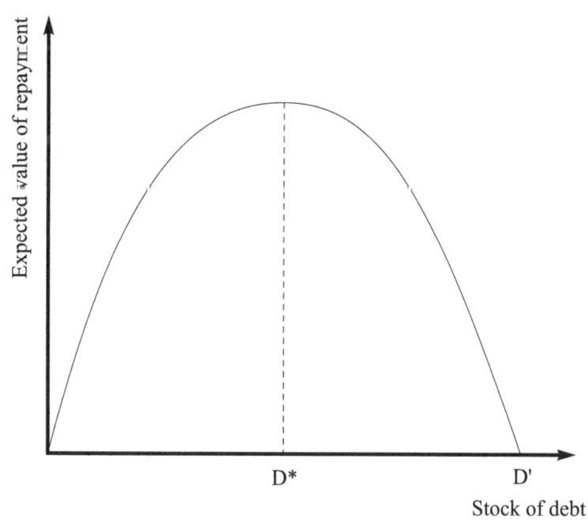


**Figure 6.2 The Debt-Laffer curve**
*Source*: Authors' elaboration.

**Box 6.2 Krugman's model of debt overhang**

Krugman (1988) develops a two period model, with an outstanding debt D, all due in the first period. If the country does not have enough resource to repay the debt, it can borrow at the opportunity cost i. The new borrowing must be repaid in the second period (otherwise there is forgiveness). Lenders are risk neutral. The maximum payments in the two periods are $x_1$ and $x_2$. The focus of the model is on the first period and in the debtor's capacity of attracting new funds.

**No uncertainty**

If $x_1 < D$, the country will borrow the amount $D - x_1$. The lenders will agree only if $(1 + i)(D - x_1) < x_2$, which means that there are no liquidity problems if the present value of the available resources is larger than the stock of debt:

$$(1) \quad x_1 + \frac{x_2}{(1+i)} > D$$

If (1) does not hold, the best solution for the creditors is an immediate write-off of the debt at a level equal to the actual resource transfer.

**Uncertainty**

Now $x_2$ is a random variable that can take two values:

$$x_2 \equiv \begin{cases} x_G & with \quad probability \quad (p) \quad \text{with} \quad x_G > x_B \\ x_B & with \quad probability \quad (1-p) \end{cases}$$

The borrowing need is $L = D - x_1$ and the interest rate offered is such that $L(1 + r) = x_G$ (it is the highest interest rate possible and the creditors will receive all the available resources in either the state of the world). The condition necessary for lending is similar to (1), with the present value of resource transfer greater than the inherited debt:

$$(2) \quad x_1 + \frac{[px_G + (1-p)x_B]}{(1+i)} > D$$

If the debt is larger (i.e., the sign in (2) is reversed), the country is unable to service its debt. Creditors are willing to prevent a liquidity crisis and accept a certain loss; this is given by the difference between the first term of (2) and the amount of resources Z that creditors can take from the country in period 1. On the contrary, they could lend enough money to prevent default in the first period, hoping that they will receive the full repayment in the second period. A simple strategy is new lending $L = D - x_1$ at the usual rate r, so that creditors will receive all the potential resources in period 1. (It is true that the expected repayment: $(px_G + (1\text{-}p)x_B)/(1+i) < L$, but it is more than what creditors could obtain without new lending). Therefore, creditors have an incentive to lend, even at an expected loss, to defend their existing claims. But they have also the incentive to apply the highest possible interest rate r (r will be higher than i if $x_G > L(1 + i)$: as long as there is a state of the world in which the present value of resource transfer is greater than the debt, creditors will charge $r > i$).

Concessional lending, however, is generally in place and it makes economic sense because it provides an incentive to economic adjustment. Using a model in which $x_2$ could assume two values (low and high) depending on the adjustment effort, it is possible to show that it could be in the interest of the creditors to charge an interest rate sufficiently low ($r < i$) to stimulate the debtor to make the highest adjustment effort.

These results have strong implications: 1) concessional lending should be generally associated with conditionality, because creditors want the debtor to make the highest effort; and 2) there is a lack of credibility in the creditors' threat of stopping lending, because the model shows that defensive lending to prevent a liquidity crisis remains in their interest.

To evaluate how the theoretical arguments supporting the debt overhang effect could be applied to the HIPCs one has to bear in mind that these models were developed as a response to the Latin American crisis of the 1980s, which affected MICs and concerned debt contracted mainly with private creditors. By contrast, the current debt crisis involves LICs, mainly located in SSA, with limited or no market access and highly dependant on concessional external lending. Notwithstanding bilateral and multilateral debt relief, they keep on receiving large inflows of external credit at highly concessional terms by multilateral institutions (Chapter 1). Hence, the continuous processes of external assistance and debt rescheduling and restructuring are expected to reduce the disincentive effect of external public debt (Bird and Milne 2003; Cordella and Ulku 2007).[4] The current situation seems to adapt better to an extensive interpretation of debt overhang. This implies that, even though a high debt may not reduce fixed capital accumulation, it could still harm the economy in multiple ways, being a disincentive on: 1) investments in human capital and new technologies; and 2) the government's willingness to adopt structural reforms (Vamvakidis 2008), such as trade and financial liberalization and fiscal adjustments. As a matter of fact, the theoretical framework of the debt overhang hypothesis can be adapted to a broader interpretation of the negative effects of debt on growth ("extended" debt overhang). The debt burden could affect the composition of government spending, penalizing capital expenditures and productive categories of current expenditures versus unproductive ones (Mahdavi 2004). Moreover, even if total investment does not change, its composition can, with effects on productivity. The uncertainty on future government actions to meet debt obligations might push investors to prefer short-term and low-risk investment to long-term and risky projects (Serven 1997). According to the so-called "*Direct Effect of Debt Hypothesis*", burdensome debt-service levels might increase the reliance on short-term investment projects in order to service the outstanding

4 Moreover, it is often argued that weak economic institutions and infrastructure, and not excessive debt burdens, are the major hindrance to investment in HIPC countries (section 7.3).

debt, without reducing substantially the investment level (Fosu 1996). In that sense, external debt could lower capital accumulation in strategic sectors – like investments in education and innovation and their long-run effects on economic growth – reducing the overall investment efficiency and productivity. The misallocation of resources, and the declining productivity, could also be the result of an increase in the underground economy (Drine and Nabi 2010); a large external debt, forcing the government to raise the tax rate to repay debt service, might cause a reduction in the size of the formal sector in favor of the less-productive informal sector, lowering the overall production efficiency of the economy. The endogenous growth model proposed by Drine and Nabi is able to explain the non-linear effect of debt on growth and seems to fit well the experience of a number of HIPCs, where a large external debt goes hand-in-hand with a great share of the shadow economy in total GDP: the underground economy accounts for more than 40 percent of GDP in Guinea, Madagascar, Ghana, Côte d'Ivoire and Nicaragua; for around 50 percent of GDP in Benin, Republic of Congo and Honduras, and for an astonishing 67 percent in Bolivia (Buhen and Schneider 2007).

An extensive interpretation of the debt overhang effect is explicitly supported by Sachs (2002), who develops a model showing how an excessive debt burden could place LICs in a poverty trap (see Box 6.3). One implication of the model is that debt relief can act as a big push towards economic development and growth. However, the recent empirical evidence is particularly critical on scaling up aid as a solution to help poor countries escaping a poverty trap (Easterly 2006; Kraay and Raddatz 2007).

A similar conclusion about the positive effect of debt relief as an instrument to ensure a fresh start for debtor countries is reached also by Koeda (2008) adopting a completely different framework. The author recognizes that the traditional models of debt overhang are specifically designed for MICs suffering from excessive (non-concessional) debt. By contrast, the current debt crisis concerns poor countries, which receive net positive resource inflows and borrow from official creditors (WB's IDA and IMF's PRGF) which are neither profit maximizers nor risk neutral, so that they are not scared off by the excessive stock of existing debt and keep on lending at a high degree of concessionality. Koeda adapts the debt overhang argument to the specific experience of LICs, developing a simple model in which the interest rate on loans depends on the debtor country's income being below or above an income cutoff point. Being trapped in a debt overhang is a function of the initial stock of debt and of a country's TFP, with highly indebted countries having a strong incentive to accumulate concessional debt and allocate resources to consumption rather than investment, stagnating below the cutoff so that they could keep on borrowing at a concessional rate and become aid dependent. One implication of this model is that debt relief has to be a once-and-for-all opportunity in order to be effective in helping countries achieving sufficient growth. If debt relief is not a one time event, at least in the poor country authorities' time horizon, debtors still have the incentive to stagnate around the cutoff point because they anticipate that they will receive future debt relief according to the same eligibility criteria.

### Box 6.3 Poverty traps, debt relief and take-offs

Using the basic assumption of non-linearities in saving, investment and production (based on the fact that, when income is under a minimum level of subsistence, the saving rate is zero) debt relief can have a positive effect on economic growth. According to the model developed by Sachs (2002), real growth is a function of the stock of physical capital k and the accumulation of k over time depends on the saving rate (s), the rate of depreciation (δ) and population growth (n, $dk/dt = s - (n + \delta)k$.). The saving rate is assumed to fall dramatically when capital stock reaches a very low level, so that the capital growth rate turns negative when k is less than k*. So, when $k < k^*$, the economy shrinks and there is a poverty trap because, even if the saving rate is positive, it is so low that output and capital stock decline to the point where the saving rate is zero and the rate of decline is equal to $(\delta + n)$. On the other hand, when $k > k^*$ the economy grows at an increasing rate because saving is greater than the amount of resources needed to replace capital per worker $(n + \delta)k$, although this increasing rate of growth is unrealistic, and not just for poor countries (Figure 6.3).

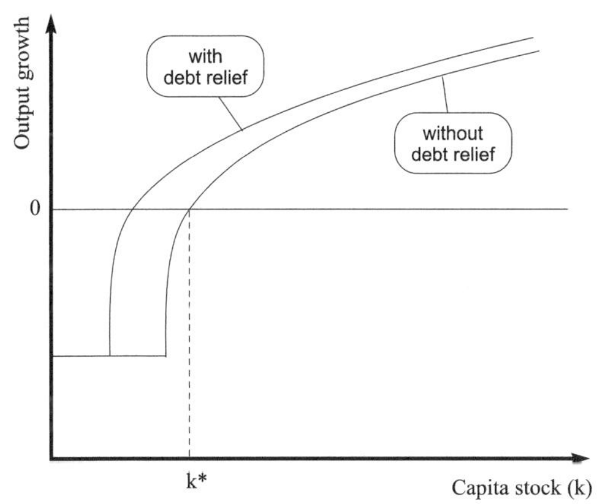


**Figure 6.3 Debt relief and output growth**
*Source*: Authors' elaboration on Sachs (2002).

For $k < k^*$ this poverty trap model seems to be consistent with the actual situation of many poor countries, where saving rates are very low, and with the debt overhang hypothesis, since a large stock of debt lowers investment and reduces the capital stock. A poverty trap could also be triggered by demographic pressure or by the fact that the marginal productivity of k could be negative when k is very low – contrary to the usual assumptions (Inada condition) – because capital stock might become productive only above a certain threshold. Furthermore, the poverty trap derives from the fact that, in absence of public investment in human capital and basic infrastructure; * also private investments are unlikely to be made.

HIPCs are likely to be in a situation with a declining output, because a high debt burden decreases the investment rate through the debt overhang effect. Debt relief shifts the curve in Figure 6.3 upward and an economy that was shrinking could start to grow. This conclusion supports the idea of a fresh start – the so-called "big push" – for HIPCs and a more comprehensive idea of debt sustainability, which should consider explicitly also the investment requirements in health, education and infrastructures. However, the critical model's assumption of strong non-linearities in saving rates is not shared by the economic literature. Kraay and Raddatz (2007) show that the empirical evidence on the relationship between saving rates and capital accumulation in developing countries does not follow an S-curve and is not consistent with a poverty trap model as the one proposed by Sachs (2002). Moreover, Easterly (2006) empirically rejects the narrative of poverty traps and take-offs during the second half of the last century which is at the ground of the Rosenstein-Rodan's big push theory of economic development recently supported by Sachs (2005).

*Note*: * This is due to the fact that public investments are determined by budgetary outlays and tax revenues are low for a LIC: very often in these countries the base of tax-payers is rather small and the rural population's economic activity is outside the formal sectors. In these circumstances, an often large share of foreign financing could be used to finance current expenditure.

### *6.1.2 The Liquidity Constraint Effect*

The negative effect of debt on growth works not only through the impact of the stock of debt, but also via the flows of service payments, which reduce funds available for investment purposes (Hofman and Reisen 1991) and are likely to crowd out investment (Cohen 1993). Depending on the degree of concessionality of the stock of external debt and on the expectation on countries effective payment of debt service, a significant share of government revenues has to be diverted to serve debt obligations, crowding out public and private investment. This effect is likely to be greater in countries with a large domestic debt, since, as we have seen in Part 2, the interest rate on internal financing and the resulting interest bill are generally higher than for foreign debt. While public investment is directly reduced by the increase in debt service payments, private investment can be crowded out because of higher tax rates, increases in the interest rate required to allocate domestic securities and lower credit to the private sector. The rationale behind the negative impact of debt payments on investments is that, if the debt obligations are expected to be met, the service payments could affect investment decisions, depending on the efficiency of the rescheduling strategy; on the other hand, if a debtor country is not expected to repay its debt as a result of a known rescheduling rule, then investments should not be crowded out. Cohen (1993) presents a model in which, for a country whose nominal debt is so large that creditors cannot commit their rescheduling strategy to follow a given rule, the crowding out effect is proportional to the amount of resources that the creditors are able to "tax away" and not to the stock of debt.[5]

Since the HIPCs, contrary to the indebted countries in the 1980s, receive net positive resource transfers, the standard disincentive effect to invest due to a large debt burden might be mitigated. Therefore, debt service payments might be the main constraint on investment and economic growth, even if the high degree of concessionality makes actual debt service a small share of government revenues in several countries. Hansen (2004) calls for more additionality (i.e., more financial aid) because his results show that both investments and growth are significantly explained by debt service and effective aid.[6]

Other than a direct crowding out effect, investment projects could be halted or postponed because of reduced credit to the private sector. The higher tax rate required to serve debt obligations reduces private saving and bank lending. Especially in countries with a significant share of domestic debt and underdeveloped financial markets, credit rationing can be the result of increasing interest rates and of the banks' preference for risk-free government securities (Chapter 3).

### *6.1.3 Effects of Uncertainty on Future Resource Flows and Debt Repayments*

The third channel through which a large external debt could affect economic performance concerns the uncertainty about future aid and resources inflows, and about debt-service payments, together with their effects on macroeconomic stability.

Risk of default, rescheduling and arrears are likely to increase the volatility of future inflows and additional lending, to encourage capital flights and to reduce indebted countries' access to international capital markets, given that the latter is conditioned on investors' perception of debt sustainability. This generates an uncertain environment, where also government policies and reforms depend on concessional lending and on rescheduling plans, domestic and foreign investors are likely to exercise the "waiting" option, even if the economy's fundamentals are good and/or improving (Claessens et al. 1997, Serven 1997). Moreover, as we have already discussed, investment decisions under uncertainty are not forward-looking and short-term low-risk investments will be preferred to long-run, high-risk and irreversible ones (Dixit and Pindyck 1994). This misallocation of resources reduces the efficiency and productivity of capital, leading to a slowdown of economic growth.

5 Debt service is shown to be proportional to the cost of debt repudiation and it crowds out investments by a factor that is equal to the intertemporal elasticity of substitution.

6 The main argument of Hansen's analysis is the importance of additionality, contrary to selectivity and conditionality invoked by many authors (see, e.g. Birdsall, Williamson and Deese 2002). His results show that when financial aid and debt payments are reduced one for one, there is no effect on economic growth and investments could fall. For a very recent review of additionality of debt relief see Powell and Bird (2009).

Debt reduction reduces uncertainty and increases confidence in the debtor country's government and in its policies, fostering economic growth. This argument is similar to the debt overhang hypothesis, but here the focus is not on the disincentives arising from the likelihood that the gains will be taxed away by foreign creditors, but on the general uncertainty that dominates the economy and biases investment choices. Claessens et al. (1997) argue that one of the conclusions that could be drawn from the experience of the Brady Plan is the crucial importance of reduced uncertainty. The removal of continual ongoing rescheduling was the main channel through which debt reduction affected growth. Debt reduction has the effect of increasing capital inflows by strengthening confidence in the government's willingness to implement reforms and new policies. This happens because investors look at debt reduction 'as an "endorsement" by the international financial community that the country is successfully pursuing sound macroeconomic policies and structural reforms' (Claessens et al. 1997: 44).

Close to this issue, there is the relationship between debt and capital flight, which leads to lower economic growth. In a model developed by Calvo (1998), returns on capital are lowered by the distortionary tax burden on capital required to service the debt. Low returns reduce investments and, as a consequence, economic growth. Facing lower future returns, domestic and international investors prefer to send (or keep) their money abroad, rather than investing in the country. Thus, in a number of countries there might be a vicious cycle (*revolving door*) between debt and capital flight: excessive foreign borrowing, increasing the likelihood of a debt crisis and worsening the investment climate (via debt overhang) might lead to capital flight, further undermining macroeconomic stability and pushing indebted countries to boost their lending abroad (Alesina and Tabellini 1989; Boyce 1992; Ndikumana and Boyce 2003; Cerra, Rishi and Saxena 2008).

Finally, large public debt might bring inflationary pressure, undermining macroeconomic stability through different channels. According to the "unpleasant monetarist arithmetic" (Sargent and Wallace 1981), governments running persistent deficits have sooner or later to finance those deficits with money creation raising inflation (see Catão and Terrones (2005) for an empirical validation of this preposition in developing countries). Moreover, according to the fiscal theory of the price level, the price level is determined exclusively by government debt, without any explicit reference to monetary policy, since a larger debt creates a wealth effect increasing the aggregate demand and inflation (see Bassetto 2008 for a brief critical review). Thus, an increase in government debt is likely to be inflationary in countries with large public debt (Kwon, McFarlane and Robinson 2006). Price levels respond to money supply and public debt dynamics, even if the latter has a much greater impact. Indeed, especially in developing countries where there is a certain degree of fiscal dominance, the presence of a large public debt increases deficit financing by money creation since a higher inflation reduces the real cost of debt in the short term, but at the cost of undermining the credibility problem and increasing the long-run costs of public debt. Even if the evidence discussed in Chapter 3 suggests that the monetary adjustment in HIPCs was quite successful, the possibility of a debt-inflation trap and the key role of inflation expectations, fiscal and policy rules and central bank independence for debt management have to be carefully considered also in heavily indebted countries.

## 6.2 Effects of External Debt on Growth: Empirical Evidence

The existing literature generally looks at cross-country analysis to assess whether, to what extent and through which channels large external debt is associated with lower economic growth rates. Lower GDP growth rates can be due to either a contraction in capital accumulation or a reduction in TFP growth. As seen in the previous section, the former effect could depend on debt service crowding out public investment or to debt overhang. The latter, instead, could be due to the misallocation of resources, lack of reforms and short-termism. In the following sub-sections, we review the most important contributions, distinguishing between stock and flow effects.

### *6.2.1 Debt Overhang*

The actual presence of debt overhang in developing countries is an empirical issue. The general theoretical framework builds on assumptions (negative resource transfers, non-linearities in saving rates) which do not necessarily hold in HIPCs, although it is possible to adapt the original framework to their specific experience. On the whole, the existing empirical evidence weakly confirms the debt overhang hypothesis, even if the link between debt and growth is not clearly defined because of some methodological issues. Thus, the relative incidence of the debt variables and the magnitude of the effects differ across different studies and lack robustness.

A large strand of literature focuses on external public debt and its effects on investment and GDP growth. Earlier studies on the 1980s debt crisis find that foreign debt has a detrimental impact on capital accumulation (Greene and Villanueva 1991; Savvides 1992; Serven and Solimano 1993). Subsequent analysis started depicting the relationship between external debt and economic growth as an inverted U-shaped curve. However, the estimated threshold varies over a broad range of values, because of different samples, empirical methodologies and indicators of debt (i.e. nominal value versus NPV). Some studies even reject the hypothesis that the stock of debt depresses investments, such as Lora (2007) who focuses on the seven largest Latin American countries and finds a positive association between public debt and public investment, although this beneficial effect is likely to be mitigated by an adverse one due to the expansion of fiscal deficit and subsequent fiscal consolidation. Other authors (Chowdhury 2004) show that both the debt burden and the debt-service obligations squeeze investments and depresses economic performance while others find evidence exclusively in support of the relevance of debt service payments.[7] Cline (1995) underlies that debt relief makes sense only when a country is on the wrong side of the Debt-Laffer curve, but this is not always the case: he shows the results of some 1980s studies which found that few countries were effectively on the right side of the hump-shaped curve. In the following, we inspect in more details the findings on the presence of a Debt-Laffer curve in developing countries. In the next chapter we provide original empirical evidence on this issue.

Clements, Bhattacharya and Nguyen (2004) investigate the relationships between external debt, investments and growth in 55 LICs, finding some empirical evidence supporting debt overhang: estimating a simple growth model and using panel data, they find that, over a certain threshold, more debt leads to lower rates of growth. Those thresholds are lower than the ones used in the HIPC program (external debt is roughly 30-37 percent of GDP, or 115-120 percent of exports). Furthermore, they show that public investments are what really matters for economic growth: a one percent increase in public investment results in a 0.2 percent increase in GDP, but this positive linkage becomes less effective as public investments increase because they lead to higher deficit and debt, which negatively affect economic growth.

Pattillo, Poirson and Ricci (2002) find a similar non-linear relationship between debt and growth, using a panel data set of 93 developing countries. As before, initial debt fosters growth but, above a certain level (D* in Figure 6.2), the marginal effect becomes negative and, over another threshold (D'), the contribution of debt to growth turns negative. Their results are consistent with the impact of external debt on growth turning negative (point D') when the ratio of the NPV of debt to exports is larger than 160-170. In general, the marginal impact becomes negative when external debt is around 35-40 percent of GDP (around 80 percent of exports), while the corresponding value estimated by Clements, Bhattacharya and Nguyen (2004) is approximately 50 percent.[8]

Also Elbadawi, Ndulu and Ndung'u (1997) find evidence of the debt overhang hypothesis in 99 developing countries: their data are consistent with an inverse-U shaped curve that has its maximum where the ratio of the current stock of debt to GDP is 0.97. Even if results can change using different specifications, the general conclusion supporting the adverse effect of debt on growth is confirmed: current deficit stimulates growth, but there is a limit above which past debt accumulation hinders output growth. Moreover, this analysis provides some support to a broader interpretation of the debt overhang hypothesis: it seems that high debt affects the

7 These studies should be taken with caution because they do not address some relevant issues, such as the degree of concessionality of the loans and the real interest rate, whose inclusion in the regression could probably change the coefficients on the debt variables.

8 The main reasons of the difference in the thresholds are probably due to the different samples (Pattillo, Poirson and Ricci (2002) consider also MICs) and the use of face value of NPV of debt.

real exchange rate, fiscal deficit and inflation, which, in turn, impact negatively on private investments; the effect on these policy variables deters reform programs and reduces the government's ability of responding to shocks.

The implications for debt relief of this non-linear relationship depend crucially on the estimates of the thresholds D* and D'. The closer D* is to the threshold of 150 used in the HIPC Initiative, the higher the contribution of debt reduction to output growth. Debt forgiveness aims at moving eligible countries from the right to the left side of the Debt-Laffer curve. Pattillo, Poirson and Ricci (2002) show that the HIPC Initiative could contribute up to a one percentage point increase in output growth and could also make the average contribution of debt to growth positive. The estimates obtained by Clements, Bhattacharya and Nguyen (2004) seem to suggest a similar or slightly higher incidence of the initiative, depending on the different estimation procedures.

These results, however, have to be taken with caution, because there are other variables, as government balance, public investment, debt service and institutional quality that may alter these conclusions. For instance, the positive impact of debt relief found by Pattillo, Poirson and Ricci (2002) might be flawed by the fact that the sample includes MICs and the computation of the impact is done for the average country. Moreover, the evidence of non-linearity is quite weak, highly dependent on the methodological approach, and probably driven by some outliers, given that the bulk of their sample is made by observations located in the downward sloping side of the curve. For example, the basic results obtained by Pattillo, Poirson and Ricci (2002, their Tables 3-6) on the inverse U-shaped curve are not generally confirmed across different specifications: the quadratic specification has both terms significant at 5 percent level of confidence only in 2 out of 16 specifications, and in both cases the growth model is estimated with the Fixed-Effects estimator, which is biased and inconsistent in a dynamic setting.[9] Besides, this strand of literature does not adequately take into account the issues of reverse causality and simultaneity, which might dramatically alter the results.

The presence of the Debt-Laffer curve is not confirmed by Presbitero (2006), who finds evidence only of a negative and linear relationship between external debt and economic growth in a sample of 69 developing countries. The point estimates of this negative and linear effect are validated using different estimators and different specifications of the model and they imply that, on average, a 10 percent increase in the debt-to-export ratio reduces the rate of per capita GDP growth by 0.12 percentage points, while a reduction of the ratio from its average level to the HIPC threshold of 150 boosts economic growth by 0.30 percentage

9 More precisely, in nine out of 16 different specifications including the quadratic term of the debt ratio neither the linear nor the quadratic term are significant. The authors do not report the test for the joint significance of the coefficients. Moreover, adopting what is generally believed to be the preferred estimator (the System-GMM, see Appendix A for a methodological discussion), the quadratic relationship is significant (at 10 percent) only in one case out of four (Pattillo, Poirson and Ricci 2002: 24-28).

points; halving the ratio from 300 percent to 150 percent will add half point to GDP growth. The inclusion of the quadratic term of the debt ratio to account for non linearities confirms that the debt-growth nexus is not shaped as an inverted-U curve, but just as a negative non-linear relation between debt and growth: the point estimates are consistent with a U-shaped curve, whose minimum is for a very high level of the debt ratio, greater than the 99th percentile of the sample, meaning that the basic relationship is negative and follows the downward sloping side of a U-shaped curve. Hence, the presence of a non-linearity could be consistent with the idea of a debt irrelevance zone for very high level of debt (Cordella, Ricci and Ruiz-Arranz 2010).[10]

In two recent papers, Cordella, Ricci and Ruiz-Arranz (2010) and Imbs and Ranciere (2008) find evidence of non-linearities in the debt-growth relationship: the former moves away from the previous literature arguing that the relationship is a "modified Debt-Laffer curve" because, over a certain threshold, the debt effect on growth is nil, creating a sort of "debt irrelevance" zone; the latter use a non-parametric technique to support the bell-shaped curve, arguing that better institutions reduce the magnitude of debt overhang. Specifically, Cordella, Ricci and Ruiz-Arranz (2010) estimate a debt-growth relationship with two breaks, finding evidence of debt overhang for intermediate levels of indebtedness. On the contrary, at low and high level of debt the relationship is not significant. Thus, over a certain threshold (a ratio between the NPV of external debt and GDP of around 60 percent), the marginal (but not the average) debt overhang is absent. Moreover, the authors show that debt overhang and the debt irrelevance zone differ according to countries' characteristics: countries with better institutions, better policies and easier market access exhibit higher thresholds than countries in worse conditions, for which the negative relationship is generally less robust. Furthermore, Cordella, Ricci and Ruiz-Arranz look explicitly at debt effects on growth in HIPCs: they find that debt overhang is a valid hypothesis only for non-HIPC countries, in which the estimated Debt-Laffer curve turns negative when the NPV of external debt is beyond 35 percent of GDP.[11] They also argue that the HIPC Initiative is shifting completion point countries from the debt-irrelevance zone (starting when the NPV of debt to GDP is above 50 to 60 percent) to the downward sloping part of the curve, so that additional debt relief is likely to spur economic growth.

10 The lack of a Debt-Laffer curve could be explained by the sample of countries, since poor countries are generally located on the wrong side of the curve. The left side of the curve, in which the effect of debt is positive, should be occupied by industrialized and low-debt countries, in which increasing debt leads to faster growth. Inn the sample used by Presbitero, 90 percent of the observations have a debt-to-export ratio larger than 70, so that they should be in the negatively-sloped side of the inverse U-shaped curve estimated by Pattillo, Poirson and Ricci (2002).

11 Splitting the sample between low and severely indebted countries, the authors find that debt overhang is still valid in low indebted countries, but not in the second sample. In sum, Cordella, Ricci and Ruiz-Arranz (2010) argue that is the level of indebtedness and not differences in policies or institutions which drives the evidence on debt overhang.

Imbs and Ranciere (2008) use kernel estimators, which have the advantage of avoiding the imposition of any restriction on the non-linearities in the debt-growth relationship, to test for the presence of the Debt-Laffer curve in developing countries. Their results are consistent with a debt overhang effect starting when the NPV of external debt exceeds 40 percent of GDP. Moreover, the authors are able to show that, once fixed effects are considered, a smaller number of countries displays a Debt-Laffer curve. Therefore, this non-linearity could be driven by some omitted time-invariant control variables which jointly determine low growth and high debt. The estimation of a growth equation controlling for different time-invariant institutional variables partially confirms this hypothesis.

Although relevant, this kind of evidence does not provide any indication about the channels through which the stock of external debt could affect economic growth. However, some authors have tried to assess whether slower growth is the result of lower capital accumulation or of declining productivity. Pattillo, Poirson and Ricci (2004) show that the non-linear relationship between debt and growth works through two main channels: physical capital and TFP. Quantitatively, for the average high-indebted country, doubling the debt will reduce the growth of output, physical capital and TFP by 1 percent. The effect of debt on growth occurs mainly through TFP and less via physical capital accumulation, while the relevance of human capital is generally negligible. An indirect evidence in support of the hypothesis that large external debt does not reduce capital accumulation, but impinges on other factors affecting TFP is provided by Presbitero (2006). The stock of external debt is found to lower the rate of economic growth, but it does not lower significantly the level of investment. Thus, the resulting lower GDP growth might be due to a slowdown of TFP growth, rather than reduced capital accumulation. The debt effect on declining productivity is confirmed by Blavy (2006), who explicitly estimates a hump-shaped relationship between total public debt and productivity, consistently with the debt overhang hypothesis. Drine and Nabi (2010) provide additional support to the non-linear effect of external debt on productivity but, differently from other contributions which focus on TFP, they consider the effect of external public debt only on production efficiency of the TFP, given the limited role of technological progress in developing countries. On the whole, a number of studies, adopting different methodologies and covering different samples, agree on the adverse effect of external indebtedness on productivity growth, consistently with short-termism due to the uncertain macroeconomic framework, with the Direct Effect of Debt Hypothesis (Fosu 1996) and with the "extended debt overhang".

In sum, the evidence of a direct link between debt and growth remains unclear, since econometric results lack robustness (Moss and Chiang 2003; Rajan 2005). In particular, many empirical studies mix low- and middle-income countries, even if the actual effects of large public external debts are likely to be heterogeneous across income levels. Empirical works should focus on more accurate investigations of the real effects of indebtedness on economic performance in the HIPCs (or for LICs). Furthermore, in order to draw a more realistic estimate of the impact of debt dynamics on economic performance, there should be a careful econometric analysis of the debt effects on investment (and not only on economic growth), of the direction of causality between debt and growth, and also of the relevance of a policy or institutional variable, which is often neglected in this sort of studies, and that could be a common determinant of both low growth and high debt (chapters 7 and 8).

All the previous works evaluate the relationship between external debt and growth, so that it is possible to estimate the contribution of a debt reduction to economic growth as an exercise of comparative statistic. To our knowledge, a recent paper by Depetris Chauvin and Kraay (2005) is the first empirical attempt to evaluate explicitly the impact of debt relief on a set of different macroeconomic variables, as growth, public spending, investment and institutional quality.[12] Looking at a sample of 62 LICs over the period 1989-2003, Depetris Chauvin and Kraay do not find any positive effect of debt relief on their dependent variables. Even acknowledging that the estimates might be flawed by statistical and data issues, their conclusions are quite pessimistic on the likelihood of debt relief to bring the expected benefits in terms of social spending and economic growth. Similar conclusions are reached also by Johansson (2010) adopting a more standard growth (and investment) regression approach and substantiated also by anecdotal evidence on HIPCs (Dömeland and Kharas 2009). In Chapter 8 we follow an approach similar to the one used by Depetris Chauvin and Kraay (2005) to evaluate the effectiveness of debt relief on different macroeconomic outcomes and on institution building in HIPCs.

### *6.2.2 Crowding Out*

Even if the theoretical argument in favor of crowding out of public investment by external debt service is straightforward, given that a larger share of revenues spent to service external debt means that less resources are available for productive investments, its actual impact in LICs and HIPCs is not obvious. LICs generally borrow at highly concessional terms (Cordella and Ulku 2007), so that the real burden of external debt service on the budget balance is small, limiting the magnitude of the crowding out effect.

The empirical findings are generally inconclusive. In a seminal contribution, Cohen (1993) rejects empirically the debt overhang hypothesis and supports the crowding out effect, whose magnitude is significant: a 1 percentage point increase in debt service reduces GDP growth by 0.35 percent. Hansen (2004) corroborates the effectiveness of the liquidity constraint, because debt service, when included together with an aid variable, has a negative impact on investment (the point estimate – 0.33 – of the crowding out effect is very close to the value found by Cohen (1993)) and growth. Similar findings are confirmed on different samples

---

12 See Chapter 8 for a detailed discussion of other papers explicitly evaluating the direct effects of debt relief.

and with alternative methodologies by Fosu (1996, 1999), with a specific reference to SSA countries, and by Chowdhury (2004) and Elbadawi et al. (1997), among others. The latter two studies show that debt-service payments have a detrimental impact on investments because the interest bill reduces import capacity and available credit, creating a disincentive for investors (Elbadawi, Ndulu and Ndung'u 1997). In a similar vein. Harrabi, Bousrih and Mohammed (2007) show that government pressure on domestic financial markets crowds out investment through a reduced credit to the private sector: in a sample of 52 African countries over the period 1988-2004, debt relief, when associated with good institutional quality, could create fiscal space and limit interest rate increases, enhancing credit to the private sector.

Despite some evidence in favour of the crowding out effect, other empirical works do not find a significant impact of debt service on growth: Pattillo, Poirson and Ricci (2002, 2004) include a debt service indicator in the growth regression, but find it not significant.[13] Clements, Bhattacharya and Nguyen (2004) show that debt service has no direct effect on growth, but find support for the crowding out effect of debt service on public investment. The magnitude of this effect is quite weak: a reduction in debt service from 8.7 percent of GDP to 3 percent increases public investment by 0.7-0.8 percent; given the growth regression estimates (1 percent more in investment means 0.2 percent increase in economic growth), this will be translated in a per capita GDP growth increase of 0.1-0.2 percent. However, when at least half of debt relief resources are directed to public investments, the same reduction in debt service can increase economic growth by 0.5 percent.

Similar evidence is found by Presbitero (2006), who estimates a growth model and an investment model for a sample of developing countries finding that debt-service payments do not have a direct impact on the GDP growth rate, while they negatively impinge on total investments. The magnitude of the crowding out effect means that a 1 percent reduction in the debt service-to-GDP ratio adds 0.20 percent to the investment ratio. In order to design efficient debt reduction programs it is important to assess whether the crowding out of investment is heterogeneous across countries. Results show that the liquidity constraint is particularly binding in the poorest countries, where the magnitude of the crowding out is more than two times larger than in the overall sample.[14]

In order to substantiate the presence of a financial constrain in the world's poorest countries, the debt-investment nexus is estimated in a sub-sample for which data on the NPV of external debt are available. The estimates confirm that debt service crowds out investment: a 1 percent increase in debt service means a

13 This result, contrary to expectations (as acknowledged by the authors themselves), could be due to the fact that the data do not measure actual payments, but rather the scheduled ones, which are often very different numbers.

14 Presbitero (2006) estimates an investment model on a sample of 69 developing countries over the period 1977-2002. A standard dynamic investment equation is estimated using yearly or non-overlapping three years averages with different estimators.

reduction in the investment ratio between 0.28 and 0.39 percent. The crowding out effect (0.39) is much larger than the limited effectiveness of foreign aid (0.15), which is consistent with the skeptical view of aid as a tool for achieving higher investment and growth rates (Bauer 1971; Easterly 2001b). The long-run equilibrium is consistent with a one-to-one relationship between debt service and investments: a reduction of debt service of 1 percent of GDP raises the investment-to-GDP ratio by 1 percent. In sum, the relevant debt effect on investment works through the liquidity constraint channel, while the stock of debt is likely to affect the quality and the efficiency of investments, not its level. From a policy perspective, a good growth-enhancing policy should prefer a reduction in debt service to increased foreign assistance.

Although the empirical literature does not show a compelling evidence in favor of the presence of a binding liquidity constraints in HIPCs, there are at least two sources of concern regarding the future evolution of debt service on investment and growth. Firstly, a sensible evaluation of the crowding out effect must include debt service on the overall public debt. As seen in Part 2, a number of HIPCs are making use to internal financing and the associated cost are already higher than external debt service. Hence, given that the rising stock of domestic debt is highly connected to the HIPC Initiative, the evaluation of the crowding out effect should not be limited to external debt. Secondly, the lack of crowding out may be due to the concessionality of external borrowing; this result critically depends on the choice between loans versus grants in concessional financing and on access to commercial lending (see Chapter 9 and sections 2.4.2 and 10.2.3). As regards the first point, the WB and the IMF should consider the interest bill both on external and domestic debt when they evaluate the debt burden (see Part 2). With respect to second point, it is worth noting that some HIPCs have already re-started borrowing at non-concessional terms. Some countries (i.e. Angola, Congo RD, Ghana, Mali, Mauritania and Rwanda) have entered non-concessional financing agreements and have issued bonds on the international capital markets (Part 4). Even if this change could be perceived as a sign of a renewed attractiveness of some HIPCs in the eyes of international lenders and could help filling the funding gap for development targets, it represent a source of concern. In the absence of sound borrowing policies, poor countries face the risks of being unable to service their debts in the near future (Chapter 10).

### 6.3 Other Effects of Debt on the Economy

An excessive debt burden has a number of adverse consequences on the domestic economy, other than its effects on capital accumulation and income growth. Firstly, a large external debt, especially with short-term maturity, is associated with a higher probability of debt distress in developing countries, even if the *debt tolerance* thresholds are heterogeneous across countries, depending on their policies and institutions (Reinhart, Rogoff and Savastano 2003; Kraay and Nehru

2006). Related to the event of a crisis, (short-term) external debt triggers capital flights, particularly when institutions are weak (Cerra, Rishi and Saxena 2008). Fofack (2009) shows that, in SSA, capital flight reached US$ 600 billions in 2004 and amounted to US$ 1000 per capita in HIPCs. His empirical analysis confirms that in the majority of SSA countries there is a co-integrating relationship between capital flight and external debt, consistent with the *revolving door* hypothesis, while in other countries the causality runs only from external debt to capital flight. Secondly, a large external debt affects the allocation of government expenditures and pro-poor spending. Lora and Olivera (2007) look at the relationship between external debt and social expenditures in a panel of 50 developing countries and find that higher total public debt and, in a limited way, debt-service payments, are associated with a reduction in social expenditures. A similar result is confirmed by Dessy and Vencatachellum (2007) for Africa: they find that debt reduction is associated with an increase in the share of a country's expenditures allocated either to public education or health in countries which have improved their institutions. Limiting the analysis at HIPC countries, Crespo Cuaresma and Vincelette (2009) provide some positive evidence of human capital accumulation in completion point countries, in terms of reduced drop out rates, proportion of young people with primary schooling and increased educational expenditures. Still focusing on the HIPCs, Schmid (2009) shows that debt relief, also thanks to lower debt service, reduces the infant mortality rate, suggesting that large external debts have adverse consequences on the socio-economic conditions of the poor.[15]

## 6.4 The Causality Issue and the Role of Institutions

The empirical evidence on the debt-growth nexus is not robust and suffers from different shortcomings. In particular, the issue of reverse causality and the role of other country-specific factors which could jointly affect economic growth and debt accumulation are often neglected. With respect to the former, we have seen through this chapter that, beyond a certain threshold, the marginal effect of external debt turns negative. However the negative correlation between debt and GDP growth could be the outcome of excessive external lending due to slow economic growth. In this sense, large debt burdens could be more a symptom rather than a cause of low economic growth. Hence, there are no sound theoretical arguments to unambiguously identify the direction of causality of the debt-growth nexus. Therefore, the two-way relationship between external debt and economic growth has to be addressed empirically in order to identify the possible causal effect of

15 As for the evidence on educational outcomes, it is difficult to disentangle the actual effect of reduced debt-service expenditures from other possible effects related to the conditionalities of the HIPC Initiatives, such as political and economic reforms and macroeconomic stability.

external debt on GDP growth and to provide strong support for the debt overhang hypothesis and for debt reduction policies.

Apart from the issue of reverse causality, also country-specific factors could affect the way in which indebtedness impinges on economic growth. Amongst the possible source of heterogeneity in the debt-growth nexus, it is critical to consider the role of institutions. As seen in Chapter 2, the DSF implemented by the WB and the IMF includes debt-burden thresholds which are a function of the CPIA index, so that countries' risk of debt distress and borrowing policies depend on the quality of their policies and institutions. In addition, recent empirical research on the effectiveness of debt overhang has taken into account the role of country-specific fixed effects and institutions, finding that debt overhang arises at different levels of indebtedness, according to countries' characteristics.

Hence, a sensible evaluation of the way in which debt accumulation affects economic growth should not ignore the role of policies and institutions, since a better institutional environment could reduce the vulnerability to debt distress episodes. In the next chapter we will test whether debt overhang is more likely to be effective in countries with strong institutions than in ones with a weak institutional framework. In the latter, agents are discouraged from undertaking investment not by fear of future high tax rates (levied to repay the debt), but by uneven regulation, state monopolies and a poor business climate. By contrast, where the basic market institutions work properly, excessive indebtedness is more likely to act as a real constraint to investment and economic growth. This hypothesis is consistent with a minimum level of institutional quality required in order to attract foreign investment, stimulate economic growth and benefit from debt relief (Asiedu 2003) and with the fact that, in indebted countries, poor institutions and lax constraints on the executive lead to capital flights and to subsequent debt accumulation and macroeconomic vulnerability (Cerra, Rishi and Saxena 2008).

# Chapter 7
# External Debt and Growth: An Empirical Investigation[1]

## 7.1 Introduction

This chapter focuses on the empirical consequences of high debt in poor countries on economic growth, building on the stream of literature reviewed in Chapter 6. In addition, on the ground of the hypothesis that this relationship could differ according to countries' specific characteristics, the chapter directly investigates the role played by institutions and policies in the debt-growth nexus. The analysis does not address the issue of the channels through which external debt affects growth,[2] nor the effects of actual debt relief, which will be investigated in the next chapter.

The international community bears large costs to finance debt relief programs. An efficient use of these resources should require a careful cost-benefit analysis. In particular, the destination of a large share of scarce resources to a limited number of countries lacking the basic infrastructures and institutions to trigger economic growth means that there will be less resources to assist other poor countries better equipped to use external assistance efficiently (Easterly 2001b; Arslanalp and Henry 2005; Jayachandran and Kremer 2006).[3] Therefore, investigating the debt-growth nexus in poor countries; it is critical to draw sensible policy recommendations. Given the large costs, policy-makers should have sound evidence that debt reduction is going to spur growth. As it stands, the current approach to debt relief proposals is based on an uniform treatment of indebted poor countries by donors; however, this is not necessarily the right or the most efficient one, since the evidence on the relationship between external debt and economic growth is not conclusive and shows the importance of country-specific characteristics (Chapter 6).

With respect to the existing literature, this chapter aims at determining whether and to what extent institutions and policies affect the debt-growth nexus. Unlike

---

1 This chapter draws on Presbitero (2009), The Debt-Growth Nexus: a Reassessment, *Economics: The-Open-Access, Open-Assessment E-Journal*, Vol. 2, 2008-30 (http://www.economics-ejournal.org/economics/journalarticles/2008-30).

2 On this, see Pattillo, Poirson and Ricci (2004) and Presbitero (2006), discussed in section 6.3.2, who both stress the relevant role played by external indebtedness of TFP.

3 This point is supported by the concerns expressed by the WB about the possibility that the costs of the HIPC Initiative and the MDRI will reduce the total amount of resources available to the IDA, undermining its lending capacity (IDA 2005).

Imbs and Ranciere (2008), we control for a time-variant institutional indicator and, instead of looking at different sub-samples (Cordella, Ricci and Ruiz-Arranz 2010), we interact the institutional variable with debt indicators in order to find a possible source of heterogeneity. The issue of reverse causality is addressed by estimating the growth model by System-GMM and smoothing the denominator of the debt ratios to eliminate the potential correlation between low growth and subsequent larger debt to GDP ratio.

Results suggest that policies and institutions are likely to affect simultaneously debt accumulation and growth. The Debt-Laffer curve, which is present in the sample of developing countries, looses statistical significance once institutional quality is controlled for. Moreover, the debt-growth nexus clearly depends on the country-specific institutional framework. Different specifications show that debt overhang is effective exclusively in countries with good policies and institutions. On the contrary, external debt seems to be irrelevant for countries with weak institutions. Larger debts and more resource transfers could explain the lack of debt overhang. A number of robustness exercises do not significantly affect these findings.

From a policy perspective, the focus on the WB overall CPIA index for institutions and policy assessment and on a parsimonious model specification could provide an insight for IFIs to develop country-specific debt relief initiatives, following the same approach behind the DSF. Further research is surely required, but our analysis substantiates the hypothesis that one-size-fits-all policies are inefficient. Debt relief could trigger economic growth exclusively in countries with sound economic and political infrastructures. In the absence of these preconditions, debt reduction would not provide the expected benefits, since institutional and other constraints hinder the growth process. This conclusion is consistent with recent findings which suggest that debt relief is likely to benefit only countries with good institutions.

## 7.2 Data and Methodology

### *7.2.1 Data*

The dataset covers 114 developing (low- and middle-income) countries (listed in Appendix, Table 7.10) over the period 1980-2004. The main sources are the WDI and the GDF published by the WB. Other data comes from the WEO and from a number of IMF Country Reports and Staff Papers.

More specifically, economic growth (*GROWTH*) is measured as the log difference in the per capita real GDP (*GDP*), from the WDI. External debt is measured in NPV terms, in order to take into account the degree of concessionality embedded in multilateral loans.[4] The historical series on the NPV of PPG external debt is a WB dataset constructed by Dikhanov (2004). From these data, we construct two measures of external debt burden: the ratios of the NPV of external debt over GDP (*DEBT/GDP*) and over exports (*DEBT/EXP*).[5] In the same vein of Cordella, Ricci and Ruiz-Arranz (2010), we take into account the possibility that the negative correlation between debt and growth is due to a causal relationship running from growth to debt (Easterly 2001c), applying the Hodrick-Prescott filter to the denominator of both measures in order to smooth the series.[6] The educational indicators – the gross primary and secondary enrolment rates – are constructed updating the Barro and Lee (2001) dataset[7] with data from the WDI. To take into account the institutional framework we make use of the CPIA index (see Box 2.3 for a description of the advantages of this choice).

To wash out any business cycle variation, we average data over non-overlapping five-year periods, ending up with five observations in time. The plot of the data helped to highlight some outliers, generally related to the first observations in former communist countries.

### *7.2.2 The Growth Model*

The hypothesis to be tested is the possibility of heterogeneous effects of debt on economic growth according to countries' policies and institutions. We estimate a simple growth equation taking into account institutional quality and interacting it with the external debt indicator. The basic model is:

$$GROWTH_{i,t} = (\alpha - 1)GDP_{i,t-1} + X_{i,t}\beta' + \delta_1 DEBT_{i,t} + \delta_2 DEBT^2_{i,t} + \eta_i + \tau_t + \varepsilon_{i,t} \quad (7.1)$$

which, given that economic growth (*GROWTH*) is measured as log difference in per capita real GDP (*GDP*), is equivalent to the dynamic panel model:

$$GDP_{i,t} = \alpha\, GDP_{i,t-1} + X_{i,t}\beta' + \delta_1 DEBT_{i,t} + \delta_2 DEBT^2_{i,t} + \eta_i + \tau_t + \varepsilon_{i,t} \quad (7.2)$$

4 Robustness exercises include also a nominal measure of external debt, from the WDI. See section 7.4.1 and Tables 7.8 and 7.9.

5 On the one hand, the ratio of external debt over exports is more informative of a country's ability to generate enough foreign currency to meet its debt obligations. On the other hand, it is more subject to the extreme volatility of exports in LICs. As a result, *DEBT/GDP* is the preferred indicator of indebtedness (a similar choice is done by Cordella, Ricci and Ruiz-Arranz 2010).

6 An alternative solution would make use of the lagged debt ratio, instead of the current one. However, this is likely to introduce an opposite bias. Nevertheless, in section 7.4.1 we show also the results obtained using the lagged debt ratios (in this case the denominators are not smoothed). This robustness exercise is important to address the critique that the partial correlation between debt and growth depends on the choice between contemporaneous, initial or lagged debt ratios (Depetris Chauvin and Kraay 2005).

7 http://www.cid.harvard.edu/ciddata/ciddata.html, last accessed April 2010.

where $X$ is a set of standard control variables including: 1) the log of total investment (*INV*); 2) the population growth rate (*POP*); 3) the log of the primary enrolment rate (*EDUC*); 4) a measure of openness (*OPEN*, the logarithm of the ratio of import plus exports over GDP); 5) the variability of inflation, defined as the standard deviation of inflation in the five-year period (*INF*), which could be thought as a measure of macroeconomic instability; and 6) the TOT growth rate (*TOT*). The debt indicator (*DEBT*), which is the variable of interest, is alternatively the ratio of the NPV of external debt over (filtered) GDP (*DEBT/GDP*) or exports (*DEBT/EXP*). A quadratic term of the debt ratio is included to allow for possible non-linearities in the debt-growth relationship. Finally, $\eta_i$ and $\tau_t$ respectively capture the country- and time-fixed effects and $\varepsilon_{i,t}$ is the classical error term. Country-specific time-invariant effects are taken into account including six regional dummies,[8] while time-fixed effects are controlled for including time dummies. Equation (7.1) is estimated with the two-step System-GMM (see Appendix A for a discussion on the methodology).

This basic setup is augmented including: 1) the institutional indicator (*CPIA*); and 2) interacting the debt indicators with the institutional one. The latter is done by simply interacting the two continuous variables and, for robustness, interacting two alternative categorical measures of institutional quality with *DEBT*. Specifically, the sample is split up between countries with good or bad policies (according to an overall CPIA index below or above the 3.5 threshold, which is the sample median) and also in three categories: weak (CPIA $\leq$ 3.25), medium (3.25 $<$ CPIA $<$ 3.75) and strong (CPIA $\geq$ 3.75) policies, according to the WB classification (IDA and IMF 2007b). The summary statistics of these variables are reported in Appendix Table 7.1. With respect to the institutional classification, observations are almost equally divided between bad versus good policies and between weak, medium and strong institutions.

## 7.3 Descriptive Evidence

Appendix Table 7.2 illustrates the pairwise correlation between real per capita GDP growth (*GROWTH*) and the variables included in the analysis. As expected, larger debt and higher inflation and population growth are correlated with lower economic growth which, instead, is fostered by investment, trade openness, education, institutions and positive changes in the TOT. The alternative measures of indebtedness are highly correlated. They all increase in periods of high inflation and are negatively correlated with the investment in physical and human capital, the level of real per capita GDP and institutional quality. The latter, finally, is better the richer a country is and it is correlated with greater investment and lower inflation.

8 Specifically, the regional dummies refer to: Europe and Central Asia, SSA, South Asia, East Asia and Pacific, Latin America and Caribbean, and North Africa and Middle East.

Appendix Table 7.3 shows that the negative correlation between external debt and economic growth could be driven by the role played by institutions and policies, which are associated with a lower external debt and higher growth rates. In particular, countries with weak institutions have an average NPV of external debt equal to 63 percent of GDP and exhibit negative growth rates. Instead, where the institutions are strong the debt ratio is equal to 35 percent and the average growth rate is 2.8 percent. Thus, this descriptive evidence suggests that excluding the measure of institutional quality from the empirical analysis could generate a decisive omitted variable bias.

Besides, in addition to considering the effects of institutions on GDP growth and external debt, it is worth noting that the relationship between debt and growth could differ according to countries' policies and institutional frameworks. Figure 7.1 clearly illustrates this point: in countries with bad policies (left panel) there is no significant correlation between external debt and economic growth, while the sub-sample of countries with good policies (right panel) shows a negative and significant correlation (-0.29).

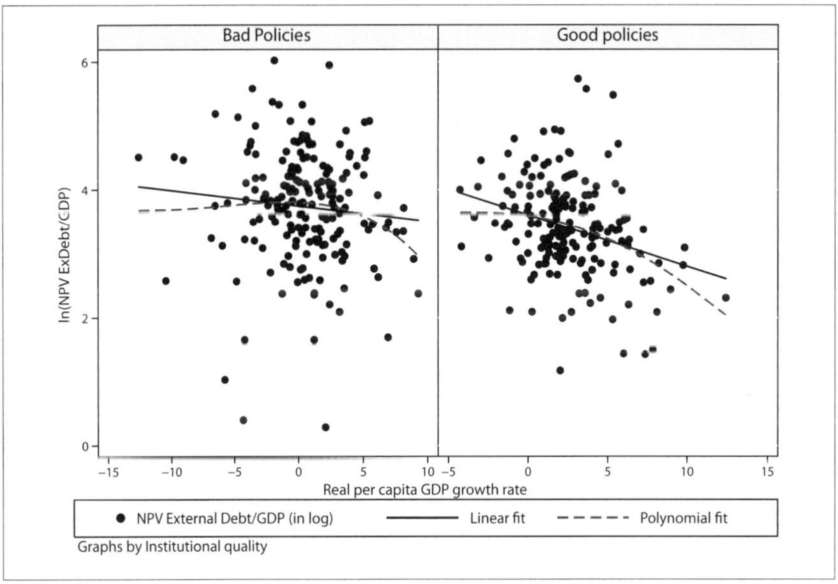


**Figure 7.1 The debt, policies and growth relationship**

*Note*: Elaboration from the dataset used in the regressions reported in Table 7.4. The left panel refers to countries with an overall CPIA score lower than 3.5, while the right panel includes countries with an overall CPIA score equal to/greater than 3.5.

*Source*: Authors' calculations.

## 7.4 Results

Appendix Tables 7.4 and 7.5 show the regression results of the estimation of the growth equation (2) measuring the debt burden, respectively, as the ratio of the NPV of external debt over (smoothed) GDP and over (smoothed) exports. These Appendix Tables provide qualitatively similar results and, in what follows, specific comments refer to Appendix Table 7.4.

Regarding the diagnostics, in all the specifications the Hansen-J statistic does not reject the OIR, confirming that the instrument set can be considered valid,[9] nor the Arellano and Bond (1991) tests for serial correlation, supporting the model's specification.[10]

Results on the control variables are broadly consistent with expectations. They show evidence of conditional convergence and of a positive effect of investment and education on economic growth, even if primary education is not always statistically significant. Trade openness exhibits a positive (but generally not statistically significant) effect on *GROWTH*. Finally, a rise in the TOT fosters economic growth, while an unstable macroeconomic environment, proxied by the volatility of inflation, is associated with lower growth rates.

Moving to the variables of interest, the first two columns show that there is evidence of non-linearities in the debt-growth relationship. The regression coefficients reported in columns (1) and (2) are consistent with a Debt-Laffer curve, whose maximum is reached at ratios of NPV of external debt over GDP equal respectively to 11 and 12. These values are very close to the ones estimated by Pattillo, Poirson and Ricci (2002: 27, column 8 of their Table 6) and by Cordella, Ricci and Ruiz-Arranz (2010), and not far from the the threshold of 20-25 calculated by Clements, Bhattacharya and Nguyen (2004). Nevertheless, the inclusion of the CPIA index (column 2) makes the relationship between debt and growth no longer significant.[11] This finding is in line with the descriptive evidence discussed in section 7.3, according to which institutional quality could simultaneously determine economic growth and the degree of indebtedness. On its own, institutional quality strongly affects the GDP growth rate: a 1 percent increase in the CPIA index almost doubles the average GDP growth rate, raising it by 1.1-1.4 percentage points. In the remaining four columns we inspect the possibility that the debt-growth relationship is heterogeneous with respect to

9 The reported Hansen OIR test refers to all the instruments being exogenous. In addition, difference-in-Hansen statistics provide additional evidence that different subsets of instruments are valid (Roodman 2009b).

10 If the model is well specified, we expect to reject the null hypothesis of no autocorrelation of the first order – AR(1) – and to not reject the hypothesis of no autocorrelation of the second order – AR(2).

11 In Appendix Table 7.5 the Debt-Laffer curve is not significant even without controlling for *CPIA*. Nevertheless, its inclusion dramatically reduces the statistical significance of the debt coefficients. This result is confirmed also in alternative specifications (Appendix Table 7.6).

institutions. Firstly, in column (3), equation (2) is augmented by adding *CPIA* and its interaction with *DEBT/GDP*. Results show that the marginal impact of external debt to economic growth is positive when the CPIA index is low and turns negative for larger values of *CPIA*. More specifically, the turning point is estimated to correspond to a CPIA score of around 2.8. In other words, the evidence suggests that countries with stronger institutions suffer most from the debt burden. This finding is confirmed by alternative specifications. In columns (4) the CPIA score is included in the regression as a dummy variable assuming value 1 (*Good CPIA*) if the institutional index is equal to/higher than 3.5 and it is interacted with the debt variable. The estimates show that the relationship between debt and growth is negative and significant only for countries with good policies. Column (5) allows for a slightly more flexible specification, since the CPIA score is inserted into the regression as a categorical variable (weak, medium and strong institutions) multiplied by *DEBT/GDP*. In this case, *GROWTH* is not affected by debt burdens in countries with weak policies (CPIA score equal to/ lower than 3.25), while a high external debt impinges on economic growth in countries with medium and strong policies. In particular, the marginal effect of debt on growth is equal to -1.1 (-1.6) for countries with medium (strong) policies.

Finally, in the last column, the specification reported in column (4) is augmented allowing for a quadratic term *DEBT/GDP* in order to inspect the possibility that a Debt-Laffer curve arises in countries with bad or good policies. In the former (*Good CPIA* = 0) there is evidence of an inverted U (hump-shaped) relationship, with a maximum at *DEBT/GDP* equal to 31 percent, while in countries with good policies higher debt is associated with lower growth rates, since the quadratic specification has a minimum for a value of *DEBT/GDP* much larger than its sample maximum.

Taking *DEBT/EXP* as a debt burden indicator delivers similar results, apart from the fact that the Debt-Laffer curves in countries with bad or good institutions loose their statistical significance.

In sum, the evidence provided by the estimation of equation (7.2) suggests that institutional quality is a key element in the debt-growth relationship. The standard Debt-Laffer curve looses its significance when the effect of policies is taken into account, suggesting that institutional quality could be a common determinant of both low growth and high debt, as suggested also by Imbs and Ranciere (2008).[12] Moreover, in line with the evidence provided by Cordella, Ricci and Ruiz-Arranz (2010), the estimates show that the debt effect on growth differs according to countries' institutions and policies. Different specifications suggest that in countries with bad policies external debt accumulation is irrelevant for

12 Differently from the estimates presented in this chapter, Imbs and Ranciere (2008) control for time-invariant institutional variables, finding evidence that government effectiveness, rule of law and bureaucratic quality make the linear debt coefficient in the OLS growth regression not significant. However, other institutional variables do not alter the negative link between external debt and growth.

economic growth, while in countries with good policies higher debt is associated with lower growth.[13] Finally, there is no strong evidence of any Debt-Laffer curve, even allowing for different effects of external debt on growth according to the institutional framework.[14]

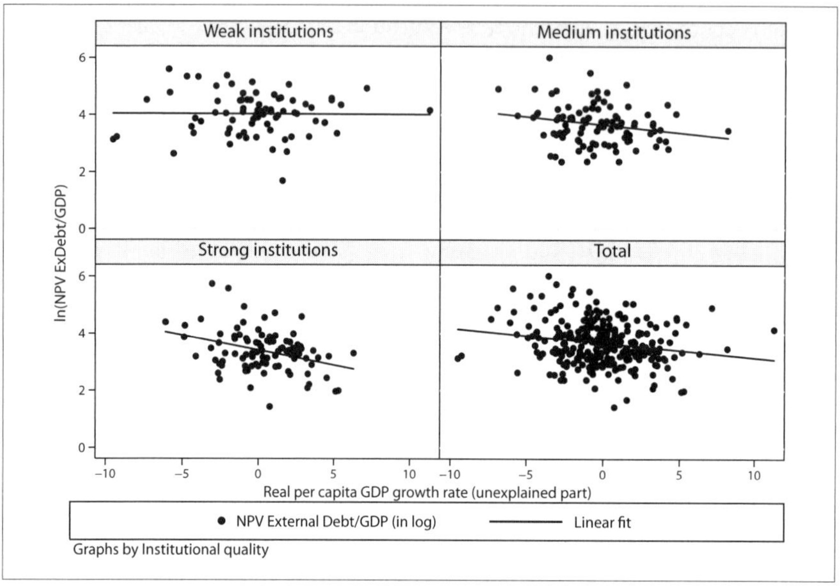


**Figure 7.2 The debt-growth nexus and institutional quality**

*Note*: Different panels refer to countries with weak ($CPIA \leq 3.25$), medium ($3.25 < CPIA < 3.75$) and strong ($CPIA \geq 3.75$) policies and institutions, and to the overall sample. The unexplained part of the real per capita GDP growth rate is the residual of equation 7.1, as estimated in column (2) of Appendix Table 7.4, excluding *DEBT/GDP* and $(DEBT/GDP)^2$.

*Source*: Authors' calculations.

13 Cordella, Ricci and Ruiz-Arranz (2010) state that "countries with very high debt and very poor policies would face a practically flat debt-growth relationship". This is the case discussed in this section, since countries with weak institutions, for which the debt-growth relationship is not significantly different from zero (see column (5) of Appendix Table 7.4), have higher debts than countries with better policies (Appendix Table 7.3). The negative link found for countries with good policies is not completely discordant from Cordella, Ricci and Ruiz-Arranz (2010)'s findings: they estimate a negative relationship at debt levels between 20 and 70 percent of GDP (below 20 the curve is positive and beyond 70 it becomes flat), which covers about the 65 percent of observation with *Good CPIA* = 1.

14 See also additional robustness results discussed in section 7.4.1.

A visual representation of this result is provided in Figure 7.2, which plots the partial correlation between external debt and economic growth for the three sub-samples of countries with weak, medium and strong institutions, conditioned on the full set of controls. The horizontal axis shows the residuals from a growth regression in which all the control variables of equation (7.2) and the overall CPIA score are included. The diagrams clearly highlights the irrelevance of external debt for growth in countries with low CPIA scores, while this relationship is linear and negative for the other countries, especially the ones with strong institutions.

To gauge the economic significance of debt overhang, a simple calculation, based on the coefficients reported in column (5) of Appendix Table 7.4, shows that a reduction in the ratio of the NPV of external debt over GDP from 60 to 20 percent (which roughly corresponds to a change from the third to the first quartile of its sample distribution) is associated with an increase in the GDP growth rate of 1.06 (1.42) in countries with medium (strong) institutions. Moreover, the effect is almost nil and statistically not significant in countries with weak institutional frameworks.

These results indicate that the link between debt and growth depends on institutional quality and that debt relief is likely to be effective only in countries with sound institutions. This finding is consistent with the conclusions reached by Dessy and Vencatachellum (2007) and Harrabi, Bousrih and Mohammed (2007), who estimate that the impact of debt relief on social expenditures and domestic credit to the private sector, respectively, is positive and significant only in countries with good institutions. The presence of debt overhang only in countries with sound institutions could also be partially explained by the role of weak institutions in magnifying the *revolving door* relationship between capital flight and further foreign borrowing (Cerra, Rishi and Saxena 2008). The lack of any significant association between external debt and economic growth in countries with weak institutions and bad policies seems to suggest that these countries do not suffer from debt overhang. In this context, economic growth is likely to be constrained by other factors and positive net resource transfers from donors could help reduce the crowding out of public investments. This interpretation is substantiated by the fact that countries with weak and medium institutions receive an amount of aid which is more than double with respect to GDP than countries with strong institutions (Appendix Table 7.3).

### *7.4.1 Robustness*

The validity of the results discussed in the previous section is tested through a number of robustness tests. In particular, the main findings are robust to changes in the methodology and in the control variable set.

With respect to the first point, reverse causality is addressed by taking lagged debt ratios instead of contemporaneous ones.[15] Results are shown in Appendix Tables 7.6 and 7.7 and are broadly consistent with the ones discussed in the previous section. In particular, when the debt burden is scaled by GDP, there is evidence that past debt is associated with subsequent lower GDP growth in countries with a CPIA score above 3.5 (column (4)). Moreover, the estimates reported in the last column are consistent with debt being irrelevant in countries with bad policies and with a Debt-Laffer curve in the ones with good policies. However, in the latter case, which differs from the results obtained in Appendix Table 7.4, one can still argue that the basic effect of debt on growth is negative, since the maximum of the curve occurs at a very low level of $(DEBT/GDP)_{t-1}$ (about the first decile of its sample distribution).

Finally, regarding the choice of the debt ratio, results are generally robust also when measuring external debt in nominal terms, as showed in Appendix Tables 7.8 and 7.9. Scaling nominal debt by (filtered) GDP or exports confirms the irrelevance of high debt for growth in countries with weak policies and institutions and the presence of debt overhang in countries with good institutional frameworks (columns (3) to (5)). Moreover, the coefficients reported in columns (6) do not reveal evidence of any Debt-Laffer curve: when significant (in Appendix Table 7.8 for *Good CPIA*), the quadratic specification has a maximum for a debt ratio below the first percentile of its sample distribution.

Then, we address the possibility that too many instruments overfit the endogenous variables in the System-GMM, generate biased estimates and weaken the Hansen test for OIR, collapsing the instrument set, as suggested by Roodman (2009b). Regression results show that the main findings are robust to a reduction in the number of instruments[16] (see Appendix Tables 7.8 and 7.9).

As regards the second point, results are generally robust to changes in the set of control variables. The inclusion of the logarithm of the ratio of M2 over GDP and measuring human capital in terms of secondary instead of primary education leaves the main results unaffected, even if secondary education proves not to be significantly correlated with GDP growth. Similar results are obtained controlling for countries' income classification (LICs vs MICs) and including a dummy for HIPCs. More importantly, we are also able to corroborate the basic findings of the chapter controlling for net transfers. The differentiated impact of debt on growth between countries with good or bad policies could be due to different levels of external assistance. However, the inclusion of the logarithm of the ratios of total debt service and official aid over GDP confirm that debt overhang impinges exclusively on countries with better policies and institutions. Finally, the limited

15 A similar strategy is followed also by Lora and Olivera (2007) to estimate the impact of debt on social expenditures.

16 Additional robustness tables are not shown, but they are available from the authors on request.

effect of debt overhang on countries with sound policies and institutions holds also when trying different categorization of the overall CPIA score.

## 7.5 Concluding Remarks

The theoretical underpinnings of the HIPC Initiative are related to the presence of debt overhang, but recent research raised some concerns regarding the idea that high debt is an actual constraint to economic growth in poor countries. In particular, Arslanalp and Henry (2006) conclude that 'The danger is that Gleneagles declaration may amount to a Pyrrhic victory: a symbolic win for advocates of debt relief that clears the conscience of the rich countries, but leaves the real problems of the poor countries unaddressed'. A failure of institutions in HIPC countries to protect investors, property rights and contracts causes debt relief efforts to have a limited impact on growth, investment and social expenditures, as we discuss in Chapter 8. While it is true that in some countries poor institutional quality actually makes external debt irrelevant for the debt-growth relationship (in 2008, 18 HIPCs were classified with weak policies and institutions), it is also the case that in some HIPCs, five in 2008, strong policies and institutions can make debt relief effective in fostering economic growth. Hence, policy-makers should follow a *growth diagnostic* approach (Hausmann, Rodrik and Velasco 2005) to identify on a country-by-country basis which are the real constraints to economic growth, disentangling between the external debt burden and the institutional framework.

Therefore, the main policy implication of this chapter is that debt relief policies should be tailored to country-specific characteristics, as already done in the DSF to evaluate the overall public debt sustainability. The dependence of debt overhang on the overall CPIA index would call for a policy design that makes the amount of debt cancellation conditional upon an actual improvements in institutional quality, which would act as a strong incentive for recipients to strengthen institutions and policies (Chapter 10).

Our analysis points to a rather clear policy indication: namely, governance-related debt relief; on this more research should be directed to refine the ranges of the thresholds for the policy and institutional index which determine the debt irrelevance and the debt overhang zones. The availability of reliable datasets on debt relief allows for the estimation of actual heterogeneous impacts of debt relief on investment and economic growth, according to country-specific policies and institutional frameworks, as discussed in Chapter 8.

Moreover, the focus of this empirical analysis is explicitly on the economic efficiency of debt relief as a valid instrument to trigger economic growth. However, debt cancellation could have had other additional effects on HIPC countries. If perceived as an endorsement of the HIPCs reform efforts by the international community, it could lead to more resource inflows and foreign investments. The recent evidence of a growing number of litigations by vulture funds against HIPCs could be interpreted as a sign that commercial creditors are becoming more confident on future growth prospects of HIPCs (Cordella, Ricci and Ruiz-Arranz 2010 and Chapter 10). Finally, policy-makers should also to take into account a number of other factors in order to implement efficient debt relief initiatives. In particular, as concerns the ineffectiveness of debt overhang in countries with a weak institutional framework, it is worth considering the concept of "odious debt" (section 10.2.2). As argued by Jayachandran and Kremer (2006), the efficiency gains derived from preventing odious debt could be larger than the ones from addressing debt overhang.

In conclusion, we argue that the evidence discussed in this chapter calls for a re-thinking of many areas of current debt relief policies, which have to avoid one-size-fits-all solutions and could consider governance-related debt relief.

## Appendix A – The Empirical Methodology

The dynamic structure of equation (7.1) makes the OLS estimator upwards biased and inconsistent, since the lagged level of income is correlated with the error term. The within transformation does not solve the problem, because of a downward bias and inconsistency (Nickell 1981). A possible GMM technique. Blundell and Bond (1998) show that when $\alpha$ in equation (7.1) approaches to one, so that the dependent variable follows a path close to a random walk, the Differenced-GMM (Arellano and Bond 1991) has poor finite sample properties and it is downwards biased, especially when $T$ is small. Bond, Hoeffler and Temple (2001) argue that this is likely to be a serious issue for autoregressive model like equation (7.1), when the per capita GDP is observed in three or five years averages and $T$ is necessarily small. Therefore, Blundell and Bond (1998) propose another estimator – the System-GMM – derived from the estimation of a system of two simultaneous equations, one in levels (with lagged first differences as instruments) and the other in first differences (with lagged levels as instruments). In multivariate dynamic panel models, the System-GMM estimator is shown to perform better than the Differenced-GMM when series are persistent ($\alpha$ close to unity) and there is a dramatic reduction in the finite sample bias due to the exploitation of additional moment conditions (Blundell, Bond and Windmeijer 2000). However, also the System-GMM is not immune to problems, since, under certain conditions, it is shown to perform worse that simple OLS on time-averaged variables to estimate the speed of convergence. However, Montecarlo simulations of growth regressions show that simple OLS overestimates the steady-state effect of right-hand side variables and the System-GMM, notwithstanding some bias, does better than the Differenced-GMM and the within-group estimators (Hauk and Wacziarg 2009). In presence of heteroscedasticity and serial correlation, the two-step System-GMM uses a consistent estimate of the weighting matrix, taking the residuals from the one-step estimate (Davidson and MacKinnon 2004). Though asymptotically more efficient, the two-step GMM presents estimates of the standard errors that tend to be severely downward biased. However, it is possible to solve this problem using the finite-sample correction to the two-step covariance matrix derived by Windmeijer (2005), which can make two-step robust GMM estimates more efficient than one-step robust ones, especially for System-GMM (Roodman 2009a).

Bond, Hoeffler and Temple (2001) provide a useful insight in the GMM estimation of dynamic growth models,[17] arguing that the pooled OLS and the Fixed-Effects estimators should be considered respectively as the upper and lower bound. As a result, whether the Differenced-GMM coefficient is close to or lower than the within group one, this is likely a sign that the estimates are biased downward (maybe because of a weak instrument problem). Thus, if this

17 One of the main problems of using the GMM estimators with macroeconomic and cross-country data is that they are generally developed for micro data, in which the spatial dimension is very large, and their properties are valid asymptotically.

is the case, the use of System-GMM is highly recommended and its estimates should lie between OLS and Fixed-Effects. This conclusion is supported by the empirical testing of the augmented Solow model (Hoeffler 2002). Presbitero (2006) estimates a model similar to equation (7.2) showing that the System-GMM is a good estimator, at least better than the Differenced-GMM, which is severely downward biased. In particular, there is evidence that using results obtained with the System-GMM confirms that: 1) the System-GMM lies between the upper and lower bound represented by OLS and Fixed-Effects; 2) there is an efficiency gain; and 3) the instrument set is valid. Whether these three conditions are met, as in this case (results not shown for reasons of space), the two-step System-GMM results can be taken as a benchmark for growth regressions.

## Appendix B – Tables

### Table 7.1 Summary statistics

| Variable | Obs. | Mean | Std. Dev. | Min. | Max. |
|---|---|---|---|---|---|
| *GROWTH* | 390 | 1.51 | 3.48 | -12.62 | 27.01 |
| *(DEBT/GDP)* | 378 | 3.57 | 0.83 | 0.29 | 6.03 |
| *(linear)* | 378 | 48.70 | 49.46 | 0.33 | 412.77 |
| $(DEBT/GDP)_{t-1}$ | 375 | 3.47 | 0.92 | 0.60 | 6.33 |
| *(linear)* | 375 | 48.08 | 52.56 | 0.99 | 584.10 |
| *(DEBT/EXP)* | 390 | 4.85 | 0.99 | 1.49 | 7.77 |
| *(linear)* | 390 | 204.09 | 268.08 | 3.45 | 2358.08 |
| $(DEBT/EXP)_{t-1}$ | 386 | 4.77 | 1.12 | -91.00 | 7.95 |
| *(linear)* | 386 | 215.89 | 328.76 | 2.17 | 2866.55 |
| *CPIA* | 390 | 3.49 | 0.75 | 1.00 | 5.60 |
| $GDP_{t-1}$ | 390 | 6.69 | 1.09 | 4.45 | 8.95 |
| *INV* | 390 | 2.97 | 0.35 | 1.72 | 4.46 |
| *POP* | 390 | 1.90 | 1.21 | -3.83 | 7.62 |
| *EDUC* | 390 | 4.51 | 0.30 | 3.21 | 5.09 |
| *OPEN* | 390 | 4.17 | 0.52 | 2.61 | 5.45 |
| *TOT* | 390 | 0.44 | 5.64 | -17.35 | 39.07 |
| *INF* | 390 | 97.89 | 687.44 | 0.23 | 9808.24 |

*Note*: Summary statistics are calculated referring to the large sample used in the regressions reported in Table 7.5, apart from *(DEBT/GDP)* and $(DEBT/GDP)_{t-1}$, which refers to Table 7.4 because of missing data. *(DEBT/GDP)* and *(DEBT/EXP)* are the debt ratios calculated with smoothed denominators, while $(DEBT/GDP)_{t-1}$ and $(DEBT/EXP)_{t-1}$ are the lagged debt ratios calculated with the actual denominators.
*Source*: Authors' calculations.

**Table 7.2 Pairwise correlations**

| | *GROWTH* | *DEBT/ GDP* | *DEBT/ EXP* | $(DEBT/GDP)_{t-1}$ | $(DEBT/EXP)_{t-1}$ | *CPIA* | $GDP_{t-1}$ |
|---|---|---|---|---|---|---|---|
| *GROWTH* | 1.00 | | | | | | |
| *DEBT/GDP* | -0.19* | 1.00 | | | | | |
| *DEBT/EXP* | -0.26* | 0.78* | 1.00 | | | | |
| $(DEBT/GDP)_{t-1}$ | -0.13* | 0.73* | 0.88* | 1.00 | | | |
| $(DEBT/EXP)_{t-1}$ | -0.11* | 0.87* | 0.63* | 0.81* | 1.00 | | |
| *CPIA* | 0.32* | -0.29* | -0.33* | -0.25* | -0.20* | 1.00 | |
| $GDP_{t-1}$ | 0.10 | -0.32* | -0.48* | -0.43* | -0.22* | 0.37* | 1.00 |
| *INV* | 0.46* | -0.05 | -0.26* | -0.17* | -0.01 | 0.26* | 0.22* |
| *POP* | -0.20* | 0.29* | 0.37* | 0.33* | 0.28* | -0.21* | -0.30* |
| *EDUC* | 0.26* | -0.12* | -0.24* | -0.18* | -0.06 | 0.24* | 0.48* |
| *OPEN* | 0.20* | -0.11* | -0.46* | -0.38* | 0.11* | 0.1 | 0.22* |
| *TOT* | 0.20* | -0.02 | -0.08 | -0.05 | -0.04 | -0.08 | 0.04 |
| *INF* | -0.25* | 0.16* | 0.19* | 0.12* | 0.11* | -0.22* | -0.03 |
| | *INV* | *POP* | *EDUC* | *OPEN* | *TOT* | *INF* | |
| *GROWTH* | | | | | | | |
| *DEBT/GDP* | | | | | | | |
| *DEBT/EXP* | | | | | | | |
| $(DEBT/GDP)_{t-1}$ | | | | | | | |
| $(DEBT/EXP)_{t-1}$ | | | | | | | |
| *CPIA* | | | | | | | |
| $GDP_{t-1}$ | 1.00 | | | | | | |
| *INV* | -0.13* | 1.00 | | | | | |
| *POP* | 0.30* | -0.22* | 1.00 | | | | |
| *EDUC* | 0.45* | -0.13* | 0.21* | 1.00 | | | |
| *TOT* | 0.05 | 0.00 | 0.03 | 0.05 | 1.00 | | |
| *INF* | -0.13* | 0.06 | -0.02 | -0.11* | -0.03 | 1.00 | |

*Note*: Correlations are calculated referring to the dataset used in the regressions reported in Table 7.4; * significant at 5 percent. *(DEBT/GDP)* and *(DEBT/EXP)* are the debt ratios calculated with smoothed denominators, while $(DEBT/GDP)_{t-1}$ and $(DEBT/EXP)_{t-1}$ are the lagged debt ratios calculated with the actual denominators.
*Source*: Authors' calculations.

**Table 7.3 External debt, GDP growth and level, by institutional quality**

| Institutional Quality (CPIA Index) | NPV Debt/GDP | Real per capita GDP growth | Real GDP per capita | Aid/GDP | Observations |
|---|---|---|---|---|---|
| Weak | 62.80 | -0.04 | 959 | 10.30 | 120 |
| Medium | 49.23 | 1.77 | 1,222 | 10.75 | 125 |
| Strong | 35.47 | 2.83 | 2,347 | 4.67 | 133 |
| Whole sample | 48.70 | 1.57 | 1,534 | 8.48 | 378 |

*Note*: Numbers refer to the dataset used in the regressions reported in Table 7.4. Numbers for Aid/GDP refers to 377 observations, given a missing value in the strong institutions category.
*Source*: Authors' calculations.

## Table 7.4 NPV of PPG external debt over GDP, System-GMM

| Dep. Var.: *GROWTH* | (1) | (2) | (3) | (4) | (5) | (6) |
|---|---|---|---|---|---|---|
| $GDP_{t-1}$ | -1.773*** | -1.499*** | -1.240*** | -2.029*** | -1.713*** | -1.744*** |
| | [0.448] | [0.535] | [0.434] | [0.396] | [0.417] | [0.404] |
| INV | 5.104*** | 4.508*** | 4.198*** | 3.775*** | 4.148*** | 4.282*** |
| | [1.012] | [1.226] | [1.131] | [1.119] | [1.147] | [1.159] |
| POP | 0.683 | 0.700 | 0.699* | 0.735** | 0.602 | 0.708* |
| | [0.512] | [0.480] | [0.403] | [0.350] | [0.451] | [0.430] |
| EDUC | 3.392** | 3.126** | 1.295 | 0.862 | 0.065 | 1.989 |
| | [1.367] | [1.283] | [1.140] | [1.428] | [1.400] | [1.488] |
| OPEN | 0.901 | 1.358 | 0.599 | 1.897** | 1.078 | 0.668 |
| | [1.226] | [1.145] | [0.848] | [0.947] | [0.710] | [0.808] |
| TOTO | 0.062** | 0.076*** | 0.077** | 0.089*** | 0.084*** | 0.090*** |
| | [0.031] | [0.026] | [0.030] | [0.028] | [0.024] | [0.029] |
| INF | -0.001*** | -0.000*** | -0.001*** | -0.001*** | -0.001*** | -0.001*** |
| | [0.000] | [0.000] | [0.000] | [0.000] | [0.000] | [0.000] |
| (DEBT/GDP) | 2.415** | 1.583 | 1.931* | -0.027 | 0.035 | 4.605** |
| | [1.232] | [1.659] | [1.098] | [0.465] | [0.470] | [2.099] |
| $(DEBT/GDP)^2$ | -0.487*** | -0.310 | | | | -0.664** |
| | [0.170] | [0.222] | | | | [0.276] |
| CPIA | | 1.112*** | 3.630*** | | | |
| | | [0.315] | [1.164] | | | |
| (DEBT/GDP) x CPIA | | | -0.690** | | | |
| | | | [0.306] | | | |
| *Good CPIA* (0,1) | | | | 7.613*** | | 16.493*** |
| | | | | [2.011] | | [5.889] |
| (DEBT/GDP) x Good CPIA | | | | -1.649*** | | -7.002** |
| | | | | [0.537] | | [3.234] |
| $(DEBT/GDP)^2$ x Good CPIA | | | | | | 0.760* |
| | | | | | | [0.430] |
| Omitted categories: *Weak CPIA* and *(DEBT/GDP) x Weak CPIA* | | | | | | |
| *Medium CPIA* (0,1) | | | | | 5.484*** | |
| | | | | | [1.996] | |
| *Strong CPIA* (0,1) | | | | | 8.031*** | |
| | | | | | [2.217] | |
| (DEBT/GDP) x Medium CPIA | | | | | -1.189** | |
| | | | | | [0.505] | |
| (DEBT/GDP) x Strong CPIA | | | | | -1.616*** | |
| | | | | | [0.574] | |

**Table 7.4 continued**

| **Dep. Var.: *GROWTH*** | **(1)** | **(2)** | **(3)** | **(4)** | **(5)** | **(6)** |
|---|---|---|---|---|---|---|
| Observations | 378 | 378 | 378 | 378 | 378 | 378 |
| Number of countries | 110 | 110 | 110 | 110 | 110 | 110 |
| Hansen OIR test | 0.408 | 0.907 | 0.784 | 0.553 | 0.984 | 0.566 |
| AR(1) | 0.002 | 0.003 | 0.006 | 0.003 | 0.004 | 0.002 |
| AR(2) | 0.404 | 0.257 | 0.706 | 0.706 | 0.748 | 0.362 |
| *(DEBT/GDP)* and *(DEBT/GDP)*$^2$ | 0.001 | 0.138 | | | | |
| With *Bad CPIA* | | | | | | 0.043 |
| With Good *CPIA* | | | | | | 0.000 |

*Note*: The table reports regression coefficients and, in brackets, the associated standard errors; * significant at 10 percent; ** significant at 5 percent; *** significant at 1 percent. The model is estimated by Two-Step System GMM, using Stata 10 SE package with XTABOND2 command. As instruments, we use all available lagged values of endogenous variables. The growth rate of the terms of trade (TOT) and the (6) geographic and (4) time dummies (included in the regressions but not shown) are taken as strictly exogenous regressors. *(DEBT/GDP)* is the ratio of the NPV of PPG external debt over (filtered) GDP. As diagnostic, the table shows the p-values of the Hansen test for overidentifying restrictions (OIR, the null is the validity of the instrument set) and of the Arellano and Bond autocorrelation tests of first and second order (AR(1) and AR(2), the null is no autocorrelation). The last three rows show the p-values of the two tailed t-test of annulment of *(DEBT/GDP)* and *(DEBT/GDP)*$^2$, when inserted individually in the regression or interacted with the dummy *Good CPIA*.
*Source*: Authors' calculations.

**Table 7.5 NPV of PPG external debt over exports, System-GMM**

| **Dep. Var.: *GROWTH*** | **(1)** | **(2)** | **(3)** | **(4)** | **(5)** | **(6)** |
|---|---|---|---|---|---|---|
| $GDP_{t-1}$ | -1.626*** | -1.619*** | -1.846*** | -2.086*** | -2.212*** | -2.139*** |
| | [0.511] | [0.423] | [0.427] | [0.586] | [0.487] | [0.501] |
| INV | 5.884*** | 4.439*** | 4.246** | 4.110*** | 4.530*** | 3.831*** |
| | [0.973] | [1.371] | [1.675] | [1.535] | [1.319] | [1.365] |
| POP | 0.454 | 0.409 | 0.573 | 0.693 | 0.479 | 0.456 |
| | [0.496] | [0.610] | [0.500] | [0.447] | [0.461] | [0.537] |
| EDUC | 3.580** | 2.903*** | 2.330** | 2.379* | 1.815 | 3.248*** |
| | [1.647] | [1.116] | [1.153] | [1.310] | [1.374] | [1.143] |
| OPEN | 0.381 | 1.208 | 1.580* | 1.519 | 1.009 | 1.283 |
| | [0.970] | [0.824] | [0.883] | [1.046] | [0.781] | [0.927] |
| TOTO | 0.063** | 0.058** | 0.067** | 0.075*** | 0.072*** | 0.061** |
| | [0.025] | [0.028] | [0.030] | [0.026] | [0.023] | [0.027] |
| INF | -0.001*** | -0.001*** | -0.001*** | -0.001*** | -0.001*** | -0.001*** |
| | [0.000] | [0.000] | [0.000] | [0.000] | [0.000] | [0.000] |
| (DEBT/EXP) | 1.719 | 2.089 | 1.192 | 0.173 | 0.730 | 4.033** |
| | [1.173] | [2.364] | [1.368] | [0.446] | [0.499] | [2.039] |
| $(DEBT/EXP)^2$ | -0.219* | -0.209 | | | | -0.377** |
| | [0.123] | [0.229] | | | | [0.191] |
| CPIA | | 1.368*** | 3.371* | | | |
| | | [0.364] | [1.939] | | | |
| (DEBT/EXP) x CPIA | | | -0.384 | | | |
| | | | [0.360] | | | |
| *Good CPIA* (0,1) | | | | 7.179** | | 16.427*** |
| | | | | [3.070] | | [6.180] |
| (DEBT/EXP) x Good CPIA | | | | -1.135** | | -5.039** |
| | | | | [0.556] | | [2.256] |
| $(DEBT/EXP)^2$ x Good CPIA | | | | | | 0.397* |
| | | | | | | [0.211] |
| Omitted categories: *Weak CPIA* and *(DEBT/EXP) x Weak CPIA* | | | | | | |
| *Medium CPIA* (0,1) | | | | | 11.474*** | |
| | | | | | [2.328] | |
| *Strong CPIA* (0,1) | | | | | 10.581*** | |
| | | | | | [3.070] | |
| (DEBT/EXP) x Medium CPIA | | | | | -2.013*** | |
| | | | | | [0.449] | |
| (DEBT/EXP) x Strong CPIA | | | | | -1.628*** | |
| | | | | | [0.590] | |

**Table 7.5 continued**

| **Dep. Var.: *GROWTH*** | **(1)** | **(2)** | **(3)** | **(4)** | **(5)** | **(6)** |
|---|---|---|---|---|---|---|
| Observations | 390 | 390 | 390 | 390 | 390 | 390 |
| Number of countries | 114 | 114 | 114 | 114 | 114 | 114 |
| Hansen OIR test | 0.440 | 0.614 | 0.597 | 0.551 | 0.926 | 0.805 |
| AR(1) | 0.002 | 0.002 | 0.000 | 0.000 | 0.001 | 0.000 |
| AR(2) | 0.425 | 0.412 | 0.861 | 0.989 | 0.576 | 0.598 |
| *(DEBT/EXP)* and *(DEBT/EXP)²* | 0.161 | 0.658 | | | | |
| With *Bad CPIA* | | | | | | 0.137 |
| With *Good CPIA* | | | | | | 0.192 |

*Note*: The table reports regression coefficients and, in brackets, the associated standard errors; * significant at 10 percent; ** significant at 5 percent; *** significant at 1 percent. The model is estimated by Two-Step System GMM, using Stata 10 SE package with XTABOND2 command. As instruments, we use all available lagged values of endogenous variables. The growth rate of terms of trade (TOT) and the (6) geographic and (4) time dummies (included in the regressions but not shown for reasons of space) are taken as strictly exogenous regressors. *(DEBT/EXP)* is the ratio of the NPV of PPG external debt over (filtered) exports. As diagnostic, the table reports the p-values of the Hansen test for overidentifying restrictions (OIR, the null is the validity of the instrument set) and of the Arellano and Bond autocorrelation tests of first and second order (AR(1) and AR(2), the null is no autocorrelation). The last three rows report the p-values of the two tailed t-test of annulment of *(DEBT/EXP)* and *(DEBT/EXP)²*, when inserted alone in the regression or interacted with the dummy *Good CPIA*.
*Source*: Authors' calculations.

**Table 7.6 Lagged NPV of PPG external debt over GDP, System-GMM**

| Dep. Var.: *GROWTH* | (1) | (2) | (3) | (4) | (5) | (6) |
|---|---|---|---|---|---|---|
| $GDP_{t-1}$ | -1.765*** | -1.669*** | -1.248*** | -1.442*** | -1.022*** | -1.668*** |
| | [0.449] | [0.536] | [0.431] | [0.426] | [0.381] | [0.435] |
| INV | 5.699*** | 4.695*** | 4.256*** | 4.192*** | 4.156*** | 4.566*** |
| | [0.950] | [1.461] | [1.076] | [1.201] | [1.044] | [1.029] |
| POP | 0.642 | 0.643 | 0.696 | 0.761 | 0.653 | 0.581 |
| | [0.433] | [0.518] | [0.547] | [0.496] | [0.465] | [0.437] |
| EDUC | 1.151 | 1.483 | 0.482 | 0.354 | -0.824 | 0.389 |
| | [1.526] | [1.718] | [1.601] | [1.844] | [1.611] | [1.702] |
| OPEN | 0.618 | 1.104 | 1.177 | 1.276 | 0.047 | 1.184 |
| | [1.115] | [1.071] | [0.888] | [1.095] | [0.779] | [0.955] |
| TOTO | 0.075** | 0.086** | 0.066*** | 0.081*** | 0.091*** | 0.093*** |
| | [0.031] | [0.036] | [0.025] | [0.029] | [0.027] | [0.028] |
| INF | -0.001*** | -0.001*** | -0.001*** | -0.001*** | -0.001*** | -0.001*** |
| | [0.000] | [0.000] | [0.000] | [0.000] | [0.000] | [0.000] |
| $(DEBT/GDP)_{t-1}$ | 2.246 | 1.473 | 2.422 | 0.748 | 0.621 | 4.600 |
| | [1.380] | [1.123] | [1.756] | [0.584] | [0.707] | [2.920] |
| $(DEBT/GDP)_{t-1}^2$ | -0.413** | -0.260* | | | | -0.562 |
| | [0.189] | [0.156] | | | | [0.390] |
| CPIA | | 1.256*** | 3.551** | | | |
| | | [0.272] | [1.549] | | | |
| $(DEBT/GDP)_{t-1}$ x CPIA | | | -0.666 | | | |
| | | | [0.424] | | | |
| *Good CPIA* (0,1) | | | | 6.049*** | | 9.195* |
| | | | | [1.681] | | [5.270] |
| $(DEBT/GDP)_{t-1}$ x Good CPIA | | | | -1.266*** | | -3.071 |
| | | | | [0.480] | | [2.915] |
| $(DEBT/GDP)_{t-1}^2$ x Good CPIA | | | | | | 0.248 |
| | | | | | | [0.401] |
| Omitted categories: *Weak CPIA* and *$(DEBT/GDP)_{t-1}$ x Weak CPIA* | | | | | | |
| *Medium CPIA* (0,1) | | | | | 3.337 | |
| | | | | | [2.485] | |
| *Strong CPIA* (0,1) | | | | | 6.119** | |
| | | | | | [2.495] | |
| $(DEBT/GDP)_{t-1}$ x Medium CPIA | | | | | -0.568 | |
| | | | | | [0.652] | |
| $(DEBT/GDP)_{t-1}$ x Strong CPIA | | | | | -1.042 | |
| | | | | | [0.642] | |

**Table 7.6 continued**

| **Dep. Var.: *GROWTH*** | **(1)** | **(2)** | **(3)** | **(4)** | **(5)** | **(6)** |
|---|---|---|---|---|---|---|
| Observations | 375 | 375 | 375 | 375 | 375 | 375 |
| Number of countries | 110 | 110 | 110 | 110 | 110 | 110 |
| Hansen OIR test | 0.460 | 0.722 | 0.691 | 0.508 | 0.843 | 0.564 |
| AR(1) | 0.009 | 0.008 | 0.007 | 0.004 | 0.006 | 0.004 |
| AR(2) | 0.981 | 0.741 | 0.941 | 0.982 | 0.969 | 0.828 |
| $(DEBT/GDP)_{t-1}$ and $(DEBT/GDP)_{t-1}^2$ | 0.019 | 0.182 | | | | |
| With *Bad CPIA* | | | | | | 0.256 |
| With Good *CPIA* | | | | | | 0.120 |

*Note*: The table reports regression coefficients and, in brackets, the associated standard errors; * significant at 10 percent; ** significant at 5 percent; *** significant at 1 percent. The model is estimated by Two-Step System GMM, using Stata 10 SE package with XTABOND2 command. As instruments, we use all available lagged values of endogenous variables. The growth rate of terms of trade (TOT) and the (6) geographic and (4) time dummies (included in the regressions but not shown for reasons of space) are taken as strictly exogenous regressors. $(DEBT/GDP)_{t-1}$ is the lagged ratio of the NPV of PPG external debt over GDP. As diagnostic, the table reports the p-values of the Hansen test for OIR restrictions (the null is the validity of the instrument set) and of the Arellano and Bond autocorrelation tests of first and second order (AR(1) and AR(2), the null is no autocorrelation). The last three rows report the p-values of the two tailed t-test of annulment of $(DEBT/GDP)_{t-1}$ and $(DEBT/GDP)_{t-1}^2$, when inserted alone in the regression or interacted with the dummy *Good CPIA*.

*Source*: Authors' calculations.

**Table 7.7 Lagged NPV of PPG external debt over exports, System-GMM**

| Dep. Var.: ***GROWTH*** | (1) | (2) | (3) | (4) | (5) | (6) |
|---|---|---|---|---|---|---|
| $GDP_{t-1}$ | -1.532*** | -1.665*** | -1.608*** | -1.576*** | -1.571** | -1.624*** |
| | [0.440] | [0.455] | [0.456] | [0.451] | [0.690] | [0.448] |
| INV | 5.250*** | 4.528*** | 4.241*** | 4.437*** | 4.340*** | 4.110*** |
| | [1.122] | [1.090] | [1.099] | [1.156] | [1.195] | [1.103] |
| POP | 0.531 | 0.415 | 0.177 | 0.500 | 0.286 | 0.419 |
| | [0.548] | [0.533] | [0.607] | [0.566] | [0.508] | [0.447] |
| EDUC | 1.808 | 1.752 | 0.890 | 0.708 | 0.124 | 0.895 |
| | [1.370] | [2.123] | [1.346] | [1.620] | [1.508] | [1.710] |
| OPEN | 1.484 | 1.401 | 2.105** | 1.901 | 1.509 | 2.041* |
| | [1.155] | [1.135] | [1.060] | [1.271] | [1.120] | [1.089] |
| TOTO | 0.062** | 0.059** | 0.057** | 0.063** | 0.065** | 0.061** |
| | [0.028] | [0.026] | [0.022] | [0.026] | [0.025] | [0.025] |
| INF | -0.001*** | -0.001*** | -0.001*** | -0.001*** | -0.001*** | -0.001*** |
| | [0.000] | [0.000] | [0.000] | [0.000] | [0.000] | [0.000] |
| $(DEBT/EXP)_{t-1}$ | 1.483 | 1.385 | 3.258** | 0.972* | 1.248** | 3.187* |
| | [1.107] | [1.093] | [1.615] | [0.590] | [0.545] | [1.859] |
| $(DEBT/EXP)_{t-1}^2$ | -0.154 | -0.122 | | | | -0.202 |
| | [0.125] | [0.116] | | | | [0.193] |
| CPIA | | 1.294*** | 5.404*** | | | |
| | | [0.316] | [1.870] | | | |
| $(DEBT/EXP)_{t-1}$ x CPIA | | | -0.848** | | | |
| | | | [0.391] | | | |
| *Good CPIA* (0,1) | | | | 6.514*** | | 12.006** |
| | | | | [2.092] | | [4.755] |
| $(DEBT/EXP)_{t-1}$ x Good CPIA | | | | -1.082**<br>[0.447] | | -2.935<br>[1.988] |
| $(DEBT/EXP)_{t-1}^2$ x Good CPIA | | | | | | 0.149<br>[0.209] |
| Omitted categories: *Weak CPIA* and *$(DEBT/EXP)_{t-1}$ x Weak CPIA* | | | | | | |
| *Medium CPIA* (0,1) | | | | | 5.936** | |
| | | | | | [2.665] | |
| *Strong CPIA* (0,1) | | | | | 10.078*** | |
| | | | | | [2.714] | |
| $(DEBT/EXP)_{t-1}$ x Medium CPIA | | | | | -0.941<br>[0.574] | |
| $(DEBT/EXP)_{t-1}$ x Strong CPIA | | | | | -1.568***<br>[0.589] | |

**Table 7.7 continued**

| **Dep. Var.: *GROWTH*** | **(1)** | **(2)** | **(3)** | **(4)** | **(5)** | **(6)** |
|---|---|---|---|---|---|---|
| Observations | 386 | 386 | 386 | 386 | 386 | 386 |
| Number of countries | 114 | 114 | 114 | 114 | 114 | 114 |
| Hansen OIR test | 0.652 | 0.681 | 0.528 | 0.398 | 0.691 | 0.410 |
| AR(1) | 0.002 | 0.002 | 0.005 | 0.000 | 0.002 | 0.000 |
| AR(2) | 0.793 | 0.497 | 0.634 | 0.634 | 0.717 | 0.629 |
| $(DEBT/EXP)_{t-1}$ and $(DEBT/EXP)_{t-1}^2$ | 0.403 | 0.390 | | | | |
| With *Bad CPIA* | | | | | | 0.041 |
| With *Good CPIA* | | | | | | 0.730 |

*Note*: The table reports regression coefficients and, in brackets, the associated standard errors; * significant at 10 percent; ** significant at 5 percent; *** significant at 1 percent. The model is estimated by Two-Step System GMM, using Stata 10 SE package with XTABOND2 command. As instruments, we use all available lagged values of endogenous variables. The growth rate of terms of trade (TOT) and the (6) geographic and (4) time dummies (included in the regressions but not shown for reasons of space) are taken as strictly exogenous regressors. $(DEBT/EXP)_{t-1}$ is the lagged ratio of the NPV of PPG external debt over exports. As diagnostic, the table reports the p-values of the Hansen test for OIR restrictions (the null is the validity of the instrument set) and of the Arellano and Bond autocorrelation tests of first and second order (AR(1) and AR(2), the null is no autocorrelation). The last three rows report the p-values of the two tailed t-test of annulment of $(DEBT/EXP)_{t-1}$ and $(DEBT/EXP)_{t-1}^2$, when inserted alone in the regression or interacted with the dummy *Good CPIA*.

*Source*: Authors' calculations.

## Table 7.8 Nominal PPG external debt over GDP, System-GMM

| **Dep. Var.:** ***GROWTH*** | **(1)** | **(2)** | **(3)** | **(4)** | **(5)** | **(6)** |
|---|---|---|---|---|---|---|
| $GDP_{t-1}$ | -1.832** | -1.742*** | -1.555*** | -1.918*** | -1.720*** | -1.917*** |
| | [0.882] | [0.423] | [0.402] | [0.368] | [0.539] | [0.508] |
| INV | 5.077** | 4.592*** | 4.281*** | 3.719*** | 4.449*** | 4.211*** |
| | [2.259] | [1.131] | [1.162] | [1.186] | [1.142] | [1.120] |
| POP | 0.648 | 0.739 | 0.887** | 0.728* | 0.578 | 0.700* |
| | [1.505] | [0.463] | [0.431] | [0.395] | [0.475] | [0.368] |
| EDUC | 3.715 | 2.423* | 1.178 | 0.767 | -0.641 | 1.765 |
| | [8.994] | [1.246] | [1.275] | [1.427] | [1.789] | [1.481] |
| OPEN | 1.171 | 1.226 | 1.092 | 1.766* | 0.943 | 1.444 |
| | [6.315] | [0.892] | [0.952] | [0.908] | [0.885] | [0.929] |
| TOTO | 0.052 | 0.071*** | 0.076** | 0.093*** | 0.085*** | 0.095*** |
| | [0.037] | [0.026] | [0.030] | [0.027] | [0.031] | [0.029] |
| INF | -0.001 | -0.001*** | -0.001*** | -0.001*** | -0.001*** | -0.001*** |
| | [0.001] | [0.000] | [0.000] | [0.000] | [0.000] | [0.000] |
| (DEBT/GDP) | 3.309 | 2.925 | 1.945* | -0.046 | 0.287 | 3.799 |
| | [8.174] | [2.590] | [1.060] | [0.486] | [0.569] | [3.353] |
| $(DEBT/GDP)^2$ | -0.538 | -0.440 | | | | -0.510 |
| | [0.990] | [0.312] | | | | [0.383] |
| CPIA | | 1.188*** | 4.356*** | | | |
| | | [0.305] | [1.250] | | | |
| (DEBT/GDP) x CPIA | | | -0.758*** | | | |
| | | | [0.282] | | | |
| *Good CPIA* (0,1) | | | | 8.893*** | | 10.285 |
| | | | | [2.502] | | [9.483] |
| (DEBT/GDP) x Good CPIA | | | | -1.716*** [0.595] | | -2.881 [4.413] |
| $(DEBT/GDP)^2$ x Good CPIA | | | | | | 0.194 [0.503] |
| Omitted categories: *Weak CPIA* and *(DEBT/GDP) x Weak CPIA* | | | | | | |
| *Medium CPIA* (0,1) | | | | | 8.709*** | |
| | | | | | [2.419] | |
| *Strong CPIA* (0,1) | | | | | 10.877*** | |
| | | | | | [2.775] | |
| (DEBT/GDP) x Medium CPIA | | | | | -1.806*** [0.568] | |
| (DEBT/GDP) x Strong CPIA | | | | | -2.115*** [0.662] | |

**Table 7.8 continued**

| Dep. Var.: *GROWTH* | (1) | (2) | (3) | (4) | (5) | (6) |
|---|---|---|---|---|---|---|
| Observations | 375 | 375 | 375 | 375 | 375 | 375 |
| Number of countries | 110 | 110 | 110 | 110 | 110 | 110 |
| Hansen OIR test | 0.412 | 0.880 | 0.688 | 0.553 | 0.946 | 0.792 |
| AR(1) | 0.012 | 0.004 | 0.010 | 0.005 | 0.006 | 0.002 |
| AR(2) | 0.678 | 0.537 | 0.769 | 0.774 | 0.593 | 0.710 |
| *(DEBT/GDP)* and *(DEBT/GDP)²* | 0.116 | 0.136 | | | | |
| With *Bad CPIA* | | | | | | 0.256 |
| With Good *CPIA* | | | | | | 0.003 |

*Note*: The table reports regression coefficients and, in brackets, the associated standard errors; * significant at 10 percent; ** significant at 5 percent; *** significant at 1 percent. The model is estimated by Two-Step System GMM, using Stata 10 SE package with XTABOND2 command. As instruments, we use all available lagged values of endogenous variables. The growth rate of terms of trade (TOT) and the (6) geographic and (4) time dummies (included in the regressions but not shown for reasons of space) are taken as strictly exogenous regressors. *(DEBT/GDP)* is the ratio of nominal PPG external debt over (filtered) GDP. As diagnostic, the table reports the p-values of the Hansen test for OIR restrictions (the null is the validity of the instrument set) and of the Arellano and Bond autocorrelation tests of first and second order (AR(1) and AR(2), the null is no autocorrelation). The last three rows report the p-values of the two tailed t-test of annulment of *(DEBT/GDP)* and *(DEBT/GDP)*$^2$, when inserted alone in the regression or interacted with the dummy *Good CPIA*.
*Source*: Authors' calculations.

**Table 7.9 Nominal PPG external debt over exports, System-GMM**

| Dep. Var.: *GROWTH* | (1) | (2) | (3) | (4) | (5) | (6) |
|---|---|---|---|---|---|---|
| $GDP_{t-1}$ | -1.535*** | -1.432*** | -1.766*** | -2.066*** | -2.334*** | -2.254*** |
| | [0.466] | [0.424] | [0.519] | [0.519] | [0.542] | [0.548] |
| INV | 5.708*** | 4.666*** | 4.434*** | 4.172*** | 4.520*** | 4.028*** |
| | [1.089] | [1.245] | [1.553] | [1.470] | [1.240] | [1.283] |
| POP | 0.393 | 0.470 | 0.699 | 0.608 | 0.517 | 0.382 |
| | [0.560] | [0.574] | [0.528] | [0.459] | [0.504] | [0.526] |
| EDUC | 2.533* | 2.038* | 1.832 | 2.451 | 1.421 | 2.663** |
| | [1.512] | [1.050] | [1.254] | [1.586] | [0.957] | [1.175] |
| OPEN | 1.447 | 1.811 | 1.988* | 1.913 | 1.528* | 1.600* |
| | [1.082] | [1.113] | [1.018] | [1.250] | [0.896] | [0.950] |
| TOTO | 0.047* | 0.056** | 0.052** | 0.068*** | 0.069*** | 0.062*** |
| | [0.028] | [0.025] | [0.026] | [0.024] | [0.025] | [0.023] |
| INF | -0.001*** | -0.000** | -0.001*** | -0.001*** | -0.001*** | -0.001*** |
| | [0.000] | [0.000] | [0.000] | [0.000] | [0.000] | [0.000] |
| (DEBT/EXP) | 4.149* | 4.060* | 1.514 | 0.180 | 0.959 | 2.901 |
| | [2.368] | [2.187] | [1.855] | [0.487] | [0.638] | [3.506] |
| $(DEBT/EXP)^2$ | -0.401* | -0.363* | | | | -0.236 |
| | [0.224] | [0.213] | | | | [0.310] |
| CPIA | | 1.414*** | 3.942 | | | |
| | | [0.350] | [2.919] | | | |
| (DEBT/EXP) x CPIA | | | -0.448 | | | |
| | | | [0.489] | | | |
| *Good CPIA* (0,1) | | | | 7.312** | | 18.667* |
| | | | | [3.220] | | [9.949] |
| (DEBT/EXP) x Good CPIA | | | | -1.056*<br>[0.545] | | -5.187<br>[3.578] |
| $(DEBT/EXP)^2$ x Good CPIA | | | | | | 0.369<br>[0.320] |
| Omitted categories: *Weak CPIA* and *(DEBT/EXP) x Weak CPIA* | | | | | | |
| *Medium CPIA* (0,1) | | | | | 14.446*** | |
| | | | | | [2.792] | |
| *Strong CPIA* (0,1) | | | | | 14.006*** | |
| | | | | | [3.753] | |
| (DEBT/EXP) x Medium CPIA | | | | | -2.360***<br>[0.505] | |
| (DEBT/EXP) x Strong CPIA | | | | | -2.043***<br>[0.665] | |

**Table 7.9 continued**

| **Dep. Var.: *GROWTH*** | **(1)** | **(2)** | **(3)** | **(4)** | **(5)** | **(6)** |
|---|---|---|---|---|---|---|
| Observations | 388 | 388 | 388 | 388 | 388 | 388 |
| Number of countries | 114 | 114 | 114 | 114 | 114 | 114 |
| Hansen OIR test | 0.279 | 0.673 | 0.700 | 0.581 | 0.919 | 0.652 |
| AR(1) | 0.002 | 0.002 | 0.000 | 0.000 | 0.000 | 0.001 |
| AR(2) | 0.485 | 0.605 | 0.988 | 0.770 | 0.368 | 0.568 |
| *(DEBT/EXP)* and *(DEBT/EXP)*$^2$ | 0.202 | 0.138 | | | | |
| With *Bad CPIA* | | | | | | 0.661 |
| With *Good CPIA* | | | | | | 0.190 |

*Note*: The table reports regression coefficients and, in brackets, the associated standard errors; * significant at 10 percent; ** significant at 5 percent; *** significant at 1 percent. The model is estimated by Two-Step System GMM, using Stata 10 SE package with XTABOND2 command. As instruments, we use all available lagged values of endogenous variables. The growth rate of terms of trade (TOT) and the (6) geographic and (4) time dummies (included in the regressions but not shown for reasons of space) are taken as strictly exogenous regressors. *(DEBT/EXP)* is the ratio of nominal PPG external debt over (filtered) exports. As diagnostic, the table reports the p-values of the Hansen test for OIR restrictions (the null is the validity of the instrument set) and of the Arellano and Bond autocorrelation tests of first and second order (AR(1) and AR(2), the null is no autocorrelation). The last three rows report the p-values of the two tailed t-test of annulment of *(DEBT/EXP)* and *(DEBT/EXP)*$^2$, when inserted alone in the regression or interacted with the dummy *Good CPIA*.

*Source*: Authors' calculations.

## Table 7.10 List of countries

| Country | WB code | Region | Country | WB code | Region |
|---|---|---|---|---|---|
| Albania | ALB | ECA | Latvia | LVA | ECA |
| Algeria | DZA | MENA | Lebanon | LBN | MENA |
| Argentina | ARG | LAC | Lesotho | LSO | SSA |
| Armenia | ARM | ECA | Lithuania | LTU | ECA |
| Azerbaijan | AZE | ECA | Macedonia, FYR | MKD | ECA |
| Bangladesh | BGD | SA | Madagascar | MDG | SSA |
| Belarus | BLR | ECA | Malawi | MWI | SSA |
| Belize | BLZ | LAC | Malaysia | MYS | EAP |
| Benin | BEN | SSA | Mali | MLI | SSA |
| Bolivia | BOL | LAC | Mauritania | MRT | SSA |
| Botswana | BWA | SSA | Mauritius | MUS | SSA |
| Brazil | BRA | LAC | Mexico | MEX | LAC |
| Bulgaria | BGR | ECA | Moldova | MDA | ECA |
| Burkina Faso | BFA | SSA | Mongolia | MNG | EAP |
| Burundi | BDI | SSA | Morocco | MAR | MENA |
| Cameroon | CMR | SSA | Mozambique | MOZ | SSA |
| Cape Verde | CPV | SSA | Nepal | NPL | SA |
| Central African Republic | CAF | SSA | Nicaragua | NIC | LAC |
| Chad | TCD | SSA | Niger | NER | SSA |
| Chile | CHL | LAC | Nigeria | NGA | SSA |
| China | CHN | EAP | Pakistan | PAK | SA |
| Colombia | COL | LAC | Panama | PAN | LAC |
| Comoros | COM | SSA | Papua New Guinea | PNG | EAP |
| Congo, Dem. Rep. | ZAR | SSA | Paraguay | PRY | LAC |
| Congo, Rep. | COG | SSA | Peru | PER | LAC |
| Costa Rica | CRI | LAC | Philippines | PHL | EAP |
| Cote d'Ivoire | CIV | SSA | Poland | POL | ECA |
| Croatia | HRV | ECA | Romania | ROM | ECA |
| Czech Republic | CZE | ECA | Russian Federation | RUS | ECA |
| Djibouti | DJI | MENA | Rwanda | RWA | SSA |
| Dominican Republic | DOM | LAC | Senegal | SEN | SSA |
| Ecuador | ECU | LAC | Sierra Leone | SLE | SSA |
| Egypt, Arab Rep. | EGY | MENA | Slovak Republic | SVK | ECA |
| El Salvador | SLV | LAC | Solomon Islands | SLB | EAP |
| Equatorial Guinea | GNQ | ECA | South Africa | ZAF | SSA |
| Eritrea | ERI | SSA | Sri Lanka | LKA | SA |
| Estonia | EST | ECA | St. Lucia | LCA | LAC |
| Ethiopia | ETH | SSA | Swaziland | SWZ | SSA |
| Gabon | GAB | SSA | Syrian Arab Republic | SYR | MENA |
| Gambia, The | GMB | SSA | Tajikistan | TJK | ECA |
| Georgia | GEO | ECA | Tanzania | TZA | SSA |
| Ghana | GHA | SSA | Thailand | THA | EAP |

**Table 7.10 continued**

| Country | WB code | Region | Country | WB code | Region |
|---|---|---|---|---|---|
| Guatemala | GTM | LAC | Togo | TGO | SSA |
| Guinea | GIN | SSA | Tonga | TON | EAP |
| Guinea-Bissau | GNB | SSA | Trinidad and Tobago | TTO | LAC |
| Guyana | GUY | LAC | Tunisia | TUN | MENA |
| Haiti | HTI | LAC | Turkey | TUR | ECA |
| Honduras | HND | LAC | Uganda | UGA | SSA |
| Hungary | HUN | ECA | Ukraine | UKR | ECA |
| India | IND | SA | Uruguay | URY | LAC |
| Indonesia | IDN | EAP | Uzbekistan | UZB | ECA |
| Jamaica | JAM | LAC | Vanuatu | VUT | EAP |
| Jordan | JOR | MENA | Venezuela, RB | VEN | LAC |
| Kazakhstan | KAZ | ECA | Vietnam | VNM | EAP |
| Kenya | KEN | SSA | Yemen, Rep. | YEM | MENA |
| Kyrgyz Republic | KGZ | ECA | Zambia | ZMB | SSA |
| Lao PDR | LAO | EAP | Zimbabwe | ZWE | SSA |

*Note*: The country code and the geographic region refer to the World Bank Country Classification (http://go.worldbank.org/K2CKM78CC0, last accessed: September 2010). ECA: Europe & Central Asia; SSA: Sub-Saharan Africa; SA: South Asia; EAP: East Asia \& Pacific; LAC: Latin America & Caribbean; MENA: North Africa & Middle East.

# Chapter 8
# An Ex-Post Evaluation of Debt Relief[1]

## 8.1 Introduction

In countries with weak institutions and unsound policies, external debt does not appear to be a binding constraint on economic growth. Therefore, given budget constraints and limited funding, debt reduction should be directed to countries with good institutions, in order to be effective and growth-enhancing. These conclusions are based on an indirect evidence which relates external debt, investment and economic growth. However, there is nothing in this relationship which assures that debt relief would necessarily boost investment and GDP growth. Therefore, given that the history of debt relief is now sufficiently long, the associated costs are soaring and the outcomes are at least uncertain, it should be of particular interest for policy-makers to evaluate how past debt relief episodes affected economic growth and other macroeconomic variables in recipient countries. Strangely, the empirical literature has devoted only limited attention to this aspect and little effort has been made in collecting reliable data on actual debt relief granted to developing countries, one notable exception being the valuable work by Depetris Chauvin and Kraay (2005). However, only looking at the direct impact of debt relief it is possible to draw more accurate indications to design more effective debt relief initiatives. To do so, however, it is necessary not only to draw lessons from past experiences (both successes and failures), but also to provide adequate incentives to debtor countries. The way in which debt relief is allocated could be a powerful tool to encourage some countries to undertake structural reforms and improve their governance in exchange for future debt cancellation. Thus, debt relief could be used to accelerate the shift from the traditional *ex-ante* conditionality to *ex-post* governance conditionality, rewarding the countries which achieved good results in improving their policies and institutions. Hence, we inspect the determinants of debt relief allocation in order to assess whether donors are moving towards some kind of *ex-post* governance conditionality and their actual ability to design adequate incentive mechanisms.

---

1 Material from this article was originally published in *Development Policy Review* 27(5), 529-559 (DOI: 10.1111/j.1467-7679.2009.00458.x). The definitive version is available at: http://www3.interscience.wiley.com/journal/122540115/abstract.

### *8.1.1 Is Debt Relief Rewarding Institution Building?*

It is generally argued that debt forgiveness should act as an incentive to recipient countries to improve their institutions and undergo adjustments leading to better policies. Traditional conditionality is based on an ex-ante commitment by debtor governments, but it suffers from a number of shortcomings, since the imperfect monitoring by donors and multilateral institutions creates an incentive for moral hazard by recipient governments. Moreover, a large number of conditions attached to aid disbursements or debt relief is perceived as intrusive in national sovereignity and it is likely to reduce the country's ownership of reform programs (Drazen 2002). The standard policy conditionality is based on the principle of making the recipient government accountable to donors and, in this way, it undermines the accountability of the government to society. Donors, through governance conditionality, could reinforce the accountability of the government to their citizens following an alternative strategy rewarding *ex-post* the countries that attained a given level of governance and that achieved significant improvements in their policies and institutional framework.

Given the large cost of debt relief, it is worth analyzing the behavior of donors in order to assess whether they were able to allocate resources to virtuous countries, adopting *ex-post* governance conditionality as guiding principle, at least in recent years. The existing literature on the determinants of debt relief shows that, in the past, debt forgiveness was not granted to countries with good governance (Neumayer 2002), even though, since 2000, debt relief programs seem to be influenced by recipients' institutional quality (Freytag and Pehnelt 2009), especially when multilateral donors are involved (Depetris Chauvin and Kraay 2007). In particular, Neumayer (2002) finds that debt forgiveness is mainly driven by countries' needs. Using a number of governance indicators, the author shows that, in a cross-section of 85 developing countries, there is only a statistical (but modest) association between the degree of voice and accountability and regulatory activity of recipient governments and the amount of debt forgiven over the period 1989-1998. On a smaller sample of 62 LICs, Depetris Chauvin and Kraay (2007) find instead that both aid and debt relief, particularly when granted by multilateral institutions, recently started to be positively correlated with policy and institutional quality. In the same vein, using more recent data for 123 developing countries from 1990 to 2004, Freytag and Pehnelt (2009) find a change in donors' behavior, which was mainly driven by "political rationality" in the nineties but mostly by "economic rationality" in the new millennium. Specifically, improvements in the rule of law and government effectiveness are positively associated with the amount of debt relief in 2000-2004, while these indicators do not appear to influence the probability of being eligible for debt forgiveness, as found also by Neumayer (2002).

### *8.1.2 The Rationale for Debt Relief*

Notwithstanding the recent decline in debt ratios, the evidence on the effectiveness of debt relief in enhancing economic growth and reducing poverty is broadly inconclusive. Depetris Chauvin and Kraay (2005) show that the $100 billion in debt relief granted by donors to LICs between 1989 and 2003 had a very limited effect on public spending, investment and growth in recipient countries.

A first argument supporting debt relief is debt overhang, but it does not seem consistent with what it has been happening in the current debt crisis. In a situation in which HIPCs keep on receiving net positive resource inflows from (non profit maximizers) official creditors, debt could limit economic growth just because it reduces the incentive of countries to invest and develop so that they can continue on meeting the eligibility criteria for debt relief and concessional lending (Koeda 2008, Chapter 6). The empirical literature reviewed in Chapter 6 suggests that the validation of the presence of debt overhang in poor countries is ambiguous. Recent studies provide evidence of a sort of debt-irrelevance zone beyond a certain debt threshold, and suggest that the Debt-Laffer curve could be a spurious relationship driven by country-specific factors jointly determining low growth rates and high debt. Specifically, our empirical analysis in Chapter 7 shows that policies and institutions are those factors and that debt overhang is effective exclusively in countries with sound institutions.

The crowding out of investments due to debt-service payments represents a second channel through which high debt could impinge on economic growth, even if its impact on GDP growth in HIPCs might be small or not significant (Cohen 1993, Fosu 1996, Loxley and Sackey 2008, Clements, Bhattacharya and Nguyen 2004 and section 6.3.1).

According to the existing evidence, there might be a positive effect of debt relief on subsequent economic growth rates, at least in countries with good institutions. Nevertheless, the theoretical arguments are not so straightforward and debt relief does not necessarily lead to an improvement in recipients' economic and social indicators.

In part, the actual effect of debt relief depends on it being an alternative source, but not a perfect substitute, of foreign aid. On the one hand, differently from foreign aid, debt relief does not consists of a direct inflow of fresh resources but in a decline in debt-service payments. This could reduce the negative effects of foreign aid due to the exchange rate over-valuation (Rajan and Subramanian 2010) and rent-seeking behavior, which could generate a sort of aid curse similar to the natural resource curse (Djankov, Montalvo and Reynal-Querol 2008). On the other hand, debt relief, similarly to foreign aid, generates a state of aid dependence in debtor countries, which could undermine institutional quality (debt relief curse), by weakening and distorting political accountability, encouraging corruption, fomenting conflict over control of funds, siphoning off scarce talent from the public sector and alleviating pressures to reform inefficient policies and institutions (Knack 2001; Moss, Pettersson and van de Walle 2008; Wood 2008).[2]

Traditional debt relief does not necessarily provide additional resources to recipient countries: when debt cancellation concerns debt that was not being serviced, it does not free up resources with respect to a situation without debt relief. By contrast, the inclusion of multilateral debt within the HIPC Initiative was a major innovation which is likely to have actually raised the amount of resource available to debtor countries. Contrary to bilateral debts, multilateral loans were serviced because a default on a multilateral debt obligation is likely to cut off the debtor country from international official or private credit (Eurodad 2005). Nevertheless, even when debt-service payments actually decrease, debt relief has a minimal impact on HIPCs' net resource transfers, which are largely driven by net lending and grants (Arslanalp and Henry 2006), consistent with the literature which does not find a robust evidence of the crowding out effect.

A further reason why debt relief could be ineffective is that it is not considered as a positive signal of countries undertaking structural reforms and changing their policies according to debt reduction initiatives. Easterly (2002) argues that investors interpreted debt relief as a signal for countries that, given their large external debt, are likely to have a high (and stable over time) discount rate against the future: this would mean that governments will keep on over-borrowing and trading off consumption today versus consumption tomorrow, heavily taxing the private sector and discouraging investors. However, this argument is strictly based on the hypothesis that debt relief does not affect the government's discount rate. Theoretically, this could be the case when gradual debt relief does not provide the right incentives, creating the opportunity for moral hazard and opportunistic behaviors. Easterly (2002) shows that the disappointing evolution of a number of policy indicators, which should have improved after debt relief, is consistent with indebted countries having high discount rates that remained unchanged before and after debt relief. However, Allen and Weinhold (2000) provide less clear-cut evidence and, more generally, Easterly's analysis, limited to the period 1979-1997, cannot exclude that the debt relief granted under the HIPC Initiative is able to change the development orientation of debtor countries' governments.

Finally, and related to the latter point, it is reasonable to assume that debt relief would become more effective with time, since governments and IFIs approach to debt relief largely advances on a learning-by-doing basis, as testified by the

2 Contrary to this point, Kanbur (2000) argues that debt relief could actually reduce aid dependence especially because of the lower energy, time and human capital wasted in debt rescheduling and negotiations with donors to keep a resource inflows large enough to repay debt obligations. Nevertheless, HIPC debt relief is not a sort of *arm's length lending*, given the number of conditions to be met under the HIPC Initiative. Moreover, even if time and effort committed by public officials to debt management could be redeployed in more productive areas after debt relief, such benefits would not become evident for many years (Moss 2006).

incremental improvements in the HIPC Initiative (i.e. from the original to the E-HIPC and finally to the MDRI) and in the DSF (Part 1).

### *8.1.3 Objectives and Structure*

The hypothesis discussed in the previous section suggest that debt relief effectiveness could be undermined by: 1) its limited impact on the government budget; 2) its negative signalling effect; and 3) worsening institutional quality. The first point should be the most effective one, given that a significant share of debt relief concerns debt which was not likely to be serviced anyway. The second explanation is consistent with the former, given that investors would have probably already discounted the write-off of the debt actually forgiven and, therefore, are not likely to change their strategies because of a formal debt relief announcement. Finally, the last point is the most critical: firstly, one should validate the link between debt relief and institutional quality and, only after that, one could investigate whether worsening institutions are another element undermining debt relief effectiveness. Only if these two hypothesis are confirmed one could argue that the larger is the debt relief's share in government revenues, the lower the incentives to invest in effective public institutions.

With respect to the last point, there is a vast literature on aid allocation showing how foreign aid and IMF lending mainly responds to political incentives and donors' strategic interests in recipient countries (Alesina and Dollar 2000; Barro and Lee 2005), even if recent trends go in the direction of increasing selectivity in terms of democracy and rule of law (Dollar and Levin 2006). By contrast, the choice of granting debt relief received limited attention, even if some authors look at the determinants of debt relief in order to assess what drives donors' behavior (Neumayer 2002; Depetris Chauvin and Kraay 2007; Freytag and Pehnelt 2009). One contribution of this chapter aims at filling this gap by estimating a two-stage model of debt relief to identify how different factors affect the likelihood of receiving debt relief and the amount of debt actually forgiven. With respect to the existing literature, this contribution updates the analysis of Neumayer (2002), still controlling for recipients' needs and explicitly focusing on HIPCs, in order to test whether HIPC relief is targeting more needy and better governed countries. Moreover, in line with Depetris Chauvin and Kraay (2007), we measure the policy and institutional framework using (among other indicators) the overall CPIA score, on which the WB lending policies are also based. This represents an advantage in the sense that we can better identify, by the *ex-post* evaluation of creditors' behaviour, whether donors moved toward consistent lending policies, rewarding countries with better policies and sounder institutions and improving debt relief effectiveness. Finally, with respect to Freytag and Pehnelt (2009), we are able to measure more precisely the actual economic effect of debt reductions, since we adopt a more accurate indicator of debt relief, calculated in NPV terms, following Depetris Chauvin and Kraay (2007), instead of face value terms.

After assessing how debt relief is allocated by donors, we expand the analysis focusing on its effectiveness. A recent strand of literature explicitly addresses the outcomes of actual debt relief on growth, investment and fiscal balance (Depetris Chauvin and Kraay 2005, Dömeland and Kharas 2009, Johansson 2010), on credit availability to the private sector (Harrabi, Bousrih and Mohammed 2007) and on social services expenditures (Dessy and Vencatachellum 2007): the results are mixed (Chapter 6).

The main contribution of this chapter is to build on this literature providing additional evidence of the consequences of debt forgiveness on different macroeconomic indicators and on institutional quality.[3] We focus on a sample of developing countries and also explicitly on HIPCs, trying to disentangle possible heterogeneous effects according to the country-specific institutional framework, given that a certain level of institutional quality is required in order to benefit from debt relief (Asiedu 2003). In particular, with respect to Depetris Chauvin and Kraay (2005), who represent the benchmark for this analysis, this chapter extends their analysis looking at the outcomes of debt relief granted at the beginning of the new millennium. This is of particular interest because those were the years when multilateral debt relief increased substantially as a result of the HIPC Initiative and also because it allows for testing whether the IFIs are learning from previous debt relief efforts and improving its effectiveness over time.

This represents an early evaluation of debt relief effectiveness and more time and data are certainly required to better establish whether HIPC debt relief was able to achieve its targets in terms of poverty reduction and sustained economic growth, without determining any negative side-effect. In particular, the 100 percent debt cancellation granted by the MDRI could be more effective than traditional debt relief in helping countries escaping a situation of aid dependence (Koeda 2008). Nevertheless, given the relevance of this issue for policy-makers and especially the hundred of millions living in poverty, making more data and analysis available could lead to better-informed decision-making and, consequently, to better results for poor countries and their citizens.

## 8.2 The Effects of Debt Relief in Poor Countries

This section presents the results of the debt relief programs in terms of debt-service reduction and poverty reduction expenditures and reviews the relevant literature on debt relief effectiveness.

---

3 Also in this case, the overall CPIA score is a good indicator in evaluating whether debt relief is actually pushing recipient governments to improve their institutions. Given that debt relief programs and lending criteria are based on these indicators, we expect debtors to improve their policy and institutional framework according to the aspects included in the CPIA score.

### *8.2.1 Debt Relief Delivered ...*

As of September 2009 the committed debt relief under the HIPC Initiative amounted to 72 billions of US dollars in nominal terms, of which 48 billions delivered to the 26 post-completion point countries and 24 billions to the nine interim HIPCs. The MDRI added other 45 billions in assistance for the 26 post-completion point countries, so that, in total, HIPC and MDRI assistance amounts to US$ 117 billions (IDA and IMF 2009 and Appendix Table 8.4).[4] To put debt relief figures in perspective, one should consider that the estimated total cost of supporting the MDG financing gap in all countries is around US$121 billion in 2006, raising to US$189 billion in 2015, while ODA was equal to US$ 103.7 billion in 2007 (95 billion without considering debt relief).

In particular, at country level, the UN Millennium Project estimates that Uganda needs US$ 33 billion to meet the MDG over the period 2005-2015, which amounts, on average, to 90 dollars per capita and 26 percent of GDP per year. Of this sum, 17 billions (13.7 percent of GDP) have to be financed through external budget support. The costs of funding the MDG represent a similar share of GDP also in Ghana (26.3 percent) and Tanzania (27.7 percent) where the external budget support should be equal, respectively, to 15.6 and 16.6 percent of GDP (Sachs et al. 2004). By contrast, as of September 2008, these countries received debt relief under the HIPC and MDRI programs only for a small share of their expected expenditures.[5]

### *8.2.2 ... and Some Results*

This section discusses the effects of debt forgiveness in poor countries. Firstly, we inspect the official data to see whether debt relief actually freed up resources in the government budget and whether this money was targeted to increasing pro-poor spending (subsection 8.2.2.1). However, more resources and more expenditures on poverty reduction, as incorporated in the PRSP, are not necessarily correlated with real improvements in the welfare of the poor: the evidence about the welfare effects of aid operating through additional public expenditures is contrasting (Gomanee et al. 2005; Gomanee, Girma and Morrissey 2005; Weiss 2008) and, with respect to HIPCs, it has been highlighted that, notwithstanding a track record

4 Since September 2009, two other countries reached completion point (Congo DR and Afghanistan), but the most recent official data on the cost of the HIPC and MDRI programs refer to September 2009. However, in this chapter we refer to the country classification under the HIPC Initiative and to data available as of September 2008.

5 In particular, debt relief for Ghana, Tanzania and Uganda totalled, respectively, US$ 7.4, 6.8 and 5.5 billion (IDA and IMF 2008). Moreover, over the period 1988-2003, those countries received, on average per year, debt relief in present value terms, ranging from 1.1 to 6.4 dollars per capita and from 0.3 to 2.9 percent of their GDP (our calculation is based on data by Depetris Chauvin and Kraay 2005).

of better policy performance and increasing pro-poor spending, heavily indebted countries are still far away from achieving the MDG (UNCTAD 2006, Dömeland and Kharas 2009). In subsection 8.2.2.2 we review the most relevant literature on debt relief effectiveness, focusing on its consequences on social spending, economic performance and on more direct measures of well-being, such as education outcomes.

*8.2.2.1 More resources*

A first result of debt relief is the relaxing of the budget constraint, with HIPCs reducing the share of debt service over GDP (and revenues). According to official WB data, from 1999 to 2007, debt service in the 33 post-decision point HIPCs decreases from 22 to 8 percent of revenues and from 3.9 to 1.5 percent of GDP. This trend is projected to continue in the following years when the ratio of debt service to GDP is expected to be below 1 percent (Figure 8.1).

Given the design of the HIPC Initiative, which strengthens the links between debt relief and poverty-reduction efforts, the savings from debt-service payments should pay for increases in poverty reduction expenditures: the latter have increased from 34.7 percent of government revenues in 1999 to 50 percent in 2005 and they are projected to raise above this threshold; as a share of GDP, pro-poor spending is estimated to increase from 7 percent in 1999 to almost 10 percent in 2012 (Figure 8.1).

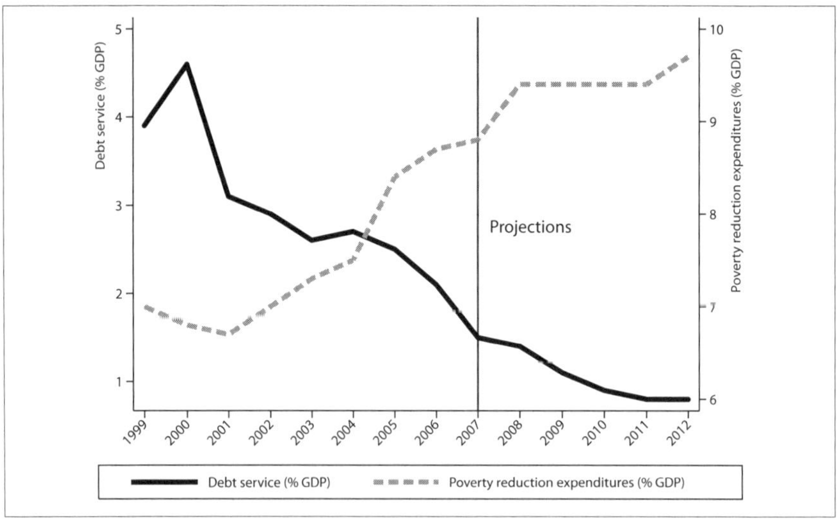


**Figure 8.1 Debt service and poverty reduction expenditures in HIPCs**

*Source*: Authors' elaboration based on IDA and IMF (2008, Table 1). Data refers to the 33 post-decision point HIPCs as of September 2008. The ratios for 2007 are preliminary, while from 2008 onwards are projections.

Notwithstanding this positive aggregate picture, the situation at country level is heterogeneous, with some countries still facing harsh financing constraints and with limited poverty-reducing expenditures, as shown in Figure 8.2. Part of this heterogeneity could be attributed to different definitions of pro-poor expenditures across countries and poor performance could be due to the fact that countries are still in the interim period, when they receive provisional relief on debt service. Nevertheless, significant differences persist between countries at completion point, when lenders actually provide the full debt relief committed at decision point. In particular, in the Congo, DR and Guinea-Bissau more than 8 percent of GDP had to be allocated to service external debt in 2007. The situation is also critical in Gambia, where debt service was 4.1 percent of GDP, in Bolivia and Sao Tome and Principe (which reached completion point in 2007, 2001 and 2007 respectively), where expenditures for debt service were above 2 percent of GDP. Moreover, notwithstanding an average reduction in debt service payments after decision point, the variability across countries increased substantially (the coefficient of variation increased from 0.64 at decision point to 1.35 in 2007).

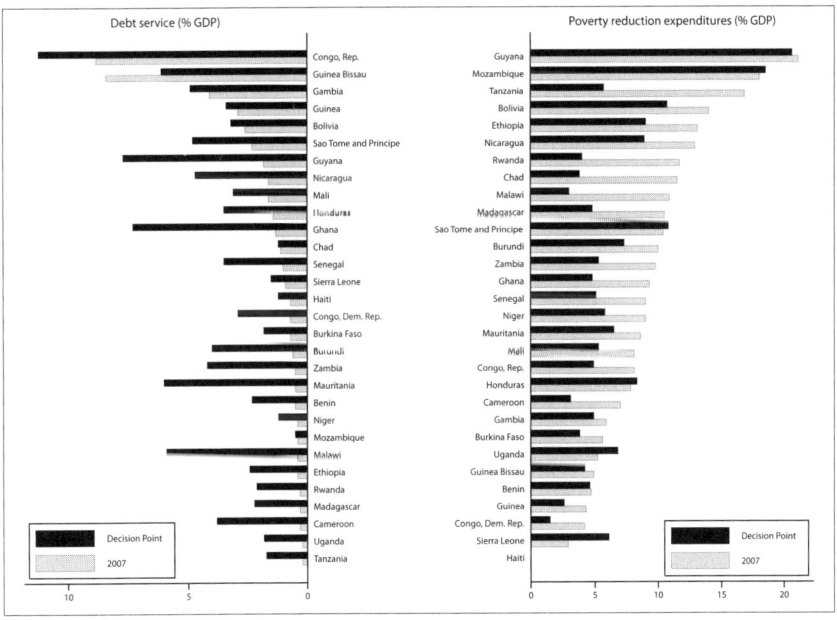


**Figure 8.2 Debt service and poverty reduction expenditures in selected HIPCs**
*Source*: Authors' calculations based on data from several HIPC Initiative and MDRI – Status of Implementation, published by the WB and the IMF. Data refer to the 30 post-decision point HIPCs as of September 2008 (Afghanistan, Central African Republic and Liberia are excluded because they reached decision point in 2007 and 2008 (Liberia)). Haiti has missing data on poverty reduction expenditures.

The opposite happened with respect to pro-poor spending, which, apart from increasing on average, became more uniform across countries (the coefficient of variation decreased from 0.65 at decision point to 0.45 in 2007). Nevertheless, there are countries lagging behind. In particular, there are interim HIPCs (such as Guinea, Congo DR and Guinea-Bissau), but also completion point countries (Benin and Sierra Leone, which reached completion point, respectively, in 2003 and 2006) which allocate less than 5 percent of GDP to poverty reduction spending. Sierra Leone, Uganda and Honduras, notwithstanding their status of completion point countries, have reduced the amount of resources spent for poverty reduction below the HIPC average of 8.8 percent of GDP.

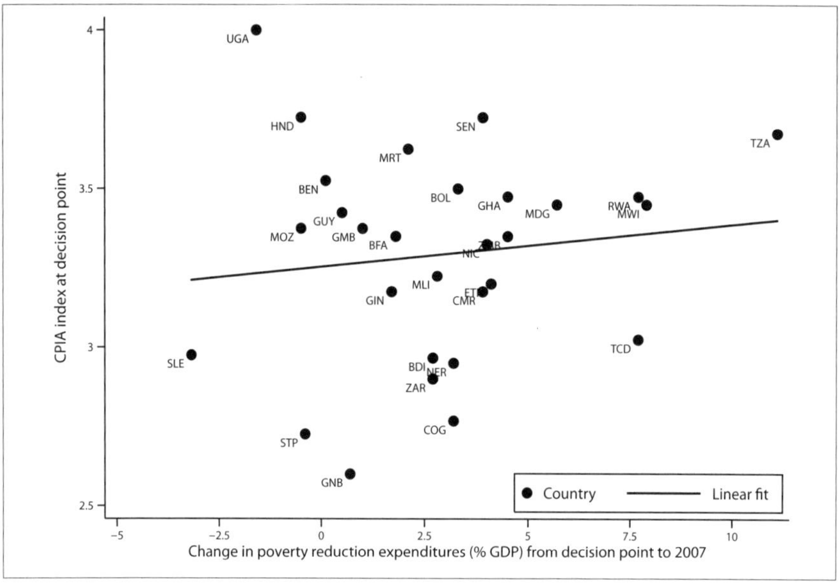


**Figure 8.3 Poverty reduction expenditures and institutional quality in HIPCs**

*Source*: Authors' calculations based on data from several HIPC Initiative and MDRI – Status of Implementation, published by the WB and the IMF. Data refers to the 29 post-decision point HIPCs as of September 2008 (Afghanistan, Central African Republic, Liberia and Haiti are excluded because they reached decision point in 2007 and 2008 or they lack data).

Finally, data on poverty reduction expenditures provide a first descriptive evidence of the importance of the policy and institutional framework in recipient countries for reaping the benefits of debt relief (Asiedu 2003). Countries with better policies are more capable, on average, of targeting resources freed up by debt relief to poverty reduction expenditure and there is a positive correlation between the change in pro-poor spending – between decision point and 2007 – and the initial quality of the policy and institutional framework, measured by the overall CPIA score (Figure 8.3).[6]

*8.2.2.2 The outcomes*

The first contribution assessing directly the impact of debt relief on growth, investment and public spending is by Depetris Chauvin and Kraay (2005). They build two alternative measures of the total amount of debt relief (in present value) over the period 1989-2003, one based on debtors' and the other on creditors' reported data. Their results on 62 LICs are rather disappointing: they found very limited evidence supporting a positive impact on public and social (health and education) spending, investment and growth rates. Furthermore, there is only weak evidence of additionality of debt relief, with countries receiving more debt relief experiencing subsequent decline in aid inflows. Finally, there is a positive association between reduction in debt and future increases in policy and institutional indicators, even if it is driven by few outliers. While Depetris Chauvin and Kraay (2005) rely on a difference-in-difference estimator to assess the impact of debt relief on a number of possible outcomes, Johansson (2010) uses a dynamic panel model to estimate a growth and an investment equation, confirming the ineffectiveness of debt relief in enhancing investment and growth, even if there is some evidence of an investment-enhancing effect of debt reduction in non-HIPCs.

Other authors have investigated the effectiveness of debt relief, focusing on African countries. Dessy and Vencatachellum (2007) analyze the relationship between debt relief and social expenditures in Africa, finding that debt reduction is associated with an increase in the share of country's expenditures allocated either to public education or health in countries which have improved their institutions. A positive effect of debt relief on the socio-economic conditions of the poor, measured by the infant mortality rate is suggested also by Schmid (2009). In addition, Crespo Cuaresma and Vincelette (2009) find some positive evidence of human capital accumulation in countries that reached completion. Comparing HIPCs at different stages of the Initiative, the authors find that drop out rates decrease after a country graduates from completion point, while educational expenditures and the proportion of young individuals with primary schooling increased after debt relief. In both cases, however, the identification problem is far from settled, since in the years of the Initiative a number of reforms were taking in place, so that it is extremely difficult to isolate the specific impact of debt relief.

A further channel through which debt relief could benefit recipient countries could be the relaxing of financing constraints for local firms. High external debt is detrimental for private sector lending because of higher interest rates and high risk premium associated with debt overhang. Furthermore, government could shift to internal financing to service external debt obligations, leading to the crowding

6 See section 8.3 for detailed information on the data used.

out of private sector investment. Harrabi, Bousrih and Mohammed (2007) test the hypothesis that debt relief, creating fiscal space and limiting the increase in the interest rates, could enhance credit to the private sector. The authors look at the experience of 52 African countries over the period 1988-2004 and find that debt relief actually alleviates government pressure on domestic financial markets. However, in the long term, debt relief reduces the crowding out effect only when associated with good institutional quality.

## 8.3 Data

The empirical analysis is based on a dataset covering 62 developing (low and lower-middle income) countries over the period 1988-2007 and built merging macroeconomic data drawn from the WB 2008 WDI with other datasets for debt relief, external and domestic debt, and institutional indicators.[7] The time series on the NPV of PPG external debt is provided by Dikhanov (2004). From these data, a measure of external debt burden is constructed scaling the NPV of external debt over GDP (*EXTERNAL DEBT*).[8] Data on domestic debt (scaled by GDP, *DomD*) comes from the dataset in Abbas (2007) on the basis of the IFS monetary surveys, for 93 LICs spanning the period 1974-2004.[9]

Data on debt relief comes from the dataset in Depetris Chauvin and Kraay (2005). These authors estimate the net change in the NPV of the stock of debt outstanding due to debt relief. With respect to the traditional data on the nominal amount of debt forgiven, this measure has the double advantage of considering adequately the changes in external debt due to reschedulings and the actual variation in the NPV of debt due to cancellation of concessional debt. As said above, they build two alternative measures of debt relief, one based on debtor-reported

7 The country coverage is based on the 1988 WB income classification, in order to avoid sample selection problems, and varies according to different exercises depending on data availability. The list of countries, together with their regional and income classification, is shown in Table 8.8

8 Alternatively, the ratio of external debt over exports could be more informative of a country's capacity to generate enough foreign currency to meet its debt obligations. However, in this chapter we need a measure of debt burden: the ratio of external debt over GDP is a better proxy and suffers less from the volatility of the denominator that the debt-to-export ratio. Moreover, as shown in Figure 1.2, the two indicators provide similar pictures. For robustness, the empirical exercises are also run using the ratio of external debt over exports and the results are broadly similar. Results are available from the author on request.

9 More formally, Abbas (2007: 18) define the public sector domestic debt as gross securitized claims on the central government (excluding the stock of securities issued by the central bank) plus all securities issued by the central bank and appearing on the liabilities side of its balance sheet. The author also reports the series of domestic debt scaled by GDP and commercial bank deposits.

data and the other on creditor-reported data. The latter indicator is constructed using data that are more accurate than the former, but have the limitation of not being comprehensive, since creditors outside the Paris Club (other than Russia) are excluded, even though some of them have provided substantial amounts of debt relief. Thus, measurements errors originate significant discrepancies between debtor- and creditor-reported data in some countries, with the latter generally underestimating the amount of debt relief. Notwithstanding these differences, the correlation between the two indicators is fairly high. We present results obtained with the debtor-based measure of debt relief, scaled by the initial stock of the NPV of external debt (*DEBT RELIEF*).[10]

The quality of policies and institutions is measured by the CPIA indicator (Box 2.3). Moreover, we also measure institutional quality using the WB WGI, covering different aspect of governance which could affect and be affected in a different ways debt forgiveness: voice and accountability, political stability, government effectiveness, regulatory quality, rule of law, and control of corruption (Kaufmann, Kraay and Mastruzzi 2008).

## 8.4 Results

This section looks, firstly, at the determinants of debt relief (subsection 8.4.1). The aims are to: 1) identify the variables affecting the donors' choice in granting debt relief and the amount of debt actually forgiven; and 2) assess whether donors are moving towards improved selectivity based on institutional quality. Then, the empirical evidence on the effects of debt relief on different macroeconomic indicators will be presented (subsection 8.4.2). Given that we are interested in any change in the effectiveness of debt relief or in donors' behavior in both the exercises, the analysis focuses on different sub-periods, in addition to analyzing the entire time period. Both sections are composed of a descriptive analysis and a regression analysis: readers not familiar with the latter can skip that part, whose findings substantiate the descriptive evidence and are summarized in the overview of Part 3 and in section 8.5.

### *8.4.1 The Determinants of Debt Relief*

#### *8.4.1.1 Descriptive evidence*

To evaluate if donors reward institution building and good policies, it is worth assessing, among the possible determinants of debt relief, the impact of the institutional framework. Available data allows us to inspect the relationship between the probability of receiving debt relief in three different sub-periods (1992-

10 Depetris Chauvin and Kraay (2005) calculate that the simple correlation between the two measures is fairly high at 0.82. For robustness, we have repeated all the exercises with the creditor-based measure.

1995, 1996-1999 and 2000-2003) and the quality of policies and institutions in the previous period. The univariate analysis suggests a selective behavior by donors, which seems to target debt relief to countries with better institutions. Appendix Table 8.1 indicates a significant difference in the overall CPIA score between countries which received debt relief and those which did not, in all sub-periods except for debt relief granted between 1996 and 1999.

A similar indication can be drawn also from the inspection of the relationship between debt relief and past institutions, limited to countries which actually had a share of their external debt forgiven (Figure 8.4). Interestingly, the lack of any statistical correlation between debt relief and past institutions is a result of completely opposite patterns over the different sub-periods. In both samples there is a negative significant correlation (-0.47) between the log of debt relief and past levels of the overall CPIA score in the first sub-period. However, this relationship becomes positive and significant starting from 1996 – it ranges from 0.20 to 0.32 for the whole sample (Figure 8.4a) and from 0.14 to 0.36 for the HIPCs (Figure (8.4b) – suggesting that the HIPC Initiative was probably successful in influencing donors to adopt lending strategies aimed at rewarding countries with better institutions and policies.

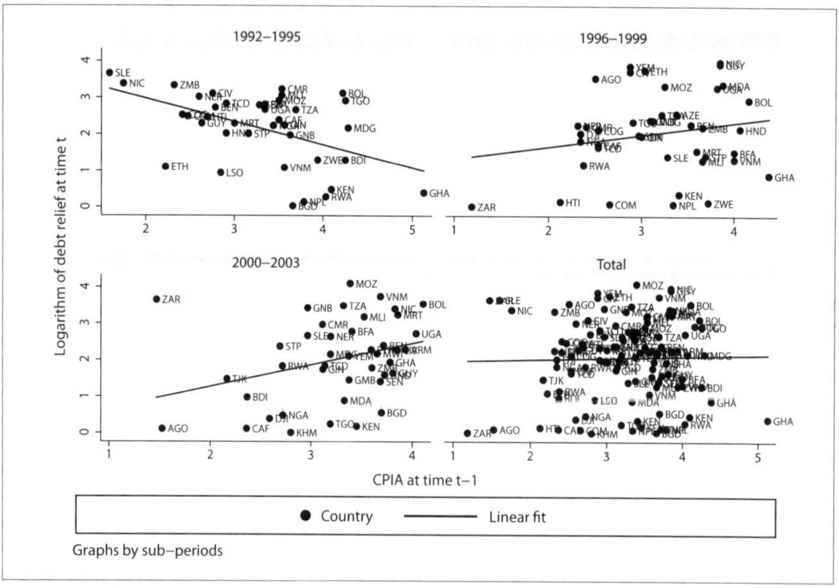


**Figure 8.4a Debt relief and past institutions – whole sample**
*Source*: Authors' calculations.

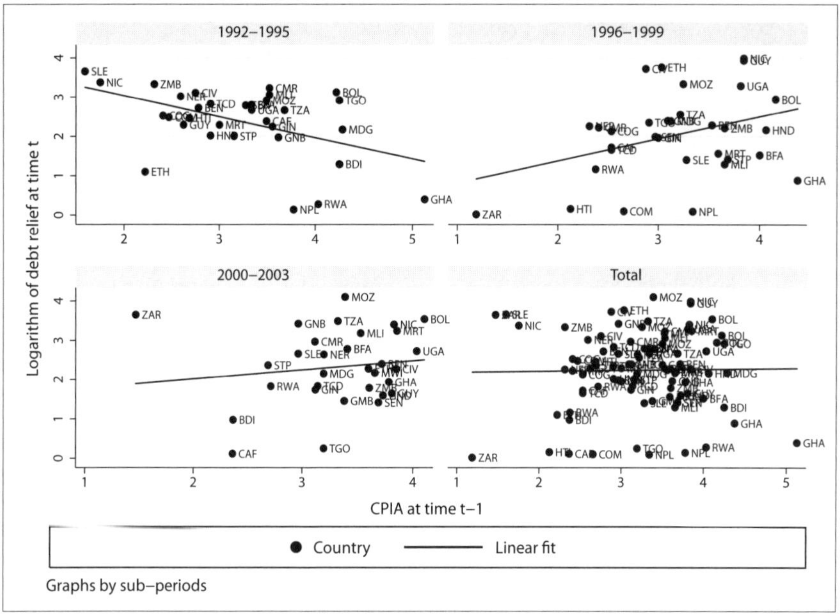


**Figure 8.4b Debt relief and past institutions – HIPCs**
*Source*: Authors' calculations.

### *8.4.1.2 Multivariate Analysis*

Using the dataset described in section 8.3 it is possible to identify which are the factors determining the choice of granting debt relief and also affecting the amount of debt forgiven. The decision of granting debt relief could be thought as a two-step process, in which the first step concerns the selection of eligible countries and the second concerns the amount of external debt actually forgiven. Hence, the whole process could be modelled using the two-step estimator developed by Heckman (1979).[11] Specifically, in the selection equation the dependent variable is the probability of a country *i* receiving a positive amount of debt relief at time *t*:

11 For our purposes, the OLS estimation suffers from a sample selection bias, given that we observe debt relief only for a selected sample which is not representative of the population. The Heckman's two-step procedure corrects for the sample selection bias. The non-random selection process is estimated with a probit model in which additional regressors influencing the selection but not the amount of debt relief are included (selection equation). The second step consists in the OLS regression of the outcome equation augmented with the "inverse Mills ratio" ($\lambda$), calculated from the selection equation, in order to control for omitted variables affecting the truncation of debt relief. As a result, estimates are unbiased and the procedure has the advantage, with respect to standard Tobit models, of not constraining the parameters to have the same effect on the probability as they do on the level of debt relief.

$$\Pr(DEBT\ RELIEF_{i,t}) = \Phi(DEBT\ RELIEF_{i,t-1}, CPIA_{i,t-1}, AID_{i,t-1}, GDP_{i,t-1}, DEBT\ SERVICE_{i,t-1}, EXTERNAL\ DEBT_{i,t-1}, HIPC_i, COLONY_i, D_t) \quad (8.1)$$

where Φ is the normal distribution function. The possible determinants of the probability of receiving debt relief refer to time t-1 and include: the amount of debt relief already received in the previous period (*DEBT RELIEF*), aid inflows (as a share of GDP, *AID*), real GDP per capita (*GDP*), total debt service (as a share of GDP, *DEBT SERVICE*), the NET of external debt over GDP (*EXTERNAL DEBT*) – all the previous ones in logs – the overall CPIA score (*CPIA*), a dummy for HIPCs (*HIPC*), and the number of years the country has been a former colony of an OECD country since 1900 (*COLONY*), to take into account political interest driving aid allocation by donors, which might want to preserve an influence on recipient countries.[12] The outcome equation expresses the amount of debt relief as a function of past levels of aid, total debt service, external debt (all expressed as the log of their ratios to GDP) and of the level of the overall CPIA score in the previous period:

$$\ln(DEBT\ RELIEF_{i,t}) = \alpha + \beta_1 CPIA_{i,t-1} + \beta_2 AID_{i,t-1} + \beta_3 DEBT\ SERVICE_{i,t-1} + \beta_4 EXTERNAL\ DEBT_{i,t-1} + D_t + \lambda_i \quad (8.2)$$

where time dummies ($D_t$) and the inverse Mills ratio estimated in equation 1 ($\lambda_i$) are included. Therefore, the excluding restrictions which are likely to affect the probability of receiving debt forgiveness but not its amount, are the real per capita GDP, the amount of debt relief in the previous period, the past colonial experience and a dummy for HIPCs. For the latter variable, we follow Freytag and Pehnelt (2009), while *COLONY* is included to taken into account possible political motivation in the allocation of debt relief (similarly, Neumayer (2002), who does not find past colonial experience being correlated with the amount of debt forgiven) and the other two variables are generally significantly correlated with the probability of receiving debt relief, but not with the quantity of debt forgiven.

Appendix Table 8.2 shows the results for the pooled cross sections over the whole period 1998-2003 as well as for the three sub-periods for the whole sample of developing countries. As regard the selection equation, results show that donors are more likely to grant debt reductions to the HIPCs and to those that already received debt relief, supporting the hypothesis of the presence of path dependence in debt relief (Michaelowa 2003; Depetris Chauvin and Kraay 2007). However, the level of indebtedness, both in terms of stocks and flows, and the level of income

12 The same measure is used, among others, by Alesina and Dollar (2000). To control also for geopolitical motivations in donors' behavior, in separate regressions we have also included the log of the minimum kilometric distance between the capital of the indebted country and either New York, Tokyo or Rotterdam. Our main findings are confirmed, even if the sample size is further reduced because of limited data availability.

are not a significant determinants of the likelihood of receiving debt relief. The result about the lack of significance of debt variables is not due to the presence of the dummy for HIPCs, since its exclusion does not turns the coefficient on external debt and debt service significant. Hence, once controlled for being HIPC and for past debt relief, there is no evidence of donors targeting more indebted and poorer countries. The number of years as former colony does not influence the probability of having debt forgiven.[13] Finally, as concerns the variable of interest, the overall CPIA score is significant at 5 percent level only in the last sub-period: from 2000 onwards, donors seem to reward countries with good policies and institutions by granting them debt relief.

Turning to the outcome equation, the picture is quite different. In this case, the larger the stock of external debt in present value terms, the greater the amount of debt cancelled in the subsequent period. This result is in contrast to the findings by Depetris Chauvin and Kraay (2007), who find that debt overhang does not seem to be a major motivation for debt relief. This contradiction could be explained by the fact that they look directly at the outcome equation, without addressing the selection into debt relief, which, instead, we find to be uncorrelated with the debt burden. Debt-service payments enter the equation with a negative and significant sign. Even if, at first glance, this result could appear contrary to expectations, it is fully consistent with the hypothesis of debt relief related to debt which was not being serviced. In other words, donors grant debt relief to countries which are most in need and with lower probability of repayment. Aid inflows are also negatively correlated with subsequent debt relief, which is still consistent with a targeting of debt relief towards countries most in need and with low repayment capacity. Finally, the analysis of the coefficients of the overall CPIA score shows a very interesting pattern, given that the positive association between institutional quality and debt reduction increases substantially over time, consistently with the descriptive evidence (Figure 8.4). Hence, these results suggest a change in donors behavior which, soon after the beginning of the HIPC Initiative, are choosing the eligible countries and the amount of debt relief on the basis of the quality of policies and institutions, rewarding countries with better governance.

Appendix Table 8.3 shows the results for the sub-sample of HIPCs. Even if the limited sample size could widen standard errors and make the estimates less reliable, it is worth assessing whether the main findings are confirmed for the HIPCs or not. Given the great effort undertaken by the international community to implement the HIPC Initiative and the emphasis on poverty reduction and institutional quality, it would be reasonable to expect HIPC relief targeting countries more in need and better governed. We find that the choice of forgiving debt is path dependent and debt relief is targeted to the countries most in need and with low repayment capacity. With respect to any change in donor's behavior in HIPCs, we find that

13 This result could be driven by the aggregation of data, since political interest could be better identified with bilateral flows (Alesina and Weder 2002), instead of looking at the total amount of external debt forgiven, which involves also multilateral creditors.

from 2000 onwards both the choice of granting debt relief and its amount depends on the policy and institutional framework. All in all, results are consistent with a better targeting of poorer countries and with a more recent selective approach by donors, which, under the increased influence of the IMF and the WB, are partially departing from political considerations in debt relief decisions, as suggested also by the results in Depetris Chauvin and Kraay (2007).

Finally, Appendix Tables 8.4 and 8.5 show the estimation of equations 1 and 2 for the debt relief granted in the sub-period 2000-2003, substituting the overall CPIA score with the individual WGI, in order to see which aspect of institutional governance matters most for debt forgiveness. Differently from the CPIA score, in the whole sample none of the governance indicators affect the probability of debt relief, while all but "control of corruption" are positively associated with larger amount of debt forgiven (Table 8.4). The quality of bureaucracy and of public service provision, as well as the ability of the government to formulate and implement sound policies and regulations are the aspects of governance which matter most in the allocation of debt relief. These effects almost vanish in the subset of HIPCs, where only differences in the implementation of sound policies and in the regulations to promote private sector development positively affect the amount of debt relief (Appendix Table 8.5).[14]

### *8.4.2 Debt Relief Effectiveness*

In the previous section we have addressed one side of the relationship between debt relief and institution building, finding that from 2000 onwards, donors started targeting debt forgiveness to countries with better policies and institutions. Another key issue is the effectiveness of debt relief. The main hypothesis to test would be the actual impact of debt relief on poverty reduction, but it is not possible at this stage to do this directly due to lack of reliable panel data on poverty incidence and human development. This section aims at assessing the debt relief effectiveness indirectly, focusing on several macroeconomic indicators related to economic development. Here we also inspect eventual improvements in debt relief program design and implementation due to (a sort of) learning by doing and improved targeting of better governed countries.

#### *8.4.2.1 Descriptive evidence*

A simple way to inspect the effectiveness of debt relief is the visual representation of the correlation between actual debt relief and subsequent changes in macroeconomic conditions. In particular, we eliminate business cycle fluctuations averaging data over five non-overlapping four-year periods (1988-1991; 1992-1995; 1996-1999; 2000-2003; 2004-2007) and measure the change in outcome Y

14 When the ratio of external debt over exports is used, results are similar to the one for the whole sample, with all governance indicators except corruption affecting the amount of debt relief.

as the difference $Y_t$-$Y_{t-1}$, while the corresponding debt relief measure refers to the period *t-1* and is divided by the initial stock of external debt (measured in NPV in the year before the four-year period).

Among the possible variables which could be affected by debt relief, we consider the following ones in order to test some simple hypotheses:

- The real growth rate of GDP per capita (*GROWTH*), calculated as log difference of the per capita GDP, measured in PPP at constant international dollars. This first exercise aims at unraveling any direct relationship between debt relief and subsequent growth.
- The investment rate (*INV*), calculated as the share of gross capital formation over GDP, to test for the presence of debt overhang.
- The ratio of FDI over GDP (*FDI*), to evaluate whether debt reduction is perceived as a positive signal by the international community, so that private investors increase their presence in the country.
- The ratio of domestic debt over GDP (*DomD*). In this case, the testable hypothesis is based on an unintended consequence of the HIPC Initiative, which is likely to determine an increase in domestic borrowing.
- The quality of policies and institutions measured, alternatively, by the overall *CPIA* and by the six WGI, to assess whether debt relief goes hand in hand with improvements in the institutional framework.

Figures 8.5 to 8.10 plot the correlation between actual debt relief and subsequent changes in the above variables in the whole sample and also in the HIPCs.[15]

Figure 8.5 shows that there is a positive and generally significant correlation between the amount of debt forgiven and subsequent changes in GDP growth in HIPCs (lower panel), while the relationship is weaker in the whole sample (upper panel). The investment rate, instead, does not seem to react to previous debt relief in both the whole sample and the HIPCs subset (Figure 8.6). Taken together, these diagrams suggest that, in HIPCs, there is a negative correlation between external debt and economic growth, even if this adverse effect does not seems to be due to lower capital accumulation, but to a TFP slowdown, consistent with the findings of Pattillo, Poirson and Ricci (2004) and Presbitero (2006) discussed in section 7.2.

15 For the last period (2004-2007) data availability on *GROWTH*, *CPIA* and *FDI* exclude 2007, while for *DomD* there is only the observation in 2004. Hence, results on this sub-period are to be taken with caution and as preliminary. More reliable are the results on the WGI which, however, can not be extended backwards before 2000.

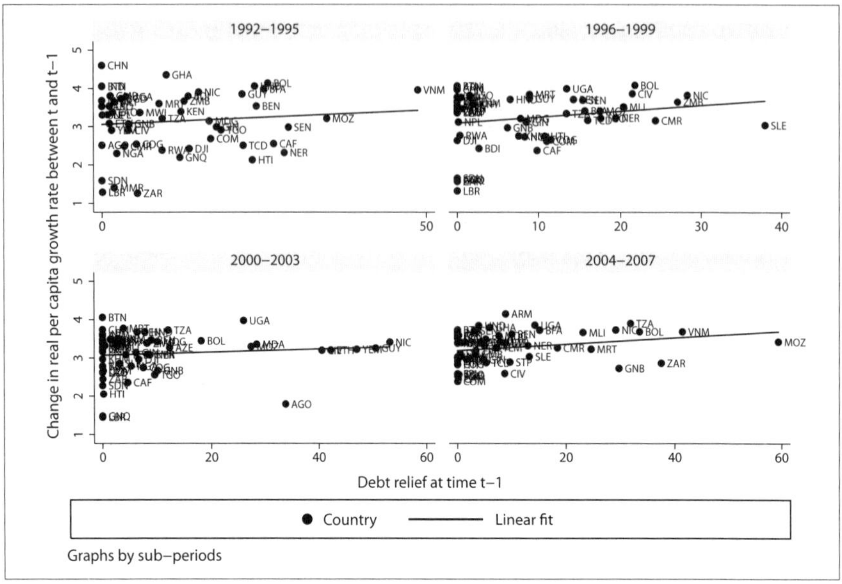


a) Whole sample

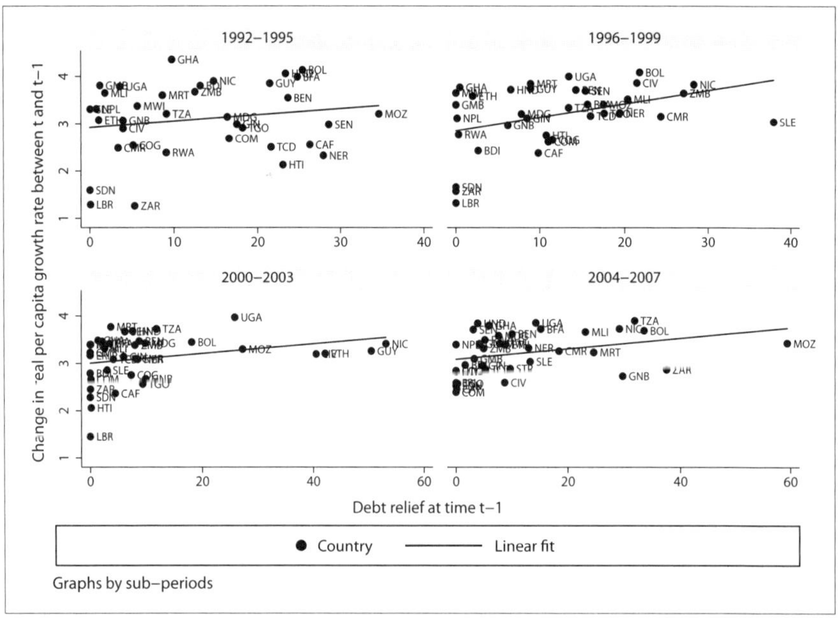


b) HIPCs

**Figure 8.5 Debt relief and subsequent growth**
*Source*: Authors' calculations.

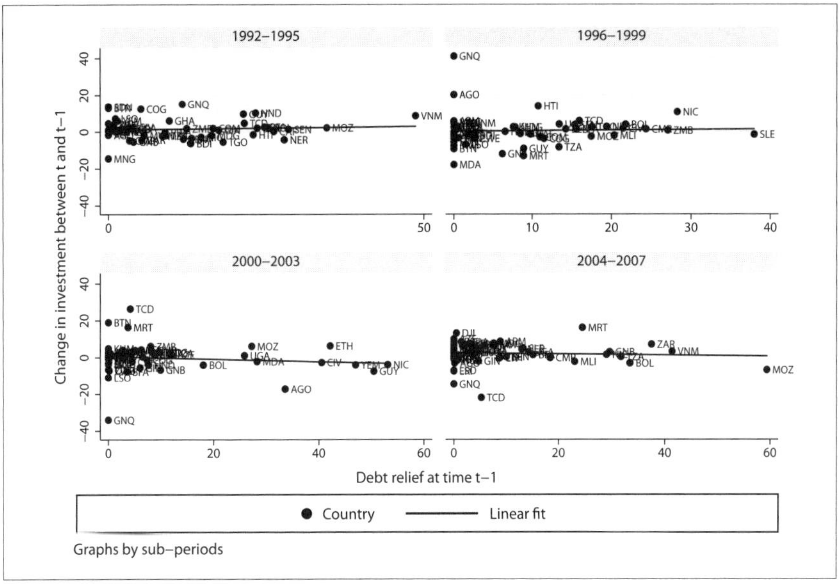


a) Whole sample

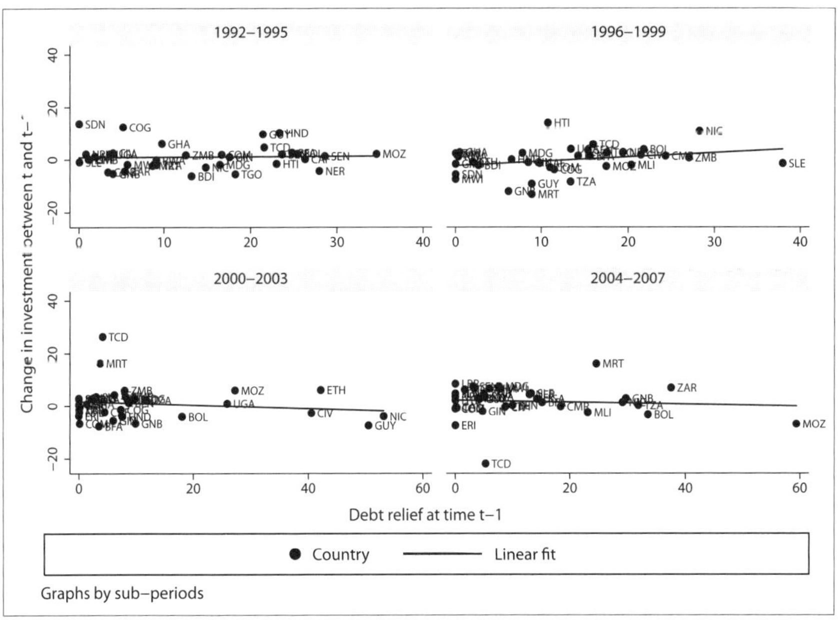


b) HIPCs

**Figure 8.6 Debt relief and subsequent investment**
*Source*: Authors' calculations.

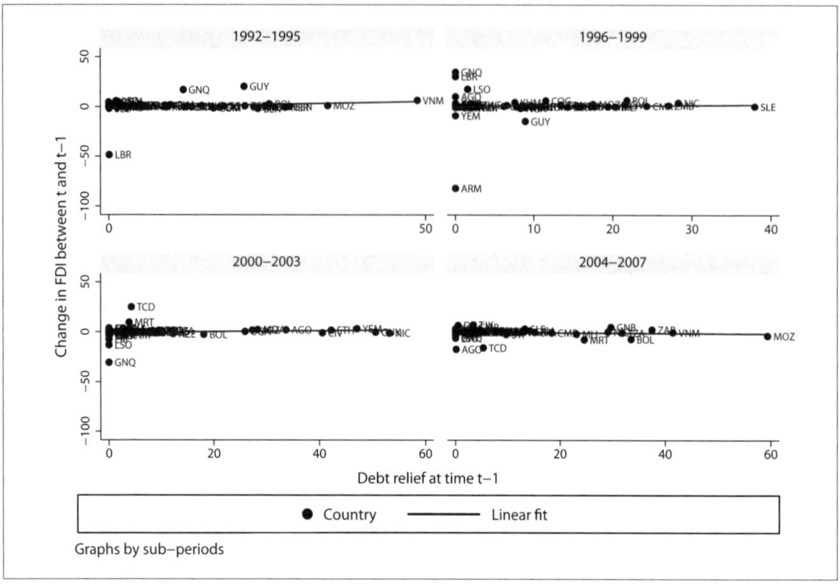


a) Whole sample

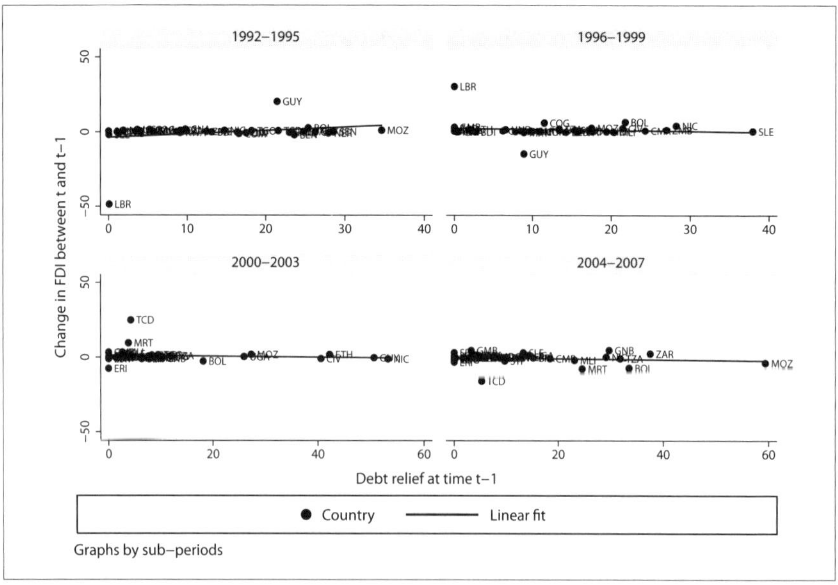


b) HIPCs

**Figure 8.7 Debt relief and subsequent FDI**

*Source*: Authors' calculations.

Figure 8.7 shows that debt relief did not enhance *FDI*. This result could be explained by the fact that part of debt actually cancelled was already discounted as debt which would have never been serviced. Hence, foreign investors do not modify their expectations on debtors' future growth prospect and do not change their investment strategy because of a formal debt relief agreement. Furthermore, in line with this possible explanation, debt relief might be interpreted by investors as a signal for countries that, given their large external debt, are likely to have a high (and stable over time) discount rate against the future: governments will keep on over-borrowing and trading off consumption today versus consumption tomorrow, heavily taxing the private sector and discouraging investors (Easterly 2002).

The lower panel of Figure 8.8 confirms the hypothesis discussed in Part 3, where we document a significant increase in domestic debt in a number of HIPCs (Chapter 4). Especially between 2000 and 2003 it is possible to observe a positive and significant correlation between the amount of debt forgiven and the subsequent increase in domestic debt as a share of GDP.[16] The increase in internal financing is an unintended consequence of the HIPC Initiative which results in high economic costs. The program was successful in bringing inflation under control but large primary deficits in a number of heavily indebted countries persisted and kept deteriorating through the nineties. This happened because a reduction of public spending is unfeasible given the extreme poverty and development targets, while an increase in government revenues is unlikely because of a limited revenue base and limited capability of tax administration (Gupta et al. 2005). Besides, traditional debt relief is likely to free up a limited amount of resources. By barring access to international capital markets, as imposed by the IDA's non-concessional borrowing policy (designed to avoid a rapid re-accumulation of debt and undermine debt sustainability), insufficient inflows of concessional loans are forcing many HIPCs to tap their domestic markets to close the financing gap. As already discussed, declining inflation, associated with increasing nominal interest rates on domestic borrowing, is making the shift from external to domestic financing particularly costly.[17] An increasing domestic debt is likely to undermine the overall public debt sustainability and to adversely impinge on the economy, through the high costs of debt service and because of a drain of resources from the private to the public sector, which is likely to crowd out private investments. The different characteristics of the other LICs included in the whole sample, and especially their access to international capital markets could explain the lack of a significant correlation between domestic debt and debt relief showed in the upper panel of Figure 8.8.

16 Between 2000 and 2003 the correlation is significant at 5 percent and it is equal to 0.35 in the whole sample and 0.58 in HIPCs. The lack of a positive relationship in the last period could be due to limited data availability.

17 This conclusion contrasts with the finding discussed by Harrabi, Bousrih and Mohammed (2007). This discrepancy could be explained by the different sample of countries analyzed, given that Harrabi, Bousrih and Mohammed look at 52 African countries, while this section focuses on HIPCs and Chapter 6 focuses on a selected number of HIPCs which are particularly exposed to domestic borrowing.

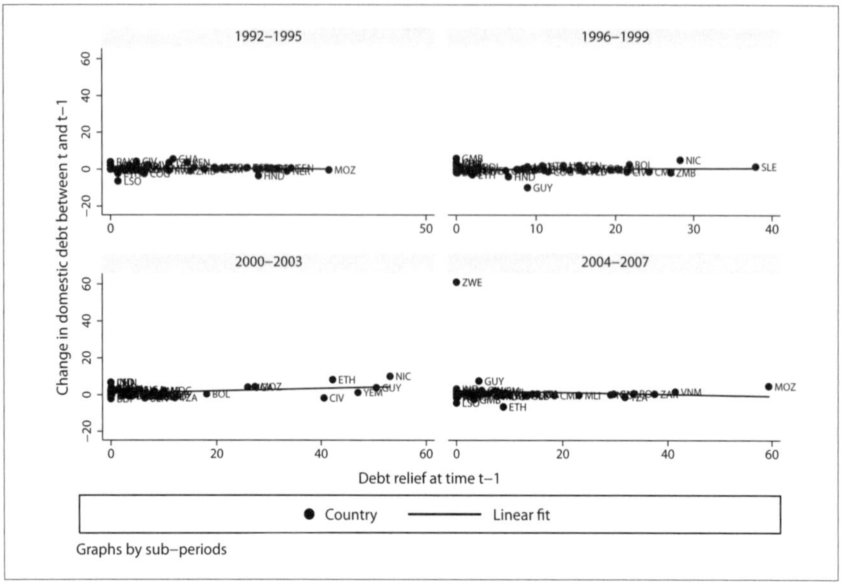


a) Whole sample

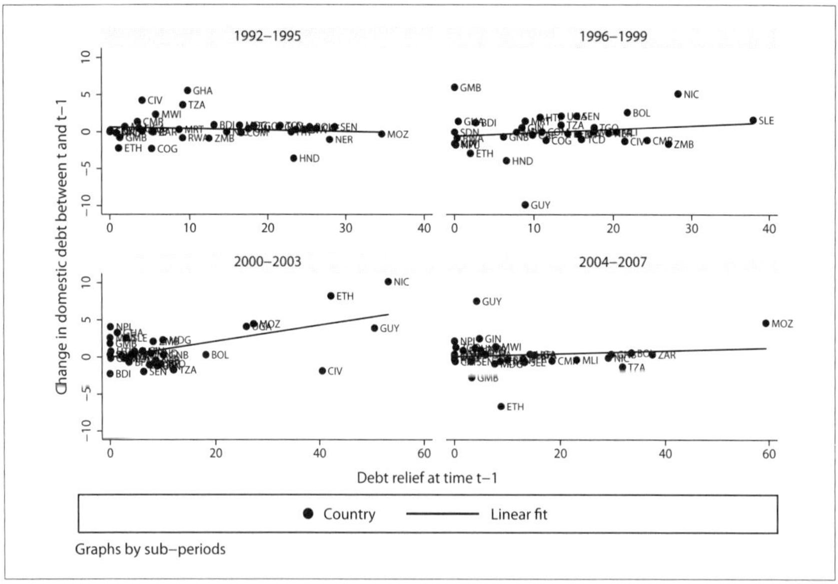


b) HIPCs

**Figure 8.8 Debt relief and subsequent domestic debt**
*Source*: Authors' calculations.

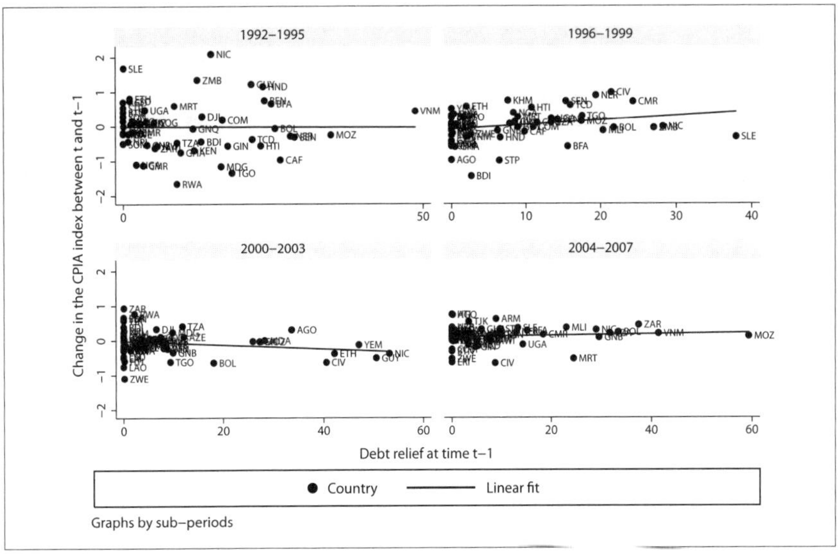


a) Whole sample

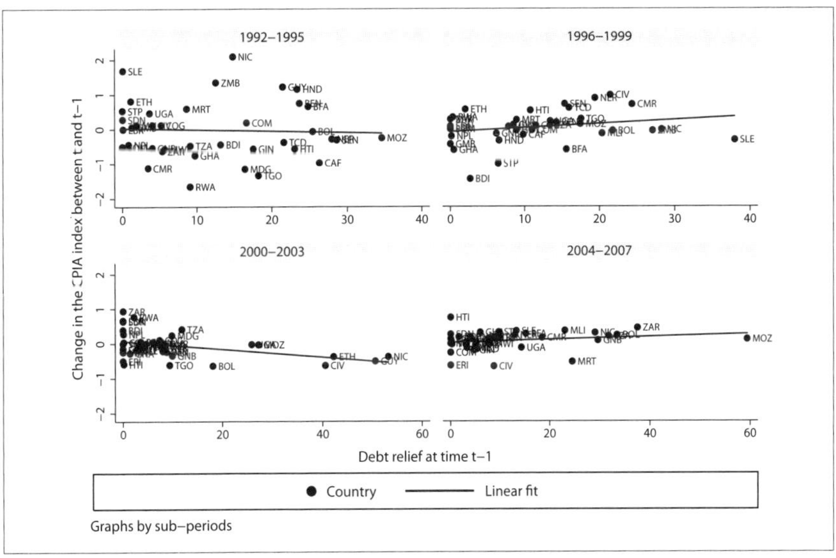


b) HIPCs

**Figure 8.9 Debt relief and the subsequent institutional framework, CPIA**
*Source*: Authors' calculations.

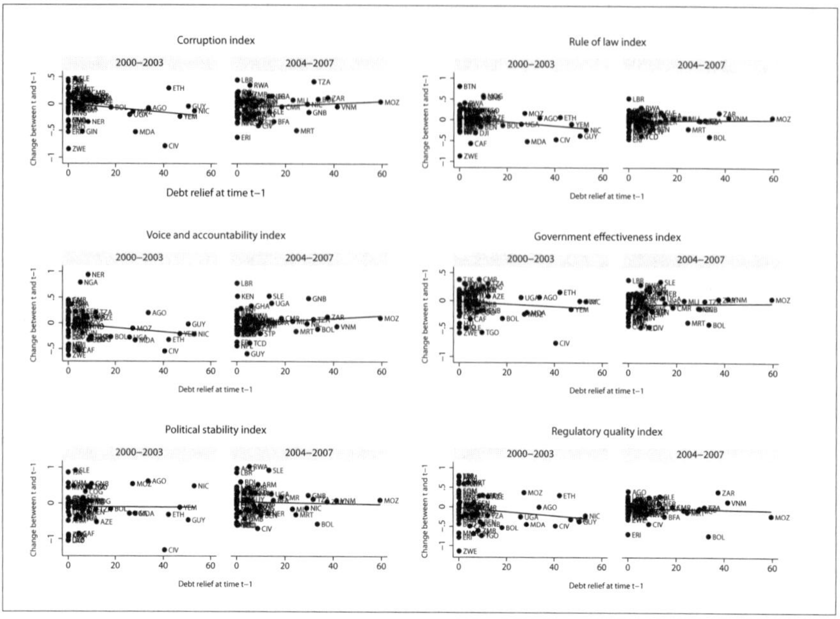


a) Whole sample

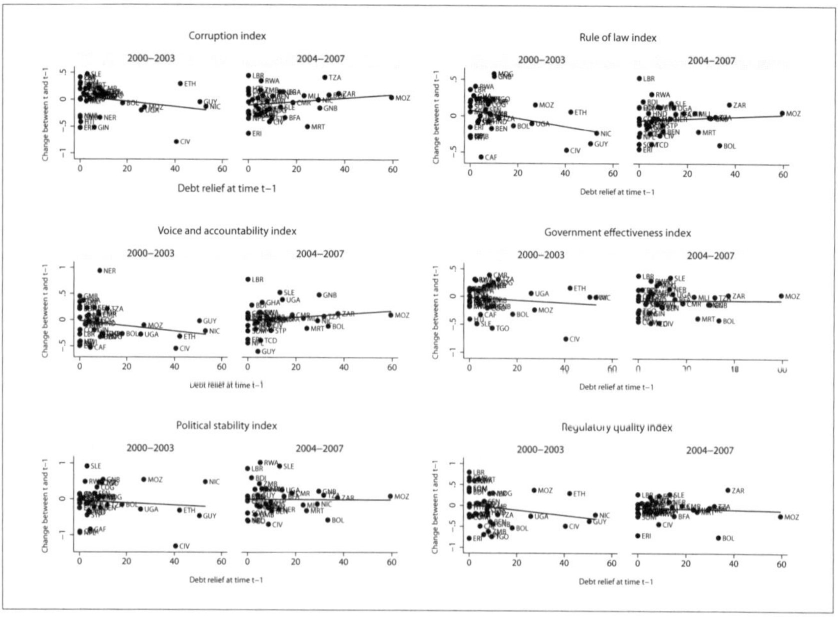


b) HIPCs

**Figure 8.10 Debt relief and the subsequent institutional framework, WGI**
*Source*: Authors' calculations.

Finally, Figures 8.9 and 8.10 focus on the critical aspect of institution building. Given the large number of conditions attached to debt reduction programs, one would expect countries that had a share of their debt forgiven improving their policies and institutions in the following periods. However, as discussed in section 8.1.2, the theoretical argument is not so straightforward, given that aid dependence could undermine institutional quality (*debt relief curse*) by weakening accountability, postponing the reform process and instigating conflicts and corruption over control of resources (Knack 2001; Moss, Pettersson and van de Walle 2008).

The descriptive analysis provides support for the latter hypothesis, given that, on the whole, there is no positive correlation between debt relief and subsequent improvements in the overall CPIA score. Also, in the period 2000-2003 there is evidence that the larger the share of outstanding external debt forgiven, the worse the performance in terms of polices and institutions (the correlation in the HIPC sample is significant and equal to -0.42), consistently with the evidence on aid discussed by Djankov, Montalvo and Reynal-Querol (2008). For robustness, Figure 8.10 measures institutional quality according to the six WGI, focusing only on their changes in the last two periods in response to debt relief in 1996-99 and 2000-03.

These years are the most interesting, since they cover the increase in debt forgiveness following the HIPC Initiative. While the indicators of regulatory quality, government effectiveness and political stability do not show any clear improvement in either period (with the correlations being sometimes negative), the picture is quite different for the indicators of corruption, rule of law and voice and accountability. In these latter cases it seems that there was a sort of reversal, with a debt relief curse during the years 2000-2003 and, instead, a positive effect of debt relief on institutional reform after 2003. More generally, especially in the HIPC sub-sample, there is a positive pattern in the correlation between debt relief and subsequent changes in governance, with the relationship turning from negative to positive or, in some cases, flat. This last result could be read as a positive signal of learning in the debt relief initiatives: the strong emphasis given by IFIs on fighting corruption and promoting the rule of law and institutional accountability seems to be having real effects.

#### *8.4.2.2 Multivariate analysis*

The evidence described in section 8.4.2.1 points to some positive effect of debt relief on economic growth and institutional reform, at least in more recent years and especially in HIPCs. the findings above could be corroborated with the following, more accurate analysis. Having five periods, we can look at the debt relief effects in a panel dataset consisting of four intervals (1992-1995; 1996-1999; 2000-2003; 2004-2007). Appendix Table 8.6 shows the coefficient β of this very simple regression for the whole sample and for HIPCs exclusively:

$$Y_{i,t} - Y_{i,t-1} = \alpha + \beta DEBT\ RELIEF_{t-1} + \gamma D_t + \varepsilon_{i,t} \tag{8.3}$$

Equation 8.3 is estimated with the within-group estimator in order to wash out country-specific fixed-effects which might jointly affect the likelihood and the amount of debt relief and the variation in Y, where the outcomes are the five macroeconomic variables discussed above.

In the whole sample of developing countries there is no evidence of any statistical significant correlation between debt relief and subsequent changes in growth, investment, FDI, institutional quality and domestic debt. Instead, when the sample is limited to the HIPCs, it turns out that past debt relief is associated with an increase in domestic debt, indicating a shift from external towards internal financing, and with a worsening of institutional quality, consistent with the debt relief curse hypothesis.

The lack of significance of the coefficient could be due to the fact that the relationship is likely to change over time, as suggested by Figures 8.5 to 8.10 discussed in the previous section. Therefore, we estimate Equation 8.3 allowing for the coefficient β to change over time, interacting $DEBT\ RELIEF_{t-1}$ with the time dummies $D_t$. The results are reported in Appendix Table 8.7 for the whole sample (upper panel) and for the HIPC sub-sample (lower panel) but they do not show any significant effect of debt relief on the variables of interest, apart from the association between debt relief and increasing domestic financing and worsening governance in HIPCs in response to the debt forgiven at the end of the Nineties, consistently with Figures 8.8 and 8.9 and with the empirical evidence on 14 HIPCs discussed in section 4.3. The lack of significance of any shift from external to internal financing in the last period could be due to poor data availability (the change in domestic debt is limited to one year only), while the lack of evidence of a debt relief curse could be a signal of an increased effectiveness of debt relief in institution building in recent years, in line with the descriptive results discussed in the previous section. Furthermore, the positive correlation between debt forgiveness and economic growth in HIPCs vanishes once country fixed-effects are taken into account, except that in the first three years of the Initiative, when also investments increased. Starting from 2000 there is no evidence of debt relief triggering economic growth, consistent with the recent critical evidence on the presence of debt overhang in HIPCs and also with the hypothesis discussed by Easterly (2002) about high and unchanged discount rates, and with the model developed by Koeda (2008), which implies that only a one-time debt cancellation could help countries escaping a situation of aid dependence.

Finally, we run two other tests for the possibility that the impact of debt relief is: 1) differentiated according to institutional quality; and 2) less effective the larger the amount of foreign aid because of the increased management effort required from local authorities and of (a sort of) aid fatigue. To do so, we interact $DEBT\ RELIEF_{t-1}$ with, respectively, the overall CPIA score in *t-1* and with $AID_{t-1}$, but results are generally not significant. The lack of non-linearities depending on policies is consistent with the finding of Depetris Chauvin and Kraay

(2005) but contrary to Harrabi, Bousrih and Mohammed (2007) and Dessy and Vencatachellum (2007).

## 8.5 Concluding Remarks

In this chapter we have presented an *ex-post* evaluation of debt relief, focusing on very recent years and on the HIPC Initiative in order to assess whether the development of such a large program by the IFIs changed the effectiveness of debt relief as well as donors' lending policies.

Firstly, we document that, since the beginning of the HIPC Initiative, bilateral and multilateral donors seem to target debt relief efforts to countries with better institutions and policies, following *ex-post* governance conditionality (Radelet 2005a; Collier 2007). This is reflected in a subsequent effectiveness of debt relief in promoting institutional reforms, suggesting that debt reduction programs are probably providing the right incentives to debtors, limiting the negative effects of aid dependence on the quality of institutions and the efficiency of the public sector. This governance-related policy shift is particularly welcome, since weak institutions and policies in HIPCs (whose average CPIA score in 2008 was lower than in low- and lower-middle income countries) are a drag on growth and on debt relief effectiveness.

The latter point is supported by the lack of any increases in economic growth, investment and FDI in response to debt relief, once country fixed-effect are taken into account. This result, consistent with the absence of debt overhang, could be explained by debt relief targeting countries with weak policies and institutions, for which the debt burden should not be the binding constraint for economic growth. In 2008, only five HIPCs had a CPIA index greater than 3.75, meaning that institutions were strong and debt overhang was withholding economic growth. In all the other countries, the evidence discussed in Chapter 7 suggests that weak policies and institutions impinged on debt relief effectiveness.[18] Moreover, debt relief generally concerns a large share of debt which was not likely to be serviced anyway, so that formal debt relief agreements do not free large enough amounts of resources for investments and do not change the incentives of foreign and domestic investors. These findings do not necessarily imply that debt relief is ineffective: more time might be probably necessary to reap the benefits of debt forgiveness and, if its effectiveness depends on institutional improvements, we might expect current debt relief to achieve better results in the near future.

By contrast, we find evidence of a shift from external to internal financing in HIPCs since the launch of the Initiative. The rising domestic debt is probably an unintended consequence of the HIPC Initiative and it is undermining overall

18 The five countries with strong institutions are Nicaragua, Tanzania, Ghana, Uganda and Bolivia. Besides, other seven countries had a CPIA index equal to 3.7, close to the upper threshold (Chapter 7).

debt sustainability and pro-poor spending. Some of the countries which have low (or declining) poverty reduction expenditures are also the ones with high or rising domestic debt. Uganda and Sierra Leone, for example, increased their ratio of domestic debt to GDP from 1.6 and 4.6 of GDP in 1996 to 9.4 and 18.2, respectively, in 2004 and, as a result, debt service on domestic debt (as a share of GDP) increased from 0.2 and 1.1 percent to 1.5 and 4.3 percent, respectively. Given debt relief and the high degree of concessionality on new loans, the amount of resources spent to service domestic debt in 2004 was around 70 percent of the total (external and domestic) public debt service and it represented the actual constraints for government expenditures.

In conclusion, our work raises some concerns on the overall effectiveness of the HIPC Initiative and of the recent MDRI in achieving their main targets. However, results have to be taken with caution because more time and data are required to accomplish a definitive evaluation of debt relief programs, especially for what concerns poverty reduction. Advocates of debt relief explicitly or implicitly assume that large external debts are a drag on domestic and foreign investments and economic growth, thus leaving indebted countries in a poverty trap. However, we do not find strong evidence of debt relief triggering investments and growth. Moreover, aggregate indicators on HIPCs' external debt service and pro-poor spending (Figure 8.2) hide a more heterogeneous picture in which some countries lag behind, and cannot be evaluated *ceteris paribus*, given that HIPC debt relief is generally associated with rising domestic debt. Finally, one should take into account that the amount of resources freed by debt forgiveness are far less than the those required for achieving the MDG. Consequently, given the current situation, expectations should be scaled down to a more realistic level.

## Appendix

### Table 8.1 Debt relief and institutions

| Periods (t) | No debt relief | | Debt relief | | t-test |
|---|---|---|---|---|---|
| | $CPIA_{t-1}$ | Obs. | $CPIA_{t-1}$ | Obs. | (p-value) |
| 1992-1995 | 2.78 | 17 | 3.28 | 38 | 0.04 |
| 1996-1999 | 2.98 | 20 | 3.16 | 41 | 0.22 |
| 2000-2003 | 2.93 | 19 | 3.24 | 42 | 0.07 |
| Total | 2.90 | 56 | 3.22 | 121 | 0.01 |

*Note*: The table reports the average values of the overall CPIA score in the period *t-1* for countries which received or not debt relief at time *t*. The last column report the p-values for the one-tailed test of the null hypothesis that the values of the CPIA scores in countries which received debt relief are higher than in countries without debt relief.
*Source*: Authors' estimates.

**Table 8.2 Determinants of debt relief, whole sample**

| | 1992-2003 | 1992-1995 | 1996-1999 | 2000-2003 |
|---|---|---|---|---|
| **Outcome equation: Dep. Var.: *DEBT RELIEF*$_t$** | | | | |
| *CPIA*$_{t-1}$ | 0.459*** | 0.022 | 0.472* | 0.878*** |
| | (-0.154) | (-0.252) | (-0.252) | (-0.239) |
| *AID*$_{t-1}$ | -0.531** | -0.350 | -0.792** | -0.065 |
| | (-0.267) | (-0.487) | (-0.384) | (0.389) |
| *DEBT SERVICE*$_{t-1}$ | -0.448*** | 0.033 | -0.046 | -1.084*** |
| | (-0.173) | (-0.307) | (-0.315) | (0.201) |
| *EXTERNAL DEBT*$_{t-1}$ | 0.629*** | -0.000 | 0.761*** | 1.032*** |
| | (-0.159) | (-0.283) | (-0.258) | (0.234) |
| **Selection equation: Dep. Var.: Pr(*DEBT RELIEF*$_t$)>0** | | | | |
| *HIPC* (0,1) | 1.152*** | 1.289* | 1.044 | 0.905 |
| | (0.330) | (-0.678) | (-0.676) | (0.609) |
| *COLONY* | -0.000 | -0.009 | -0.000 | 0.009 |
| | (-0.005) | (-0.012) | (-0.011) | (0.010) |
| ln(*DEBT RELIEF*)$_{t-1}$ | 0.534*** | 0.779*** | 0.617*** | 0.482** |
| | (-0.112) | (-0.255) | (-0.216) | (0.234) |
| *CPIA*$_{t-1}$ | 0.144 | -0.298 | 0.146 | 1.106** |
| | (-0.202) | (-0.358) | (-0.388) | (0.473) |
| *AID*$_{t-1}$ | -0.044 | 0.264 | -0.288 | 0.486 |
| | (-0.354) | (-0.693) | (-0.605) | (0.855) |
| *DEBT SERVICE*$_{t-1}$ | 0.067 | -0.081 | 0.084 | 0.458 |
| | (-0.278) | (-0.554) | (-0.494) | (0.529) |
| *GDP*$_{t-1}$ | 0.169 | 0.004 | 0.614 | -0.680 |
| | (-0.278) | (-0.552) | (-0.575) | (0.581) |
| *EXTERNAL DEBT*$_{t-1}$ | 0.267 | 0.322 | 0.192 | 0.480 |
| | (-0.213) | (-0.452) | (-0.368) | (0.465) |
| $\lambda$ | 0.152 | -0.124 | 0.727*** | 0.156 |
| | (-0.220) | (-0.450) | (-0.281) | (-0.295) |
| Observations | 161 | 50 | 53 | 58 |
| Censored | 76 | 24 | 25 | 27 |

*Note*: The table reports regression coefficients and, in brackets, the associated standard errors; * significant at 10 percent; ** significant at 5 percent; *** significant at 1 percent. The model is estimated by Two-Step Heckman, using Stata 10 SE package with HECKMAN command. Time dummies (in the first column) and the constant are included.
*Source*: Authors' estimates.

**Table 8.3 Determinants of debt relief, HIPC sample**

| | 1992-2003 | 1992-1995 | 1996-1999 | 2000-2003 |
|---|---|---|---|---|
| **Outcome equation: Dep. Var.: *DEBT RELIEF*$_t$** | | | | |
| *CPIA*$_{t-1}$ | 0.252 | 0.024 | 0.252 | 0.947* |
| | (0.157) | (0.201) | (0.259) | (0.554) |
| *AID*$_{t-1}$ | -0.433 | -0.367 | -0.352 | -0.123 |
| | (0.271) | (0.470) | (0.444) | (0.431) |
| *DEBT SERVICE*$_{t-1}$ | -0.455*** | -0.181 | -0.307 | -1.202*** |
| | (0.175) | (0.238) | (0.304) | (0.362) |
| *EXTERNAL DEBT*$_{t-1}$ | 0.635*** | 0.210 | 0.889*** | 1.051*** |
| | (0.155) | (0.241) | (0.291) | (0.343) |
| **Selection equation: Dep. Var.: Pr(*DEBT RELIEF*$_t$)>0** | | | | |
| *COLONY* | -0.002 | -0.007 | -0.008 | 0.012 |
| | (0.007) | (0.012) | (0.014) | (0.015) |
| ln(*DEBT RELIEF*)$_{t-1}$ | 0.736*** | 0.607** | 1.158*** | 0.304 |
| | (0.163) | (0.281) | (0.387) | (0.447) |
| *CPIA*$_{t-1}$ | -0.171 | -0.412 | -0.441 | 2.794** |
| | (0.288) | (0.424) | (0.745) | (1.416) |
| *AID*$_{t-1}$ | -0.196 | 0.483 | -0.628 | -0.719 |
| | (0.517) | (1.019) | (0.959) | (1.391) |
| *DEBT SERVICE*$_{t-1}$ | 0.589 | 0.164 | 1.339 | -0.391 |
| | (0.398) | (0.585) | (1.175) | (1.091) |
| *GDP*$_{t-1}$ | -0.368 | 0.111 | -1.079 | -1.253 |
| | (0.358) | (0.611) | (1.032) | (0.790) |
| *EXTERNAL DEBT*$_{t-1}$ | -0.020 | -0.076 | -0.240 | 1.305 |
| | (0.277) | (0.562) | (0.612) | (0.965) |
| $\lambda$ | -0.297 | 0.057 | -0.167 | 0.131 |
| | (0.271) | (0.368) | (0.382) | (0.653) |
| Observations | 108 | 36 | 35 | 37 |
| Censored | 32 | 12 | 10 | 10 |

*Note*: The table reports regression coefficients and, in brackets, the associated standard errors; * significant at 10 percent; ** significant at 5 percent; *** significant at 1 percent. The model is estimated by Two-Step Heckman, using Stata 10 SE package with HECKMAN command. Time dummies (in the first column) and the constant are included.
*Source*: Authors' estimates.

**Table 8.4 Determinants of debt relief, whole sample, 2000-2003**

| | Corruption | Government | Regulation | Rule of Law | Stability | Voice |
|---|---|---|---|---|---|---|
| **Outcome equation: Dep. Var.: *DEBT RELIEF*$_t$** | | | | | | |
| *GOVERNANCE*$_{t-1}$ | 0.306 | 1.036*** | 0.791*** | 0.620** | 0.429*** | 0.413* |
| | (0.350) | (0.311) | (0.220) | (0.303) | (0.148) | (0.226) |
| *AID*$_{t-1}$ | 0.333 | 0.108 | 0.078 | 0.223 | 0.155 | 0.077 |
| | (0.471) | (0.408) | (0.418) | (0.449) | (0.425) | (0.487) |
| *DEBT SERVICE*$_{t-1}$ | -0.855*** | -1.134*** | -1.114*** | -1.024*** | -0.992*** | -0.896*** |
| | (0.263) | (0.230) | (0.239) | (0.258) | (0.232) | (0.249) |
| *EXTERNAL DEBT*$_{t-1}$ | 0.644** | 0.890*** | 0.957*** | 0.859*** | 0.756*** | 0.677*** |
| | (0.258) | (0.227) | (0.227) | (0.269) | (0.220) | (0.234) |
| **Selection equation: Dep. Var.: Pr(*DEBT RELIEF*$_t$)>0** | | | | | | |
| *HIPC* (0,1) | 1.008* | 1.078* | 1.027* | 1.013* | 1.009* | 0.988* |
| | (0.566) | (0.579) | (0.577) | (0.567) | (0.566) | (0.575) |
| *COLONY* | 0.008 | 0.008 | 0.008 | 0.008 | 0.007 | 0.008 |
| | (0.008) | (0.009) | (0.009) | (0.009) | (0.008) | (0.008) |
| ln(*DEBT RELIEF*)$_{t-1}$ | 0.455** | 0.483** | 0.478** | 0.468** | 0.467** | 0.455** |
| | (0.200) | (0.207) | (0.211) | (0.202) | (0.199) | (0.198) |
| *GOVERNANCE*$_{t-1}$ | 0.320 | 0.840 | -0.118 | 0.433 | 0.166 | 0.068 |
| | (0.532) | (0.637) | (0.483) | (0.551) | (0.288) | (0.438) |
| *AID*$_{t-1}$ | 0.563 | 0.564 | 0.758 | 0.619 | 0.607 | 0.691 |
| | (0.808) | (0.785) | (0.785) | (0.771) | (0.798) | (0.806) |
| *DEBT SERVICE*$_{t-1}$ | 0.774 | 0.588 | 0.898* | 0.655 | 0.796* | 0.828* |
| | (0.489) | (0.518) | (0.518) | (0.530) | (0.482) | (0.491) |
| *GDP*$_{t-1}$ | -0.439 | -0.522 | -0.380 | -0.403 | -0.476 | -0.415 |
| | (0.482) | (0.511) | (0.487) | (0.485) | (0.499) | (0.483) |
| *EXTERNAL DEBT*$_{t-1}$ | -0.023 | 0.098 | -0.190 | 0.064 | -0.071 | -0.116 |
| | (0.378) | (0.381) | (0.403) | (0.419) | (0.347) | (0.344) |
| $\lambda$ | 0.176 | 0.129 | 0.386 | 0.088 | 0.057 | 0.218 |
| | (0.334) | (0.283) | (0.283) | (0.323) | (0.304) | (0.326) |
| Observations | 58 | 58 | 58 | 58 | 58 | 58 |
| Censored | 27 | 27 | 27 | 27 | 27 | 27 |

*Note*: The table reports regression coefficients and, in brackets, the associated standard errors; * significant at 10 percent; ** significant at 5 percent; *** significant at 1 percent. *GOVERNANCE* refers to the six WGI reported at the top of each column. The model is estimated by Two-Step Heckman, using Stata 10 SE package with HECKMAN command. *Source*: Authors' estimates.

**Table 8.5 Determinants of debt relief, HIPC sample, 2000-2003**

| | Corruption | Government | Regulation | Rule of Law | Stability | Voice |
|---|---|---|---|---|---|---|
| **Outcome equation: Dep. Var.: *DEBT RELIEF*$_t$** | | | | | | |
| *GOVERNANCE*$_{t-1}$ | -0.171 | 0.723* | 0.684** | 0.111 | 0.183 | 0.231 |
| | (0.395) | (0.407) | (0.267) | (0.368) | (0.194) | (0.247) |
| *AID*$_{t-1}$ | 0.123 | -0.058 | -0.220 | 0.019 | 0.017 | -0.121 |
| | (0.500) | (0.467) | (0.472) | (0.511) | (0.490) | (0.505) |
| *DEBT SERVICE*$_{t-1}$ | -0.593* | -0.984*** | -1.132*** | -0.762** | -0.821*** | -0.827*** |
| | (0.318) | (0.299) | (0.331) | (0.338) | (0.313) | (0.301) |
| *EXTERNAL DEBT*$_{t-1}$ | 0.555** | 0.845*** | 0.990*** | 0.689** | 0.707*** | 0.698*** |
| | (0.269) | (0.249) | (0.267) | (0.295) | (0.250) | (0.244) |
| **Selection equation: Dep. Var.: Pr(*DEBT RELIEF*$_t$)>0** | | | | | | |
| *COLONY* | 0.008 | 0.009 | 0.007 | 0.008 | 0.005 | 0.010 |
| | (0.013) | (0.013) | (0.013) | (0.013) | (0.013) | (0.013) |
| ln(*DEBT RELIEF*)$_{t-1}$ | 0.631* | 0.566* | 0.668* | 0.600* | 0.589* | 0.555* |
| | (0.346) | (0.328) | (0.373) | (0.331) | (0.324) | (0.319) |
| *GOVERNANCE*$_{t-1}$ | 0.710 | 1.166 | -0.351 | 0.451 | 0.235 | 0.595 |
| | (0.888) | (1.051) | (0.732) | (0.837) | (0.400) | (0.667) |
| *AID*$_{t-1}$ | -0.187 | 0.046 | 0.343 | 0.156 | 0.075 | -0.137 |
| | (1.207) | (1.140) | (1.155) | (1.094) | (1.134) | (1.208) |
| *DEBT SERVICE*$_{t-1}$ | 1.189 | 0.940 | 1.572* | 1.134 | 1.337* | 1.317* |
| | (0.726) | (0.812) | (0.804) | (0.849) | (0.717) | (0.725) |
| *GDP*$_{t-1}$ | -1.053 | -1.052 | -0.915 | -0.939 | -1.096 | -1.120 |
| | (0.676) | (0.665) | (0.672) | (0.655) | (0.701) | (0.688) |
| *EXTERNAL DEBT*$_{t-1}$ | 0.029 | 0.114 | -0.466 | -0.045 | -0.165 | -0.135 |
| | (0.565) | (0.546) | (0.582) | (0.589) | (0.443) | (0.454) |
| $\lambda$ | -0.353 | -0.142 | -0.089 | -0.434 | -0.341 | -0.446 |
| | (0.596) | (0.596) | (0.530) | (0.604) | (0.580) | (0.581) |
| Observations | 37 | 37 | 37 | 37 | 37 | 37 |
| Censored | 10 | 10 | 10 | 10 | 10 | 10 |

*Note*: The table reports regression coefficients and, in brackets, the associated standard errors; * significant at 10 percent; ** significant at 5 percent; *** significant at 1 percent. *GOVERNANCE* refers to the six WGI reported at the top of each column. The model is estimated by Two-Step Heckman, using Stata 10 SE package with HECKMAN command. *Source*: Authors' estimates.

**Table 8.6 The effects of debt relief**

| Dep. Var.: Change in: | (1) *GROWTH* | (2) *INV* | (3) *FDI* | (4) *DomD* | (5) *CPIA* |
|---|---|---|---|---|---|
| *Whole sample* | | | | | |
| *DEBT RELIEF*$_{t-1}$ | 0.002 | -0.030 | 0.039 | 0.041 | -0.006 |
| | [0.002] | [0.060] | [0.070] | [0.043] | [0.004] |
| Observations | 220 | 221 | 223 | 183 | 230 |
| Number of countries | 60 | 60 | 60 | 48 | 62 |
| *HIPC countries* | | | | | |
| *DEBT RELIEF*$_{t-1}$ | 0.002 | 0.015 | -0.020 | 0.054** | -0.011** |
| | [0.003] | [0.056] | [0.063] | [0.022] | [0.005] |
| Observations | 146 | 143 | 145 | 136 | 152 |
| Number of countries | 38 | 37 | 38 | 35 | 39 |

*Note*: The table reports regression coefficients and, in brackets, the associated standard errors; * significant at 10 percent; ** significant at 5 percent; *** significant at 1 percent. The model is estimated by Within Group, using Stata 10 SE package with XTREG command.
*Source*: Authors' estimates.

**Table 8.7 The effects of debt relief, different sub-periods**

| Dep. Var.: Change in: | (1) *GROWTH* | (2) *INV* | (3) *FDI* | (4) *DomD* | (5) *CPIA* |
|---|---|---|---|---|---|
| *Whole sample* | | | | | |
| 1992-95 | 0.001 | 0.010 | 0.165 | 0.053 | -0.002 |
| 1996-99 | 0.012*** | 0.039 | 0.014 | 0.078 | 0.006 |
| 2000-03 | -0.001 | -0.076 | 0.025 | 0.092 | -0.013** |
| 2004-07 | 0.004 | -0.023 | -0.018 | -0.044 | -0.001 |
| *HIPC countries* | | | | | |
| 1992-95 | 0.002 | 0.036 | 0.306** | -0.019 | -0.006 |
| 1996-99 | 0.015** | 0.219* | -0.114 | 0.062 | 0.001 |
| 2000-03 | -0.004 | -0.060 | -0.085 | 0.122*** | -0.024*** |
| 2004-07 | 0.005 | 0.014 | -0.086 | 0.011 | -0.002 |

*Note*: The table reports regression coefficients and, in brackets, the associated standard errors; * significant at 10 percent; ** significant at 5 percent; *** significant at 1 percent. The model is estimated by Within Group, using Stata 10 SE package with XTREG command.
*Source*: Authors' estimates.

**Table 8.8 Country coverage**

| Country | Code | Income | Region | HIPC | Country | Code | Income | Region | HIPC |
|---|---|---|---|---|---|---|---|---|---|
| Angola | AGO | LMIC | SSA | 0 | Lesotho | LSO | LIC | SSA | 0 |
| Armenia | ARM | LMIC | ECA | 0 | Moldova | MDA | LMIC | ECA | 0 |
| Azerbaijan | AZE | LMIC | ECA | 0 | Madagascar | MDG | LIC | SSA | 1 |
| Burundi | BDI | LIC | SSA | 1 | Mali | MLI | LIC | SSA | 1 |
| Benin | BEN | LIC | SSA | 1 | Myanmar | MMR | LIC | EA | 0 |
| Burkina Faso | BFA | LIC | SSA | 1 | Mongolia | MNG | LMIC | EA | 0 |
| Bangladesh | BGD | LIC | SA | 0 | Mozambique | MOZ | LIC | SSA | 1 |
| Bolivia | BOL | LMIC | LAC | 1 | Mauritania | MRT | LIC | SSA | 1 |
| Bhutan | BTN | LIC | SA | 0 | Malawi | MWI | LIC | SSA | 1 |
| Central African Rep. | CAF | LIC | SSA | 1 | Niger | NER | LIC | SSA | 1 |
| China | CHN | LIC | EA | 0 | Nigeria | NGA | LIC | SSA | 0 |
| Cote d'Ivoire | CIV | LMIC | SSA | 1 | Nicaragua | NIC | LMIC | LAC | 1 |
| Cameroon | CMR | LMIC | SSA | 1 | Nepal | NPL | LIC | SA | 1 |
| Congo, Rep. | COG | LMIC | SSA | 1 | Pakistan | PAK | LIC | SA | 0 |
| Comoros | COM | LIC | SSA | 1 | Rwanda | RWA | LIC | SSA | 1 |
| Djibouti | DJI | LMIC | MENA | 0 | Sudan | SDN | LIC | SSA | 1 |
| Eritrea | ERI | LIC | SSA | 1 | Senegal | SEN | LMIC | SSA | 1 |
| Ethiopia | ETH | LIC | SSA | 1 | Sierra Leone | SLE | LIC | SSA | 1 |
| Ghana | GHA | LIC | SSA | 1 | Somalia | SOM | LIC | SSA | 1 |
| Guinea | GIN | LIC | SSA | 1 | Sao Tome and Principe | STP | LIC | SSA | 1 |
| Gambia, The | GMB | LIC | SSA | 1 | Chad | TCD | LIC | SSA | 1 |
| Guinca-Bissau | GND | LIC | SSA | 1 | Togo | TGO | LIC | SSA | 1 |
| Equatorial Guinea | GNQ | LIC | 1 | 0 | Tanzania | TZA | LIC | SSA | 1 |
| Guyana | GUY | LIC | LAC | 1 | Uganda | UGA | LIC | SSA | 1 |
| Honduras | HND | LMIC | LAC | 1 | Ukraine | UKR | LMIC | ECA | 0 |
| Haiti | HTI | LIC | LAC | 1 | Uzbekistan | UZB | LMIC | ECA | 0 |
| India | IND | LIC | SA | 0 | Vietnam | VNM | LIC | EA | 0 |
| Kenya | KEN | LIC | SSA | 0 | Yemen, Rep. | YEM | LMIC | MENA | 0 |
| Cambodia | KHM | LIC | EA | 0 | Congo, Dem. Rep. | ZAR | LIC | SSA | 1 |
| Lao PDR | LAO | LIC | EA | 0 | Zambia | ZMB | LIC | SSA | 1 |
| Liberia | LBR | LIC | SSA | 1 | Zimbabwe | ZWE | LMIC | SSA | 0 |

*Note*: The country code, the regional and income categories refer to the WB Country Classification in 1988 (http://go.worldbank.org/K2CKM78CC0). ECA: Europe and Central Asia; SSA: Sub-Saharan Africa; SA: South Asia; EAP: East Asia and Pacific; LAC: Latin America and Caribbean; MENA: North Africa and Middle East. LIC: Low Income Country; LMIC: Lower Middle-Income Country.

# PART 4
# The Challenges Ahead

### Overview

Part 4 deals with some open issues of debt relief programs. The first one is the management of the global economic and financial crisis in LICs, where it was transmitted with a time lag and, at the time of writing, is not yet over. We argue that the crisis represents a serious threat to public debt sustainability and poverty reduction targets in several HIPCs, already hit by the food crisis which worsened the BOP in several non oil-exporting countries. In Chapter 9 we outline the channels through which the financial crisis has spread to LICs, focusing on the severe contraction of external finance – foreign aid, remittances, private capital flows – which, coupled with declining budget revenues and increasing public expenditures, has resulted in a widening financing gap. The likely increase in domestic and external borrowing, together with a sharp contraction in export revenues and GDP growth can have unpleasant consequences on debt sustainability. Debt relief, especially thanks to the MDRI debt write-off, has granted completion point HIPCs a fresh start which is reflected in lower debt ratios and reduced risks of debt distress in the wake of the global crisis. Nevertheless, the picture is not so encouraging since, at the end of June 2009, no pre-decision point or interim HIPCs had a low probability of debt distress and, even among completion point countries, almost one out of five was at a high risk of debt distress (IDA and IMF 2009). In other words, their initial conditions make indebted countries extremely vulnerable to the global financial crisis, whose impact is of the order of a GDP growth slowdown of 2.5 percent with respect to the pre-crisis estimates. In Chapter 9 we show that the downward revision in GDP and export growth are already reflected in a worsening debt sustainability scenario in many HIPCs. Further (and likely) downward revisions and increasing borrowing, especially if non-concessional, could open the door to another round of debt distress episodes.

This scenario makes some of the future challenges discussed in Chapter 10 more pressing. In particular, the role of private creditors and non-concessional lending has to be carefully evaluated in the DSF. Access to international capital markets by some HIPCs – thanks to a lower debt burden, and the moral hazard by non-Paris Club and private creditors, which take advantage of the higher borrowing capacity – could provide the needed additional resources, but they also worsen future debt sustainability and increase the crowding out and debt overhang effects. The data we have collected on actual and projected domestic and foreign financing do not show any sign of a downward trend after the MDRI. Total financing is estimated to be higher in 2009 than in the years before the debt cancellation, with a worse outlook in the poorest countries. Therefore, multilateral institutions should focus on the development of appropriate lending strategies, based on some sort of mix between loans and grants, with a limited and conditioned access to commercial lending and on different tools for improved debt management strategies and reform programs. More generally, given also the risks posed by odious debt and vulture funds in many HIPCs, we believe that donors should pledge to take account of debt sustainability issues in their lending practices and endorse a Charter for Responsible Lending, including binding requirements for creditors not to sell sovereign debts issued by debt relief-eligible countries without explicit approval of the debtors.

Finally, we outline two sorts of policy recommendations. Firstly, we propose an extended DSF which should include all the alternative sources of financing, including domestic debt, non-concessional lending and remittances, in addition to external debt, in a fully-fledged budget constraint. At the cost of limiting the simplicity and communicability of the current DSA, we believe that the framework should take into account many possible feedback effects and interactions among variables, in order to draw more realistic indications on the possible evolution of total public debt. We also suggest to strengthen the linkages between the DSA and poverty reduction strategies and to give more weight to debt flows, given that debt-service payments can crowd out or change the composition of investment and social spending. Finally, we urge the international community to develop a legal framework to deal with private creditors and to increase cooperation among donors, especially with the ones outside the Paris Club.

Secondly, we call for a *growth diagnostic* approach to debt relief initiatives, which should be tailored to country-specific characteristics. Not only debt sustainability, the amount and composition of new lending, but also eligibility criteria and actual debt cancellations should be a function of institutional quality. We believe that debt relief effectiveness can be strengthened if the IFIs: 1) avoid one-size-fits-all solutions; 2) consider different eligible countries, with large debt but sound institutions, other than the actual HIPCs; and 3) make the amount of debt cancellation conditional upon actual improvements in institutional quality, in order to give the right incentives to debtors to strengthen institutions and debt management capacity.

# Chapter 9
# The Global Economic and Financial Crisis and the HIPCs[1]

## 9.1 Introduction

As seen so far, the various debt relief initiatives of the last decades were only partially successful in reducing external debt dependence in poor countries, increasing poverty reduction and social expenditures, and putting heavily indebted countries on a debt-sustainable path. Results in terms of higher investments and enhanced economic growth are less evident. In any case, even the positive but limited results cannot be taken for granted, since there are many sources of vulnerability, such as rising domestic debt (Part 2) and the predatory role of new lenders and vulture funds lawsuits, which we discuss in Chapter 10. On the top of that, external exogenous shocks are always a threat to poverty reduction policies and debt sustainability in poor countries, because of limited fiscal space and policy options.

The analysis of the consequences of the global economic and financial crisis (2008-2010) on LICs is of particular interest not only because of its unprecedented financial severity and global scale, but also because it forces poor countries to deal with multiple exogenous shocks simultaneously: mitigating the effects of a reduction in trade, capital inflows and possible foreign assistance is going to be a very hard task. In the following, we try to spell out the way in which the global crisis has affected and still weighs on developing countries, focusing on overall debt sustainability and the progress and targets of the HIPC and MDRI Initiatives.

## 9.2 The Transmission Channels

Although the epicenter of the current turmoil has been the financial industry of the richest countries and the recession is hitting harder in Europe and the United States, it is now evident that dramatic long-run consequences are likely to be suffered by LICs. Even if poor countries are not so directly interconnected to the world financial system, so that they can escape the direct contagion channel, they are exposed to many other sources of vulnerability and lack the appropriate resources

1 This chapter was originally published as a journal article in *Rivista Bancaria – Minerva Bancaria* LXV (5-6): 35-64. The chapter includes minor modifications. The definitive version is available at: http://www.rivistabancaria.it/presbitero.pdf.

and instruments to face the crisis.[2] More broadly, developing countries are the least to blame for the outbreak of the financial crisis, but they likely to suffer the most dramatic and long-lasting consequences. In the words of a Malawian cotton farmer: "I feel cheated as I wonder how economic problems somewhere in America can make my cash crop suffer here in Malawi. It's a shame that I cannot boil and eat it" (Oxfam 2010). Poor countries' vulnerability to a collapse in industrialized countries' output is due to their extraordinary dependence on volatile resources, such as exports of primary commodities, private capital inflows, remittances and foreign assistance (Mold, Paulo and Prizzon 2009; IMF 2009a; WB 2009a). Besides, the financial crisis has spread to in many poor countries, especially in SSA, which were and are still affected by the food crisis.[3] The impact of the financial turmoil is extremely heterogeneous among poor countries, depending on their economic structure, external dependence and institutional framework. Nonetheless, there are different common indirect channels through which the current financial turmoil and the recession in the rich world could affect poor countries.

### *9.2.1 Trade*

The most important source of vulnerability is the critical dependence of poor countries on export revenues and their narrow export base, since commodities still account for about 70 percent of LICs exports. Thus, the sharp decline in the world demand following the crisis has dramatic consequences on the volume of exports. Moreover, the fall in commodity prices during the crisis, has to be taken into account. The IMF (2009a) projections show a sharp fall in exports, from 26.6 to 21.8 percent of GDP and a deterioration in the terms of trade. The fall in the price of copper, for instance, has hurt the economy of Zambia, whose foreign exchange earnings are generated for three quarters by copper mining: some large investment projects are put on hold, poverty rates increase and debt sustainability is at risk. However, some price movements, such as the early decline of the imports bills for fertilizers, food and oil have helped (non-oil producing) LICs' current account. The WB (2009a) estimates that between July 2008 and May 2009 the terms of

2 By contrast, the bailout of the financial industry in OECD countries amounts to a huge amount of public money. Even a tiny percentage of it could have been spent on a number of different aid programs (i.e. the 700 billion dollars program originally proposed to bail out Wall Street is about seven fold the global level of annual official development assistance).

3 International commodity prices increased substantially from 2005 to mid-2008, when they collapsed. However, since 2009 prices are following again an upward trend and they are much above their pre-crisis level (see http://www.imf.org/external/np/res/commod/index.asp, last accessed April 2010). Furthermore, local food prices in many countries have not fallen: according to the most recent survey conducted by the World Food Program, in 73 percent of the countries monitored, the overall cost of the food basket is more than 20 percent above the five-year averages.

trade deteriorated for 18 African countries, but improved for 26 countries, mainly oil importers.

### 9.2.2 External Finance

The second transmission channel is the dependence on external finance. The relative weight of different sources of capital inflows to LICs is substantially changed in the last years. While ODA reached a peak in the early nineties, but then declined, both net FDI and workers' remittances increased substantially, representing around 2 percent of GDP in 2000. In the last decade, remittances grew at an even faster pace and became the second source of external finance in poor countries, amounting to more than 5 percent of national GDPs, almost twice the net inflows of FDI and not much smaller than foreign assistance (Figure 9.1).[4]

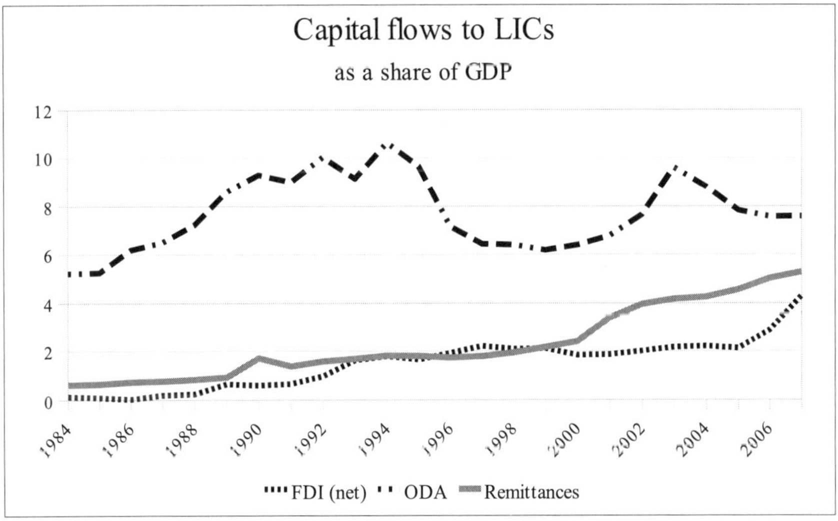


**Figure 9.1 Changes in capital inflows to LICs**
*Source*: Authors' elaborations based on WDI (2009).

The intensity at which the crisis is affecting capital inflows to poor countries depends on their correlation with the business cycle and on their resilience to the

4 In SSA countries the flow of remittances in 2006 was similar to the one of FDI, while aid was still more than three times larger (Gupta, Pattillo and Wagh 2009). The picture is different considering the whole sample of developing countries, where, in 2008, remittances reached 328 billion of dollars, more than 50 percent of FDI and twice the amount of ODA.

recession in industrialized countries. On the whole, capital flows are generally perceived as strongly pro-cyclical, so that they should contract following the global crisis. However, the flow of remittances should be somewhat less correlated with economic conditions in the home and host countries and less volatile than official aid and FDI, smoothing consumption and investment in poor countries. In light of this, poor countries might be better equipped to deal with the crisis than in the past. However, to verify this hypothesis one must look at past experiences and at the preliminary data on the effect of the current global turmoil on global development finance.

On the whole, the world crisis is likely to generate a reduction in capital flows to developing countries. According to the Institute of International Finance, net private capital flows to poor countries has slowed from almost US$ 1 trillion in 2007 to US$ 165 billion in 2009. Even if private capital flows to Africa account for a negligible share of global flows, their decline for African countries is substantial: the WB estimates that net private capital inflows to SSA countries contracted by 35 percent in 2008 with respect to 2007 (at US$ 36 billion) as in 2005 (WB 2009a). Some African LICs have recently gained access to the international bond market and the private debt market, but the crisis has dried up this financing channel, delaying the construction of important infrastructures, such as toll roads and gas pipelines. HIPCs, in particular, have benefited from lower debt ratios and institutional reforms for exploring new forms of borrowing, including lending at commercial terms (Chapter 3). On the whole, African countries raised in 2007 US$ 6.5 billion in international bonds, while in 2008 they raised nothing.

**Foreign assistance**

As shown in Figure 9.2, LICs and especially HIPCs are highly dependent on bilateral and multilateral aid flows – especially the latter ones – representing around 8 percent of GDP. Given that, as typically happened in the past, developing countries' access to private international financial markets dries up precisely when their economies are hit by a shock (Kaminsky, Reinhart and Vegh 2004), foreign aid should increase and act as a sort insurance mechanism, smoothing consumption and providing large welfare gains in poor crisis-hit countries (Pallage, Robe and Bérubé. 2006). However, notwithstanding the pronouncements by IFIs and donors, ODA is not likely to be scaled up as a response to the crisis. During the 1972-3 global recession aid fell by 15 percent before bouncing back. But in 1990-93 aid plummeted by nearly 25 percent in a five-year period, and did not return to its 1992 levels until 2003. Humanitarian aid followed the same pattern. A recent analysis limited to the United States estimates a potential decline in ODA ranging from 13 to 30 percent depending on the severity of the current crisis (Mendoza, Jones and Vergara 2009). The IMF estimates on foreign assistance show a decline with respect to 2008, while anecdotal evidence on donors suggest that some of them, such as Austria, Ireland and Italy, are already reducing their disbursements, while others are "front-loading" their aid efforts, meaning that they are borrowing from future years to keep aid flows steady now, so that foreign assistance might fall further after 2009.[5] Looking at past experiences, this outcome could be partially explained by the poor role of aid as an insurance mechanism against GDP shortfalls (Pallage and Robe 2001; Bulir and Hamann 2008) and also by the negative response of aid disbursements in industrialized countries after a domestic crisis (Roodman 2008; Frot 2009; Dang, Knack and Rogers 2009). Using data from past crisis, Frot (2009) estimates that five years after an adverse growth shock of 1 percentage point, aid may fall by as much as US$ 7 billion. A similar exercise carried out by the WB finds that aid flows are positively correlated with donor country's income and falls by an average of 20-25 percent in response to a banking crisis, rebounding to the original level only a decade after the crisis' inception (Dang, Knack and Rogers 2009).

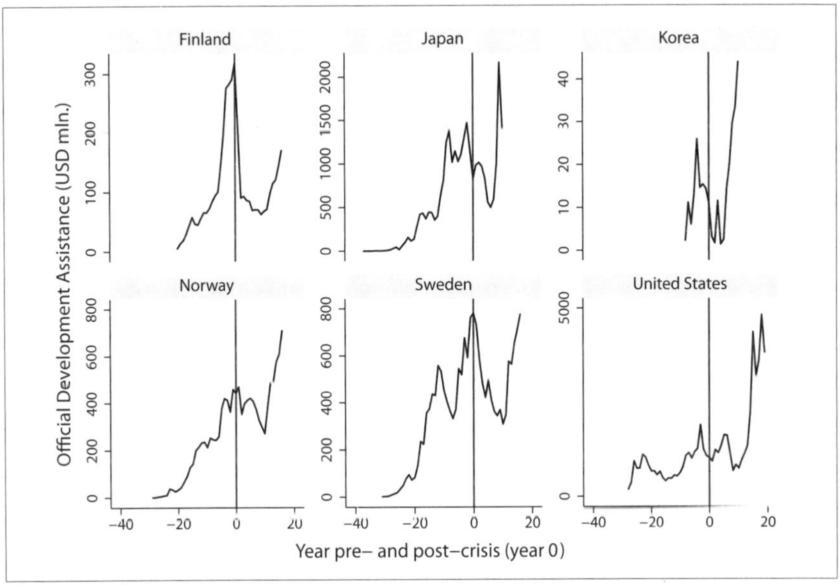


**Figure 9.2 Crisis and ODA, the past experience**
*Source*: Authors' elaboration on OECD, WB and Laeven and Valencia (2008) data.

To better gauge the impact of past crisis on foreign assistance to Africa, we replicate the exercise presented in Frot (2009) on the whole sample of developing countries, by plotting the evolution of the ODA flows to SSA countries by the

5 The US budget for fiscal year 2011 indicates a reduction in overseas aid in order to limit the explosion of the US debt. By contrast, even with a shrinking economy, the UK has left the overseas aid unchanged at GDP 9.1 billion of pounds for 2010, as projected in 2007.

most important donors which were affected by a crisis during the past fifty years (Figure 9.2).[6] The diagrams are instructive in the sense that they can provide a benchmark of how major donors reacted in the past to a (regional) crisis. However, the global nature and the intensity of the global crisis is likely to have different, and probably stronger, consequences, as testified by the IMF projections. In any case, the picture is not encouraging. Finland and Sweden dramatically reduced their aid assistance and were still below the pre-crisis level after two decades. The US have experienced a massive increase in ODA since 2000, while, before that, their disbursements were still below the level reached at the times of the Saving & Loans crisis.

**Workers' remittances**

Even in the best-case scenario, foreign aid is not likely to increase and act as a shock absorber for poor countries, filling the financing gap due to the fall in capital inflows. In recent years, remittances by international migrants grew at double-digit annual rate and emerged as another, market-driven, insurance mechanism for developing countries. Remittances by international migrants to LICs amounted to more than 60 billion dollars in 2007, representing around 7 percent of GDP in the average SSA country, and more than 12 percent in Latin America.[7] In some poor countries, such as Tajikistan, Guyana, Honduras and Haiti, remittances account for more than 20 percent of output and they are even more important than aid flows. Their rapid increase is seen as a favorable evolution in the composition of development finance, since remittances are generally associated with development and growth through a number of channels, such as capital accumulation, allocation efficiency, entrepreneurship, financial development, education and infant mortality (Adams and Page 2005, Giuliano and Ruiz Arranz 2009, Chami et al. 2008, Gupta, Pattillo and Wagh 2009). A contraction in world remittances can have strong negative effects on the receiving countries. On the one hand, if remittances are counter cyclical with respect to the country of origin, they should help smoothing consumption and investment intertemporally, mitigating the impact of a local crisis. On the other hand, the positive correlation between the flow of remittances and the GDP of the host country and the limited role played by altruism as a determinant of remittances flows reduce the role of remittances as a shock absorber in case of a global crisis (Frankel 2009). Because of rising unemployment in western countries, migrants' remittances are likely to decrease: the crisis induced a contraction in remittances flows to the developing world from 5 to 8 percent in 2009 (Ratha and Mohapatra 2009). A larger reduction is estimated by Calì and Dell'Erba (2009),

6 ODA data are drawn from the DAC dataset compiled by the OCSE and they are in constant 2000 US dollars (data are deflated using the GDP deflator published in the WDI). A financial crisis episode is defined following the recent dataset constructed by Laeven and Valencia (2008, http://www.luclaeven.com/Data.htm).

7 See also the WB website on Migration and Remittances data at: http://go.worldbank.org/QOWEWD6TA0 (last accessed April 2010).

who calculate a drop in remittances ranging from 8 to 12 percent in 2009, but a rapid recovery in 2010. Looking at previous experiences of banking crisis in the host country, they conclude that many episodes seem to have a substantially negative effect on subsequent remittance flows, even if in the majority of cases this effect is short-lived. In any case, remittances are likely to remain more resilient than other sources of capital inflows in poor countries. The availability of up-to-date monthly data on remittances inflows in selected HIPCs shows that there is not yet a convincing evidence of a decline in response to the crisis, especially for the two largest recipients (Uganda and Nicaragua, Figure 9.3).

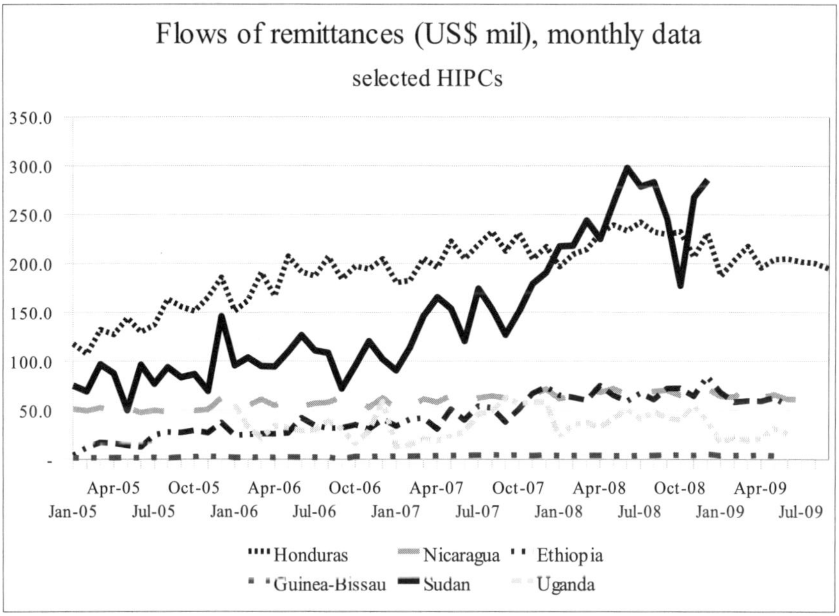


**Figure 9.3 Workers' remittances to heavily indebted and poor countries**
*Source*: Authors' elaboration based on data from Migration and Remittances Team, Development Prospects Group, WB (http://www.worldbank.org/prospects/migrationand remittances).

**Foreign direct investment**
FDIs, even if generally targeted to MICs, are becoming an important element of external finance also in LICs, especially since 2005. Notwithstanding the general presumption of FDI being a better and more stable source of external financing than portfolio and debt flows, they are pro-cyclical, as testified by their reduction in 2008 and 2009. UNCTAD (2009a) estimates that global FDI halved in the first quarter of 2009, on a year-to-year basis. This reduction interests also inflows to

developing countries, where, however, FDI continued to rise in 2008, albeit at a slower pace than in previous years. In developing Africa FDI increased since 2000 for eight consecutive years, financing more than 40 percent of gross fixed capital formation, before a slowdown in the second half of 2008 (UNCTAD 2009b). The IMF projected for 2009 a fall in FDI inflows to LICs of around 20-25 percent with respect to their 2008 level (IMF 2009a). Thus a number of countries will have to scale down large infrastructure projects, especially natural resource-abundant countries, where a number of exploration and exploitation projects, started in response to the surge in commodity prices, will be postponed. According to the WB, for example, Congo DR is estimated to loose US$ 1.8 billion in FDI because of the financial crisis.

### *9.2.3 Credit and Capital Markets*

Finally, even if LICs' financial systems are not directly part of the financial crisis, the extremely large foreign participation in the banking system does have adverse effects on small business finance and entrepreneurship. The share of foreign-owned banking assets is about 50 percent or more in SSA and Europe and Central Asia, and more than one third in Latin America.[8] Large multinational banks are likely to generate cream-skimming effects which penalize small and informationally opaque borrowers (Detragiache, Tressel and Gupta 2008; Gormley 2010). Moreover, during a financial crisis multinational banks are likely to rein in their credit supply in order to focus on the home-country market, transmitting the home-country financial shock to the host country (Peek and Rosengren 1997). Total lending by foreign-owned banks contracted by 13.6 percent in the second semester of 2008, more than three times the contraction registered by domestic banks, even if there are significant differences across countries, with foreign banks acting as a stabilizers in the Middle East and, partially, in Latin America (Galindo, Izquierdo and Rojas-Suarez 2010). Tightening credit conditions in bank lending are observed in several HIPCs, such as in Ghana and Zambia (WB 2009b). Local financial markets have also been hit by the crisis, since the deterioration in the functioning of US and European interbank markets forced investors to deleverage and reduce their positions in African bond, money and equity markets to raise liquidity. In some African countries declines in equity prices, currency depreciation and higher interbank rates have been observed (IMF 2009g, World Bank 2009a).[9]

---

8 See the WB website at: http://go.worldbank.org/X23UD9QUX0 (last accessed April 2010).

9 The WB (2009a) estimates that the currency of the average SSA country depreciated by 25 percent against the dollar and that bond spreads widened considerably in 2008-2009, being between 220 and 375 basis point higher than their pre-crisis level in Gabon and Ghana.

## 9.3 The Financing Gap and the Responses by the IFIs

According to a number of different estimates provided by international organizations and NGOs, developing countries are going to face a financing gap of around US$ 140-700 billion, depending on the severity of the crisis, the policy responses and the materializing of different scenarios. The IMF estimates that LICs will have to deal with a balance of payment negative shock of around US$ 165 billion, resulting from a fall in exports, FDI, remittances and from adverse price food and fuel changes. Once the loss of reserves is taken into account, this shock will result in additional financing needs of about US$ 25 billion in 2009. A bad case scenario, in which a number of shocks take place simultaneously, is also simulated and, in this case, total financing needs for LIC will amount to US$ 138 billion. Focusing on the whole sample of developing countries, the WB estimated that in 2009 many countries (between 59 and 69) had difficulties meeting external financing needs, estimated at one trillion dollars. While the overall financing gap in 2009 should be between US$ 350 billion to US$ 635 billion, in SSA external financing needs should amount to around US$ 150 billion, mainly due to current account deficits, and the financing gap is estimated to be less than US$ 100 billion.

The severity of the crisis in LICs is exacerbated by the national governments' lack of appropriate tools to face the crisis. Apart from a few poor countries which were able to accumulate stock of international reserves or to reduce public debt in recent years, the majority of developing countries have limited resources to fund any fiscal stimulus, having no room for countercyclical policies without weakening debt sustainability. Moreover, expansionary fiscal policies in developing countries are riskier than in industrialized countries, since for the former there is a very limited body of analytical and empirical evidence on the effectiveness of the fiscal multiplier and the few available studies point to a smaller effect of a fiscal stimulus, particularly in heavily indebted countries (Ilzetzki and Végh 2008; Ilzetzki, Mendoza and Végh 2009). In developing countries with a recent record of central bank independence, a fiscal expansion could result in financing deficits with money creation, loosing the hard-gained credibility and threatening the pursuit of price stability (Reinhart and Reinhart 2009). A different opinion is expressed in the IMF African Regional Economic Outlook: "a number of sub-Saharan African countries would have scope for a fiscal expansion [and a] few countries may also have scope for discretionary fiscal stimulus to sustain demand" (IMF 2009g: 21). This statement is based on an analysis which assumes that low or moderate risks of debt distress in almost two third of SSA countries can create room for fiscal expansion. However, as we discuss in the next section, the current crisis is severely affecting debt dynamics, so that many countries in the coming years can be more vulnerable to fiscal deficits and will have limited scope for expansionary policies, especially if donor assistance will not be scaled up. Anyway, some SSA countries could actually implement discretionary fiscal stimulus to sustain aggregate demand, giving priority to the financing of social safety nets programs. Nevertheless, fiscal policies should consider the specific economic and financial characteristics of SSA countries: limited access to international capital markets and thin domestic financial markets could make fiscal policy less effective and might lead to a crowding out of private investment (Berg et al. 2009 and Chapter 3).

Given the limited room for counter-cyclical policies, the role of donors and the international community in poor countries becomes fundamental. With the unfolding of the crisis, the WB and the IMF have developed alternative strategies aimed at mitigating the effects of the global recession, improving the lending capacity and the pool of resources available to LICs.

The economic crisis and the subsequent higher demand for funds from poor countries has forced the IMF to undertake a substantial revision of its lending instruments to poor countries and to double its borrowing limits, in order to meet the increased needs of LICs.[10] According to the IMF, its new initiatives are expected to boost concessional lending to US$ 17 billion through 2014. Since 2008, new lending by the IMF to low income (PRGF-eligible) countries amounted to US$ 4.3 billion and new loans appear to be economically driven and targeted to poor countries most hit by the crisis (Presbitero and Zazzaro 2010).

The ESF, originally created to provide financial support to countries facing an exogenous shock, was modified in September 2008 and April 2009 in order to made it faster to access, easier and more flexible to use, and to enable it to provide increased financing. Specifically, a *rapid access component* allows a country to quickly gain access to a concessional loan equal to up to half of its quota, with limited conditionality (the borrower country only needs to commit to appropriate policies to address the shock), while the *high access component* refers to 150 percent of the quota, disbursed under the usual arrangements. Many poor countries have already accessed the modified ESF to avoid jeopardizing their hard-won economic results because of the current crisis. Tanzania, for instance, will receive US$ 336 million to support its reserves and its balance of payment, under temporary stress because of declining cotton prices, tourism revenues and FDI. Cameroon received US$ 144 million to finance important investments and health and education expenditures, which could have been delayed because of tighter external financing conditions in addition to lower export and fiscal revenues. The IMF approved arrangements under the ESF also for other countries, such as Mozambique, Kenya, Ethiopia and Senegal, to shield them from the effects of the global economic downturn and offset the deterioration of their balance of payments.

A more comprehensive and important step was taken on July 2009, when the IMF establishes a PRGT, expected to be effective by late 2009, replacing and expanding the previous PRGF-ESF Trust. The new trust includes tools to provide flexible medium-term support, as well as instruments designed to meet countries

10 The IMF provides financial assistance to LIC at concessional rates (0.5 percent) through the PRGF and the ESF. For more details on IMF lending activities, see: http://www.imf.org/external/np/exr/facts/howlend.htm (last accessed April 2010). A detailed review of the IMF financing activities in LICs and of the ongoing reform proposals is in IMF (2009i).

short-term precautionary and emergency needs. Besides, the focus on growth and poverty alleviation will be strengthened and the IMF will provide exceptional interest relief to countries most severely affected by the global crisis. Specifically, the new structure (IMF 2009h) consists of:

- The Extended Credit Facility (ECF). This facility, the successor to the PRGF, will allow the Fund to provide sustained program engagement and financing for countries facing protracted balance of payments difficulties.
- The Standby Credit Facility (SCF). Similar to the Stand-By Arrangement (SBA) widely used by emerging markets, the SCF will provide financial assistance and policy support to LICs with shorter-term or episodic financing needs emanating from a range of sources. It also allows for precautionary use, in cases where there is a potential rather than an actual financing need.
- The Rapid Credit Facility (RCF). This will rapidly provide a limited amount of financing in response to urgent needs, with reduced conditionality particularly appropriate to the transitory nature of the financing need or instances in which policy implementation capacity is constrained.

Similarly, the WB is undertaking a number of reforms to increase and speed up its assistance and lending to LICs.[11] In December 2008, the WB made US$ 2 billion available to finance spending in basic infrastructure, health and schooling and social safety net programs to protect the poor in the hardest hit countries. In April 2009 it was announced that investment in safety nets and other social protection programs would triple over the following two years. Between July 2008 and June 2009, the WB committed US$ 58.8 billion to help crisis-hit developing countries: 14 billion (+25 percent with respect to 2008) consisted of interest-free loans and grants to the world's 79 poorest countries provided through the IDA (the 56 percent of those funds were channelled to SSA countries). Finally, the WB is supporting a Vulnerability Fund, calling for the developed countries to offer the 0.7 percent of their economic stimulus packages to a fund providing financial assistance to developing countries suffering for the global downturn, which can not afford bailouts and fiscal deficits.

## 9.4 Another Debt Crisis?

The current financial turmoil and the associated reduction in trade, foreign aid and capital flows might trigger another debt crisis in LICs. On one side, government revenues are going to decline: according to the IMF, central government revenues

11 A broad presentation of the WB initiatives set up to deal with the financial crisis is available at: http://www.worldbank.org/financialcrisis/bankinitiatives.htm (last accessed April 2010).

in LICs have declined from 24.2 percent of GDP in 2007 to 22 percent in 2009. On the other side, public spending is rising in order to sustain the overall economy. Subsidies to domestic exporters and to SOEs, financing schemes to avoid the credit crunch and social spending to mitigate the impact of the crisis on poverty are all contributing to the rise in public expenditures. These two contrasting trends worsen the fiscal balance.

Increasing financing requirements, coupled with a decline in international aid and remittances, is going to push developing countries to finance their deficits borrowing abroad or issuing domestic debt. External and domestic borrowing is becoming more expensive because of the rise in interest rates, which follows the withdrawal of foreign investors from poor countries, and the decline in domestic savings. Even countries able to access the international financial markets have been affected by the liquidity shortage: Ghana, Kenya, Tanzania and Uganda have put on hold their debut Eurobond until market conditions improve. Moreover, the outflows of capital are putting downward pressures on the exchange rates, increasing the cost of foreign currency denominated external and domestic debt. The rising cost of debt service will worsen the fiscal deficit even further, generating a vicious cycle.

Differently from the past, this time many poor countries can cope with the crisis starting from better initial conditions, thanks to sounder fiscal positions, reduced debt burdens, lower inflation, a lower dependence on foreign assistance, thanks to a rising share of remittances and comfortable reserve cushions. However, notwithstanding an improvement in the debt sustainability outlook, several HIPCs, especially the ones in the interim phase of the process, are still vulnerable to external shocks (Dömeland and Braga 2009). Those same countries have already been hit by the 2007-2008 food crisis (which is still not over), are still afflicted by widespread poverty, food insecurity, fragility and conflicts, and have highly differentiated initial conditions, especially between oil exporter and importer.[12] With a number of countries with debt ratios close to the 60 (150) percent of GDP (exports) thresholds and at moderate or high risk of debt distress, the projected rise in financing requirements could undermine the positive achievements of debt reduction policies. The expected future increase in world interest rates, that could drive the exit strategy in industrialized countries, would aggravate the cost of public debt and make its sustainability at risk. Debt ratios could quickly bounce back to their pre-debt relief levels, given that the global crisis is adversely affecting both the numerator and the denominator of the debt ratios: public debt is expanding because of a quantity effect (more lending), but also because of a price effect (in the case of foreign currency-denominated debt), which works through the depreciation of the exchange rate. The denominator, being either exports or GDP, is declining as a result of the global recession and the fall in world trade. In

12 In example, oil and metal producers are the worstly affected by the recent reversal in commodity prices, even if many of them were able to accumulate a fiscal cushion during the boom years which is now alleviating the impact of the crisis (IMF 2009a).

addition, the value of exports has diminished due to the fall in commodity prices, which has worsened the TOT in many LICs. The stress tests run under the DSF do not contemplate multiple adverse external shocks nor one of such a magnitude. Therefore, new *ad-hoc* simulations and specific policy responses are required.

As data are released and projections updated, the decline in exports and GDP is actually worse than expected, exposing many poor countries to a severe shock which could bring them to an unsustainable debt path.

Table 9.1 shows the data on economic growth for the 39 HIPCs, collected from the IMF WEO database. The comparison between the last pre-crisis estimates (IMF 2008d) and recent data and projections, released in the April 2009 WEO[13] (IMF 2009f) displays the severity of the crisis and makes it clear that the assumptions of the DSF are generally overly optimistic and that the financial crisis can adversely affect the future evolution of total public debt (Figure 9.4). For the whole sample of HIPCs, the WEO estimates a slowdown of economic growth from 5 in 2008 to 3.5 percent in 2009 and 4.3 in 2010. By contrast, the 2008 estimates were still consistent with a growth acceleration from 5.6 to 6.2 percent over 2008-2010. The largest downward revisions are concentrated in 2009, where the average HIPC is projected to grow 2.5 percent less than the April 2008 estimated growth rate. The picture is quite heterogeneous, with differences among completion and decision point countries, as well as between countries within those groups. Specifically, if we look at the short term (revision for 2009 and 2010), data suggest that completion point countries are better equipped than the others to cope with the crisis: eight out of the ten most adversely affected by the crisis are decision or pre-decision point countries (Congo DR, Sudan, Liberia, Senegal, Haiti, Central African Republic, Kyrgyz Republic and Afghanistan), while only Madagascar and Mauritania underwent a sharp downward revision of their growth prospects.[14]

To better gauge the actual impact of the crisis on public debt dynamics, we have compared the DSA done after the MDRI with the most recent one, for countries for which a very recent DSA is available. Even if the long-run increase in external debt seems generally not worrying, so that the risk of debt distress episodes appears often unchanged, the comparison shows a severe deterioration of the debt dynamics in response to the worsened macroeconomic situation. Thus, additional downward revisions of these projections on growth, exports and external assistance are bound to have more alarming effects, possibly triggering perverse debt dynamics. The 2007 DSA for Ghana (IMF 2007a) assumed a real GDP growth rate of 7 percent over the period 2006-2011, and of 5.8 percent thereafter.

13 Data are available via the Internet at: http://www.imf.org/external/pubs/ft/weo/2009/01/weodata/index.aspx, last accessed April 2010.

14 According to the IMF, the economic outlook for Mauritania, which qualified for the MDRI in June 2006, is uncertain because of the sanctions imposed after the 2005 coup and a loosening of fiscal policies (the recent drop in iron ore prices is expected to exert further pressures on international reserves and the government fiscal balance). The downward revisions for Madagascar are due to its large dependence on oil.

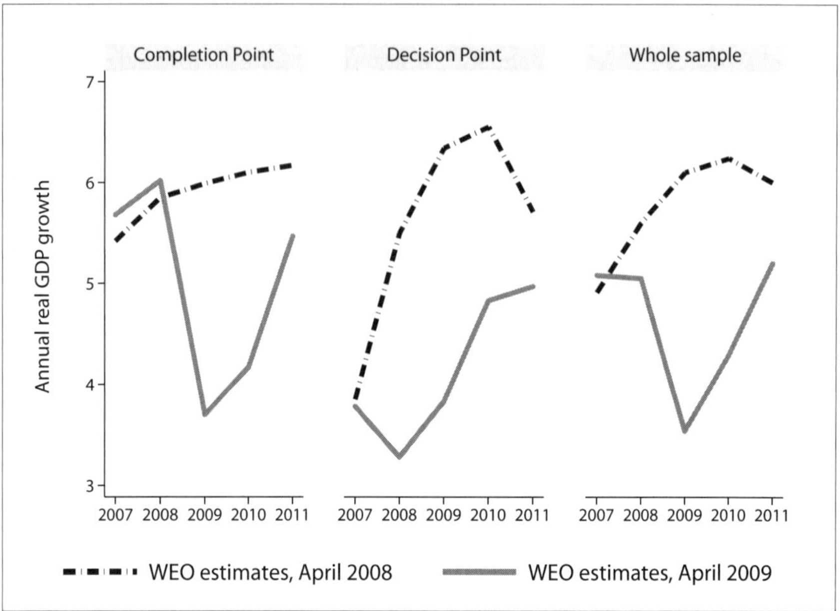


**Figure 9.4 The effect of the global crisis on HIPCs' economic growth**
*Source*: Authors' calculations based on IMF WEO (April 2008 and April 2009). Somalia is excluded because of missing data. HIPC classification as of June 2009.

**Table 9.1 Economic growth forecasts for HIPCs pre- and post-crisis**

| Country | April 2009 WEO growth projections | | | | Change with respect to April 2008 WEO | | | |
|---|---|---|---|---|---|---|---|---|
| | 2008 | 2009 | 2010 | 2011 | 2008 | 2009 | 2010 | 2011 |
| Afghanistan, Rep. of. | 3.35 | 8.96 | 7.01 | 8.10 | -5.28 | 0.56 | -0.18 | 0.90 |
| Benin | 4.98 | 3.84 | 3.04 | 5.65 | -0.38 | -1.81 | -2.65 | -0.03 |
| Bolivia | 5.92 | 2.20 | 2.90 | 3.30 | 1.22 | -2.80 | -2.20 | -2.70 |
| Burkina Faso | 5.00 | 3.54 | 4.09 | 5.32 | 0.98 | -2.76 | -1.89 | -0.64 |
| Burundi | 4.53 | 3.53 | 3.83 | 3.84 | -1.36 | -2.14 | -2.16 | -2.21 |
| Cameroon | 3.45 | 2.44 | 2.64 | 4.00 | -1.05 | -2.16 | -2.13 | -1.40 |
| Central African Republic | 2.20 | 2.40 | 3.10 | 4.00 | -2.70 | -2.60 | -1.90 | -1.00 |
| Chad | -0.41 | 2.83 | 2.51 | 2.93 | -2.18 | 0.37 | -0.22 | 0.45 |
| Comoros | 0.98 | 0.84 | 1.49 | 2.50 | -0.63 | -2.16 | -3.01 | -2.00 |
| Congo, Democratic Republic of | 6.20 | 2.70 | 5.54 | 7.97 | -2.65 | -8.93 | -6.23 | -1.00 |
| Congo, Republic of | 5.57 | 9.55 | 11.87 | 1.05 | -3.64 | -1.03 | 1.62 | -1.66 |
| Côte d'Ivoire | 2.33 | 3.70 | 4.23 | 4.68 | -0.58 | -1.42 | -1.38 | -1.50 |
| Eritrea | 1.03 | 1.14 | 4.72 | 5.24 | -0.18 | -0.91 | -1.30 | -0.14 |
| Ethiopia | 11.61 | 6.52 | 6.54 | 6.99 | 3.20 | -0.60 | -0.72 | -0.53 |

**Table 9.1 continued**

| Country | April 2009 WEO growth projections | | | | Change with respect to April 2008 WEO | | | |
|---|---|---|---|---|---|---|---|---|
| | 2008 | 2009 | 2010 | 2011 | 2008 | 2009 | 2010 | 2011 |
| Gambia, The | 5.86 | 3.98 | 4.42 | 5.14 | -0.64 | -2.52 | -1.57 | -0.86 |
| Ghana | 7.16 | 4.50 | 4.72 | 16.78 | 0.31 | -2.97 | -2.75 | 9.34 |
| Guinea | 3.96 | 2.55 | 4.14 | 4.69 | -0.92 | -2.66 | -1.34 | -1.02 |
| Guinea-Bissau | 3.33 | 1.90 | 3.10 | 3.76 | 0.10 | -1.22 | -0.25 | -0.18 |
| Guyana | 3.23 | 2.60 | 3.45 | 5.78 | -1.37 | -1.90 | -0.85 | 1.18 |
| Haiti | 1.30 | 1.00 | 2.00 | 3.20 | -2.40 | -3.00 | -2.00 | -0.80 |
| Honduras | 4.00 | 1.50 | 1.90 | 2.20 | -0.85 | -3.10 | -2.60 | -2.20 |
| Kyrgyz Republic | 7.60 | 0.94 | 2.93 | 4.05 | 0.65 | -5.56 | -3.07 | -1.45 |
| Liberia | 7.13 | 4.87 | 7.53 | 10.27 | -2.34 | -5.32 | -5.14 | -2.31 |
| Madagascar | 5.04 | -0.18 | 2.03 | 3.71 | -1.76 | -7.43 | -7.53 | -4.61 |
| Malawi | 9.70 | 6.90 | 6.00 | 5.13 | 2.55 | 0.72 | -1.20 | -2.85 |
| Mali | 4.99 | 3.88 | 4.09 | 4.64 | 0.72 | -1.25 | -1.43 | -1.51 |
| Mauritania | 2.23 | 2.35 | 4.69 | 5.70 | -3.91 | -4.42 | -0.56 | 0.74 |
| Mozambique | 6.18 | 4.30 | 4.00 | 4.50 | -0.85 | -2.69 | -3.05 | -2.00 |
| Nicaragua | 3.00 | 0.50 | 1.00 | 2.00 | -1.00 | -3.70 | -3.70 | -3.00 |
| Niger | 9.52 | 3.02 | 4.51 | 4.46 | 5.08 | -1.50 | -0.49 | -0.74 |
| Rwanda | 11.23 | 5.60 | 5.79 | 5.88 | 5.23 | 0.05 | 0.33 | 0.17 |
| São Tomé and Príncipe | 5.80 | 5.00 | 6.00 | 7.00 | -0.20 | -1.00 | -0.50 | 0.00 |
| Senegal | 2.49 | 3.12 | 3.43 | 4.35 | -2.88 | -2.81 | -2.45 | -1.17 |
| Sierra Leone | 5.52 | 4.49 | 5.30 | 5.97 | -0.96 | -2.03 | -1.02 | 0.00 |
| Sudan | 6.84 | 3.96 | 5.04 | 5.03 | -0.71 | -8.72 | -3.56 | -2.76 |
| Tanzania | 7.46 | 4.97 | 5.66 | 7.17 | -0.31 | -3.03 | -2.35 | -0.83 |
| Togo | 1.10 | 1.69 | 2.15 | 4.05 | -1.90 | -2.31 | -1.85 | 0.05 |
| Uganda | 9.53 | 6.20 | 5.50 | 6.70 | 2.43 | -0.80 | -1.50 | -0.30 |
| Zambia | 6.02 | 4.04 | 4.55 | 5.03 | -0.28 | -2.31 | -1.31 | -0.80 |
| | | | **Country averages** | | | | | |
| HIPC whole sample | 5.05 | 3.54 | 4.29 | 5.20 | -0.55 | -2.56 | -1.95 | -0.80 |
| *Completion point countries* | *6.02* | *3.70* | *4.17* | *5.47* | *0.16* | *-2.29* | *-1.93* | *-0.71* |
| *Decision point countries* | *3.28* | *3.83* | *4.83* | *4.97* | *-2.23* | *-2.51* | *-1.72* | *-0.73* |

*Source*: Authors' calculations based on IMF WEO (April 2008 and April 2009). Somalia is excluded because of missing data. HIPC classification as of June 2009.

According to this assumption, after MDRI relief, PPG external debt was equal to 22.3 percent of GDP in 2006 and it would have increased to 27.5 percent in 2012. By contrast, the most recent DSA (IMF 2009b) updates the assumptions setting the output growth below 5 percent in 2009 and 2010. This results in an even more divergent debt dynamic, since PPG external debt, revised at 17.3 percent of GDP in 2006, raises to 41.5 and 47.7 percent in 2009 and 2010, respectively. A similar pattern is observable also in other HIPCs. In the 2006 DSA for Benin, the assumption on the annual GDP growth rate was set at 5.3 percent over 2006-2011, so that PPG external debt was projected to increase from 12.7 to 16.1 percent of GDP (IMF 2007b). By contrast, actual growth rates in 2006-2008 were well below the target and in 2009-2010 output is expected to growth at 3.8 and 3.0 percent, respectively. Thus, according to the most recent DSA (IMF 2009c), the Benin debt-to-GDP ratio is estimated to reach 21.4 in 2011, more than 5 percentage points above the previous projection. In Mozambique, the revision of the growth rates leads to an increase of the ratio of PPG external debt over GDP from 22.5 in 2008 to 35.1 in 2010, while the pre-crisis estimates where consistent with a debt ratio of 24.7 in 2010 (IMF 2007c and 2009d). Similarly, in Senegal the 2007 DSA projected an almost stable debt to GDP ratio under the baseline scenario (from 17.3 in 2006 to 19.6 in 2010), while the most recent DSA updates the 2010 ratio at 26, since in 2006-2008 output grew annually at a 3.2 percent rate instead that at the projected 4.8 percent (IMF 2007d and 2009e).

Hence, given uncertain borrowing policies and with still limited liquidity facilities by the IFIs to help countries to go through (hopefully) temporary liquidity problems, vulnerable countries are going to face aggravated risks of future debt distress episodes and rising public debt. In addition to that, this scenario could undermine past and current debt relief efforts made by the international community and it might reduce, or even wipe out, progress achieved so far, scaling down public investments and pro-poor spending and endangering economic growth.

## 9.5 Outlook

At the time of writing, many emerging markets have already started growing close to pre-crisis rates. However, while OECD countries have the resources and the instrument to cope with the global crisis and mitigate its effects on displaced workers and the poor, the poorest countries are still well below their trend of output growth and lack the appropriate tools to deal with these multiple external shocks. Thus, the poorest people in the poorest countries are the most exposed to the global recession: not only they lack sufficient safety nets for immediate help but also, more importantly, they are going to be dramatically affected in the long run by the likely reduction in social spending. A new generation of poor might not benefit from the recent (limited) progress in education and health, with severe consequences for individuals, their local communities and for poor countries' growth prospects.[15] Recent WB estimates suggest that lower growth rates would trap an additional 89 million people into poverty, in addition to the 130-155 million

15 Harper et al. (2009) discuss the effect of the crisis on children, stressing their vulnerability and the irreversible long-run effects of child malnutrition, infant mortality and school dropout on future poverty rates, inequality and economic growth. The author shows data from a previous study suggesting that a 1 percent decrease in per capita GDP has been linked to an increase in infant mortality of between 17 and 44 per thousand children born.

people pushed into poverty in 2008 because of the soaring food and fuel prices (WB 2009b). As stated by the WB president, Robert Zoellick,

> *this is obviously* going to have an effect on the Millennium Development Goals, and just to take one example of infant mortality, we estimate that as a result of the sharply lower economic growth rates, that between 200,000 and 400,000 more children a year may die, and that's out of a total of about 1.4 to 2.8 million children that perish each year. (Zoellick 2009)

Also the IMF's managing director of the Dominique Strauss-Kahn, is

> deeply concerned by the potential humanitarian costs of this crisis. […] Starting from what is only a financial crisis, we may at the end have much bigger consequences than only income and growth consequences. For these reasons, low-income countries have to safeguard the funds they have for education and infrastructure, while boosting safety nets to protect the most vulnerable. (Brookings Institution 2009: 9 10)

To address this potentially dramatic situation, the rich world and the IFIs should reshape their policy agenda, devoting much more attention and providing more resources and assistance to LICs. Some recent steps made by the multilateral institutions, such as the Vulnerability Fund proposal advanced by the WB, the IMF's PRGT, and the call for a temporary debt moratorium on all LICs' official debt (UNCTAD 2009a) are commendable and encouraging, but probably not enough. As stressed also by Strauss-Kahn,

> it's clear that the financing needs are substantial, and they are very urgent. […] The international community [has] to provide the financing the most vulnerable countries need to preserve their hard-earned gain, and also to prevent a humanitarian crisis. Of course, the primary responsibility to me lies with bilateral donors who must ensure that the aid flows are scaled up, not down. (Brookings Institution 2009:14)

However, the recent G8 summit in L'Aquila in July 2009 confirms the usual "abundance of promises and commitments, without sufficient details and clear mechanisms that would ensure effective implementation" (De Rienzo 2009): the 2005 Gleneagles commitments to double aid to Africa are re-stated, but it is still unclear when the promised additional resources will become available. At the same summit, donors pledged to halve the cost of remittances in five years. Given the increasing importance of migrants' remittances as a source of development finance in many LICs and their advantage over aid in targeting the basic needs of the poor, efforts in lowering the cost of sending remittances could act as an important policy tool (Freund and Spadafora 2008). According to WB data, sending US$ 200 dollars to the country of origin costs, on average, over US$ 20 (Beck and

Martinez Peria 2009). It has been calculated that if the international money-transfer cost could be reduced by 5 percent relative to the transferred value, recipients in developing countries could receive additional US$ 12 billion each year. This benefit, representing more than a tenth of the annual flows of ODA, might be achieved at a lower (political) cost than an increase in foreign assistance of the same amount. Moreover, under the hypothesis that remittances are somewhat less pro-cyclical and more effective than aid in fostering development, this policy could also achieve better results.

Finally, even from a self-interested point of view, the rich world should realize that it is in its own interest to help developing countries coping with the crisis. The threat of another debt crisis, rising political instability and social unrest, which generally follow a severe economic downturn, not to mention the increase in transnational criminal activities, should be sound and economically rational arguments to urge rich countries to scale up their involvement in LICs.

# Chapter 10
# Some Proposals for a Comprehensive Approach to Debt Sustainability and Debt Relief

## 10.1 Introduction

This chapter brings together the issues we have developed throughout the book in order to point out some critical elements of the DSF and the debt relief initiatives, and to provide some policy suggestions to policy-makers – especially national authorities, IFIs and the donors' community – for future debt relief policies. Firstly, we discuss the possible evolution of new lending by countries which have had their debt cancelled. We highlight the emerging role of new lenders, which are not part of the Paris Club, and of private creditors, whose behavior might undermine some of the achievements of the HIPC Initiative and the MDRI.

Secondly, we advance some policy suggestions. Against the backdrop of the limitations of the current DSF discussed in Part 1 and the relevance of debt stock and flows for poor countries' economic performance, we propose an extended DSF which should include all the alternative sources of financing, in addition to external debt, into a fully-fledged budget constraint. The framework should allow for the assessment of possible feedback effects and interactions among variables. The possible crowding out of investment and social spending, due to interest payments on total public debt, would call for more emphasis on debt flows indicators and closer linkages to poverty reduction strategies and their financing requirements. A legal framework to deal with private creditors and more cooperation among donors, especially with the ones outside the Paris Club, should be pursued to avoid the build up of unsustainable debts. Finally, the evidence discussed on debt overhang and debt relief effectiveness requires a country-specific approach to debt relief policies, in the same vein of the DSF.

## 10.2 Lending to LICs

The G8 Gleneagles Accords in 2005 and the institution of the MDRI for complete debt cancellation for the poorest countries constituted a turning point: efforts by the international community lost momentum, while some issues which could weaken public debt sustainability remain unresolved; namely, creditors' coordination, reduced participation by commercial creditors to multilateral agreements, and the emergence of so-called vulture funds.

### *10.2.1 Moral Hazard and Donors' Coordination*

Up until now, we have seen that external debt could affect the economy of LICs mainly through the debt overhang and the crowding out effects and the macroeconomic uncertainty it brings. We have also seen that debt relief, at least until now, has not achieved positive results in terms of growth and investments. The effectiveness of debt relief could be weakened also by moral hazard, meaning that debt relief might induce debtors to overspend, believing that creditors have taken a softer stance and will be more willing to forgive future debt, when the likelihood to obtain a repayment decreases substantially.

A large body of literature has investigated the effects of debtor moral hazard related to IMF financing (Vaubel 1983; Dreher and Vaubel 2004), which is based on the fact that countries could pursue over-expansionary domestic policies on the basis of their potential access to IMF financing (Bird 2007). The same concept could be applied to the HIPC Initiative, since the program could raise the incentive, for debtor countries, to finance excessive expenditures with external debt, on the expectations of future debt cancellation also by multilateral institutions. Besides, other than debtor moral hazard, debt reduction by the IFIs could foster creditor moral hazard; this is due to the fact that the expectation of (non-commercial and/or non-Paris Club) debt reduction "encourages private international capital markets to underestimate the risks associated with lending to individual countries or groups of countries and therefore to overlend" (Bird 2007: 693). This issue is not broadly supported by the empirical evidence and it should be more severe for MICs, which have easier access to international capital markets. However, creditor moral hazard could be a problem also for countries that graduated from the HIPC and MDRI initiatives, especially for the ones where debt relief has created some borrowing space and the ones able to have access to the international capital markets and the IDA's Non-Concessional Borrowing Policy. Large debt reduction and lower debt ratios increase the capacity for new lending, attracting non-concessional financing. In this case, debt relief could work as a subsidy to lenders offering non-concessional loans, creating a *free-riding* problem among creditors, which, as acknowledged by the multilateral institutions, undermines the efforts made to achieve long-term debt sustainability (WB 2006, Reisen and Ndoye 2008). The WB and the IMF are actively searching to collaborate with non-Paris Club bilateral creditors, which, on average, have provided only one third of debt relief expected under the HIPC Initiative.[1]

---

1 Costa Rica, Guatemala, Taiwan, Kuwait, China, Algeria, Saudi Arabia and Libya are the main non-Paris Club creditors (IDA and IMF 2007a).

The increasing economic engagement of China in Africa, especially in resource-rich countries, is also a source of concern for post-MDRI debt sustainability, because of its increasing non-concessional lending (Moss and Rose 2006; Wang and Bio-Tchané 2008; Dahle Huse and Muyakwa 2008; Reisen and Ndoye 2008). The state-owned Export-Import (ExIm) Bank of China is significantly expanding in Africa (by 15-20 percent yearly), especially in the infrastructure sectors, supporting Chinese enterprises' investment activities and not imposing all the conditions generally attached to more traditional aid assistance. Even if China financing provides much-needed capital, fosters economic and export growth, increases public revenues and can create policy space, its role could undermine the international efforts to promote better governance, export diversification, labor standards and public debt sustainability. Because of lack of transparency and information on China loans to African countries, it is difficult to assess precisely how China's lending is affecting debt sustainability. However, some country studies are instructive: the China's $5 billion loan to Congo DR in 2007, for example, is highly controversial and highlights how new lending could jeopardize debt sustainability, given that Congo DR external debt was $11.5 billions as of December 2006. The WB and the IMF estimate that, in 2007, China held claims with 20 post-completion point countries, representing about 8 percent of HIPC debt relief by non-Paris Club creditors, and signed debt relief agreements with many HIPCs, delivering only 34 percent of its expected debt relief.[2]

### *10.2.2 Odious Debt, Vulture Funds and Responsible Lending*

The limited donors' coordination and the lack of an international legal framework to deal with debt issues are magnified by the critical problems of odious debt, responsible lending and vulture funds litigations, which are taken as example by debt relief campaigners to call for an increase in the debt reduction effort and for a greater attention to prudent lending practices (Hurley 2008).

The growing and widespread interest in odious debt is testified by the civil society campaign for the cancellation of the Iraqi and Haitian debt, by the chapters in the WB's book on debt relief by Primo Braga and Dömeland (2009) and by the Working Group for the prevention of odious debt, established at the Center for Global Development, co-chaired by John Williamson, Michael Kremer and Seema Jayachandran.

2 On the China's role in Africa see the special issue of the *European Journal of Development Research* (Volume 21, Issue 4, 2009) and Dahle Huse and Muyakwa (2008) for a more detailed description on lending to African countries and, especially, Zambia. Reisen and Ndoye (2008) suggest that, since China's presence is concentrated in resource-abundant countries, such as Angola and Sudan, its lending might not represent a real issue, since it is collateralized and these countries could benefit from the build up of international reserves and from the growth in exports and GDP which comes with China non-concessional loans.

The doctrine of odious debt originated in 1898 after the Spanish-American War, when the US argued that neither Cuba nor the US itself should be held responsible for debt the colonial rulers had incurred without the consent of the Cuban people and not used for their benefit. A formalization of the concept of odious debt was given in 1927 by Alexander Sack, who underlined the absence of consent on the part of the people, the lack of any significant benefit to them and the awareness of the situation by the creditor. Still now, many creditors lend to a government without regard to its legitimacy, allowing 'illegitimate' governments to saddle their countries with debt and burdening the successor governments with repayments. Countries repay odious debt to avoid the seizure of their foreign assets and the loss of reputation following a default, which could dramatically increase the cost of financing and lower the country's attractiveness for foreign investor. As a result, several LICs are shouldering debt incurred by rulers who borrowed without the people's consent and used the funds either to repress the people or for personal gain.

To avoid this outcome, Jayachandran and Kremer (2006) propose the use of *ex-ante* loan sanctions which would put creditors on notice that any future loans to a regime would be considered the responsibility of that regime and would not be considered transferable to successor governments. Moreover, lending to odious regimes could be eliminated by designing the right incentives for lenders and borrowers: odious debt contracts could be made legally unenforceable and foreign aid to successor regimes could be made contingent on non-repayment of odious debt. As a result, creditors would benefit from knowing the *rules of the game* in advance and "dictators would no longer be able to borrow, use the proceeds for illegitimate purposes, and then saddle the people with their debts" (Kremer and Jayachandran 2002). While this proposal looks sensible and thoughtful, a lot of work would have to be done to make it politically and practically feasible, so that at the moment policy initiative for the write-off of illegitimate or odious debt are sporadic and on a voluntary basis. This is a research area for law and economics which deserves careful scrutiny.

The second critical aspect we deal with is the activity of the so-called vulture funds, which, similarly to non-Paris Club bilateral creditors, can free ride on the multilateral effort to reduce debt, undermining the achievements of debt relief initiatives. Vulture funds are private companies that seek to profit by buying bad debt at a very low price and then attempt to recover the full amount, often by suing through Western courts and undermining the debt relief efforts of the international community.

The biggest limit of the debt relief initiatives lies in the absence of an international architecture for sovereign debt restructuring: the activity of vulture funds originates from this gap and could endanger even the limited results achieved by the HIPC Initiative and the MDRI. In general, vulture funds are speculative funds operating on stock and secondary bond markets to buy debt at risk of insolvency or stock of quasi-bankrupt firms: they provide market liquidity in difficult situations, thereby improving market efficiency, as happened during the Asian crisis. Moreover, their activity could facilitate the discovery of malpractices and corruption, thereby stimulating poor countries' governments to improve public sector governance. However, the threat of legal actions could lead to practices aimed at avoiding asset confiscation, thereby reducing transparency.

For HIPCs, vulture funds' activity can be destabilizing, because they buy sovereign debt at risk of insolvency, issued by poor countries to commercial creditors and sovereign countries who are not part of the HIPC Initiative. Transactions are carried out below nominal price and vulture funds maximize returns by denying debt restructuring and bringing to court the debtor country to get the full value of debt plus interests (Seager and Lewis 2007; Committee on Foreign Affairs 2007).

This is not a new story in the global debt arena: for example, in 1996 the Elliot Associates fund bought Peruvian debt for US$ 11 million. After refusing the debt restructuring under the Brady Plan, it obtained by a US Appeal Court that Peru be condemned to pay US$ 58 million. Recently, the same fund has undertaken legal action against the government of Congo DR to get US$ 400 million for debt bought for US$ 10 million (see Foroohar (2008) for an overview on the activity of Paul Singer's Elliott Associates hedge fund).

Vulture funds activity with respect to HIPCs and other poor countries is not only ethically reproachable, but it has also negative economic consequences: vulture funds weaken the efforts of the international community to generate resources to invest in public infrastructure, health and education. A well-known case involved the Donegal International fund and the governments of Zambia and Romania. In 1979 Zambia contracted with Romania a commercial debt of US$ 15 million to buy agricultural machinery. Later Zambia defaulted on its debt and it was not re-negotiated within the Paris Club. In 1999 Romania sold this debt – nominally valued at US$ 30 million – to the Donegal fund for US$ 3.2 million, notwithstanding a slightly higher Zambian bid. After an early legal attempt based in the Virgin Islands, Donegal started a new legal action in Britain asking for US$ 55 million. In April 2007 the British High Court condemned Zambia to pay US$ 15.4, a sum equivalent to half the debt relief agreed under the HIPC Initiative in 2006 and 66 percent of the 2007 budget for new teachers (see Eurodad 2008 for more details).

The Zambian case is probably the best know, but many other countries are involved. Recent IMF and WB data record 44 legal actions by commercial creditors, for a total value of over 1.5 billion US dollars, against 11 HIPC countries, already forced to pay almost one billion dollars (IDA and IMF 2007b; Debt Relief International 2007). For instance, Niger has been condemned to reimburse more than one half of the amount it invests in health and education; Cameroon forced reimbursements amount to almost 100 percent of annual fiscal revenues. The case of Liberia is particularly worrying: after 20 years of political instability and civil war, it became one of the poorest and most indebted countries in the world. Before reaching completion point in June 2010, in February 2008 Liberia obtained the first debt relief by IFIs, but the stock of external debt, accumulated under the regimes of Samuel Doe and Charles Taylor, remained high; one third was in the hands of commercial creditors. Ministry of Finance estimates indicate that around US$ 1.5 billion of commercial debt outstanding in 2008 was held by hedge funds, exposing Liberia to high social risks and costs in case vulture funds take legal actions. A British court, in fact, recently ruled in favor of two vulture funds, awarding them USD 20 million for a debt bought at 1 percent of that sum, seriously jeopardizing the Liberia's recovery from civil war.

Heightened awareness of these issues and pressure from NGOs and civil society have induced the international community to become more prudent and responsible in its lending behavior. Paris Club countries are committed to avoid selling their credits toward HIPC countries to those who are not (and do not intend to be) members of the HIPC Initiative, and invited other creditors to do the same.

Recently the G8 declared it would develop a Charter for Responsible Lending – to be endorsed also by G20 countries – based on prudent lending practices to limit the re-accumulation of high debt as a consequence of excessive lending or the activity of vulture funds ("Responsible lenders ensure that their lending decisions meet the need for funds of recipient countries [...] in order to avoid the return to the lend-and-forgive cycles [... and] help avoid the risk of litigation against HIPC"). In addition, there are even stronger positions taken by individual countries, like Germany and the UK.

In the short term two policy measures could be effective. Firstly, the WB extension of its DRF to 2012 allows each country to obtain resources and support to buy back commercial debt.[3] The support of the DRF, for instance, helped Liberia to slash its foreign debt, buying back in April 2009 USD 1.2 billion in commercial debt from its private commercial creditors at a 97 percent discount of its face value and without costs for its people. However, in order to minimize vulture funds' interventions, the DRF should be strengthened and eligibility extended to all HIPCs, independently from the stage of advancement in the debt relief program. Secondly, adequate legal assistance could be provided to prevent such legal controversies and when they actually arise.

Broader and more ambitious (but less feasible) measures could include at least one of the following: a first one could aim at legal measures for the cancellation of outstanding odious debt, for the avoidance of illegitimate/odious lending and to prevent vulture funds from acquiring sovereign debt or going to court. In this respect, Belgium approved a resolution in January 2008 to safeguard development financing and debt relief from actions undertaken by vulture funds. A second measure could aim at international agreements, first voluntary and then mandatory, to define and adopt legal standards for the lending activity to poor countries, protecting debtor countries from legal action of minority creditors (this framework was drafted in 2001 by Anne Krueger in the proposal for the creation of the SDRM (Krueger 2002)). The international financial community, pressed by NGOs and civil society, is currently committed to the issue of responsible

3 For a description of the DRF, see the WB website at: http://go.worldbank.org/2CRHS4N500 (last accessed April 2010).

lending, which has gained importance in recent years, also because of the activity of vulture funds. Unfortunately, in this case, any initiative suffers from the lack of any binding agreement between donors, so that additional efforts should be made to enlarge the pool of responsible lenders and limit the risks of free-riding among creditors. Research and interest on the doctrine of odious debt, responsible lending and creditors co-responsibility in lending to poor countries were stimulated by the decision of the Norwegian government to cancel, in October 2006, US$ 80 million in debt owed by five countries (Ecuador, Egypt, Jamaica, Perù and Sierra Leone) because credit had been extended irresponsibly without due consideration for the needs of recipient countries, so that the Norwegian government assumed a shared responsibility for the subsequent debt accumulation (Hurley 2008, Nehru and Thomas 2009).

The actual development of a Charter for Responsible Lending – to increase transparency and forbid the sale of sovereign debt on the secondary market without the explicit permission of the debtor country – as proposed also by the European Network on Debt and Development (Eurodad 2008; Hurley 2008), would be recommendable. In particular, in May 2007, the Paris Club creditors committed themselves "to avoid selling their claims on HIPC countries to other creditors who do not intend to provide debt relief under the HIPC initiative, and urge[d] other creditors to follow suit" (Paris Club 2007); the OECD issued guidelines to promote responsible lending practices for export credits to LICs (OECD 2008), and, at the Heiligendamm summit, the G8 countries made an invitation to all donors "to take account of debt sustainability issues in all their lending practices and share fully information on their lending to low-income countries (as envisaged by the Charter of Responsible Lending endorsed by the G8 Finance Ministers)" (G8 Summit Meetings 2007).

### *10.2.3 New Lending After the MDRI*

One of the objectives of the HIPC Initiative is to ensure that poor countries would move towards a debt sustainable path. The 100 percent MDRI multilateral debt write-off is bringing debt ratios in completion point countries to low levels, far below the (discussed) sustainability thresholds. Nonetheless, this kind of policies does non necessarily assure the achievement of long-run debt sustainability. As we have seen in Chapter 3, even in the simplest framework, debt sustainability is grounded on the solvency condition, which requires that "the current debt *plus* the present discounted value of all expenditures does not exceed the present discounted value of all revenues" (Wyplosz 2007: 3). Thus, even assuming a starting level of zero debt, future sustainability depends on the evolution of government financing: without increase in growth (and/or a sharp contraction of fiscal deficits) and a sound debt management strategy, public debt is likely to increase. However, as long as the economy grows at a rate higher than the (risk- and exchange rate-adjusted) real interest rate, the debt-to-GDP ratio will not explode. Therefore, debt relief programs could be positively evaluated if, apart from their other targets, they were able to trigger economic growth and limit excessive future borrowing. While it seems that HIPCs have accelerated their growth rate, even if it is not clear whether this depends on debt relief programs rather than on the positive evolution of their TOT until 2007, the achievement of fiscal consolidation is less evident.[4] As discussed in section 4.4, the HIPC Initiative was successful in bringing inflation under control, while the delay in reducing fiscal deficits induced greater reliance on domestic financing. Moreover, the financing gap can be financed with foreign borrowing: in 2007 the share of non-concessional debt in total external debt in SSA was higher than in 2000. If this is the case, and if the fiscal authorities do not reduce the deficit, debt ratios are likely to revert to pre-debt relief levels. What happened in Bolivia, as well as in other heavily indebted countries, is particularly instructive (Figure 10.1). Until the MDRI debt write-off, the stock of external debt followed an U-shaped path, meaning that different round of debt relief where not able to achieve debt sustainability. Moreover, since launch of the HIPC Initiative, domestic debt is partially compensating for the reduction in external debt. This kind of experience, which is not unique among HIPCs, should be taken in serious consideration to develop sound borrowing policies after the MDRI in order to avoid the re-accumulation of unsustainable public debt, especially in countries where debt relief has created significant borrowing space.

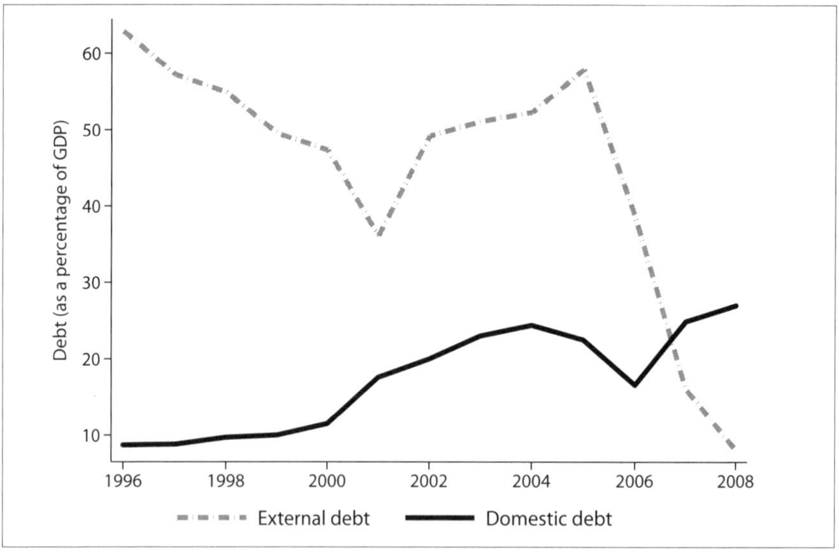


**Figure 10.1 Bolivia, net external debt (in percent of GDP)**
*Source*: Authors' elaboration on IMF data.

4 Both economic growth and the budget balance have been under stress because of the global financial crisis. Here we abstract from this additional factor, discussed in Chapter 9.

The WB and the IMF are putting strong emphasis on LICs' borrowing policies and debt management. The choice of the appropriate mix between grants and loans in IDA allocation, based on country-specific risk of debt distress, is specifically devoted to design safe borrowing practices. Moreover, given the augmented creditworthiness in several HIPCs – which has granted them access to international capital markets and private capital flows – the WB has developed the IDA's Non-Concessional Borrowing Policy and the IMF is reviewing its lending policies in LICs: both institutions are adopting a more flexible approach, which could increase the pool of available resources to the most vulnerable countries (Chapter 9). Finally, the launch of the DMF in November 2008 by the WB in partnership with the IMF and other institutions aims at strengthening debt management capacity and institutions in poor countries: thanks to different tools and programs of learning and training, poor countries should be assisted in the development and implementation of medium-term debt management strategies and reform programs.[5]

Notwithstanding this widespread interest in debt management and borrowing policies, to our knowledge there is a very limited empirical evidence on debtor countries' behavior. At the time of writing, more than three years have elapsed since the MDRI. Thus, it is instructive to look at the lending behavior of those countries in order to assess whether the trend of their actual financing requirements is changing.

To avoid the build up of unsustainable (and growth-limiting) debt, recipient countries should improve their fiscal and current account balances. If this is not the case, meaning that debt relief initiatives were not able to improve fiscal management and implement appropriate structural reforms, the financing gap will persist and countries will keep on relying on foreign lending and/or domestic debt markets. We have made a simple comparison of the share of internal and external financing over GDP in the years before and after the achievement of the 100 percent MDRI debt cancellation. We have collected data (and projections) on foreign and domestic financing from 2004 to 2010, for 16 of the 24 countries which reached completion point before 2009 from a number of IMF country reports.[6]

As illustrated in Figure 10.2, the evolution of foreign and total financing does not show any downward trend in the years following the MDRI, a result recently confirmed by Leo (2009). By contrast total financing is estimated to be higher in

5 For a presentation of the DMF and the DeMPA, see the WB website at: http://go.worldbank.org/8P70EDTP80 (last accessed April 2010). See also IMF and World Bank (2009b).

6 For three (Guyana, Honduras and Nicaragua) of the 24 countries we do not have sufficient information. In order to have an homogeneous sample of countries which had their debt cancelled at the beginning of 2006, we have excluded Gambia, Malawi, Sao Tomè and Principe and Sierra Leone, since they received MDRI relief in late 2006 or in 2007. Hence, the sample includes Benin, Bolivia, Burkina Faso, Cameroon, Ethiopia, Ghana, Madagascar, Mali, Mauritania, Mozambique, Niger, Rwanda, Senegal, Tanzania, Uganda and Zambia. Because of the crisis, projections should be taken with caution.

2009 than in the years before the debt cancellation, while foreign financing, after a brief reduction, is projected to re-bounce back to its pre-debt relief levels in 2009 and 2010. Besides, the situation is generally worse for the poorest countries: if we limit the sample to countries whose income is below the one-dollar-a-day threshold, foreign and total financing is larger, leading to serious concerns about future debt sustainability. Certainly, it is still early to expect the new tools such as the DeMPA, to be effective in improving countries' fiscal discipline and public debt management. Besides, results are likely to be highly heterogeneous and an aggregate study could hide some success stories. Nonetheless, we believe that, until new data become available, more (and more sophisticated) research is certainly required in order to assess the effectiveness of the IMF and WB lending polices in poor and indebted countries, monitoring not only the amount of new borrowing, but also its destination.

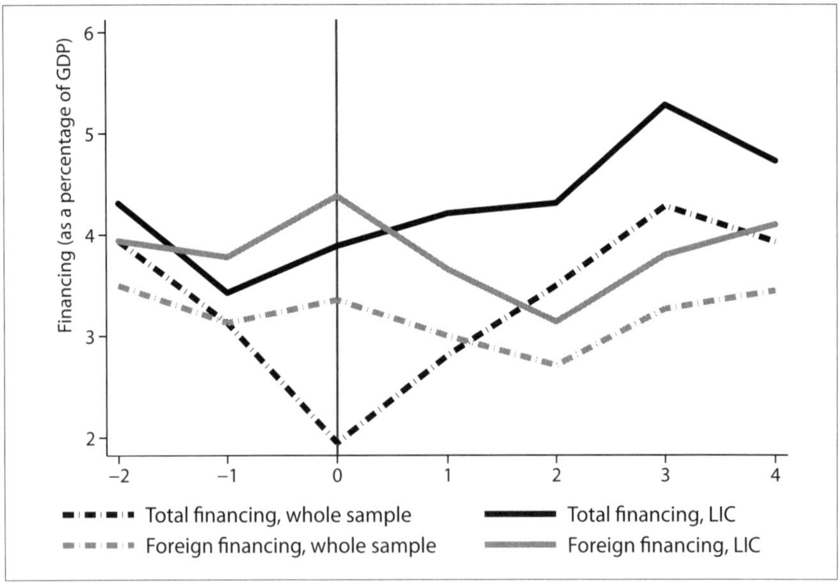


**Figure 10.2 Lending after the MDRI**
*Source*: Authors' calculations based on IMF Country Reports. The dotted lines refer to the whole sample of 16 HIPCs, while the solid lines exclude countries with per capita income above US$ 380 (Benin, Bolivia, Cameroon, Mauritania, Senegal and Zambia).

In sum, debt relief is strictly connected with moral hazard issues, since over-borrowing does not necessarily finance the most efficient projects, resulting in an inefficient allocation of capital. As a consequence, multilateral institutions should be careful in designing appropriate policies taking the these additional complexities of debt relief into consideration. A certain degree of conditionality is required to lessen the debtor moral hazard, while some incentive mechanisms limiting (but not excluding, like the standard HIPC program does) non-concessional borrowing by countries that obtained debt reductions are required to avoid creditor moral hazard.

## 10.3 An Extended Debt Sustainability Framework

The basic accounting approach to debt sustainability, as embedded in the standard WB-IMF DSF, will not necessarily deliver debt sustainability, if not by chance. The dominant financial framework represents a rigorous tool to project the evolution of external public debt, but it does not internalize all the relevant feedback effects of debt on the functioning of the economy nor does it consider the development needs of LICs. Thus, we argue that a comprehensive debt sustainability framework requires a fully-fledged government budget constraint, which includes not only the external position, but also (at least) domestic debt and exchange rates. The theory of debt is, indeed, generally concerned with the government budget constraint and the evolution of debt (domestic and external) indicators along with other relevant macroeconomic variables. An appropriately extended DFS should be based on a government budget constraint that links fiscal deficit, public debt, output growth, inflation and the BOP. The usual IFIs DSF should be modified to include these blocks, paying attention to the need for evaluating the above-mentioned feedback effects. This is particularly relevant for the assessment of debt sustainability under alternative scenarios: if multiple shocks and their interactions are not considered, the debt projections might be based on unrealistic assumptions and miss key macroeconomic elements, as the current financial crisis has shown (Chapter 9).

The risk of default, rescheduling and arrears, which are likely to increase volatility of future inflows and uncertainty about future policies, must be carefully evaluated to reduce the level of macroeconomic instability. Other than the negative direct effect of large indebtedness on economic growth, multilateral institutions should consider how the volatility of resource inflows impacts on different kinds of investments, such as human capital, on the adoption of structural reforms and on fiscal adjustments, via the extended debt overhang. Concerning specifically the incorporation of the risk of default in the DSA, Gray et al. (2008) apply the concepts and methods of the contingent claim approach to develop a new framework for public debt sustainability. Though their framework is ideally suited for emerging economies, it could be adapted to LICs, representing an innovative tool to include uncertainty in the DSA.

As embedded in the current DSF, country-specific debt thresholds, which define the need for and magnitude of debt relief (and grant financing), are justified by the relevance of the debt management institutions and policies and by the heterogeneity of the debt overhang effect, as shown in the empirical analysis presented in Chapter 7. Nevertheless, the definition of these debt thresholds should be determined not only on the basis of institutional quality, but also on country-specific patterns of investments and consumption, the exchange rate and monetary regime, the speed and structure of fiscal adjustments, and the structure of the BOP, with great attention being given to the elasticity of imports and exports, their structure, and the dependence on the international prices of agricultural and raw material, among other things.

We recommend that, notwithstanding the recent focus of IFIs on domestic debt, the extended DSF should deepen the analysis on overall domestic debt, on the ground of high financing costs and possible negative impact on the BOP in case of default, exchange rate effects and specific interest rate effects, which include the consequences of domestic borrowing on medium- and long-term rates (Part 2). Particular attention should be paid to the analysis of the public deficit financing, considering all possible sources of financing (including remittances), the characteristics of domestic financial markets, and their feedback effects on future public deficits, monetary policy and inflation. The creation and the development of domestic debt (and, more generally financial) markets should be pursued, since financial markets are a necessary condition to improve access to finance for local entrepreneur and SMEs and to foster economic growth (Demirguc-Kunt, Beck and Honohan 2008). However, these reforms must be gradual and conditioned upon the achievements of a certain degree of macroeconomic stability and institutional development. The creation of a large investor base and a the development of longer maturity structure should be two other important targets of fiscal consolidation policies, which could mitigate the adverse effects of domestic debt on interest rates. In this context, it is essential for the IFIs to keep on relaxing the prohibition of borrowing in the international capital markets, and to formulate country-specific and flexible foreign borrowing limitation. In particular, while it is true that borrowing on the market is more expensive than borrowing on concessional terms, when additional resources are essential, international borrowing should be allowed and the appropriate comparison should be made between the cost of domestic versus foreign borrowing (which includes exchange rate risk).

For policy and research purposes, it is essential to increase data availability on domestic debt and, more generally, on deficit financing in LICs on a cross-country basis and with a sufficiently long time span. At the moment, to our knowledge, there are only: 1) a detailed dataset on securitized domestic debt, covering a limited number of country on a comparable basis, but provides some additional information on instruments, maturities and holders (Chapter 4); 2) the dataset on public debt for 89 developing countries compiled by Panizza (2008), who distinguishes between domestic and external central government debt stocks; 3) the Christensen's (2005) dataset on domestic debt in 27 SSA countries; and 4) the dataset presented in Abbas (2007), which has the advantage of the largest coverage in time and across countries, but has data only on the stock of domestic debt. Ideally, one would need a large dataset as the latter, complemented with much additional information on debt service, debt composition, maturity and currency denomination.

Moreover, even if the stock of debt may not be a real disincentive, especially in countries with a weak institutional framework (as several HIPCs are), debt service could be an actual constraint to investments. The increasing domestic debt and its large interest bill in many HIPCs, as well as the recent access to international capital markets and to non-concessional borrowing by some poor countries, is going to exacerbate possible crowding out effects, related not only to investments, but also to social spending, possibly jeopardizing debt sustainability. In this context, a detailed analysis of the inflows and outflows of foreign currency must be an integral part of a country's liquidity management, in close coordination between the fiscal authorities and the central bank, in order to avoid or minimize the temporary liquidity constraint of servicing public debt. Therefore, country-specific debt service thresholds could be implemented not only to evaluate the risk of debt distress (and determine the grants-loans mix), but also to identify eligibility criteria and the actual amount of debt relief.

With respect to the latter issue, another relevant aspect to be addressed by IFIs is the weak link between the DSF and poverty reduction strategies, which results in the heterogeneous and not always encouraging performance of debt relief initiatives, with many HIPCs lagging behind in terms of poverty reduction expenditures and development financing (Chapter 8). Apart from considering the crowding out of pro-poor spending due to excessive interest payments on public (external and domestic) debt, which soak up a large share of the (limited) government revenues, debt forgiveness targets should take into account the amount of resources needed to reach specific targets of growth and poverty reductions. Public debt sustainability has to be evaluated keeping those targets in mind. At present, resources freed up by debt relief are assumed to be spent on health, education, nutrition and infrastructures according to government plans. The lack of specific sectoral expenditure targets increases uncertainty about economic growth and future borrowing; therefore, debt sustainability cannot be assured. Following the economic approach to debt sustainability (section 2.2.3), the WB-IMF analysis should explicitly calculate the amount of resources to be re-directed to specific sectoral targets, spur economic growth and reduce poverty after debt relief. The amount of debt to be cancelled should be a function of these targets, even if one must keep in mind that the amount of resources related to debt relief initiatives are only a small fraction of the much-needed funds required to finance the MDG.

Bringing together the considerations made in the last two sections, the extended framework to be devised by the IFIs should also include binding agreements with/for private creditors, to avoid that resources freed up with debt reduction by multilateral institutions and Paris Club countries can be appropriated in court by private creditors via vulture funds or other financial intermediaries. We notice that the lack of a binding legal framework for restructuring sovereign debt is the most relevant constraint to this recommendation. In this vein, the aborted SDRM proposal included a mechanism that would deter disruptive litigation by creditors during the debt restructuring negotiation and prevented minority creditors from blocking the majority agreements and from enforcing the terms of the original debt contracts. Given that implementing a binding agreements can only be done in the medium term, we argue that in the short term the international community could improve self-regulation: measures and codes on responsible lending should be more binding and extended to the largest pool of donors (and not exclusively to OECD countries) in order to reach international standards of responsible lending.

## 10.4 Debt Relief Policies

In the previous section we have discussed different ways in which the current DSA could be improved. More generally, we conclude suggesting a different approach to debt relief. In Part 3, we inspected the debt-growth nexus in order to assess the channels through which external debt could impinge on economic growth and to analyse whether, to what extent and under which conditions debt relief policies could be effective in promoting economic development and institution building. Our results imply that debt relief, if any, is likely to be effective only in countries with sound institutions, while the lack of any significant association between external debt and economic growth in countries with weak institutions and bad policies seems to suggest that these countries do not suffer from debt overhang. A first evaluation of debt relief provides mixed and generally not-encouraging results. On the one hand, there is no evidence of debt relief triggering economic growth, stimulate investment and reduce poverty, which could be partially explained by the poor institutional quality of many HIPCs and by the low amount of debt relief compared with the development needs. On the other hand, it seems that, since the launch of the HIPC Initiative, debt reduction is, at the same time, promoting and rewarding the development of sound institutions, starting a virtuous circle, thanks to which institution building could foster economic growth and lead to a sustainable debt path.

On the ground of these pieces of evidence and of the previous discussion, we call for a re-thinking of many areas of current debt relief policies. Future programs should follow a *growth diagnostic* approach aimed at identifying whether external debt is an actual constraint to economic growth and, if so, the channels through which the debt burden impairs the economy. In particular, is there a problem of reduced capital accumulation or lower TFP? In the latter case, is this due to short-termism, to a lack of structural reforms, or to a rise of the informal economy? As a result, debt relief initiatives should be tailored to country-specific characteristics, following the same approach adopted in the DSF to evaluate the overall public debt sustainability. Not only the amount and the composition of new lending, but also eligibility criteria and actual debt cancellations should also be a function of institutional quality, according to a governance-based debt relief. The avoidance of one-size-fits-all solutions, the consideration of different countries other than the actual HIPC-eligible ones, and a policy design that makes the amount of debt cancellation conditional upon actual improvements in institutional quality are likely to provide debtors' with the right incentives to strengthen institutions and debt management capacity and to increase debt relief effectiveness. These objectives can be achieved also thanks to deeper linkages with poverty reduction programs; to the definition of prudent borrowing policies, which can not ignore, on a flexible base, non-concessional lending; and to the implementation of an extended DSF based on a fully-fledged budged constraint, considering all sources of deficit financing and their effects on the economy. This kind of framework could deliver a more efficient use of a very limited pool of resources and improve support for the poorest people in the poorest countries by granting them freedom from hunger and access to basic health and education.

# Afterword

Debt relief for the poorest countries has been in the forefront of the development agenda for the past 20 years. Thanks to the advocacy of star actors (Angelina Jolie), star musicians (Bono), star professors (Jeffrey Sachs), and countless others, debt relief for the poorest countries has come to be viewed by many as a moral imperative. In an interview with the *Financial Times* on July 6, 2004, Jeffrey Sachs eloquently summed up this view: "No civilised country should try to collect the debts of people that are dying of hunger and disease and poverty". The creditors of the world's poorest countries, mostly bilateral and multilateral aid agencies, have responded with significant amounts of debt relief. While measuring the total amount of debt relief over the past 20 years is tricky, it is likely to easily top $100 billion.

Against this background, Arnone and Presbitero's book is a careful, thoughtful, and useful tour of the issues of public debt accumulation and debt relief in low-income countries (LICs). Rather than rely on rhetoric, the book sets itself the task of providing a balanced and evidence-based viewpoint of the relevant issues. This is essential in an area as conceptually complex and empirically murky as debt relief. I would like to illustrate these complexities, and the accompanying need for careful analysis such as that offered by Arnone and Presbitero, by briefly discussing two paradoxes that quickly emerge when one starts to think about debt relief.

## Paradox 1: The Debt that Wasn't

A first paradox of LIC debt is that, in an important sense, it never really was debt in the first place. This is because much of the debt owed by LICs was highly concessional. By concessional, I mean that much of the debt owed by LICs was lent by multilateral and bilateral aid donors, on highly favourable terms involving low or zero interest rates and long grace periods, as a way of providing financial assistance to the recipients. A simple example is useful to illustrate the issues. Suppose that a country receives a zero-interest loan of $100m from an aid donor that it has to repay next year. To see why this is really not a debt for the recipient country, imagine that the recipient takes $91m and invests it in US T-Bills that pay a 10 percent interest rate, and spends the remaining $9m on building schools and vaccinating kids. The next year when the loan must be repaid, the $91m invested in US T-Bills is now worth $100m ($91m + 10 percent of $91m = $9m in interest). This money can be used to fully repay the loan, and the country has received a gift of \$9m for development spending that never needs to be repaid. In the jargon of debt experts, the \$91m set aside and invested in US T-bills is the present value of the loan, and the \$9m that the country receives for free thanks to the interest subsidy is the grant element of the loan. Viewed in this way, a concessional loan cannot be a "burden" for the receiving country. Rather it represents a gift from the donor to the receiving country. Admittedly the gift is "only" \$9m, not \$100m, but it is a gift nonetheless.

As shown in Table A.1, these grant elements or gifts are in very large in reality. This table refers to an aggregate of the 27 LICs that have made it to the Completion Point of the Heavily Indebted Poor Countries (HIPC) debt relief process.[1] The first row shows that, as a group, these countries owed \$15b to their creditors in 1970, and by 1990 this figure had ballooned to \$92b. Thanks to debt relief beginning mostly in the 1990s, first from Paris Club bilateral creditors, and then from multilateral creditors in the HIPC process, total external debt fell by almost exactly half, to \$45b in 2008. The second row of this table reports total new borrowing. Between 1970 and 2008, this group of countries received \$241b in new loans. Of course, some of these new loans were eventually repaid, and some were eventually forgiven, so that these countries ended up in 2008 with only \$45b in debt. The crucial point here is that these new loans were on average highly concessional, just like in the simple example above, and so can usefully be thought of in part as gifts to the recipient countries. Since the World Bank reports the grant element of all new borrowing in each year, we can see exactly how large this gift was. The grant element of the \$241b in new loans is reported in the third row of Table A.1, and totals fully \$115b over the period 1970-2008 for this group of countries.[2]

The numbers in this table are remarkable because they suggest that the entire run-up of LIC debt and the complicated process of rescheduling and forgiving it over the past 40 years could in principle have been avoided completely. Suppose that starting in 1970, this group of countries receiving \$240b in concessional loans had followed the strategy described above of investing the present value of each new loan in US T-Bills, and had used the proceeds to repay the loans as they came due. Then this group of countries would have been able to spend a total of \$115b on building schools, vaccinating kids, and countless other worthwhile development projects, and would have ended up in 2008 with not a penny more in external debt than they started out with in 1970![3]

1 There are in fact 28 countries in AP's Table 1.2, but I have dropped Afghanistan for which data availability is a problem.

2 There are reasons why this estimate of the size of the "gift" might be too high or too low. On the one hand, the discount rate used by the World Bank to calculate the grant element is high, at 10 percent, and this implies the "gift" might be overstated (by way of comparison the average US 30-year T-Bill rate is 8.5 percent). On the other hand, the "gift" might be understated if one takes into account the fact that many recipients of concessional debt might not have been able to borrow anything at all on market terms.

3 Indeed, the new Debt Sustainability Framework of the World Bank and IMF, ably discussed by Arnone and Presbitero in Chapter 2, can be thought of as precisely a way of

**Table A.1 Debt, new borrowing, and grant elements for 27 HIPC countries**

| **Billions constant 2000 US Dollars** | | | |
|---|---|---|---|
| Total long-term debt outstanding | *1970* | *1990* | *2008* |
| | 15 | 91 | 45 |
| Cumulative new borrowing | *1970-1990* | *1990-2008* | *1970-2008* |
| | 147 | 94 | 241 |
| Cumulative grant element | *1970-1990* | *1990-2008* | *1970-2008* |
| | 55 | 60 | 115 |

*Note*: Table refers to an aggregate of 27 HIPC countries listed in Table 1.2, excluding Afghanistan. Data are taken from the Global Development Finance publication of the World Bank (http://data.worldbank.org). Series codes are DT.DOD.DLXF.CD (Long-term debt outstanding), DT.DIS.DLXF.CD (Total disbursements on long-term debt) and DT.GRE.DPPG (Average grant element on new external debt committments).
*Source*: Author's calculations.

Yet this did not happen, and what went wrong is a long and complicated story well beyond the scope of a short comment. Some of the blame surely lies with the providers of concessional loans, who did not do enough to ensure that the loans were wisely allocated across countries and wisely invested by the recipients. And some of the blame surely also lies with recipient governments, who were only too glad to receive and spend loans that would fall due well after they had left office, and that they might very well have expected to be forgiven anyhow. And both the suppliers and users of concessional loans surely were at times overoptimistic about the returns to the projects that they financed, and the extent to which these returns could be recaptured in the form of tax revenues that could in turn be used to pay down the debt. Nevertheless, any careful analysis of the debt difficulties of LICs needs to be grounded in the observation that, *ex-ante* at least, the debts incurred were entirely repayable.

## Paradox 2: Hiccups for HIPCs

A second paradox of debt relief is that it may have done little to improve the long-run fiscal sustainability in the countries benefitting from debt relief.[4] Table 2 provides a simple example to illustrate the issue. Imagine a country that, before

delivering the grant element of loans to countries with high debt burdens where further debt accumulation would be undesirable.

4 This observation is not new, and is carefully spelled out in an excellent paper whose title I borrow here: C. Burnside and D. Fanizza (2005), "Hiccups for HIPCS", *Contributions to Macroeconomics* 5(1), Article 4.

debt relief, starts out with a debt outstanding of $200m (this is the first row in Table A.2), of which $20m falls due in the current year. Suppose also that the government collects $50m in tax revenue and plans to spend another $40m on various public projects over the course of the year. Clearly this country is headed for fiscal trouble: since it will spend a total of $60m on debt service and other spending, but it takes in only $50m in taxes, its public debt is set to expand by $10m. If this pattern of spending in excess of revenues continues, over time the public debt will balloon until eventually some painful correction in the form of more taxes or less spending is required.

**Table A.2 Hypothetical debt relief scenarios**

| Millions USD | Initial debt | Debt service due | Taxes | Non-interest spending | Final debt |
|---|---|---|---|---|---|
| Before debt relief | 200 | 20 | 50 | 40 | 210 |
| After debt relief | 100 | 10 | 50 | 40 | 100 |
| After debt relief with conditionality | 100 | 10 | 50 | 50 | 110 |

*Source*: Author's calculations.

Now imagine that the country benefits from debt relief that eliminates half of its public debt. The second row in Table A.2 shows the outcome. Debt service falling due also halves from $20m to $10m, and if spending and tax revenues remain the same and generate a primary surplus of $10m, this precisely covers debt service. The overall effect that public debt remains constant at $100m, and the country is no longer on track to having its public debt expand without limit.

But the outcome is very different if the donor providing debt relief requires the recipient to use the "savings" generated by debt relief to increase development spending, as was the case with HIPC debt relief. The third row of Table A.2 shows that this ostensibly sensible requirement can lead to problems down the road. Debt service due after debt relief is still only $10m, but now the government increases spending by $10m, to $50m. Since tax revenues are still only $50m, the government primary budget surplus is zero and it cannot cover its remaining debt service obligations. And so public debt is on track to expand again without limit, unless eventually there is some increase in taxes and or decrease in spending. Obviously the country is immediately better off following debt relief, as it is able to benefit from increased development spending. But in the longer term the same fundamental force that led to high debt in the first place is still present: the government is spending more than it takes in in tax revenues, and eventually debt problems will re-emerge.

Of course this is a very simplistic example that abstracts from many considerations that would make the conclusions less stark. It could be that after debt relief, the country is able to collect taxes more effectively, and so is better able to cover its total interest and non-interest expenditures. It could also very well be the case that aid donors recognize that the need for public development spending in the country simply exceeds the ability of the government to finance, and so the donors agree to provide grants to the recipient country to fill the gap. But at the same time the example in Table A.2 is not entirely unrealistic. In Figure 8.1 Arnone and Presbitero document precisely this pattern of debt service declines and commensurate spending increases that can undermine long-term fiscal sustainability. According to World Bank and IMF projections, between 1999 and 2012 debt service as a share of GDP in HIPC countries will decline from 4 percent to 1 percent, while "poverty reduction expenditures" will rise by exactly the same amount, from 7 to 10 percent of GDP.

These issues at the heart of several chapters in Arnone and Presbitero's book. In Chapter 2 they carefully discuss fiscal and debt sustainability analysis of the sort that motivates my discussion here: indeed the simple question of whether a pattern of spending and taxes is consistent with a stable public debt is discussed explicitly in Box 2.1. In Chapters 4 and 5 they rightly emphasize concerns about the accumulation of domestic and external debt following debt relief. And finally their empirical findings in Chapters 7 and 8 that show that debt relief is more likely to be effective in countries with good institutions is also consistent with this view: with strong public institutions, better and more sustainable fiscal decisions that prevent over accumulation of debt are more likely to be taken.

Beyond these two paradoxes, the broader issue that the reader of this book should consider – and will learn much about – is that public indebtedness should not be thought of as a problem in itself, but rather as a symptom of more fundamental political and socioeconomic forces that cause governments to spend more than they take in. Unless these underlying problems are addressed as well resulting in some combination of more taxes, less spending, or more foreign aid, debt relief alone is unlikely to achieve its desired objective of reducing the debt burdens of the world's poorest countries.

Aart Kraay[5]
Lead Economist, Development Research Group, The World Bank
Washington, DC

5 I am grateful to Luis Serven and Vikram Nehru for helpful comments. The views expressed here are the authors and do not reflect those of the World Bank, its Executive Directors, or the countries they represent.

# Bibliography


Abbas, S.M.A. 2005. Public Debt Sustainability and Growth in Sub-Saharan Africa (Post-HIPC): The Role of Domestic Debt, *GDN Project on Macroeconomics of Low Income Countries*, February 2005.

Abbas, S.M.A. 2007. Public Domestic Debt and Economic Growth in Lower Income Countries, unpublished, University of Oxford.

Abbas, S.M.A. and Christensen, J.E. 2010. The Role of Domestic Debt Markets in Economic Growth: An Empirical Investigation for Low-Income Countries and Emerging Markets, *IMF Staff Papers*, 57(1), 209-55.

Acemoglu, D. and Robinson, J. 2008. The Role of Institutions in Growth and Development, Commission on Growth and Development, Working Paper No. 10.

Adam, C.S. and Bevan, D.L. 2006. Aid and the Supply Side: Public Investment, Export Performance and Dutch Disease in Low-Income Countries, *World Bank Economic Review*, 20(2), 261-90.

Adams, R.H. and Page, J. 2005. Do International Migration and Remittances Reduce Poverty in Developing Countries? *World Development*, 33(10), 1645-69.

Addison, T., Hansen, H. and Tarp, F. 2004, *Debt Relief for Poor Countries*. New York: Palgrave Macmillan.

Agenor, P.R. 2005. *The Economics of Adjustment and Growth*. Cambridge, MA: Harvard University Press.

Agenor, P.R. and Montiel, P.J. 1999. *Development Macroeconomics*, 2nd ed. Princeton, NJ: Princeton University Press.

Alesina, A. and Dollar, D. 2000. Who Gives Foreign Aid to Whom and Why? *Journal of Economic Growth*, 5(1), 33-63.

Alesina, A. and Tabellini, G. 1989. External Debt, Capital Flight and Political Risk, *Journal of International Economics*, 27(3-4), 199-220.

Alesina, A. and Weder, B. 2002. Do Corrupt Governments Receive Less Foreign Aid? *American Economic Review*, 92(4), 1126-37.

Allen, T. and Weinhold, D. 2000. Dropping the Debt for the New Millennium: Is it Such a Good Idea? *Journal of International Development*, 12(6), 857-75.

Arellano, M. and Bond, S. 1991. Some Tests of Specification for Panel Data: Monte Carlo Evidence and an Application to Employment Equations, *Review of Economic Studies*, 58(2), 277-97.

Arnone, M., Bandiera, L. and Presbitero, A.F. 2005. Debt Sustainability Framework in HIPCs: A Critical Assessment and Suggested Improvements, unpublished (revised 2008).

Arnone, M. and Presbitero, A.F. 2007. External Debt Sustainability and Domestic Debt in Heavily Indebted Poor Countries, *Rivista Internazionale di Scienze Sociali*, 2, 187-213.

Arnone, M. and Ugolini, P. 2005. *Primary Dealers in Government Securities*. Washington, DC: International Monetary Fund.

Arslanalp, S. and Henry, P.B. 2005. Is Debt Relief Efficient? *The Journal of Finance*, LX(2), 1017-51.

Arslanalp, S. and Henry, P.B. 2006. Policy Watch: Debt Relief, *Journal of Economic Perspectives*, 20(1), 207-20.

Asiedu, E. 2003. Debt Relief and Institutional Reform: A Focus on Heavily Indebted Poor Countries, *The Quarterly Review of Economics and Finance*, 43(4), 614-26.

Baqir, R. 2002. Social Sector Spending in a Panel of Countries, *IMF Working Paper*, 02/35.

Barro, R.J. and Lee, J.W. 2001. International Data on Educational Attainment: Updates and Implications, *Oxford Economic Papers*, 53(3), 541-63.

Barro, R.J. and Lee, J.W. 2005. IMF Programs: Who is Chosen and What are the Effects? *Journal of Monetary Economics*, 52(7), 1245-69.

Bassetto, M. 2008, Fiscal Theory of the Price Level, in *The New Palgrave Dictionary of Economics*, edited by S.N. Durlauf and L.E. Blume. New York: Palgrave Macmillan.

Bauer, P.T. 1971. *Dissent on Development: Studies and Debates in Development Economics*. London: Weidenfeld and Nicholson.

Beaugrand, P., Loko, B. and Mlachila, M. 2002. The Choice between External and Domestic Debt in Financing Budget Deficits: The Case of Central and West African Countries, *IMF Working Paper*, 02/79.

Beck, T. and Martinez Peria, M.S. 2009. What Explain the Cost of Remittances? An Examination Across 119 Country Corridors, *Policy Research Working Paper*, 5072, The World Bank.

Beddies, C., Dömeland, D., Le Manchec, M.H. and Mooney, H. 2009. Debt Sustainability in Low-Income Countries: Recent Experience and Challenges Ahead, in *Debt Relief and Beyond. Lessons Learned and Challenges Ahead*, edited by C.A. Primo Braga and D. Dömeland. Washington, DC: The World Bank, 35-48.

Berg, A., Funke, N., Hajdenberg, A., Lledo, V., Ossowski, R., Schindler, M., Spilimbergo, A., Tareq, S. and Yackovlev, I. 2009. Fiscal Policy in Sub-Saharan Africa in Response to the Impact of the Global Crisis, *IMF Staff Position Note*, 09/10.

Bird, G. 2007. The IMF: A Bird's Eye View of its Role and Operations, *Journal of Economic Surveys*, 21(4), 683-745.

Bird, G. and Milne, A. 2003. Debt Relief for Low Income Countries: Is it Effective and Efficient? *The World Economy*, 26(1), 43-59.

Birdsall, N., Williamson J. and Deese, B. 2002. *Delivering Debt Relief: From IMF Gold to a New Aid Architecture*. Washington, DC: Institute for International Economics.

Blavy, R. 2006. Public Debt and Productivity: The Difficult Quest for Jamaica, *IMF Working Paper*, 06/235.

Blejer, M. and Kahn, M. 1984. Government Policy and Private Investment in Developing Counties, *IMF Staff Papers*, 31(2), 379-403.

Blundell, R. and Bond, S.R. 1998. Initial Conditions and Moment Restrictions in Dynamic Panel Data Models, *Journal of Econometrics*, 87(1), 115-43.

Blundell, R., Bond, S.R. and Windmeijer, F. 2000. Estimation in Dynamic Panel Data Models: Improving on the Performance of the Standard GMM Estimator, *IFS Working Papers*, W00/12.

Bond, S.R., Hoeffler, A. and Temple, J. 2001. GMM Estimation of Empirical Growth Models, *CEPR Discussion Papers*, 3048.

Boote, A.R. and Thugge, K. 1997. Debt Relief for Low-Income Countries: The HIPC Initiative, *IMF Working Paper*, 97/24.

Borensztein, E., Levy Yeyati, E. and Panizza, U. 2006. *Living with Debt How to Limit the Risks of Sovereign Finance.* Cambridge, MA: Harvard University Press.

Boyce, J. 1992. The Revolving Door? External Debt and Capital Flight: A Philippine Case Study, *World Development*, 20(3), 335-349.

Brookings Institution 2009. The Impact of the Financial Crisis on Low-Income Countries, 3 March 2009, Washington, DC. Available at: http://www.brookings.edu/~/media/Files/events/2009/0303_imf/20090303_imf.pdf.

Buehn, A. and Schneider, F. 2007. Shadow Economies and Corruption all Over The World: Revised Estimates for 120 Countries, *Economics: The Open-Access, Open-Assessment E-Journal*, 1, 2007-9 (Version 2).

Bulir, A. and Hamann, A.J. 2008. Volatility of Development Aid: From the Frying Pan into the Fire? *World Development*, 36(10), 2048-66.

Bulow, J. and Rogoff, K. 1990. Cleaning Up Third World Debt without Getting Taken to the Cleaners, *Journal of Economic Perspectives*, 4(1), 31-42.

Bulow, J. and Rogoff, K. 2005. Grants versus Loans for Development Banks, *American Economic Review*, 95(2), 393-7.

Burnside, C. and Fanizza, D. 2005. Hiccups for HIPCs? *Contributions to Macroeconomics*, 5(1), Article 4.

Calì, M. and Dell'Erba, S. 2009. The Global Financial Crisis and Remittances – What Past Evidence Suggests, *ODI Working Paper*, 303.

Calvo, G.A. 1988. Growth, Debt and Economic Transformation: The Capital Flight Problem, in *New Theories in Growth and Development*, edited by F. Coricelli, M. di Matteo and F. Hahn. New York: St. Martin's Press.

Cassimon, D., Moreno-Dodson, B. and Wodon, Q. 2008. Debt Sustainability for Low-Income Countries. A Review of Standard and Alternative Concepts, in *Public Finance for Poverty Reduction: Concepts and Case Studies from Latin*

*America and Africa*, edited by B. Moreno Dodson and Q. Wodon. Washington, DC: The World Bank, 21-56.

Catão, L.A.V. and Terrones, M.E. 2005. Fiscal Deficits and Inflation, *Journal of Monetary Economics*, 52(3), 529-54.

Cerra, V., Rishi, M. and Saxena, S. 2008. Robbing the Riches: Capital Flight, Institutions and Debt, *The Journal of Development Studies*, 44(8), 1190-213.

Chami, R., Barajas, A., Cosimano, T., Fullenkamp, C., Gapen, M. and Montiel, P. 2008. Macroeconomic Consequences of Remittances, *IMF Occasional Paper*, 259.

Chenery, H.B. and Strout, A.M. 1966. Foreign Assistance and Economic Development, *American Economic Review*, 56(4), 679-733.

Chowdhury, A.R. 2004. External Debt, Growth and the HIPC Initiative: Is the Country Choice too Narrow? in *Debt Relief for Poor Countries*, edited by T. Addison, H. Hansen and F. Tarp. New York: Palgrave Macmillan, 158-80.

Christensen, J. 2005. Special Data Section Domestic Debt Markets in Sub-Saharan Africa, *IMF Staff Papers*, 52(3), 518-38.

Claessens, S., Detragiache, E., Kanbur, R. and Wickham, P. 1997. Analytical Aspects of the Debt Problems of Heavily Indebted Poor Countries, in *External Finance for Low-Income Countries*, edited by Z. Iqbal and R. Kanbur. Washington, DC: International Monetary Fund, 21-48.

Clements, B.J., Bhattacharya, R. and Nguyen, T.Q. 2004. External Debt, Public Investment and Growth in Low-Income Countries, in *Helping Countries Develop: The Role of Fiscal Policy*, edited by S. Gupta, B. Clements and G. Inchauste. Washington, DC: International Monetary Fund.

Clements, B., Gupta, S., Pivovarsky, A. and Tiongson, E.R. 2004. Foreign Aid: Grants versus Loans, *Finance and Development*, 4(September), 46-49.

Cline, W. 1995. *International Debt Re-Examined.* Washington, DC: Institute for International Economics.

Cline, W.R. 2003. HIPC Debt Sustainability and Post-Relief Lending Policy, *Issue Paper on Debt Sustainability*, HIPC Unit, The World Bank, August.

Cohen, D. 1990. Debt Relief: Implications of Secondary Market Discounts and Debt Overhangs, *World Bank Economic Review*, 2(1), 77-104.

Cohen, D. 1993. Low Investment and Large LDC Debt in the 1980s, *American Economic Review*, 83(3), 437-49.

Cohen, D. 2001. The HIPC Initiative: True and False Promises, *International Finance*, 4(3), 363-80.

Cohen, D., Jacquet, P. and Reisen, H. 2007. Loans or Grants? *Review of World Economics*, 143(4), 764-82.

Collier, P. 2007. *The Bottom Billion*. New York: Oxford University Press.

Committee on Foreign Affairs 2007. *Vulture Funds and the Threat to Debt Relief in Africa: A Call to Action at the G-8 and Beyond*, hearing before the subcommittee on Africa and global health. Washington, DC: US Government Printing Office.

Cordella, T., Ricci, L.A. and Ruiz-Arranz, M. 2010. Debt Overhang or Debt Irrelevance? *IMF Staff Papers*, 57(1), 1-24.

Cordella, T. and Ulku, H. 2007. Grants vs Loans, *IMF Staff Papers*, 54(1), 139-62.

Crespo Cuaresma, J. and Vincelette, G.A. 2009. Debt Relief and Education in Heavily Indebted Poor Countries, in *Debt Relief and Beyond. Lessons Learned and Challenges Ahead*, edited by C.A. Primo Braga and D. Dömeland. Washington, DC: The World Bank, 35-48.

Cukierman, A., Edwards, S. and Tabellini, G. 1992. Seigniorage and Political Instability, *American Economic Review*, 82(3), 537-55.

Dahle Huse, M. and Muyakwa, S.L. 2008. *China in Africa: Lending, Policy Space and Governance*. Norwegian Campaign for Debt Cancellation and Norwegian Council for Africa.

Dang, H., Knack, S. and Rogers, H. 2009. International Aid and Financial Crises in Donor Countries, *Policy Research Working Paper*, 5162, The World Bank.

Das, U.S., Papaioannou, M.G. and Trebesch, C. 2009. Sovereign Default Risk and Private Sector Access to Capital in Emerging Markets, in *Debt Relief and Beyond. Lessons Learned and Challenges Ahead*, edited by C.A. Primo Braga and D. Dömeland. Washington, DC: The World Bank, 141-80.

Daseking, C. and Powell, R. 1999. From Toronto Terms to the HIPC Initiative – A Brief History of Debt Relief for Low-Income Countries, *IMF Working Papers*, 99/142.

Daseking, C. and Joshi, B. 2006. Debt and New Financing in Low-Income Countries – Looking Back, Thinking Ahead, in *The Macroeconomic Management of Foreign Aid: Opportunities and Pitfalls*, edited by P. Isard, L. Lipschitz, A. Mourmouras and B. Yontcheva. Washington, DC: International Monetary Fund.

Davidson, R. and MacKinnon, J.G. 2004. *Econometric Theory and Methods*. New York: Oxford University Press.

De Renzio, P. 2009. *The G8 and Poor Countries: Promises, Just Promises?* Available at: http://www.globaleconomicgovernance.org/blog/2009/07/the-g8-and-poor-countries-promises-just-promises/.

Del Valle, C. and Ugolini, P. 2003. The Development of Domestic Markets for Government Bonds, in *The Future of Capital Markets in Developing Countries*, edited by R.E. Litan, M. Pomerlano and V. Sundararajan. Washington, DC: Brookings Institution Press.

Debt Relief International. 2007. *Negotiating Debt Reduction in the HIPC Initiative and Beyond*. London: Debt Relief International.

Demirguc-Kunt, A., Beck, T. and Honohan, P. 2008. *Finance for All? Policies and Pitfalls in Expanding Access*. Washington, DC: The World Bank.

Depetris Chauvin, N. and Kraay, A. 2005. What has 100 Billion Dollars Worth of Debt Relief Done for Low-Income Countries? unpublished, The World Bank.

Depetris Chauvin, N. and Kraay, A. 2007. Who Gets Debt Relief? *Journal of the European Economic Association*, 5(2-3), 333-42.

Dessy, S.E. and Vencatachellum, D. 2007. Debt Relief and Social Services Expenditure: The African Experience, 1989-2003, *African Development Review*, 19(1), 200-16.

Detragiache, E., Tressel, T. and Gupta, P. 2008. Foreign Banks in Poor Countries: Theory and Evidence, *Journal of Finance*, 63(5), 2123-60.

Dikhanov, Y. 2004. Historical Present Value of Debt in Developing Economies: 1980-2002, unpublished, The World Bank.

Dixit, A.H. and Pindyck, R.S. 1994. *Investment Under Uncertainty*. Princeton, NJ: Princeton University Press.

Djankov, S., Montalvo, J. and Reynal-Querol, M. 2008. The Curse of Aid, *Journal of Economic Growth*, 13(3), 169-94.

Dollar, D. and Levin, V. 2006. The Increasing Selectivity of Foreign Aid, 1984-2003, *World Development*, 34(12), 2034-46.

Dömeland, D. and Kharas, H. 2009. Debt Relief and Sustainable Financing to Meet the MDGs, in *Debt Relief and Beyond. Lessons Learned and Challenges Ahead*, edited by C.A. Primo Braga and D. Dömeland. Washington, DC: The World Bank, 117-40.

Dooley, M. 1989. Debt Relief and Leveraged Buy-Outs, *International Economic Review*, 30(1), 71-5.

Doucouliagos, H. and Paldam, M. 2009. The Aid Effectiveness Literature: The Sad Results of 40 Years of Research, *Journal of Economic Surveys*, 23(3), 433-61.

Drazen, A. 2002. Conditionality and Ownership in IMF Lending: A Political Economy Approach, *IMF Staff Papers*, 49(Special Issue), 36-67.

Dreher, A. and Vaubel, R. 2004. Do IMF and IBRD Cause Moral Hazard and Political Business Cycles? Evidence from Panel Data, *Open Economies Review*, 15(1), 5-22.

Drine, I. and Sami Nabi, M. 2010. Public External Debt, Informality and Production Efficiency in Developing Countries, *Economic Modelling*, 27(2), 487-495.

Easterly, W. 1999. The Ghost of Financing Gap: Testing the Growth Model of the International Financial Institutions, *Journal of Development Economics*, 60(2), 423-38.

Easterly, W. 2001a, Think Again: Debt Relief, *Foreign Policy*, 127, 20-26.

Easterly, W. 2001b, *The Elusive Quest for Growth: Economists Adventures and Misadventure in the Tropics*. Cambridge, MA: The MIT Press.

Easterly, W. 2001c. Growth Implosions and Debt Explosions: Do Growth Slowdowns Cause Public Debt Crises? *Contributions to Macroeconomics*, 1(1), Article 1.

Easterly, W. 2002. How Did Heavily Indebted Poor Countries become Heavily Indebted? Reviewing Two Decades of Debt Relief, *World Development*, 30(10), 1677-1696.

Easterly, W. 2006. Reliving the 50s: The Big Push, Poverty Traps and Take-Offs in Economic Development, *Journal of Economic Growth*, 11(2), 289-318.

Easterly, W. and Pfutze, T. 2008. Where Does the Money Go? Best and Worst Practices in Foreign Aid, *Journal of Economic Perspective*, 22(2), 29-52.

Easterly, W. and Schmidt-Hebbel, K. 1991. The Macroeconomics of Public Sector Deficits, *World Bank Country Economic Department Working Paper*, 775.

Easterly, W. and Schmidt-Hebbel, K. 1993. Fiscal Deficits and Macroeconomics Performance in Developing Countries, *World Bank Research Observer*, 8(2), 211-37.

Eaton, J. 2002. *The HIPC Initiative: The Goals, Additionality, Eligibility and Debt Sustainability*. Washington, DC: The World Bank.

Edwards, S. 2002. Debt Relief and the Current Account: An Analysis of the HIPC Initiative, *The World Economy*, 26(4), 513-31.

Edwards, S. 2003. Debt Relief and Fiscal Sustainability, *Review of World Economics*, 139(1), 38-65.

Eichengreen, B. and Hausmann, R. 1999. Exchange Rates and Financial Fragility, *Proceedings*, Federal Reserve Bank of Kansas City, 329-68.

Elbadawi, I.A., Ndulu, B.N. and Ndung'u, N. 1997. Debt Overhang and Economic Growth in Sub-Saharan Africa, in *External Finance for Low-Income Countries*, edited by Z. Iqbal and R. Kanbur. Washington, DC: International Monetary Fund, 49-72.

Eurodad. 2001. *Putting Poverty Reduction First*. European Network on Debt and Development.

Eurodad. 2005. *Paying for 100% Multilateral Debt Cancellation: Current Proposals Explained*, European Network on Debt and Development.

Eurodad. 2008. *Taming the Vultures: Are New Measures Enough to Protect Debt Relief Gains?* European Network on Debt and Development.

Eurodad. 2009. *Review of the DSF: Bank & Fund Declare Countries can Borrow More*, European Network on Debt and Development.

Evans, H. 1999. Debt Relief for the Poorest Countries: Why Did it Take so Long? *Development Policy Review*, 17(3), 267-79.

Fedelino, A. and Kudina, A. 2003. Fiscal Sustainability in African HIPC Countries: A Policy Dilemma? *IMF Working Paper*, 03/187.

Fofack, I. 2009. Causality between External Debt and Capital Flight in Sub-Saharan Africa, *Policy Research Working Paper*, 5042, The World Bank.

Foroohar, K. 2008. The Opportunist, *Bloomberg Markets*, February.

Fosu, A.K. 1996. The Impact of External Debt on Economic Growth in Sub-Saharan Africa, *Journal of Development Economics*, 21(1), 93-117.

Fosu, A.K. 1999. The External Debt Burden and Economic Growth in the 1980s: Evidence from Sub-Saharan Africa, *Canadian Journal of Development Studies*, 20(2), 307-18.

Frankel, J.A. 2009. Are Bilateral Remittances Countercyclical? *NBER Working Papers*, 15419.

Freund, C. and Spadafora, N. 2008. Remittances, Transaction Costs and Informality, *Journal of Development Economics*, 86(2), 356-66.

Freytag, A. and Pehnelt, G. 2009. Debt Relief and Governance Quality in Developing Countries, *World Development*, 37(1), 62-80.

Frot E. (2009). The Consequences of Financial Crisis Aid, unpublished, SITE/ Stockholm School of Economics.

G8 Summit Meetings. 2007. Growth and Responsibility in Africa, *Summit Declaration*, Heilegendamm, 8 June.

Galindo, A., Izquierdo, A. and Rojas-Suarez, L. 2010. Financial Integration and Foreign Banks in Latin America: How do they Impact the Transmission of External Financial Shocks? *RES Working Papers*, 4651, Inter-American Development Bank.

Gamarra, B., Pollock, M. and Primo Braga, C.A. 2009. Debt Relief to Low-Income Countries: A Retrospective, in *Debt Relief and Beyond. Lessons Learned and Challenges Ahead*, edited by C.A. Primo Braga and D. Dömeland. Washington, DC: The World Bank, 11-34.

Gautam, M. 2003. *Debt Relief for the Poorest. An OED Review of the HIPC Initiative.* Washington, DC: The World Bank.

Geginat, C. and Kraay, A. 2007. Does IDA Engage in Defensive Lending? *Policy Research Working Paper*, 4328, The World Bank.

Giuliano, P. and Ruiz-Arranz, M. 2009. Remittances, Financial Development and Growth, *Journal of Development Economics*, 90(1), 144-152.

Gomanee, K., Girma, S. and Morrissey, O. 2005. Aid, Public Spending and Human Welfare: Evidence From Quantile Regressions, *Journal of International Development*, 17(3), 299-309.

Gomanee, K., Morrissey, O., Mosley, P. and Verschoor, A. 2005. Aid, Government Expenditure and Aggregate Welfare, *World Development*, 33(3), 355-70.

Gormley, T.A. 2010. The Impact of Foreign Bank Entry in Emerging Markets: Evidence from India, *Journal of Financial Intermediation*, 19(1), 26-51.

Gray, D., Lim, C.H., Loukoianova, E. and Malone, S. 2008. A Risk-Based Debt Sustainability Framework: Incorporating Balance Sheets and Uncertainty, *IMF Working Paper*, 08/40.

Greene, J. and Vilanueva, D. 1991. Private Investment in Developing Countries, *IMF Staff Papers*, 38(1), 33-58.

Gunning, J.W. and Mash, R. 1998. Fiscal Implications of Debt and Debt Relief: Issues Paper, unpublished, Centre for the Study of African Economies.

Gunter, B.G. 2003. Achieving Long-Term Debt Sustainability in all Heavily Indebted Poor Countries (HIPCs), Discussion Paper prepared for the G-24 XVI Technical Meeting, February 2003. Available at: http://www.g24.org/ guntetgm.pdf.

Gunter, B.G., Rahman, J. and Shy, H. 2009. Linking Social Development with the Capacity to Carry Debt: Towards an MDG-Consistent Debt-Sustainability Concept, *Development Policy Review*, 27(3), 269-86.

Gupta, S., Clements, B., Baldacci, E. and Mulas-Granados, C. 2004. The Persistence of Fiscal Adjustments in Developing Countries, *Applied Economics Letters*, 11(4), 209-12.

Gupta, S., Clements, B., Baldacci, E. and Mulas-Granados, C. 2005. Fiscal Policy, Expenditure Composition and Growth in Low-Income Countries, *Journal of International Money and Finance*, 24(3), 441-63.

Gupta, S., Pattillo, C. and Wagh, S. 2009. Effects of Remittances on Poverty and Financial Development in Sub-Saharan Africa, *Journal of Development Economics*, 37(1), 104-15.

Gupta, S., Powell, R. and Yang, Y. 2006. *Macroeconomic Challenges of Scaling Up Aid to Africa – A Checklist for Practitioners*. Washington, DC: International Monetary Fund.

Guscina, A. 2008. Impact of Macroeconomic, Political and Institutional Factors on the Structure of Government Debt in Emerging Market Countries, *IMF Working Paper*, 08/205.

Hanmer, L. and Shelton, R. 2001. *Sustainable Debt: What has HIPC Delivered?* Paper for the WIDER Conference on Debt Relief, Helsinki, August 2001.

Hansen, H. 2004. The Impact of External Aid and External Debt on Growth and Investment, in *Debt Relief for Poor Countries*, edited by T. Addison, H. Hansen and F. Tarp. New York: Palgrave Macmillan, 134-57.

Hanson, J.A. 2007. The Growth in Government Domestic Debt: Changing Burdens and Risks, *Policy Research Working Paper*, 4348, The World Bank.

Harper, C., Jones, N., McKay, A. and Espey, J. 2009. Children in Times of Economic Crisis: Past Lessons, Future Policies, *ODI Background Note*, Overseas Development Institute.

Harrabi, S., Bousrih, L. and Mohammed, S. 2007. Debt Relief and Credit to the Private Sector in African Countries, *African Development Review*, 19(3), 469-80.

Hausmann, R. and Panizza, U. 2003. The Determinants of Original Sin: An Empirical Investigation, *Journal of International Money and Finance*, 22(7), 957-90.

Hausmann, R., Rodrik, D. and Velasco A. 2005. Growth Diagnostics, unpublished, *John F. Kennedy School of Government*, Harvard University.

Hauk, W.R. and Wacziarg, R. 2009. A Monte Carlo Study of Growth Regressions, *Journal of Economic Growth*, 14(2), 103-47.

Heckman, J.J. 1979. Sample Selection Bias as a Specification Error, *Econometrica*, 47(1), 153-61.

Hicks, N.L. 1989. Expenditure Reductions in High-Debts Countries, *Finance and Development*, 26, 35-7.

Hjertholm, P. 2004. HIPC Debt Sustainability Thresholds: Revisiting the Case for a Uniform Formula for Debt Relief, *Journal of Restructuring Finance*, 1(1), 13-33.

Hoeffler, A.E. 2002. The Augmented Solow Model and the African Growth Debate, *Oxford Bulletin of Economics and Statistics*, 64(2), 135-58.

Hofman, B. and Reisen, H. 1991. Some Evidence on Debt-Related Determinants of Investment and Consumption in Heavily Indebted Countries, *Review of World Economics*, 127(2), 281-99.

Hostland, D. 2009. Low-Income Countries' Access to Private Debt Markets, *World Bank Policy Research Working Paper*, 4289.

Hurley, G. 2008. *Eurodad Charter on Responsible Financing.* Brussels: Eurodad.

Hussain, M., Berg, A. and Aiyar, S. 2009. The Macroeconomic Management of Increased Aid: Policy Lessons from Recent Experience, *Review of Development Economics*, 13(1), 491-509.

IEG. 2006. *Debt Relief for the Poorest – An Evaluation Update of the HIPC Initiative*. Washington, DC: The World Bank.

IDA. 2007. *Country Policy and Institutional Assessment – 2007 Assessment Questionnaire*. Washington, DC: The World Bank.

IDA and IMF. 2001. The Challenge of Maintaining Long-Term External Debt Sustainability, April 20, 2001.

IDA and IMF. 2004a. Debt Sustainability in Low-Income Countries – Proposal for an Operational Framework and Policy Implications, February 3, 2004.

IDA and IMF. 2004b. Debt Sustainability in Low-Income Countries: Further Considerations on an Operational Framework and Policy Implications, September 10, 2004.

IDA and IMF. 2007a. Enhanced Heavily Indebted Poor Countries (HIPC) Initiative-Status Non-Paris Club Official Bilateral Creditors Participation, The World Bank and IMF.

IDA and IMF. 2007b. Staff Guidance Note on the Application of the Joint Bank-Fund Debt Sustainability Framework for Low-Income Countries, The World Bank and IMF.

IDA and IMF. 2008. Heavily Indebted Poor Countries (HIPC) Initiative and Multilateral Debt Relief Initiative (MDRI) – Status of Implementation, The World Bank and the IMF.

IDA and IMF. 2009. Heavily Indebted Poor Countries (HIPC) Initiative and Multilateral Debt Relief Initiative (MDRI) – Status of Implementation, The World Bank and the IMF.

IFIC. 2000. *Report of the International Financial Institution Advisory Commission* ("Meltzer Commission Report"). Washington, DC: International Financial Institutions Advisory Commission.

Ilzetzki, E., Mendoza, E.G. and Végh, C.A. 2009. How Big are Fiscal Multipliers? *CEPR Policy Insight*, 39.

Ilzetzki, E. and Végh, C.A. 2008. Pro-Cyclical Fiscal Policy in Developing Countries: Truth or Fiction? *NBER Working Paper*, 14191.

Imbs, J. and Ranciere, R. 2008. The Overhang Hangover, unpublished, *HEC Lausanne*.

IMF. 1998. Costa Rica: Recent Economic Development, *IMF Country Report*, 98/45.

IMF. 2002a. Assessing Sustainability, May 28, 2002.

IMF. 2002b. Nicaragua: Selected Issues and Statistical Appendix, *IMF Country Report*, 02/269.

IMF. 2003. Ghana: Selected Issues, *Country Report*, 03/134.

IMF. 2004a. Zambia: Selected Issues and Statistical Appendix, *IMF Country Report*, 04/160.

IMF. 2004b. Tanzania: Selected Issues and Statistical Appendix, *IMF Country Report*, 04/284.

IMF. 2004c. Costa Rica: 2004 Article IV Consultation-Staff Report; Staff Statement; Public Information Notice on the Executive Board Discussion; and Statement by the Executive Director for Costa Rica, *IMF Country Report*, 04/284.

IMF. 2004d. Malawi: Selected Issues and Statistical Appendix, *IMF Country Report*, 04/390.

IMF. 2005a. Arab Republic of Egypt: Selected Issues, *IMF Country Report*, 05/179.

IMF. 2005b. Indonesia: Selected Issues, *IMF Country Report*, 05/327.

IMF. 2006a. The Managing Director's Report on Implementing the Fund's Medium Term Strategy, April 5, 2006.

IMF. 2006b. Nicaragua: 2005 Article IV Consultation, *IMF Country Report*, 06/174.

IMF. 2007a. Ghana: 2007 Article IV Consultation, *IMF Country Report*, 07/210.

IMF. 2007b. Benin: 2007 Article IV Consultation, *IMF Country Report*, 07/6.

IMF. 2007c. Mozambique: 2007 Article IV Consultation, *IMF Country Report*, 07/262.

IMF. 2007d. Senegal: 2006 Article IV Consultation, *IMF Country Report*, 07/335.

IMF. 2007e. Bolivia: Selected Issues, *IMF Country Report*, 07/249.

IMF. 2008a. Zambia: Selected Issues, *IMF Country Report*, 08/29.

IMF. 2008b. Zambia: Statistical Appendix, *IMF Country Report*, 08/30.

IMF. 2008c. Malawi: Staff Report, *IMF Country Report*, 08/3.

IMF. 2008d. *World Economic Outlook April 2008*, Washington, DC: International Monetary Fund.

IMF. 2009a. *The Implication of the Global Financial Crisis for Low-Income Countries*, Washington, DC: International Monetary Fund.

IMF. 2009b. Ghana: 2009 Article IV Consultation, *IMF Country Report*, 09/256.

IMF. 2009c. Benin: Staff Report, *IMF Country Report*, 09/252.

IMF. 2009d. Mozambique: 2009 Article IV Consultation, *IMF Country Report*, 09/227.

IMF. 2009e. Senegal: Staff Report, *IMF Country Report*, 09/205.

IMF. 2009f. *World Economic Outlook April 2009*. Washington, DC: International Monetary Fund.

IMF. 2009g. *Regional Economic Outlook: Sub-Saharan Africa*, April 2009. Washington, DC: International Monetary Fund.

IMF. 2009h. IMF Reforms Financial Facilities for Low-Income Countries, *Public Information Notice*, 09/94, July 29.

IMF. 2009i. The Fund's Facilities and Financing Framework for Low-Income Countries, February 25, 2009.

IMF. 2009l. Malawi: Staff Report, *IMF Country Report*, 09/16.

IMF. 2009m. Tanzania: 2009 Article IV Consultation, *IMF Country Report*, 09/179.

IMF. 2009n. Bolivia: 2008 Article IV Consultation, *IMF Country Report*, 09/27.

IMF and the World Bank. 2001. *Developing Government Bond Markets: A Handbook*. Washington, DC: The World Bank and International Monetary Fund.

IMF and the World Bank. 2006. Applying the Debt Sustainability Framework for Low-Income Countries Post Debt Relief, November 6, 2006.

IMF and the World Bank. 2009. A Review of Some Aspects of the Low-Income Country Debt Sustainability Framework, August 5, 2009.

Jayachandran, S. and Kremer, M. 2006. Odious Debt, *American Economic Review*, 96(1), 82-92.

Johansson, P. 2010. Debt Relief, Investment and Growth. *World Development*, 38(9), 1204-16.

Jubilee Debt Campaign 2009. *A New Debt Crisis?* London: Jubilee Debt Campaign.

Kaminsky, G.L., Reinhart, C.M. and Végh, C.A. 2005. When it Rains, it Pours: Procyclical Capital Flows and Macroeconomic Policies, *NBER Macroeconomics Annual 2004*, 19, 11-82.

Kanbur, R. 2000. Aid, Conditionality and Debt in Africa, in *Foreign Aid and Development: Lessons Learnt and Directions for the Future*, edited by F. Tarp. New York: Routledge.

Katsouris, C. 1999. Creditors Making "Major Changes" in Debt Relief for Poor Countries, *Africa Recovery*, 13(2-3), 1-15.

Kaufmann, D., Kraay, A. and Mastruzzi, M. 2008. Governance Matters VII: Aggregate and Individual Governance Indicators 1996-2007. *Policy Research Working Paper*, 4654, The World Bank.

Keynes, J.M. 1919. *The Economic Consequences of The Peace*. London: Macmillan.

Khan, M.S. and Kumar, M.S. 1997. Public and Private Investment and the Convergence of Per Capita Incomes in Developing Countries, *Oxford Bulletin of Economics and Statistics*, 59(1), 69-88.

Knack, S. 2001. Aid Dependence and The Quality of Governance: Cross-Country Empirical Tests, *Southern Economic Journal*, 68(2), 310329.

Koeda, J. 2008. A Debt Overhang Model for Low-Income Countries, *IMF Staff Papers*, 55(4), 654-78.

Kose, M.A., Prasad, E.S., Rogoff, K. and Wei, S. 2009. Financial Globalization: A Reappraisal, *IMF Staff Papers*, 56(1), 8-62.

Kraay, A. and Nehru, V. 2006. When is External Debt Sustainable? *The World Bank Economic Review*, 20(3), 341-65.

Kraay, A. and Raddatz, C. 2007. Poverty Traps, Aid and Growth, *Journal of Development Economics*, 82(2), 315-37.

Kremer, M. and Jayachandran, S. 2002. Odious Debt, *Finance and Development*, June.

Krueger, A.O. 2002. A New Approach to Sovereign Debt Restructuring, unpublished, *International Monetary Fund*, April.

Krugman, P. 1988. Financing vs Forgiving a Debt Overhang, *Journal of Development Economics*, 29(3), 253-68.

Kwon, G., McFarlane, L. and Robinson W. 2006. Public Debt, Money Supply and Inflation: A Cross-Country Study and its Application to Jamaica, *IMF Working Paper*, 06/121.

Laeven, L. and Valencia, F. 2008. Systemic Banking Crisis: A New Database, *IMF Working Paper*, 08/224.

Levy Yeyati, E. and Panizza, U. 2010. The Elusive Costs of Sovereign Defaults, *Journal of Development Economics*, forthcoming.

Ley, E. 2009. Fiscal (and External) Sustainability, unpublished, The World Bank. Available at: http://siteresources.worldbank.org/INTDEBTDEPT/Resources/468980-1207588563500/4864698-1207588597197/FSPrimer.pdf.

Lora, E. 2007. Public Investment in Infrastructure in Latin America: Is Debt the Culprit? *RES Working Papers*, 4502, Inter-American Development Bank.

Lora, E. and Olivera, M. 2007. Public Debt and Social Expenditure: Friends or Foes? *Emerging Markets Review*, 8(4), 299-10.

Loxley, J. and Sackey, H.A. 2008. Aid Effectiveness in Africa, *African Development Review*, 20(2), 163-99.

Mahdavi, S. 2004. Shifts in the Composition of Government Spending in Response to External Debt Burden, *World Development*, 32(7), 1139-57.

Marchesi, S. and Missale, A. 2004. What Does Motivate Lending and Aid to The HIPCs? *Development Studies Working Paper*, 189, Centro Studi Luca d'Agliano.

Martin, M. 2002. Debt Relief and Poverty Reduction: Do we Need a HIPC III? unpublished, North-South Institute and Debt Relief International.

Martin, M. 2004. Assessing the HIPC Initiative: The Key HIPC Debates, in *HIPC Debt Relief. Myths and Reality*, edited by J.J. Teunissed and A. Akkerman. The Hague: Forum on Debt and Development (FONDAD), 11-47.

Mendoza, R.U., Jones, R. and Vergara, G. 2009. Will the Global Financial Crisis Lead to Lower Foreign Aid? A First Look at United States ODA, *Fordham Economics Discussion Paper Series*, Dp2009-01.

Michaelowa, K. 2003. The Political Economy of the Enhanced HIPC-Initiative, *Public Choice*, 114(3-4), 461-76.

Mold, A., Paulo, S. and Prizzon, A. 2009. Taking Stock of the Credit Crunch: Implications for Development Finance and Global Governance, *OECD Development Center Working Paper*, 277.

Mongardini, J. and Samake, I. 2009. The Macroeconomics of Scaling Up Aid: The Gleneagles Initiative for Benin, *IMF Working Paper*, 09/115.

Moss, T. 2006. Will Debt Relief Make a Difference? Impact and Expectations of The Multilateral Debt Relief Initiative, *Center for Global Development Working Paper*, 88.

Moss, T.J. and Chiang, H.S. 2003. The Other Costs of High Debt in Poor Countries: Growth, Policy Dynamics and Institutions, *Issue Paper on Debt Sustainability*, 3, Center for Global Development.

Moss, T. and Rose, S. 2006. China ExIm Bank and Africa: New Lending, New Challenges, Center for Global Development Notes, November 2006.

Moss, T., Pettersson, G. and van de Walle, N. 2008. An Aid-Institutions Paradox? A Review Essay on Aid Dependency and State Building in Sub-Saharan Africa, in *Reinventing Foreign Aid*, edited by W. Easterly. Cambridge, MA: MIT Press, 255-82.

Moyo, D. 2009. *Dead Aid*. New York: Farrar, Straus and Giroux.

Ndikumana, L. and Boyce, J.K. 2003. Public Debts and Private Assets: Explaining Capital Flight from Sub-Saharan African Countries, *World Development*, 31(1), 107-30.

Neumayer, E. 2002. Is Good Governance Rewarded? A Cross-National Analysis of Debt Forgiveness, *World Development*, 30(6), 913-30.

Nickell, S.J. 1981. Biases in Dynamic Models with Fixed Effects, *Econometrica*, 49(6), 1417-26.

Nwachukwu, J. 2008. The Prospects for Foreign Debt Sustainability in Post-Completion-Point Countries: Implications of the HIPC-MDRI Framework, *Development Policy Review*, 26(2), 171-88.

Odedokun, M. 2004. Multilateral and Bilateral Loans Versus Grants: Issues and Evidence, *World Economy*, 27(February), 239-63.

OECD. 2008a. Principles and Guidelines to Promote Sustainable Lending Practices in The Provision of Official Export Credits to Low-Income Countries, *Trade Committee*, 20 February.

OXFAM. 2010. *The Global Economic Crisis and Developing Countries*. Oxfam International.

Pallage, S. and Robe, M.A. 2001. Foreign Aid and the Business Cycle, *Review of International Economics*, 9(4), 641-72.

Pallage, S., Robe, M.A. and Bérubé, C. 2006. The Potential of Foreign Aid as Insurance, *IMF Staff Papers*, 53(3), 453-75.

Panizza, U. 2008. Domestic and External Public Debt in Developing Countries, *UNCTAD Discussion Paper*, 188.

Panizza, U., Sturzenegger, F. and Zettelmeyer, J. 2009. The Economics and Law of Sovereign Debt and Default, *Journal of Economic Literature*, 47(3), 651-98.

Paris Club. 2007. Press Release of the Paris Club on the Threats Posed by Some Litigating Creditors to Heavily Indebted Poor Countries, 22 May.

Pasinetti, L. 1998. The Myth (or Folly) of the 3% Deficit-GDP Maastricht 'Parameter', *The Cambridge Journal of Economics*, 22(1), 103-16.

Pattillo, C.A., Poirson, H. and Ricci, L.A. 2002. External Debt and Growth, *IMF Working Paper*, 02/69.

Pattillo, C.A., Poirson, H. and Ricci, L.A. 2004. What are the Channels Through Which External Debt Affects Growth? *IMF Working Paper*, 04/15.

Peek, J. and Rosengren, E.S. 1997. The International Transmission of Financial Shocks: The Case of Japan, *American Economic Review*, 87(4), 495-505.

Powell, R. and Bird, G. 2009. Aid and Debt Relief in Africa: Have they Been Substitutes or Complements? *World Development*, 38(3), 219-27.

Prasad, E., Rajan, R.G. and Subramanian, A. 2006. Patterns on International Capital Flows and their Implications for Economic Development, *Proceedings*, Federal Reserve Bank of Kansas City, 119-58.

Presbitero, A.F. 2006. The Debt-Growth Nexus: A Dynamic Panel Data Estimation, *Rivista Italiana degli Economisti*, 3(4), 417-62.

Presbitero, A.F. 2008. The Debt-Growth Nexus: A Reassessment, *Economics: The Open-Access, Open-Assessment E-Journal*, 2(2008-30).

Presbitero, A.F. 2009a. Debt-Relief Effectiveness and Institution-Building, *Development Policy Review*, 27(5), 529-59.

Presbitero, A.F. 2009b. The 2008-2009 Financial Crisis and the HIPCs: Another Debt Crisis? *Rivista Bancaria – Minerva Bancaria*, LXV(5-6), 35-64.

Presbitero, A.F. And Zazzaro, A. 2010. The Global Crisis in Low- and Middle-Income Countries: How the IMF Responded, in *The Global Economic Crisis: New Perspectives on the Critique of Economic Theory and Policy*, edited by E. Brancaccio and G. Fontana. London: Routledge.

Primo Braga, C.A. and Dömeland, D. 2009. *Debt Relief and Beyond – Lessons Learned and Challenges Ahead*. Washington, DC: The World Bank.

Radelet, S. 2005a, From Pushing Reforms to Pulling Reforms: The Role of Challenge Programs in Foreign Aid Policy, Center for Global Development, *Issue Paper on Debt Sustainability*, 53.

Radelet, S. 2005b. Grants for the World's Poorest: How the World Bank Should Distribute its Funds, unpublished, Center for Global Development Notes, June.

Radelet, S. and Chiang, H. 2003. Providing New Financing to Low-Income Countries with High Levels of Debt: Some Considerations, *Issue Paper on Debt Sustainability*, 2, Center for Global Development.

Rajan, R.G. and Subramanian, A. 2008. Aid and Growth: What Does the Cross-Country Evidence Really Show? *Review of Economics and Statistics*, 40(8), 643-65.

Rajan, R.G. and Subramanian, A. 2010. Aid, Dutch Disease and Manufacturing Growth, *Journal of Development Economics*, forthcoming.

Rajan, R.G., 2005, Debt Relief and Growth, *Finance and Development*, 42(2), 56.

Ratha, D. and Mohapatra, S. 2009. Revised Outlook for Remittance Flows 2009-2011: Remittances Expected to Fall by 5 to 8 percent in 2009, *Migration and Development Brief*, 9, The World Bank.

Reinhart, C.M., Rogoff, K.S. and Savastano, M.S. 2003. Debt Intolerance. *Brookings Papers on Economic Activity*, 34(2003-1), 1-74.

Reinhart C.M and Rogoff, K.S. 2009. *This Time is Different*. Princeton, NJ: Princeton University Press.

Reinhart, C.M. and Reinhart, V. 2009. Is there scope for fiscal stimulus for debt-intolerant countries? Available at: http://www.voxeu.org/index.php?q=node/3893.

Reisen, H. and Ndoye, S. 2008. Prudent versus Imprudent Lending to Africa: From Debt Relief to Emerging Lenders, *OECD Development Centre Working Paper*, 268.

Rodrik, D. 2008. The Real Exchange Rate and Economic Growth, *Brookings Papers on Economic Activity*, 2008(2), 365-412.

Roodman, D. 2006. Aid Project Proliferation and Absorptive Capacity, *Center for Global Development Working Paper*, 75.

Roodman, D. 2008. History Says Financial Crisis Will Suppress Aid, *Global Development: Views from the Center.*

Roodman, D. 2009a. How to Do xtabond2: An Introduction to Difference and System GMM in Stata, *Stata Journal*, 9(1), 86-136.

Roodman, D. 2009b. A Note on the Theme of too Many Instruments, *Oxford Bullettin of Economics and Statistics*, 71(1), 135-58.

Roubini, N. 2001. Debt Sustainability: How to Assess Whether a Country is Insolvent, unpublished, *Stern School of Business*.

Sachs, J.D. 1989. The Debt Overhang of Developing Countries, in Debt, Stabilization and Development, edited by G.A. Calvo, R. Findlay, P. Kouri and J. Braga de Macedo. Oxford: Basil Blackwell.

Sachs, J.D. 2002. Resolving the Debt Crisis of Low-Income Countries, *Brookings Papers on Economic Activity*, 1, 257-86.

Sachs J.D. 2005. *The End of Poverty*. New York: Penguin Press.

Sanford, J.E. 2002. World Bank: IDA Loans or IDA Grants? *World Development*, 30(5), 741-62.

Sargent, T.J. and Wallace, N. 1981. Some Unpleasant Monetarist Arithmetic, *Federal Reserve Bank of Minneapolis Quarterly Review*, 5, 1-17.

Savvides, A. 1992. Investment Slowdown in Developing Countries During the 1980s: Debt Overhang or Foreign Capital Inflows? *Kyklos*, 45(3), 363-78.

Schmid, J.P. 2009. Is Debt Relief Good for the Poor? The Effects of the HIPC Initiative on Infant Mortality, in *Debt Relief and Beyond. Lessons Learned and Challenges Ahead*, edited by C.A. Primo Braga and D. Dömeland. Washington, DC: The World Bank, 49-70.

Seager, A. and Lewis, J. 2007. How Top London Law Firms Help Vulture Funds Devour their Prey, *The Guardian*, 17 October.

Serven, L. 1997. Irreversibility, Uncertainty and Private Investment: Analytical Issues and Some Lessons for Africa, *Journal of African Economies*, 6(3), 229-68.

Serven, L. and Solimano, A. 1991. Adjustment Policies and Investment Performance in Developing Countries: Theory, Country Experiences and Policy Implications, *Policy Research Working Paper*, 606, The World Bank.

Sun, Y. 2004. External Debt Sustainability in HIPC Completion Point Countries: An Update, *IMF Working Paper*, 04/160.

Teunissen, J.J. 2004. Introduction, in *HIPC Debt Relief. Myths and Reality*, edited by J.J. Teunissed and A. Akkerman. The Hague: Forum on Debt and Development (FONDAD), 1-10.

UNCTAD. 2004, *Debt Sustainability: Oasis or Mirage?* Geneva: United Nations.

UNCTAD. 2006. *Trade and Development Report 2006*. New York and Geneva: United Nations.

UNCTAD. 2008. *Trade and Development Report 2008*. Geneva: United Nations.

UNCTAD. 2009a. *Trade and Development Report 2009*. Geneva: United Nations.

UNCTAD. 2009b. *World Investment Report*. Geneva: United Nations.

United Nations. 2009. *The Millennium Development Goals Report 2009*, New York.

Vamvakidis, A. 2008. External Debt and Economic Reform: Does a Pain Reliever Delay the Necessary Treatment? *Journal of Economic Policy Reform*, 11(3), 187-99.

Vaubel, R. 1983. The Moral Hazard of IMF Lending, *The World Economy*, 6(3), 291-304.

Wang, J. and Bio-Tchané, A. 2008. Africa's Burgeoning Ties with China, *Finance and Development*, 45(1).

Weiss, J. 2008. The Aid Paradigm for Poverty Reduction: Does it Make Sense? *Development Policy Review*, 26(4), 407-26.

Windmeijer, F. 2005. A Finite Sample Correction for the Variance of Linear Efficient Two-Step GMM Estimators, *Journal of Econometrics* 126(1), 25-51.

Wood, A. 2008. How Donors Should Cap Aid in Africa, *Financial Times*, September 4.

World Bank. 2006. IDA Countries And Non-Concessional Debt: Dealing with the "Free Rider" Problem in IDA14 Grant-Recipient and Post-MDRI Countries, June 19, 2006.

World Bank. 2009a. *Global Development Finance 2009*. Washington, DC: The World Bank.

World Bank. 2009b. Protecting Progress: The Challenge Facing Low-Income Countries in the Global Recession, Background Paper prepared by World Bank Group staff for the G-20 Leaders' Meeting, Pittsburgh, USA, September 24-25, 2009.

Wyplosz, C. 2007. Debt Sustainability Assessment: The IMF Approach and Alternatives, *HEI Working Paper*, 03/2007, Graduate Institute of International Studies.

Yang, J. and Nyberg, D. 2009. External Debt Sustainability in HIPC Completion Point Countries: An Update, *IMF Working Paper*, 09/128.

Zoellick, R.B. 2009. Roundtable with Media, *G7 Finance Ministers Meeting*, Rome, 13 February 2009. Available at: http://go.worldbank.org/0YHVV64T90.

# Index

Page numbers in *italics* refer to figures and tables.

# Global Finance Series

*Full series list*

**Making Global Economic Governance Effective: Hard and Soft Law Institutions in a Crowded World**
Edited by John Kirton, Marina Larionova and Paolo Savona
ISBN 978-0-7546-7671-3

**G8 against Transnational Organized Crime**
Amandine Scherrer
ISBN 978-0-7546-7544-0

**Governing Global Derivatives: Challenges and Risks**
Chiara Oldani
ISBN 978-0-7546-7464-1

**Financing Development: The G8 and UN Contribution**
Edited by Michele Fratianni, John J. Kirton and Paolo Savona
ISBN 978-0-7546-4676-1

**The New Economic Diplomacy: Decision-Making and Negotiation in International Economic Relations (Second Edition)**
Edited by Nicholas Bayne and Stephen Woolcock
ISBN 978-0-7546-7047-6 (hbk)
ISBN 978-0-7546-7048-3 (pbk)

**The G8 System and the G20: Evolution, Role and Documentation**
Peter I. Hajnal
ISBN 978-0-7546-4550-4

**Corporate, Public and Global Governance: The G8 Contribution**
Edited by Michele Fratianni, Paolo Savona and John J. Kirton
ISBN 978-0-7546-4046-2

**Elements of the Euro Area: Integrating Financial Markets**
Edited by Jesper Berg, Mauro Grande and Francesco Paolo Mongelli
ISBN 978-0-7546-4320-3

**New Perspectives on Global Governance: Why America Needs the G8**
Edited by Michele Fratianni, John J. Kirton, Alan M. Rugman and Paolo Savona
ISBN 978-0-7546-4477-4

**Global Financial Crime: Terrorism, Money Laundering and Offshore Centres**
Edited by Donato Masciandaro
ISBN 978-0-7546-3707-3

**Sustaining Global Growth and Development: G7 and IMF Governance**
Edited by Michele Fratianni, Paolo Savona and John J. Kirton
ISBN 978-0-7546-3529-1

**Governing Global Finance: New Challenges, G7 and IMF Contributions**
Edited by Michele Fratianni, Paolo Savona and John J. Kirton
ISBN 978-0-7546-0880-6